MATHI

A Concise Course in Pure Mathematics

A Concise Course in Pure Mathematics

R. I. PORTER
M.B.E., M.A.

Bell & Hyman

First published in 1985 by
Bell & Hyman Limited
Denmark House
37–39 Queen Elizabeth Street
London SE1 2QB

British Library Cataloguing in Publication Data

Porter, R.I.
A concise course in pure mathematics.
1. Mathematics—Examinations, questions, etc.
I. Title
510′.76 QA43

ISBN 0 7135 2466 9

Printed in Great Britain at The Thetford Press Limited, Thetford, Norfolk

Contents

ANALYSIS AND NUMERICAL ANALYSIS

COORDINATE GEOMETRY

MATRICES

VECTORS

Preface

This book comprising statements of basic results and methods in Pure Mathematics together with sets of illustrative examples had originally the sole objective of providing a concise, instructive and helpful revision course for students in the latter stages of preparation for an examination in A level mathematics or its equivalent. However it is hoped that the book will have a wider usefulness in serving as a supplementary course book for teachers and students using either a modern textbook with insufficient examples or a popular but older book which does not include "modern" topics. It covers most, if not all, of the material included in recently published examination syllabuses which have been designed to bring together the modern and traditional approaches to advanced level Pure Mathematics.

Topics are dealt with in sections and are grouped under the main heads of Algebra, Trigonometry, Complex numbers, Analysis and numerical analysis, Coordinate geometry, Matrices and Vectors. Numerous worked examples to illustrate the principles and operations involved and a set of graded examples, marked (A), are provided in each section. At intervals, miscellaneous examples of a more testing nature, marked (B), covering topics involved in the immediately preceding sections are included.

I am grateful for the helpful advice of my daughter, Mrs Elizabeth Lucas, B.Sc.. In addition to reviewing the material and contents she has helped to check the answers.

1985 R. I. PORTER

Algebra

IMPORTANT RESULTS AND METHODS

Factors

$a^2-b^2=(a-b)(a+b)$; $a^3-b^3=(a-b)(a^2+ab+b^2)$;
$a^3+b^3=(a+b)(a^2-ab+b^2)$.

Polynomials

A polynomial of degree n, where n is a positive integer, is a function of the form $a_0x^n+a_1x^{n-1}+a_2x^{n-2}+\ldots+a_{n-1}x+a_n$, where the coefficients $a_0, a_1, a_2, \ldots, a_n$ are constants.

Proper fractions

If $p(x)$ is a polynomial of degree m and $q(x)$ a polynomial of degree n, the fraction $p(x)/q(x)$ is *proper* if m is less than n.

To change from an improper to a proper fraction, use a long division process as illustrated in the following example.

Example 1. Express the fraction $(x^3-2x^2+x+3)/(x^2-x-2)$ *in terms of a proper fraction.*

Dividing,

$$\begin{array}{r} x^2-x-2)\,x^3-2x^2+x+3\,(x-1 \\ \underline{x^3-x^2-2x} \\ -x^2+3x+3 \\ \underline{-x^2+x+2} \\ 2x+1 \end{array} \text{ — remainder.}$$

So

$$\frac{x^3-2x^2+x+3}{x^2-x-2}=x-1+\frac{2x+1}{x^2-x-2}.$$

Remainder and factor theorems

When polynomial $f(x)$ is divided by $(x-a)$, the remainder is $f(a)$; more generally if the division is by $(px-q)$, the remainder is $f(q/p)$.

Consequently, if $f(a)=0$, $(x-a)$ is a factor of $f(x)$ and more generally if $f(q/p)=0$, $(px-q)$ is a factor of $f(x)$ and conversely.

Example 2. Prove that $(x-2)$ *is a factor of* $2x^3-5x^2+5x-6$ *and complete the factorisation.*

Writing $f(x) = 2x^3-5x^2+5x-6$; $f(2) = 16-20+10-6 = 0$.

$\therefore$ $(x-2)$ is a factor of $f(x)$.

By division, $2x^3-5x^2+5x-6 = (x-2)(2x^2-x+3)$.

Surds

The methods of simplifying terms containing surds are used in the following exercises:

(i) $\sqrt{32} = \sqrt{(16\times 2)} = 4\sqrt{2}$;

(ii) $\sqrt{27}-\sqrt{12} = 3\sqrt{3}-2\sqrt{3} = \sqrt{3}$;

(iii) $\sqrt{2}/(\sqrt{2}-1) = \sqrt{2}(\sqrt{2}+1)/(\sqrt{2}-1)(\sqrt{2}+1) = 2+\sqrt{2}$.

The method used to rationalise the denominator of a fraction involving surds should be carefully noted.

Process of completing the square

$$x^2+ax = \left(x+\frac{a}{2}\right)^2-\frac{a^2}{4};$$

$$ax^2+bx = a\left(x^2+\frac{b}{a}x\right)$$

$$= a\left[\left(x+\frac{b}{2a}\right)^2-\frac{b^2}{4a^2}\right].$$

Example 3. Express $x^2+y^2-4x+6y+1$ *in the form* $(x+a)^2+(y+b)^2+c$.

We have $x^2-4x = (x-2)^2-4$; $y^2+6y = (y+3)^2-9$.

Expression $= (x-2)^2+(y+3)^2-12$.

Mathematical induction

This is a method of proving stated theorems or results involving the *natural* numbers $1, 2, 3, \ldots, n$. The method involves two steps: (i) verification that the stated result is true for $n = 1$; (ii) on the assumption that the result is true for a particular value of n, say $n = r$, the proof that the result is also true for $n = r+1$.

The important application of this method to finite series is dealt with in a later section. Other applications are illustrated in the following examples.

Example 4. If n *is a* $+^{\text{ve}}$ *integer, prove that* $f(n) = 5^n-1$ *is divisible by 4.*

(i) When $n = 1$, $f(1) = 5-1 = 4$: so the result is true for $n = 1$;

(ii) assume the result is true for $n = r$, i.e. that $f(r) = 4g(r)$ where $g(r)$ is some function of r.

To establish on this assumption that $f(r+1)$ is also divisible by 4, we show that this property holds for the difference $f(r+1)-f(r)$. Generally in this type of example some linear relation of the form $af(r+1)+bf(r)$ can be used as required by the particular example. Here

$$f(r+1)-f(r) = 5^{r+1}-1-(5^r-1) = 5^{r+1}-5^r$$
$$= 5^r(5-1) \qquad = 4.5^r.$$
$$f(r+1) = f(r)+4.5^r$$
$$= 4(g(r)+5^r).$$

So $f(r+1)$ is divisible by 4, establishing that if the result is true for one value of n it is also true for the next highest value of n. As the result is true for $n = 1$, it is true for $n = 2, 3, \ldots$.

Example 5. Show that $3^n \geqslant 1+2n$, where n is a positive integer.

Write $f(n) = 3^n-1-2n$ and establish that $f(n) \geqslant 0$.

(i) When $n = 1$, $f(1) = 0$; so the result is true for $n = 1$;
(ii) assume the result is true for $n = r$, i.e. that $3^r-1-2r \geqslant 0$.

Then
$$f(r+1) = 3^{r+1}-1-2(r+1)$$
$$= 3^{r+1}-3-2r;$$
so
$$f(r+1) > 3^{r+1}-3-6r \text{ as } r \geqslant 1,$$
i.e.
$$f(r+1) > 3f(r).$$

So $f(r+1) \geqslant 0$ and the result follows in the usual way.

(A) EXAMPLES 1

1. Factorise: (i) x^2-4y^2; (ii) x^3-8y^3; (iii) x^3+8y^3; (iv) x^4-y^4.
2. Simplify: (i) $(p^3+q^3)/(p+q)$; (ii) $(ap^2-aq^2)/(2ap-2aq)$, $p \neq q$; (iii) $(cp^3-cq^3)/(cp^2-cq^2)$, $p \neq q$.
3. Express each of the following in terms of a proper fraction: (i) $x/(x+1)$; (ii) $3x/(x-1)$; (iii) $x^2/(x+1)$; (iv) $x^2/(x^2+1)$; (v) $(x^2-1)/(x^2+4)$; (vi) $x^3/(1+x^2)$; (vii) $(2x^2-x+2)/[(x-1)(x+2)]$.
4. (i) Simplify $4\sqrt{5}-\sqrt{20}$; (ii) expand $(2\sqrt{5}+3)(\sqrt{5}-1)$.
5. Find the remainders when the following functions are divided by $x-2$: (i) x^2+4x+3; (ii) x^3-x-4; (iii) x^4-3x^2-4x+1.
6. Express the following fractions each in the form $a+b\sqrt{n}$, where a, b are rational: (i) $2/\sqrt{3}$; (ii) $1/2\sqrt{2}$; (iii) $1/(\sqrt{3}-1)$; (iv) $\sqrt{2}/(2\sqrt{2}+1)$; (v) $1/(\sqrt{3}+\sqrt{2})$; (vi) $(\sqrt{2}-1)/(\sqrt{2}+1)$; (vii) $1/[(\sqrt{3}+1)^2]$.
7. If $p \neq q$, find y from the equations: $yp-x = ap^2$, $yq-x = aq^2$.
8. Find the value of the constant a if the remainder when the function x^5-ax^3+2 is divided by $x+1$ is 4.
9. Express each of the following in terms of a perfect square: (i) x^2-8x; (ii) y^2+10y; (iii) y^2+5y; (iv) $2x^2+6x$; (v) $4y-y^2$; (vi) $2x^2-5x$; (vii) ax^2+2gx.
10. If $f(n) = 3^{2n}+7$, where n is a positive integer, show that $f(n+1)-f(n)$ is divisible by 8. Hence prove by induction that $f(n)$ is always divisible by 8.
11. For what value of c is $x-2$ a factor of $(x+2)^5+4x+c$?
12. Express: (i) $x^2+y^2+2x-6y+3$ in the form $(x+p)^2+(y+q)^2+r$; (ii) $2x^2+2y^2-4x+6y+1$ in the form $a(x+p)^2+a(y+q)^2+r$.
13. Use the factor theorem to find a linear factor of each of the following expressions and complete the factorisation in each case: (i) x^3-x^2+x-1; (ii) x^3+x^2+x+1; (iii) x^3-3x+2; (iv) x^3+x^2-x+2.
14. Evaluate $[1/(\sqrt{3}+\sqrt{2})-1/(\sqrt{3}-\sqrt{2})]^2$.
15. Prove by induction that: (i) $3^{2n}-5$ is divisible by 4; (ii) $2^{3n}+6$ is divisible by 7, n being a positive integer.

16. When the function ax^2+bx+c is divided successively by $x-1$, $x-2$ and $x-3$, the respective remainders are -1, 4 and 11. Determine the values of the constants a, b, c.
17. Express $(1+\sqrt{3})/[(2+\sqrt{3})(3\sqrt{3}+5)]$ in the form $a+b\sqrt{3}$, where a, b are rational.
18. Given that x^2-x-6 is a factor of $x^4+ax^3-9x^2+bx-6$, find the values of the constants a and b and complete the factorisation of the expression.
19. If $x+1/x = p$, show that $x^2+1/x^2 = p^2-2$ and express x^3+1/x^3 in terms of p.
20. Prove by mathematical induction that $2^n \geqslant 1+n$ for $n \geqslant 1$, by writing $f(n) = 2^n-1-n$ and showing that $f(n+1) > 2f(n)$.
21. If $a_n = 2a_{n-1}$ and $a_1 = 2$, establish by induction that $a_n = 2^n$ for $n \geqslant 1$.

EQUATIONS AND INEQUALITIES

Quadratic equations

General form: $$ax^2+bx+c = 0.$$

Roots: $$x = \frac{-b\pm\sqrt{(b^2-4ac)}}{2a}.$$

Nature of roots:
real and different if $b^2-4ac > 0$;
real and equal if $b^2-4ac = 0$;
complex (not real) if $b^2-4ac < 0$.

Sum and product of roots: if the roots are α, β,

$$\textit{then } \alpha+\beta = -\frac{b}{a}, \ \alpha\beta = \frac{c}{a}.$$

Using the latter results, the values of symmetrical expressions such as $\alpha^2+\beta^2$, $\alpha^3+\beta^3$, $\alpha^4+\beta^4$, $\alpha/\beta+\beta/\alpha$ are obtained by using the identities $\alpha^2+\beta^2 = (\alpha+\beta)^2-2\alpha\beta$, $\alpha^3+\beta^3 = (\alpha+\beta)(\alpha^2-\alpha\beta+\beta^2)$, $\alpha^4+\beta^4 = (\alpha^2+\beta^2)^2-2\alpha^2\beta^2$, $\alpha/\beta+\beta/\alpha = (\alpha^2+\beta^2)/\alpha\beta$.

Note

(i) As α, β are the roots of the equation remember that $a\alpha^2+b\alpha+c = 0$ and $a\beta^2+b\beta+c = 0$;
(ii) the roots are of opposite signs if a and c have opposite signs—this condition ensures that the roots are real and their product is negative; the roots are of the same sign if $b^2-4ac \geqslant 0$ and a and c are of the same sign;
(iii) the roots are both positive if $b^2-4ac \geqslant 0$ and a and c have the same sign which differs from that of b.

Quadratic equation in terms of its roots

General form: x^2-x *(sum of roots)* + *product of roots* $= 0$.

Example 6. If the equations $x^2+px+q = 0$, $x^2-2px-3q = 0$ where $p \neq q$, have a common root, show that $16q = 3p^2$.

Let the roots of the equations be α, β and α, γ respectively.

Then $\alpha+\beta = -p$, $\alpha\beta = q$ and $\alpha+\gamma = 2p$, $\alpha\gamma = -3q$.

Eliminating α from the first and third equations gives $\gamma-\beta = 3p$ and from the second and fourth equations gives $\gamma = -3\beta$. Hence $\beta = -3p/4$, $\gamma = 9p/4$ and so $\alpha = -p/4$.

Substituting for α and β in the second equation, $(-p/4)(-3p/4) = q$

or $$16q = 3p^2, \text{ the required condition.}$$

Example 7. Show that the roots of the equation $2x^2+3x-5 = m(x-1)$ are real for all real values of m.

Rearranging the equation, $2x^2+x(3-m)+m-5 = 0$.

With the usual notation,
$$b^2-4ac = (3-m)^2-8(m-5)$$
$$= m^2-14m+49$$
$$= (m-7)^2.$$

$\therefore b^2-4ac \geqslant 0$ for all real values of m and consequently the roots of the given equation are real.

Linear simultaneous equations

The elementary method used in the solution of linear simultaneous equations in two unknowns can readily be extended to the cases of three or four unknowns.

Example 8. Solve the equations (i) $a+b+c = 4$; (ii) $4a+2b+c = 12$; (iii) $9a+3b+c = 26$.

Eliminating c by subtracting equations (i) from (ii) and (ii) from (iii) leads to the equations $3a+b = 8$, $5a+b = 14$.

The solution of these equations is $a = 3$, $b = -1$ and consequently $c = 2$.

Non-linear simultaneous equations

The solutions of non-linear simultaneous equations in two or three unknowns are effected by using the method of substitution.

Example 9. Solve the equations $8y = xy-6$, $8y^2 = x^2y^2+4$.

Here we could write $x = (8y+6)/y$ using the first equation and substitute this value for x in the second equation but it is simpler to write the first equation as $xy = 8y+6$ and substitute for xy in the second equation, giving

$$8y^2 = (8y+6)^2+4$$

i.e. $$2y^2 = (4y+3)^2+1,$$

$$7y^2+12y+5 = 0.$$

By factorising, $$y = -\frac{5}{7}, -1,$$

and $$x = -\frac{2}{5}, 2.$$

Inequalities

A basic principle in the solution of inequalities is to avoid multiplication or division by a negative number or by a term which could be negative.

The methods of solving inequalities in one variable are in general similar to those used for the solution of the corresponding equalities or equations, care always being taken to adhere to the principle stated above. Linear and quadratic inequalities are readily handled by analytical methods as are inequalities involving higher polynomial functions which can be factorised. Inequalities involving rational algebraic functions, logarithmic, exponential or trigonometric functions are often best dealt with by using graphical or semi-graphical methods.

In the case of inequalities involving two variables the fact that the square of a real quantity is $\geqslant 0$ is frequently used.

The following worked examples serve to illustrate the different methods.

Example 10. Find the ranges of values of x for which: (i) $4-3x < 0$; (ii) $(x-1)(2-x) \geqslant 0$; (iii) $x^2-4x < 5$.

(i) $$4-3x < 0;\ 4 < 3x \rightarrow x > \frac{4}{3}.$$

(ii) $$(x-1)(2-x) \geqslant 0.$$

The equality has solutions $x = 1$, $x = 2$. For a value of x between 1 and 2 $(x-1)$ is positive and $(2-x)$ is also positive; consequently $(x-1)(2-x)$ is positive.

$$\therefore \quad (x-1)(2-x) \geqslant 0 \quad \text{for} \quad 1 \leqslant x \leqslant 2.$$

(iii) $$x^2-4x-5 < 0.$$

Factorising, $$(x-5)(x+1) < 0.$$

The solution of the corresponding equation is $x = -1, 5$. For a value of x between -1 and 5, the function $(x-5)(x+1)$ is negative.

$$\therefore \quad x^2-4x < 5 \quad \text{for} \quad -1 < x < 5.$$

Example 11. Show that the inequality $x^2+5 > 4x$ is satisfied for all real values of x.

$$x^2+5 > 4x,$$

i.e. $$x^2-4x+5 > 0.$$

Completing the square in this case where the quadratic function has not simple rational factors, $(x-2)^2+1 > 0$.

As $(x-2)^2 \geqslant 0$ for all real values of x, the inequality is satisfied for all real values of x.

Example 12. Find the ranges of values of x for which $2/x > x+1$, $x \neq 0$.

Sketch graphs of $y = 2/x$ and $y = x+1$ are shown in Fig. 1.

Solving the equation $2/x = x+1$, i.e. $x^2+x-2 = 0$, gives the x-coordinates of A, B as $-2, 1$ respectively.

Using this result together with the sketch graphs it is clear that the given inequality is satisfied for $x < -2$ and $0 < x < 1$.

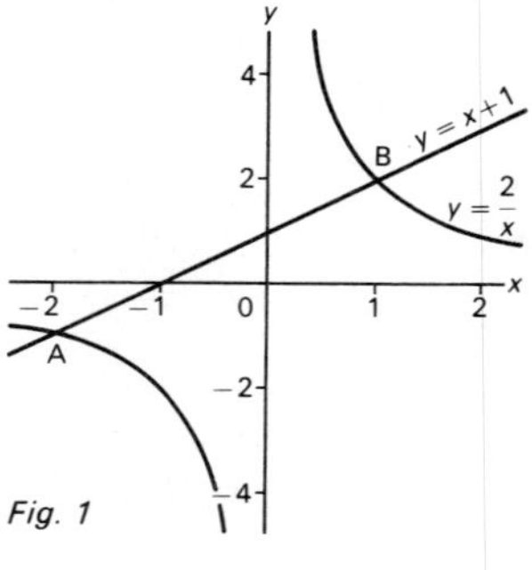

Fig. 1

Alternatively an analytical solution can be obtained

by expressing the inequality in the form $\frac{2}{x}-x-1>0$,

i.e. $$\frac{2-x-x^2}{x}>0, \text{ or } \frac{(2+x)(1-x)}{x}>0$$

and finding the ranges of values of x for which both numerator and denominator of the L.H.S. are $+^{\text{ve}}$ $(0<x<1)$ and both numerator and denominator are $-^{\text{ve}}$ $(x<-2)$.

Example 13. Find the range of values of the constant k for which the function $3x^2+2kxy+3y^2$ is positive for real values of x and y.

The inequality to be solved is $$3x^2+2kxy+3y^2>0,$$

i.e. $$x^2+\frac{2kxy}{3}+y^2>0.$$

Completing the square, $$\left(x+\frac{ky}{3}\right)^2-\frac{k^2}{9}y^2+y^2>0.$$

This inequality is always satisfied if $1-\frac{k^2}{9}>0$, $k^2<9$, $-3<k<3$.

Example 14. If x, y, z are positive and unequal, prove that: (i) $x+y>2\sqrt{(xy)}$; (ii) $(x+y)(y+z)(z+x)>8xyz$.

(i) $$(\sqrt{x}-\sqrt{y})^2 = x+y-2\sqrt{(xy)},$$

as $(\sqrt{x}-\sqrt{y})^2>0$, $$x+y>2\sqrt{(xy)}.$$

(ii) Using the result (i),

$$(x+y)(y+z)(z+x)>2\sqrt{(xy)}\cdot 2\sqrt{(yz)}\cdot 2\sqrt{(zx)},$$

i.e. $$(x+y)(y+z)(z+x)>8xyz.$$

(A) EXAMPLES 2

1. Determine the nature of the roots of the equations: (i) $x^2+x-3=0$; (ii) $2x^2-x=5$; (iii) $x^2+x=1$; (iv) $x^2+x+1=0$; (v) $m^2x^2-2mx+1=0$, m real.
2. Solve the inequalities: (i) $5x-4>0$; (ii) $3-2x\leqslant 0$; (iii) $-3x\geqslant 6$; (iv) $3x/4<1$.
3. If α, β are the roots of the equation $x^2-5x+2=0$, find the values of: (i) $\alpha^2+\beta^2$; (ii) $\alpha^3+\beta^3$; (iii) $\alpha^4+\beta^4$; (iv) $\alpha^2/\beta+\beta^2/\alpha$.
4. If α, β are the roots of the equation $4x^2-x-3=0$, show that: (i) $\alpha^2=(\alpha+3)/4$; (ii) $4\beta^3=\beta^2+3\beta$.
5. What is the sign of the roots of the equation $3x^2-11x+2=0$?
6. If m is real, solve the inequalities: (i) $m(2-m)<0$; (ii) $m^2\geqslant 2m$; (iii) $m^2-2\leqslant m$; (iv) $(m-1)^2-4>0$.
7. Solve the simultaneous equations $x+y+z=2$, $2x-y+z=5$, $3x+2y+z=3$.
8. If α, β are the roots of the equation $2x^2+5x-1=0$, find the equation with roots α^2 and β^2.
9. For what values of m has the equation $x^2(2-m)+x(m-6)+2m+8=0$ equal roots?
10. Find the ranges of real values of x for which: (i) $x^2>6-x$; (ii) $x^2<x+2$. Deduce that there are no values of x for which $6-x<x^2<x+2$. Illustrate this result graphically.
11. Find the relationship between the constants a and b if one root of the equation $x^2+ax+b=0$ is double the other.

12. Solve the equations: (i) $x/3+3/y = x/4-4/y = 1$; (ii) $x-y = 1, x^2+xy = 6$.
13. Show that the inequality $[(x+1)(2-x)]/x > 0$ is satisfied for $0 < x < 2$ and $x < -1$.
14. If α, β are the roots of the equation $x^2-3x-7 = 0$, form the equation whose roots are α^2+1/β^2, β^2+1/α^2.
15. Find the ranges of real values of x for which: (i) $-3 < 2x+1 < 3$; (ii) $-5x < x^2+6 < 5x$.
16. Given $x = p$, $x = q$ satisfy the equation $x^2+ax+b = k(x^2-bx+a)$, find the value of $p/q+q/p$ in terms of the constants a, b, k, assuming $k \neq 1$ or b/a.
17. Solve the inequalities: (i) $(x-1)(x-2) > 0$; (ii) $(x-1)(x-2)(x-3) > 0$.
18. If $k < 0$, show that the roots of the equation $x^2+2x+1 = k$ are not real.
19. Find the values of x, y and z if $2x-5y-z = -4, x+3y+2z = 5, 3x-y-z = -10$.
20. Use a sketch graph of $y = 2/x$ to solve the inequalities: (i) $2/x < -1$; (ii) $(4-x)/x > 0$ for real values of x.
21. One root of the equation $x^2-px-8 = 0$ is the square of the other. Find the value of p.
22. If α, β are the roots of the equation $a(x^2-1)+2bx = 0$, show that the same equation has roots $2\alpha+1/\beta$, $2\beta+1/\alpha$.
23. Given that $1-px+qx^2 \equiv (1-\alpha x)(1-\beta x)$ obtain expressions for: (i) $\alpha^2+\beta^2$; (ii) $\alpha/\beta+\beta/\alpha$ in terms of p and q.
24. If $f: x \to x(x-1)$, $g: x \to (x-1)(2x-3)$, find the set of real values of x for which $f(x) \geqslant g(x)$.
25. Use a semi-graphical method to solve the inequality $2/(x-1) > x, x \neq 1$.
26. Solve the equations $2x = 3y = -4z, x^2-9y^2-4z+8 = 0$.
27. Prove that the roots of the equation $4x^2+4(2-m)x+3m-8 = 0$ are not real if $3 < m < 4$.
28. Find the ranges of real values of x for which: (i) $(x-2)/(x-3) > 4, x \neq 3$; (ii) $(x^2+6)/x > 5, x \neq 0$.
29. If α, β are the roots of the equation $x^2+qx+r = 0$, form the equation with roots $(\alpha-1)^2$ and $(\beta-1)^2$.
30. If x is real, find the ranges of values of k for which: (i) $2x^2+4x+k > 0$; (ii) $2x^2+2kx+4.5 > 0$; (iii) both inequalities are satisfied.
31. Find the ranges of real values of x for which: (i) $1/(2-x) < 1, x \neq 2$; (ii) $-1 < (3x+4)/(x-6) < 1$, $x \neq 6$; (iii) $4/x > x/(x-1), x \neq 0, 1$.

LINEAR RELATIONS

The straight line law

If on plotting values of a variable y against values of a second variable x, a straight line graph is obtained, then y and x are related by a linear equation of the form

$$y = a+bx, \text{ where } a, b \text{ are constants.}$$

In experimental work, observed values of the variables concerned will not be exact but it is possible to establish a linear relationship if one exists and the best approximation to the values of a, b, by drawing the straight line which most closely fits the plotted points.

Non-linear laws

Non-linear laws can often be reduced to a linear form by change of variable. For example, if there is a law of the form $y^3 = a+bx^2$ connecting x and y, the law reduced to the linear form $Y = a+bX$, where $Y = y^3$, $X = x^2$. So to establish a law of this form, plot y^3 against x^2 and obtain a straight line graph.

Additional examples of non-linear laws

(i) $1/x+1/y = 1/a$, where a is constant; plot values of $1/y$ against $1/x$;
(ii) $y = ae^{bx}$, where a, b are constants; plot values of $\ln y$ against x;

(iii) $y = ax^n$, where a, n are constants; plot values of $\lg y$ against $\lg x$;
(iv) $y = ax + b/x$, where a, b are constants; plot values of xy against x^2.

Example 15. The number of bacteria N in a culture at time t hours is given by the table:

t	0	1	2	3
N	100	700	5500	40 300

Establish an approximate law of the form $N = N_0 e^{kt}$ and determine suitable values for the constants N_0 and k.

The law $N = N_0 e^{kt}$ is reduced to a linear form by taking logarithms. In this particular case because of the large values of N, logarithms to base 10 will be more convenient than logarithms to base e. We have

$$\lg N = \lg N_0 + kt \lg e,$$

and to obtain a straight line graph, $\lg N$ is plotted against t (Fig. 2). From the graph, when

$$t = 0, \lg N = 2; N_0 = 100;$$

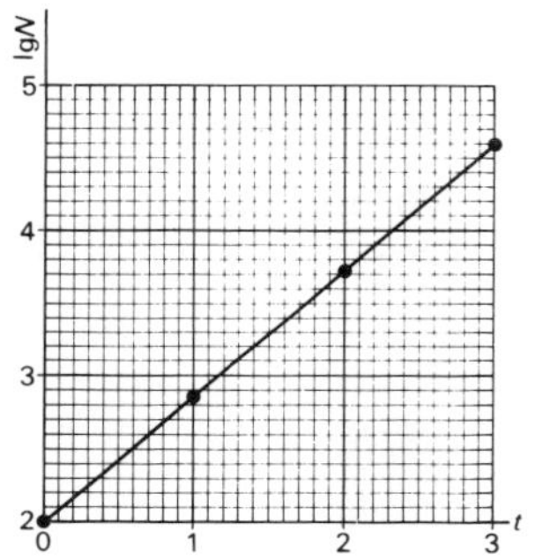

Fig. 2

when

$$t = 3, \lg N = 4.6; 3k \ln e = 2.6, k \approx 2.$$

So an approximate law

$$N = 100e^{2t}$$

is established.

(A) EXAMPLES 3

1. For each of the following relationships where a, b are constants, state the variables which must be plotted to give a straight line graph: (i) $y = a + bx^2$; (ii) $y^2 = a + bx$; (iii) $y = a + b/x$; (iv) $1/y = a + b/x^2$; (v) $y = ax^b$; (vi) $y \doteq ae^{bx}$; (vii) $y = ab^x$; (viii) $x^2 y = a$; (ix) $y = ax + bx^2$; (x) $y = ax + b/x$.
2. The following corresponding values of variables P and V were obtained

P	290	560	1144	1810	2300
V	7.5	10.5	13.5	16.5	18.0

Establish the approximate law $P = a + bV^3$ and obtain values for a and b.

3. The following pairs of values of x and y satisfy approximately a law of the form $y = ax^n$. Find approximate values of the constants a and n.

x	10.4	11.2	12.5	14.8	16.8
y	1.42	1.45	1.50	1.57	1.63

4. The total absorption x mol. of a certain gas by another chemical varies with the time t min. according to the following table:

x	2	4	6	7
t	12	49	106	147

Show that there is an approximate law of the form $t = kx^n$ relating t and x. Obtain values for the constants k and n.

5. The mean distance D of the planets from the sun and their periods of revolution T years are given in the following table, the distance of the earth from the sun being taken as one unit.

	Mercury	Venus	Earth	Mars	Jupiter	Saturn	Uranus	Neptune	Pluto
T	0.241	0.615	1.00	1.88	11.9	29.5	84.0	165	265
D	0.387	0.723	1.00	1.52	5.20	9.54	19.2	30.1	41.3

Show that there is an approximate law of the form $T = aD^b$ and find values for the constants a and b.

6. Corresponding values of variables x and y are given in the following table:

x	1.6	3.0	4.8	7.0	9.6
y	2.0	3.0	4.0	5.0	6.0

By plotting x/y against y, obtain a relation connecting x and y.

MODULUS, QUADRATIC AND RATIONAL FUNCTIONS

Modulus functions

The modulus of x, $|x|$ = the numerical value of x, so

$$|3| = |-3| = 3; \text{ when } x = 1, |x-3| = 2; \ |x^2| = x^2.$$

Example 16. Find x if $|x-1| = 2$.

We have $x-1 = 2$ or $x-1 = -2$.

So $x = 3, -1$.

Graph of the function $|f(x)|$

To obtain the graph of $y = |f(x)|$, draw the graph of $y = f(x)$ and reflect the parts of the graph where y is negative in the x-axis.

Example 17. Sketch the graphs of: (i) $y = |x+1|$; *(ii)* $y = |x-1|$; *(iii)* $y = |x+1|-|x-1|$.

The graphs are shown in Fig. 3 below; the graph of $y = |x+1|-|x-1|$ being obtained from the graphs of $y = |x+1|$ and $y = |x-1|$.

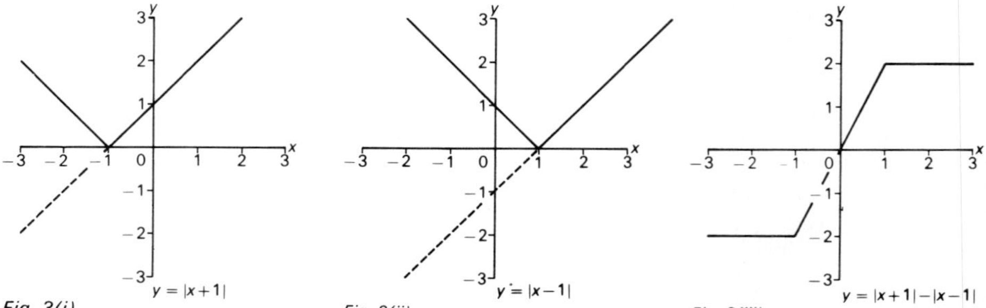

Fig. 3(i) Fig. 3(ii) Fig. 3(iii)

Quadratic functions

General form $ax^2 + bx + c$.

The graph of $y = ax^2 + bx + c$ is a parabola with axis parallel to the y-axis. The vertex is downwards or upwards according as a is positive or negative.

Expression in terms of a perfect square

Completing the square $$ax^2+bx+c = a\left[x^2+\frac{b}{a}x+\frac{c}{a}\right]$$
$$= a\left[\left(x+\frac{b}{2a}\right)^2-\frac{b^2}{4a^2}+\frac{c}{a}\right]$$
$$= a\left[\left(x+\frac{b}{2a}\right)^2+\frac{4ac-b^2}{4a^2}\right].$$

It follows that:

(i) *the function ax^2+bx+c is of invariable sign for real values of x if b^2-4ac is negative. When this condition is satisfied, the function is positive or negative according as a is positive or negative;*

(ii) *the function ax^2+bx+c is expressible as a perfect square if $b^2-4ac = 0$.*

Example 18. *For what range of values of k is the function $(5-k)x^2+3x+k$ positive for all real values of x?*

With the usual notation, the quadratic function is positive if $b^2-4ac < 0$ and $a > 0$. So in this case,

$$3^2-4(5-k)(k) < 0,$$
$$4k^2-20k+9 < 0,$$
$$(2k-1)(2k-9) < 0,$$

i.e. $$\frac{1}{2} < k < \frac{9}{2}; \qquad \text{(i)}$$

and $$5-k > 0,$$
$$k < 5. \qquad \text{(ii)}$$

Conditions (i) and (ii) are satisfied if $1/2 < k < 9/2$. So for this range of values the function is positive.

Example 19. *Determine the two values of m for which the function $2x^2-6x+8-m(x^2-x-2)$ can be expressed in the form $p(x-q)^2$ and for each value find the corresponding values of p and q.*

Collecting the terms, $$\text{function} = x^2(2-m)+x(m-6)+2m+8.$$

With the usual notation, the quadratic function is expressible as a perfect square if $b^2-4ac = 0$. In this case,

$$(m-6)^2-4(2-m)(2m+8) = 0,$$
$$9m^2+4m-28 = 0,$$
$$(9m-14)(m+2) = 0,$$
$$m = -2, \frac{14}{9}.$$

When $m = -2$, function $= 4x^2 - 8x + 4 = 4(x-1)^2$; $p = 4, q = 1$.

When $m = \frac{14}{9}$, function $= \frac{4x^2}{9} - \frac{40x}{9} + \frac{100}{9} = \frac{4(x-5)^2}{9}$; $p = \frac{4}{9}, q = 5$.

Maximum or minimum values

The maximum or minimum value of a quadratic function is readily found by expressing the function in the form $a(x+b)^2 + c$.

Example 20. Express the function $6x - 4 - 3x^2$ in the form $a(x-b)^2 + c$ and write down the coordinates of the maximum point on the curve $y = 6x - 4 - 3x^2$.

Completing the square,
$$6x - 4 - 3x^2 = -3\left[x^2 - 2x + \frac{4}{3}\right],$$
$$= -3\left[(x-1)^2 + \frac{1}{3}\right],$$
$$= -3(x-1)^2 - 1.$$

As $(x-1)^2 \geqslant 0$, the function has a maximum value of -1 when $x = 1$. So the point $(1, -1)$ is the maximum point on the curve $y = 6x - 4 - 3x^2$.

Rational functions

These are functions of the form $p(x)/q(x)$, where $p(x)$, $q(x)$ are polynomials. Only linear rational functions of the form $(ax+b)/(cx+d)$ will be considered here.

Graphs of linear rational functions

Graphs of functions of the type $y = (ax+b)/(cx+d)$ will be of one or other of the forms shown in Fig. 4, where the asymptotes are parallel to the axes.

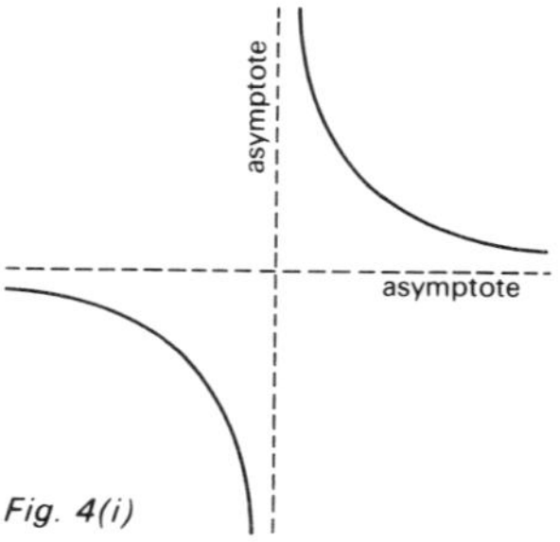

Fig. 4(i)

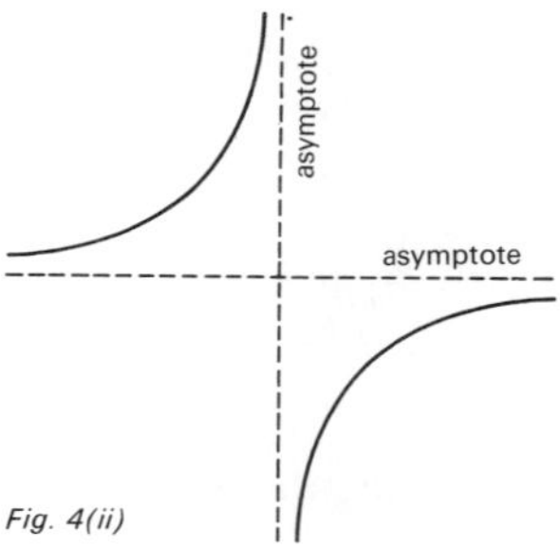

Fig. 4(ii)

The method of finding the equations of the asymptotes is illustrated in the following example.

Example 21. Find the asymptotes of the curve $y = (1-2x)/(1+x)$ and sketch the curve.

The value of x which makes the denominator of the fraction $(1-2x)/(1+x)$ zero, i.e. $x = -1$, gives the asymptote parallel to the y-axis. When sketching the curve, it should be noted that as $x \to -1$ from below, $y \to -\infty$ and as $x \to -1$ from above, $y \to +\infty$.

To obtain the asymptote parallel to the x-axis, rearrange the equation to give $x = (1-y)/(2+y)$ and so $y = -2$ is an asymptote. To help determine the relationship of the curve to its asymptotes find, if possible, the points of intersection of the curve with the axes; in this case $(0, 1)$ and $(1/2, 0)$. To obtain a more accurate graph, take a few additional values for x, say -4, -3, -2, 1 and 2. The graph is shown in Fig. 5.

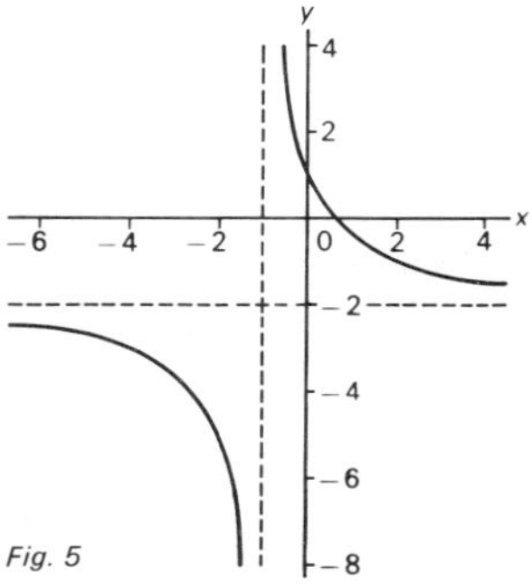

Fig. 5

(A) EXAMPLES 4

1. Sketch the graphs of: (i) $y = |x|$; (ii) $y = |x-2|$; (iii) $y = |x|-|x-2|$; for $-2 \leqslant x \leqslant 4$.
2. Express each of the following functions in the form $p(x+q)^2+r$ and find its sign for all real values of x: (i) x^2+2x+2; (ii) $x^2-6x+10$; (iii) $2x-3-x^2$; (iv) $2x^2+8x+9$; (v) $4x^2-4x+3$; (vi) $2x-3-2x^2$.
3. Sketch the graphs of: (i) $y = x(2-x)$; $y = |x(2-x)|$; for $-2 \leqslant x \leqslant 4$.
4. Find the values of x if $|2x-3| = 5$.
5. Express in the form $a(x+by)^2+cy^2$ each of the expressions: (i) $x^2+4xy+5y^2$; (ii) $2x^2+2xy+y^2$; (iii) $3xy-x^2-y^2$.
6. Express the function x^2-6x+5 in the form $p(x+q)^2+r$ and determine its minimum value. Sketch the graph of $y = x^2-6x+5$.
7. Find: (i) the value of the constant a for which $x^2-2x+a-2$ can be expressed as a perfect square; (ii) the range of values of a for which the function is positive for all real values of x.
8. For each of the following curves find the equations of the asymptotes and sketch the curve: (i) $y = 2x/(x-1)$; (ii) $y = (3x-1)/x$; (iii) $y = 2/(2-x)$; (iv) $y+3 = 6/(x-1)$; (v) $y = 1-2/(x+2)$.
9. For what values of the constant k can the function $(5-k)x^2+3x+k$ be expressed in the form $a(x+b)^2$?
10. Express the function $4x-1-x^2$ in the form $a(x-b)^2+c$ and hence write down the coordinates of the turning point on the curve $y = 4x-1-x^2$.
11. Find the ranges of values of x for which: (i) $|x-1| \leqslant 5$; (ii) $|x-1|^2 \leqslant 4$.
12. Sketch the graph of $y = (1+x)/(1-x)$ and find the range of values of y if x is in the interval $-1 < x < 1$.
13. Show that the function $4x^2+4x(2-m)+3m-8$ is positive for all real values of x, so long as $3 < m < 4$.
14. Show that the expression $(3x-2)^2+k(x-1)(x-2)$ can be put in the form of a perfect square $a(x+b)^2$ when k has one of two possible values. Find these values and the corresponding ones of a and b.
15. Sketch the graphs of; (i) $y = |(x+2)/x|$; (ii) $y = |x/(x+2)|$.
16. Find the range of values of λ for which the function $4\lambda x^2+4(\lambda+1)x+3\lambda+3$ is of invariable sign for all real values of x.
17. If x, p, q are real, show that the function $x^2+(p-q)x+p^2+pq+q^2$ is positive.

EXPONENTIAL AND LOGARITHMIC FUNCTIONS

Exponential functions

The general exponential function is a^x, where $a > 0$. The function e^x is of special importance and is referred to as *the* exponential function.

Graphs

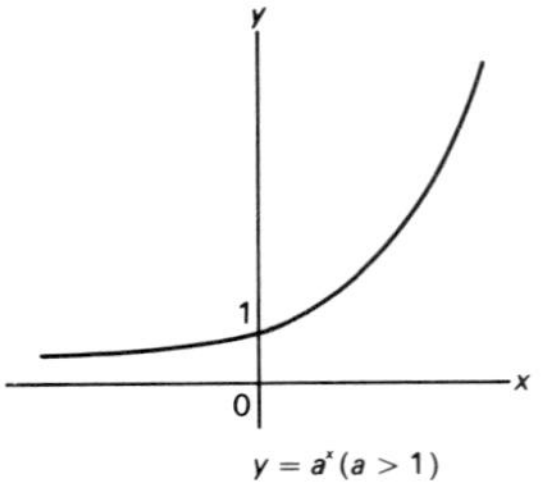

$y = a^x\,(a > 1)$

Fig. 6(i)

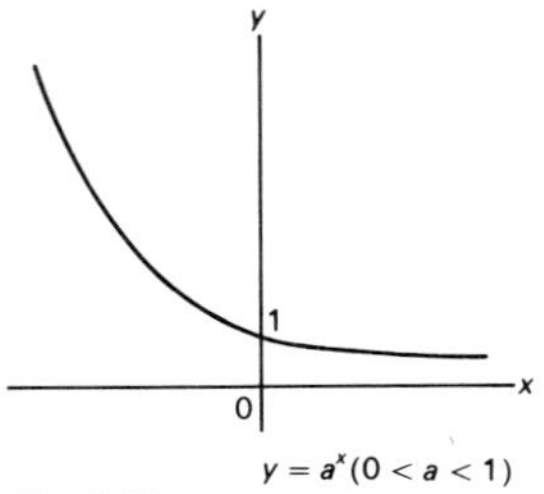

$y = a^x\,(0 < a < 1)$

Fig. 6(ii)

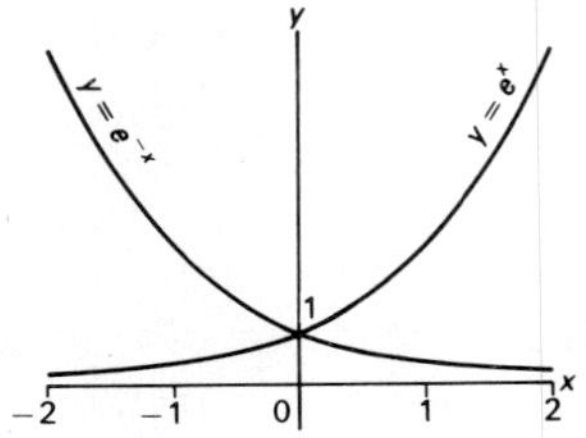

$y = e^x$ and $y = e^{-x}$

Fig. 6(iii)

Note

(i) Exponential functions are positive for all real values of x;
(ii) $a^{1/n} = \sqrt[n]{a}$, where n is a positive integer; $a^0 = 1$; $a^{-n} = a^{1/n}$.

Laws

$$a^x \times a^y = a^{x+y};$$

$$a^x \div a^y = a^{x-y};$$

$$(a^x)^y = a^{xy}.$$

Example 22. Solve the equation $2^{2x} - 3.2^{x+1/2} + 2^2 = 0$.

Writing $2^x = y$ and noting that $2^{x+1/2} = \sqrt{2}.2^x$ and $2^{2x} = (2^x)^2$, the equation becomes

$$y^2 - 3\sqrt{2}y + 4 = 0,$$

giving

$$y = \sqrt{2}, 2\sqrt{2}.$$

So

$$2^x = \sqrt{2} = 2^{1/2};\ x = \frac{1}{2},$$

$$2^x = 2\sqrt{2} = 2^{3/2};\ x = \frac{3}{2}.$$

Logarithmic functions

The basic logarithmic function is $\log_a x$, where the base a is positive; an important special case is the function $\log_e x$, written $\ln x$.

It should be noted that exponential and logarithmic functions are inverse functions, for if $y = a^x$, $x = \log_a y$.

Graphs

Note

(i) $\log_a x$ only exists for positive values of x;
(ii) $\log_a 1 = 0$;
(iii) $\log_a (a^x)$ and $a^{\log_a x} = x$.

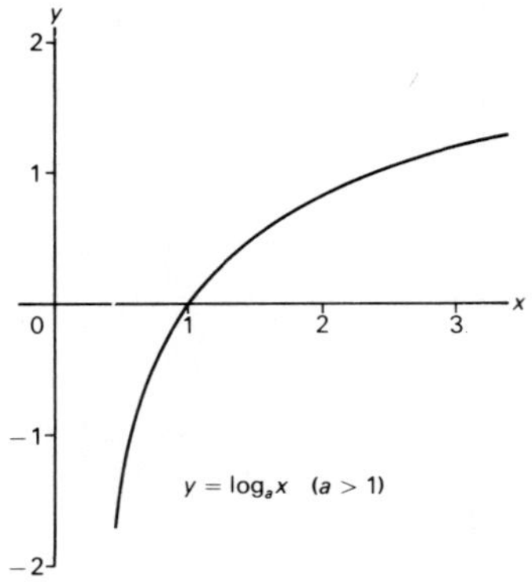

Fig. 7(i)

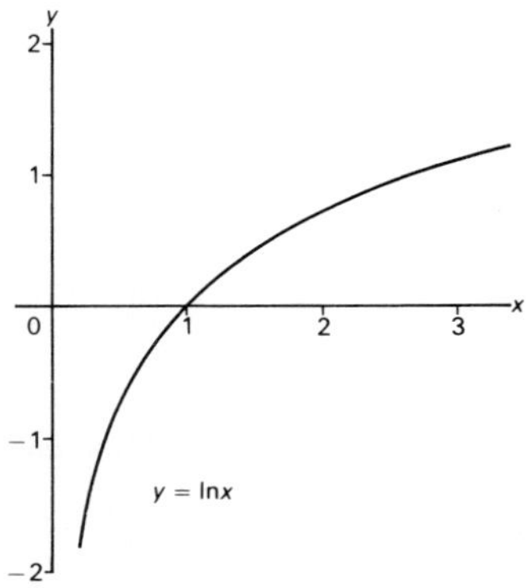

Fig. 7(ii)

Laws

$$\log_a x + \log_a y = \log_a xy;$$

$$\log_a x - \log_a y = \log_a x/y;$$

$$\log_a(x^k) = k\log_a x.$$

Special case, $$\log_a(1/x) = -\log_a x.$$

Change of base law

$$\log_a x = \frac{\log_b x}{\log_b a}.$$

Special case taking $a = y$ and $b = x$,

$$\log_y x = \frac{1}{\log_x y}.$$

Example 23. Simplify: (i) $\ln\sqrt{(1-x^2)/(1+x^2)}$; (ii) $\ln(e^{\sqrt{x}})$; (iii) $e^{-2\ln x}$.

(i) $\ln[\sqrt{(1-x^2)/(1+x^2)}] = \ln[(1-x^2)/(1+x^2)]/2 = [\ln(1-x^2) - \ln(1+x^2)]/2$;
(ii) $\ln(e^{\sqrt{x}}) = \sqrt{x}$;
(iii) $e^{-2\ln x} = e^{\ln 1/x^2} = 1/x^2$.

Example 24. Solve the equations $\log_x y + 2\log_y x = 3$, $\log_3 y + \log_9 x = 3$.

Replacing $\log_y x$ by $1/\log_x y$ in the first equation and writing $z = \log_x y$ gives

$$z^2 - 3z + 2 = 0,$$

$$z = 1, 2.$$

So $\log_x y = 1$, i.e. $y = x$; $\log_x y = 2$, i.e. $y = x^2$.

In the second equation, replacing $\log_3 y$ by $2\log_9 y$ or $\log_9 y^2$ and combining the terms, $\log_9(y^2x) = 3$ or

$$y^2x = 9^3.$$

So when $y = x$,

$$y^3 = 9^3,\ y = 9,\ x = 9;$$

and when $y = x^2$,

$$x^5 = 9^3,\ x = 9^{3/5},\ y = 9^{6/5}.$$

(A) EXAMPLES 5

1. Simplify: (i) $2^x \times 8^y$; (ii) $\log_a(1/a)$; (iii) $\ln\sqrt{e}$; (iv) $2^{\log_2 x}$; (v) $\ln\sqrt{[(1+x)/(1-x)]}$; (vi) $e^{1/2\ln 2}$; (vii) $\ln e^{\sqrt{x}}$; (viii) $\log_a 8/\log_a 2$.
2. Find x if: (i) $\log_x 16 = 2$; (ii) $\log_{16} x = 2$.
3. Solve the equation $(2.4)^x = (5.3)^{x-1}$.
4. Express $\log_4(x^2y^3)$ in terms of $\log_2 x$ and $\log_2 y$.
5. If $\log_y x = 1/2$, what is the value of $\log_x y$? Express y in terms of x.
6. Find the two possible values of x if $(\log_2 x)^2 = 4$.
7. Given $\log_9 x = n$, find the values of: (i) $\log_9 3x$; (ii) $\log_3 x$; (iii) $\log_x 81$.
8. Find the values of x and y if $2^x 4^{-y} = 2$ and $3^{-x} 9^{2y} = 3$.
9. For what values of x does $9\log_x 5 = \log_5 x$?
10. Given $\log_3 6 = m$ and $\log_6 5 = n$, obtain the values of $\log_3 2$, $\log_3 5$ and $\log_3 30$ in terms of m and n.
11. Solve the equation $3^{x-2} = 1.8$, giving the value of x correct to four significant figures.
12. Given $\log_a 2 = m$ and $2^{x-2} = a/8$, show that $m(x+1) = 1$.
13. Simplify: (i) $\ln 1/\sqrt{e}$; (ii) $e^{2\ln x}$; (iii) $e^{1/2\ln(1+x)}$.
14. Given $\log_a(xy^3) = m$ and $\log_a(x^2y) = n$, find the value of $\log_a\sqrt{(xy)}$ in terms of m and n.
15. Find y if $1/\lg y + 2\lg 5 = 4$, where $\lg y = \log_{10} y$.
16. Solve the equation $\log_4 x + \log_x 4 = 2.5$.
17. A curve with equation $y = ax^n$, where a, n are constants, passes through the points (2,96), (3,729). Find the values of a and n.
18. Solve the equation $3^{2x} - 3^{x+2} + 8 = 0$.
19. If α, β are the roots of the equation $ax^2+bx+c = 0$, show that $\log(ax^2+bx+c) = \log a + \log(x-\alpha) + \log(x-\beta)$.
20. Find the integer n if $\log_8 n = \log_2 3 + 2\log_4 3 + 1$.
21. Solve the equation $\log_8(x/2)\log_8 2 = \log_2 x$.

FUNCTIONS AND COMPOSITE FUNCTIONS

Functions of a real variable

If a relation between two variables y and x is such that when x is given, y is uniquely determined, then y is said to be a function of x.

A function of x is usually written as $f(x)$; if more than one function is involved, $f(x)$ and $g(x)$ can be used to denote them.

For a particular function defined for all real values of x, say $x(x-2)$, we can write

$$f(x) = x(x-2)$$

for all real values of x, or in more formal notation:

$$f: x \to x(x-2),\quad x \in \mathbb{R}.$$

Domain and range

The *domain* of a function $f(x)$ is the range of values of x for which the function is defined; a *sub-domain* is a part of the domain.

The *range*, or *set of images*, of a function is the range of possible values the function can take for values of x in the domain or sub-domain involved.

Example 25. State the domain and find the range of each of the functions (i) $f(x) = \sqrt{(4-x^2)}$*; (ii)* $f(x) = \ln(1+x)$*; (iii)* $f(x) = x^2-3x+2$*, where x is real.*

(i) Clearly $\sqrt{(4-x^2)}$ is not defined if $x^2 > 4$ and so its domain is $-2 \leqslant x \leqslant 2$. The range is given by $0 \leqslant f(x) \leqslant 2$;
(ii) here $(1+x)$ must be > 0, so the domain is $x > -1$. The function can take all real values and so the range is given by $-\infty < f(x) < +\infty$;
(iii) the function x^2-3x+2 is defined for all real values of x, i.e. $x \in \mathbb{R}$. To find the range use the method of completing the square

$$f(x) = x^2-3x+2 = \left(x-\frac{3}{2}\right)^2-\frac{1}{4}.$$

The function has a minimum value of $-1/4$ and so the range is given by $f(x) \geqslant -1/4$.

Special types of function

One-one or injective functions. If a function $y = f(x)$ is such that no value of y can be obtained from more than one value of x, the function is said to be a *one-one* or *injective function*, e.g.

$$y = \frac{x}{x-1} \quad \text{and} \quad y = 2^x \text{ are one-one functions.}$$

Even and odd functions. A function $f(x)$ is *even* if $f(-x) = f(x)$ and *odd* if $f(-x) = -f(x)$, e.g.

$$\frac{1}{x^2+1} \text{ is an even function,}$$

$$\frac{x}{x^2+1} \text{ is an odd function and}$$

$$\frac{1}{x+1} \text{ is neither even nor odd.}$$

If $f(x)$ is a function neither even nor odd as for example $f(x) = e^x$, then $f(x)$ can be expressed as the sum of an even and an odd function as:

$$f(x) = \frac{1}{2}[f(x)+f(-x)]+\frac{1}{2}[f(x)-f(-x)],$$

where the first bracket in an even function and the second bracket an odd function, e.g.

$$e^x = \frac{1}{2}(e^x+e^{-x})+\frac{1}{2}(e^x-e^{-x}).$$

Periodic functions. If the value of a function $f(x)$ repeats itself at regular intervals of x, the function is said to be *periodic*. So if $f(x+a) = f(x)$ where a is a positive constant, then $f(x)$ is periodic; the least value of a is called the period of function. The most common periodic functions are the trigonometric functions which will be dealt with in a later section.

Graphs

The graphs of some important algebraic functions have been dealt with in previous sections. In general, graphs provide a valuable means of illustrating and investigating properties of given functions. They can be drawn or sketched from given functional relationships over stated domains, e.g. $y = xe^{-x}$, $x \geqslant 0$, or from more specific data as is illustrated in the following example.

Example 26. The function f is defined by: (i) f has domain $\mathbb{R}$; (ii) f is even; (iii) f is periodic with period 2; (iv) $f(x) = 2x^3$ for $0 \leqslant x \leqslant 1$. Sketch the graph of $y = f(x)$ for $-3 \leqslant x \leqslant 3$.

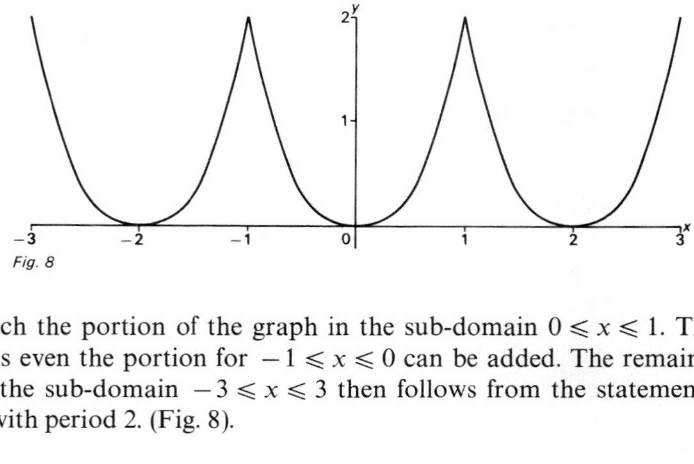

Fig. 8

First sketch the portion of the graph in the sub-domain $0 \leqslant x \leqslant 1$. Then as the function is even the portion for $-1 \leqslant x \leqslant 0$ can be added. The remainder of the graph in the sub-domain $-3 \leqslant x \leqslant 3$ then follows from the statement that f is periodic with period 2. (Fig. 8).

Transformations of the graph of $y = f(x)$

Taking a as a non-zero constant:

(i) $y = f(x)+a$; the graph of $y = f(x)$ is moved a distance a in the direction of the y-axis or alternatively the graph of $y = f(x)$ becomes the graph of $y = f(x)+a$ by moving the x-axis parallel to itself through a new origin at the point $(0, -a)$;

(ii) $y = f(x-a)$; the graph of $y = f(x)$ becomes the graph of $y = f(x-a)$ when the y-axis is moved parallel to itself through a new origin at the point $(-a, 0)$;

(iii) $y = af(x)$; the graph of $y = f(x)$ is changed by a scale factor of a in the direction of the y-axis or more simply the graph of $y = f(x)$ becomes the graph of $y = af(x)$ by multiplying the scale on the y-axis by a;

(iv) $y = f(ax)$; the graph of $y = f(x)$ is changed by a scale factor of $1/a$ in the direction of the x-axis or more simply the graph of $y = f(x)$ becomes the graph of $y = f(ax)$ when the scale on the x-axis is multiplied by $1/a$.

Example 27. Express $f(x) = 2x^2 - 8x + 9$ in the form $a(x-p)^2 + q$. Show that the graph of $y = 2x^2 - 8x + 9$ may be obtained from the graph of $y = x^2$ by appropriate translations and scalings.

Completing the square,
$$f(x) = 2\left[x^2 - 4x + \frac{9}{2}\right],$$
$$= 2\left[(x-2)^2 - 4 + \frac{9}{2}\right],$$
$$= 2(x-2)^2 + 1.$$

To obtain the graph of $y = 2x^2 - 8x + 9$ from that of $y = x^2$ (Fig. 9(i)); move the origin to the point $(-2, 0)$ (Fig. 9(ii)); multiply the y-scale by 2 (Fig. 9(iii)); finally move the origin to the point $(0, -1)$ with respect to the new scales (Fig. 9(iv)).

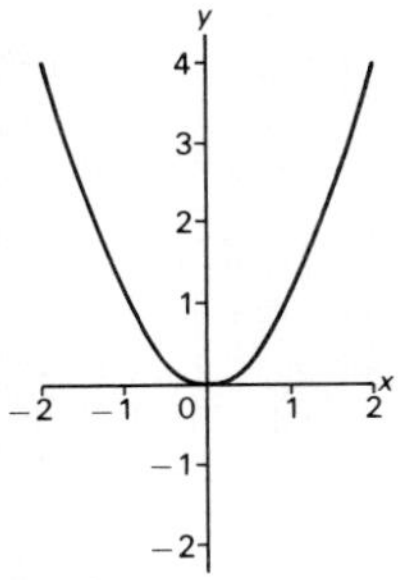

Fig. 9(i)

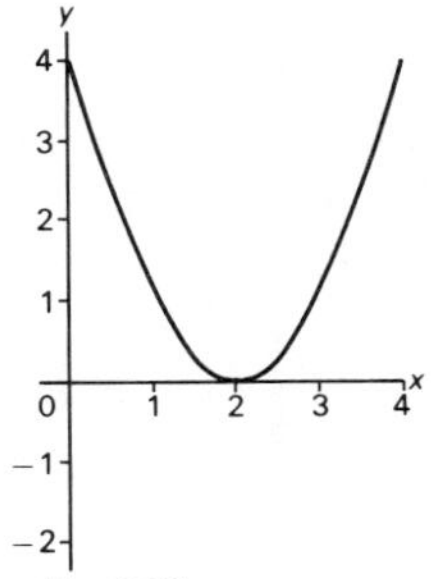

Fig. 9(ii)

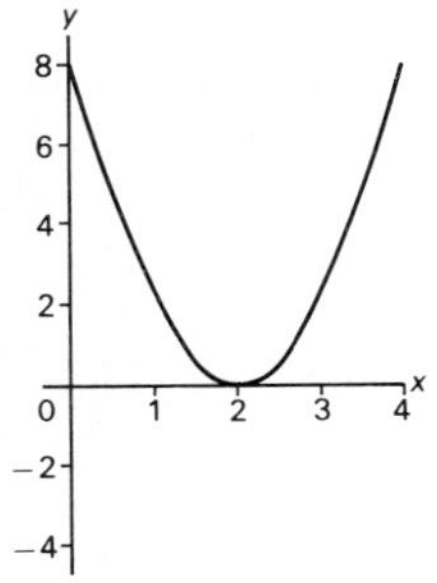

Fig. 9(iii)

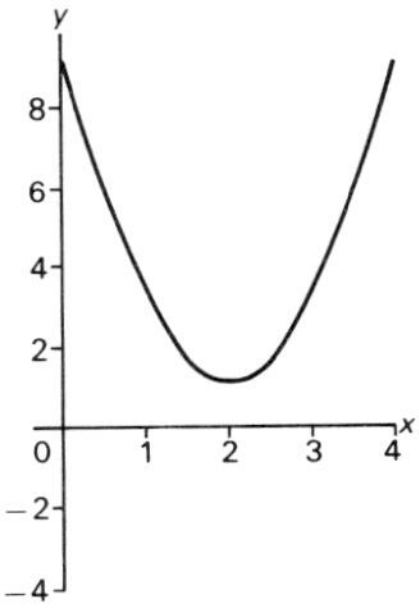

Fig. 9(iv)

Inverse functions

If $y = f(x)$ is a $1-1$ function of x there exists a function $y = f^{-1}(x)$, called the *inverse function* of $f(x)$; the ordered pairs (x, y) of the inverse function are the ordered pairs (y, x) of the given function.

The graph of $y = f^{-1}(x)$ is the reflection of the graph of $y = f(x)$ in the line $y = x$; the domain and range of f become the range and domain respectively of f^{-1}. To obtain the inverse function in a given case, switch the variables to give $x = f(y)$ and solve for y to give $y = f^{-1}(x)$.

Example 28. Given $f(x) = 2x/(x-1)$, $x \in \mathbb{R}$, $x \neq 1$, find the inverse function $f^{-1}(x)$ stating its domain and range. Sketch the graphs of $y = f(x)$ and $y = f^{-1}(x)$.

$$y = f(x) = \frac{2x}{x-1}.$$

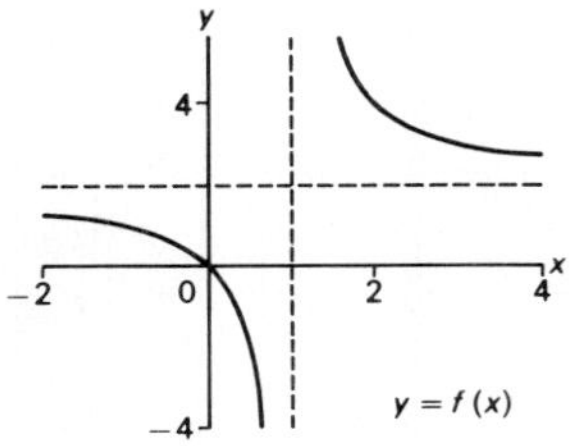

Fig. 10(i)

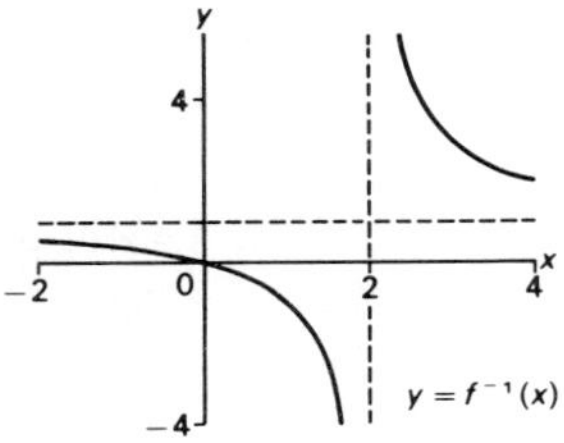

Fig. 10(ii)

Interchanging x and y, $$x = \frac{2y}{y-1}.$$

Solving for y, $$y = f^{-1}(x) = \frac{x}{x-2}.$$

The domain of f^{-1} is $x \in \mathbb{R}$, $x \neq 2$; i.e. the range of f; the range of f^{-1} is $y \in \mathbb{R}$, $y \neq 1$; i.e. the domain of f.

Sketch graphs of $y = f(x)$ and $y = f^{-1}(x)$ are shown in Fig. 10.

Special cases of inverse functions

In some cases where a function $f(x)$ is not $1-1$ it is possible to restrict its domain so that the restricted function does have an inverse. Take for example the function $y = f(x) = x(x-2)$ whose graph is shown in Fig. 11. The domain of $f(x)$ is all real values of x and its range is given by $-1 \leqslant f(x)$. Clearly $f(x)$ is not a $1-1$ function as a value of $y \geqslant -1$ is obtained from two values of x. By restricting the domain to either $x \geqslant 1$ or $x \leqslant 1$, the restricted function is $1-1$ and has an inverse. We will take the case $x \geqslant 1$.

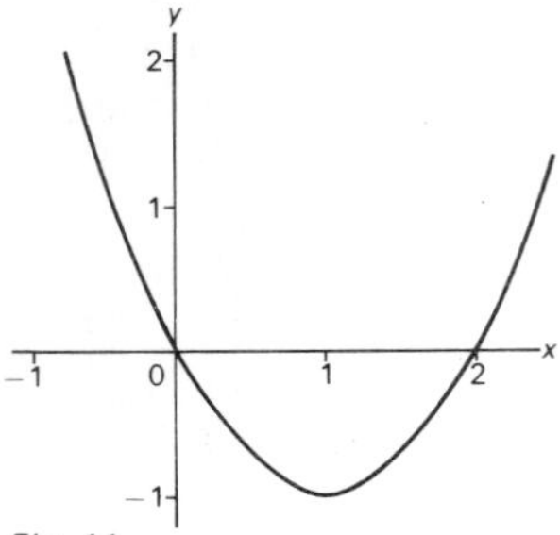

Fig. 11

Then interchanging x and y, $$x = y(y-2),$$

$$y^2 - 2y - x = 0,$$

$$y = \frac{2 \pm \sqrt{(4+4x)}}{2},$$

$$= 1 \pm \sqrt{(1+x)}.$$

But the domain of the restricted function $f(x)$ is $x \geqslant 1$, so the range of the inverse function is $f^{-1}(x) \geqslant 1$. Consequently $y = 1 + \sqrt{(1+x)}$, i.e.

$$f^{-1}(x) = 1 + \sqrt{(1+x)},\ x \geqslant -1.$$

Clearly if the other sub-domain $x \leqslant 1$ had been chosen, the inverse function would have been $1 - \sqrt{(1+x)}$.

Combinations of functions

Consider the functions $f(x)$, $g(x)$ with domains d_f, d_g respectively, then the functions $f(x)+g(x)$, $f(x)-g(x)$, $f(x)\cdot g(x)$ and $f(x)/g(x)$ will be defined for values of x common to d_f and d_g with the exception that in the quotient function $f(x)/g(x)$ the values of x for which $g(x) = 0$ must be excluded.

Composite functions

The composite function of functions g and f written $g_0 f$ or sometimes gf, is defined as the function $g(f(x))$; similarly the composite function of f and g, $f_0 g$ or fg, is defined as $f(g(x))$, e.g. given

$$f(x) = 4x + 7,\ g(x) = 3x^2 - 2x + 1,$$

then $$(g_0 f)(x) = 3(4x+7)^2 - 2(4x+7) + 1,$$
$$= 48x^2 + 160x + 134.$$
$$(f_0 g)(x) = 4(3x^2 - 2x + 1) + 7,$$
$$= 12x^2 - 8x + 11.$$

Clearly $g_0 f$ is only defined for values of x for which the value of $f(x)$ falls within the domain of $g(x)$ and similarly for the composite function $f_0 g$.

Inverses of composite functions
If the inverse functions $f^{-1}, g^{-1}, (g_0 f)^{-1}$ exist, then
$$(g_0 f)^{-1} = f_0^{-1} g^{-1},$$
and if $(f_0 g)^{-1}$ also exists
$$(f_0 g)^{-1} = g_0^{-1} f^{-1}.$$

Example 29. The functions f and g are defined by $f(x) = e^{-x}$ for x real and positive and $g(x) = 1/(1-x)$, for x real and <1. Write down the composite functions $g_0 f$ and $f_0 g$ stating in each case the domain and the range. Also determine the inverse functions $(g_0 f)^{-1}$ and $(f_0 g)^{-1}$, verifying the result $(g_0 f)^{-1} = f_0^{-1} g^{-1}$.

The composite function
$$y = (g_0 f)(x) = \frac{1}{1-e^{-x}}$$
is defined for real values of x for which the value of e^{-x}, defined for $x > 0$, is <1; i.e. for $x > 0$. So the domain of $g_0 f$ is $x > 0$, and the range is given by $y > 1$.

The composite function
$$y = (f_0 g)(x) = e^{-\left(\frac{1}{1-x}\right)}$$
is defined for real values of x for which the value of $1/(1-x)$, defined for $x < 1$, is > 0; i.e. for $x < 1$. So the domain of $f_0 g$ is $x < 1$ and the range is given by $0 < y < 1$.

To find $(g_0 f)^{-1}$, write $$x = \frac{1}{1-e^{-y}},$$
then $$y = (g_0 f)^{-1}(x) = \ln \frac{x}{x-1} \quad \text{for } x > 1.$$

To find $(f_0 g)^{-1}$, write $$x = e^{-\left(\frac{1}{1-y}\right)},$$
then $$y = (f_0 g)^{-1}(x) = \frac{1+\ln x}{\ln x} \quad \text{for } 0 < x < 1.$$

Also $f^{-1}(x) = \ln(1/x)$ for $0 < x < 1$ and $g^{-1}(x) = (x-1)/x$ for $x > 0$, so
$$(f_0^{-1} g^{-1})(x) = \ln \frac{x}{x-1} \quad \text{for } x > 1,$$
$$= (g_0 f)^{-1}(x).$$

(A) EXAMPLES 6

In each of the examples 1–12 find the domain and range of the function $f(x)$ for real values of x and sketch the graph of $y = f(x)$ in the given sub-domain.

1. $f(x) = x^2 - 2x;\ -1 \leqslant x \leqslant 3$.
2. $f(x) = e^{-x};\ 0 \leqslant x \leqslant 5$.
3. $f(x) = 4\sqrt{x};\ 0 \leqslant x \leqslant 9$.
4. $f(x) = \sqrt{(1+x^2)};\ -3 \leqslant x \leqslant 3$.
5. $f(x) = \sqrt{(9-x^2)};\ -3 \leqslant x \leqslant 3$.
6. $f(x) = x^{-1/2};\ 0 < x \leqslant 4$.
7. $f(x) = 1/x^2;\ -3 \leqslant x \leqslant 3,\ x \neq 0$.
8. $f(x) = \dfrac{2}{1+x};\ -4 \leqslant x \leqslant 2,\ x \neq -1$.
9. $f(x) = |x-1|;\ -2 \leqslant x \leqslant 4$.
10. $f(x) = \ln(1+x);\ 0 \leqslant x \leqslant 5$.
11. $f(x) = |x(x-2)|;\ -3 \leqslant x \leqslant 3$.
12. $f(x) = |\ln x|;\ e^{-2} \leqslant x \leqslant e^2$.
13. Does the relation $x^2 + y^3 = 4$ determine: (i) y as a function of x; (ii) y as a 1–1 function of x, assuming x and y are real?
14. The functions f and g are defined on the set of real numbers by $f{:}x \to |x^2-4|$, $g{:}x \to 4$. Draw the graphs of f and g for $-3 \leqslant x \leqslant 3$ and state the range of values of x for which $f \leqslant g$.
15. Find the ranges of the functions: (i) $y = x^2 - 3x + 2$; (ii) $y = 4x - x^2$; (iii) $y = 2x^2 - 10x + 13$ for real values of x.
16. State whether the following functions are odd, even or neither: (i) $3x^3 + x$; (ii) x^{-2}; (iii) $2x^2 + 1$; (iv) $x/(x^2+1)$; (v) $x/(x+2)$; (vi) $x^2/(x-1)$; (vii) x^2e^{-x}; (viii) xe^{-x^2}.
17. If $f(x) = x/(x-1)$, $x \neq 1$, show that the function $f(x) + f(-x)$ is even and the function $f(x) - f(-x)$ is odd.
18. Find the domain and the range of the functions defined by the equations: (i) $y = \sqrt{(x-x^2)}$; (ii) $y = -\sqrt{(x-x^2)}$ and sketch the graph in each case.
19. The function f is defined for real values of x satisfying $-2 \leqslant x \leqslant 4$ by

$$f{:}x \to \begin{cases} x(2-x) & \text{for} \quad -1 \leqslant x \leqslant 3, \\ -2 & \text{for} \quad -3 \leqslant x < -1 \text{ and } 3 < x \leqslant 4. \end{cases}$$

Sketch the graph of the function.

20. Show that the function $f(x) = x - [x]$, where $[x]$ denotes the greatest possible integer $\leqslant x$, is periodic with a period of unity and sketch the graph of $y = f(x)$.
21. Find the domain and the range and sketch the graph of each of the functions defined by the equations: (i) $y = 4/(2-x), x \neq 2$; (ii) $y = x/(x+1), x \neq 1$; (iii) $y = |(1+2x)/(x-1)|, x \neq 1$.
22. The function f is defined by: (i) f has domain $\mathbb{R}$; (ii) f is even; (iii) f is periodic with period 2; (iv) for $0 \leqslant x \leqslant 1, f(x) = \sqrt{x}$. Sketch the graph of $f(x)$ for $-4 \leqslant x \leqslant 4$.
23. Show how the graphs of the straight lines: (i) $y = x + 4$; (ii) $y = 2x + 1$; (iii) $2y = x - 4$ can be obtained from the graph of $y = x$ by appropriate translations and scalings.
24. Express each of the functions: (i) $f(x) = x^2 + 2x + 1$; (ii) $f(x) = x^2 + 2x + 3$; (iii) $f(x) = 2x^2 + 4x + 3$ in the form $a(x+p)^2 + q$. Show in each case that the graph of $y = f(x)$ can be obtained from the graph of $y = x^2$ by appropriate translations and scalings.
25. In each of the following cases find the inverse function $f^{-1}(x)$ and state its domain and range. Also sketch the graphs of $y = f^{-1}(x)$ and $y = f(x)$ on the same diagram: (i) $f(x) = 3x + 1$, $x \in \mathbb{R}$; (ii) $f(x) = e^x, x \in \mathbb{R}$; (iii) $f(x) = 1/(x-1), x \in \mathbb{R}$ but $\neq 1$; (iv) $f(x) = \ln(1+x), x \in \mathbb{R}$ and > -1.
26. Show that the function $y = f(x) = x^2$ defined for all real values of x does not have an inverse. Find the sub-domains for x such that the restricted function does have an inverse and find the inverse in each case.
27. Given $f(x) = x/(x+1)$ for $x \in \mathbb{R}$ but $\neq -1$, find $f^{-1}(x)$ and sketch the graphs of $y = f(x)$ and $y = f^{-1}(x)$.
28. The function $f(x) = x(x-4)$ is defined over the domain $x \in \mathbb{R}$. Show that: (i) $f(x)$ has not an inverse over this domain; (ii) an inverse function $f^{-1}(x)$ does exist when $f(x)$ is restricted to one or other of two sub-domains to be stated and find $f^{-1}(x)$ in these cases.
29. In each of the following cases the functions f and g are defined for $x \in \mathbb{R}$ with the exceptions stated, find the composite functions $g_0 f$ and $f_0 g$, stating the domain and range in each case.
   (i) $f(x) = x^2 + 2, g(x) = 2x - 1$;
   (ii) $f(x) = e^x, g(x) = x - 2$;
   (iii) $f(x) = 1/(1-x), x \neq 1, g(x) = x^2$;
   (iv) $f(x) = \ln x, x > 0, g(x) = |x|$;
   (v) $f(x) = x/(1+x), x \neq -1, g(x) = e^{-x}$;
   (vi) $f(x) = \sqrt{x}, x \geqslant 0, g(x) = |x-1|$.

30. Given $f(x) = 1/(x+1), x > -1, g(x) = \ln x, x > 0$, find the composite functions $g_0 f$ and $f_0 g$ stating their domains and ranges. Also find the inverse functions $f^{-1}, g^{-1}, (g_0 f)^{-1}$ and $(f_0 g)^{-1}$ and verify that $(g_0 f)^{-1} = f_0^{-1} g^{-1}, (f_0 g)^{-1} = g_0^{-1} f^{-1}$.

(B) MISCELLANEOUS EXAMPLES

1. Find the values of the constants a and b if $x^2 - x - 2$ is a factor of $f(x) = 2x^4 + ax^3 - 4x^2 + bx - 2$ and complete the factorisation of $f(x)$.
2. Show that $1/(3+2\sqrt{2})^3 + 1/(3-2\sqrt{2})^3 = 198$.
3. Prove that the equations $(x+a)y = 1, (y+b)x = 1$ have no real solutions if $-4 < ab < 0$.
4. If $\log_4 m = a, \log_{12} m = b$, prove that $\log_3 48 = (a+b)/(a-b)$.
5. Find the values of the constant λ if the roots α, β of the equation $5x^2 + (2\lambda + 1)x + \lambda - 2 = 0$ are such that $2\alpha + 5\beta = 1$.
6. Sketch the graph of $y = f(x) = (x+1)/(x-2), x \neq 2$. Find the inverse function f^{-1} and also sketch the graph of $y = f^{-1}(x)$.
7. Solve the inequalities: (i) $(x+1)(x-1) > 0$; (ii) $(x+1)(x-1)(x-2) > 0$; (iii) $(x-2)/(x-3) > 4$.
8.

x	1	2	3	4	5	6
y	2.7	6.8	12.3	19.6	28.0	37.8

The table gives pairs of simultaneous values of two variables x, y. Show graphically that the values satisfy an approximate formula $y = ax + bx^2$ and find values for the constants a and b.

9. Find the range of values of the constant k for which the function $x^2 + 2x(1-k) + 3k - 5$ is of invariable sign for all real values of x. What is the sign?
10. Prove that the equation $a^2x^2 + (4ac - b^2)x + c^2 = 0$ has positive roots if the roots of the equation $ax^2 + bx + c = 0$ are real.
11. Find the value of the integer n if $2 \log_{27} n = \log_9 16 + 2$.
12. Given that $1 + \omega + \omega^2 = 0$ show that: (i) $\omega^3 = 1$; (ii) $1/(1+\omega) = (1 - \omega + \omega^2)/2 = -\omega$.
13. Sketch the graphs of: (i) $y = 2x/(x-1)$; (ii) $y = |2x/(x-1)|$; (iii) $y^2 = 2x/(x-1), x \neq 1$.
14. Express the function $4x - 1 - x^2$ in the form $p(x-q)^2 + r$. Find the coordinates of: (i) the maximum point on the curve $y = 4x - 1 - x^2$; (ii) the minimum point on the curve $y = (4x - 1 - x^2)^{-1}$.
15. Find the ranges of real values of x for which: (i) $|(3x+4)/(x-6)| < 1$; (ii) $(x^2+3)/(x+3) > 1$.
16. Express $f(x) = 2x^2 + 4x + 5$ in the form $a(x+p)^2 + q$. Show that the graph of $y = f(x)$ may be obtained from the graph of $y = x^2$ by appropriate translations and scalings.
17. Find the values of a and b if $\log_2(ab^2) = -2$ and $\log_2 a \log_2 b = -12$.
18. If $f(x) = x^3 - ax^2 - 4a^2x + 4a^3$, using the factor theorem or otherwise show that $(x-a)$ is a factor of $f(x)$. Complete the factorisation of $f(x)$ and if $a > 0$, find the ranges of values of x for which $f(x)$ is positive.
19. If n is a positive integer, prove by induction that $f(n) = 7^n(3n+1) - 1$ is always divisible by 9.
20. Find the values of the constant k for which the equations $x^2 + kx - 6k = 0, x^2 - 2x - k = 0$ have a common root.
21. Given $y = ax^2 + bx + c$ and $y = -2, -26, -17$ when $x = 1, -1, 2$ respectively, find the values of the constants a, b, c and show that y is negative for all real values of x.
22. The functions f and g are defined by $f(x) = e^{2x}, g(x) = x - 1$ for $x \in \mathbb{R}$. Write down the composite function $g_0 f$ and state its domain and range. Also find the inverse function $(g_0 f)^{-1}$ and sketch the graphs of the composite function and its inverse.
23. Solve the equations $\log_x y + 3 \log_y x = 4, 2 \log_4 x + \log_2 y = 2$.
24. Given $y = a(x+b)^2 + c$, where $a \neq 0, b, c$ are constants, write down the coordinates of the turning point on the graph of this equation. State the conditions that: (i) the curve touches the x-axis; (ii) the curve does not meet the x-axis.
25. Sketch the graph of $y = (9-4x)/(2-x), x \neq 2$ and use it to find the range of values of x for which $y > 9$. On the sketch show the region for which $0 \leqslant x \leqslant 2, 0 \leqslant y \leqslant 9$ and $y \leqslant (9-4x)/(2-x)$.
26. By eliminating a^2 from the equations $x^2 - 6xy + 11y^2 = 3a^2, x^2 - 2xy - 3y^2 = 5a^2$, find two values for the ratio $x:y$ and hence solve the equations for x, y in terms of a.
27. Functions f and g are defined for real values of x as follows: $f: x \rightarrow e^{-2x}, x > 0; g: x \rightarrow 1/(2-x)$,

$x < 2$. State the ranges of the functions f, g and $g_0 f$ and find expressions for the inverses of the functions giving domain and range in each case.

28. If the remainder when $f(x) \equiv x^3+ax^2+bx+c$, where a, b, c are constants, is divided by $(x+1)(x-2)$ is $8x+4$, show that $f(x) \equiv (x+1)(x-2)g(x)+8x+4$ where $g(x)$ is some other function of x. By taking suitable values for x, find two equations connecting a, b and c. If it is also given that $f(x)$ has a factor $(x-1)$, find the values of a, b, c and solve the equation $f(x) = 0$.
29. Show that the function ax^2+bx+c can be expressed in the form $a(x+p)^2+q$ and deduce that it is a perfect square if $b^2-4ac = 0$. Show that the function $x^2+8xy-5y^2-k(x^2+y^2)$ can be expressed in the form $a(x+by)^2$ if k has one of two possible values. Find these values and the corresponding values of a and b.
30. The functions f, g are defined by $f{:}x \to 1/(x-2), x \neq 2, g{:}x \to x/(x^2-4), x^2 \neq 4$, x being real. State whether f and g are odd or even functions or neither. Give a reason why g^{-1} does not exist and find an expression for f^{-1}. Sketch the graphs of f and f^{-1} using the same axes.
31. If $u_1 = 0$ and $u_{r+1} = (1+x)u_r - rx$ for all positive integral values of r, prove by induction that $u_n = [1+nx-(1+x)^n]/x$.
32. When a polynomial $f(x)$ is divided by $x-2$ the remainder is 3 and when it is divided by $(x+1)$ the remainder is 6. State the values of $f(2)$ and $f(-1)$. If the remainder when the polynomial is divided by $(x-2)(x+1)$ is $ax+b$, where a, b are constants, express $f(x)$ in terms of the quotient $g(x)$ and the remainder and hence find the values of a and b.

BINOMIAL THEOREM

Binomial theorem

If n is a positive integer,

$$(a+b)^n = a^n + \binom{n}{1}a^{n-1}b + \binom{n}{2}a^{n-2}b^2 + \binom{n}{3}a^{n-3}b^3 + \ldots + \binom{n}{r}a^{n-r}b^r + \ldots + b^n,$$

where $\binom{n}{r}$ is an alternative notation for ${}_nC_r$, the number of combinations of n unlike quantities taken r at a time;

$$\binom{n}{1} = n; \binom{n}{2} = \frac{n(n-1)}{2!}; \binom{n}{3} = \frac{n(n-1)(n-2)}{3!};$$

$$\ldots \binom{n}{r} = \frac{n(n-1)(n-2)\ldots(n-r+1)}{r!}.$$

Note

(i) For small values of n, the following rule for working out successive coefficients is useful:

Value of n	Coefficients
2	1 $\overset{\text{add}}{\longrightarrow}$ 2 $\overset{\text{add}}{\longrightarrow}$ 1
	↓ ↓
3	1 → 3 → 3 → 1
	↓ ↓ ↓
4	1 4 6 4 1
5	1 5 10 10 5 1
6	1 6 15 20 15 6 1

So $(a+b)^5 = a^5+5a^4b+10a^3b^2+10a^2b^3+5ab^4+b^5$.

(ii) To expand a trinomial expression $(a+b+c)^n$. Write $(b+c) = x$, expand the binomial $(a+x)^n$, replace x by $(b+c)$ in the expansion and then expand the resulting terms $(b+c)^2$, $(b+c)^3$, $(b+c)^4, \ldots$.

Example 30. Expand $(1-2x)^5$.

Using the coefficients given above

$$\begin{aligned}(1-2x)^5 &= 1^5+5.1^4\cdot(-2x)+10.1^3\cdot(-2x)^2+10.1^2\cdot(-2x)^3\\ &\quad +5.1\cdot(-2x)^4+(-2x)^5,\\ &= 1-10x+40x^2-80x^3+80x^4-32x^5.\end{aligned}$$

Example 31. Find the term independent of x in the expansion of $(3x-5/x^3)^8$.

$$\left(3x-\frac{5}{x^3}\right)^8 = (3x)^8+8(3x)^7\left(-\frac{5}{x^3}\right)+\frac{8.7}{2}(3x)^6\left(-\frac{5}{x^3}\right)^2+\ldots;$$

the term independent of x is $8.7/2\,(3x)^6(-5/x^3)^2$; i.e. 700×3^6.

Example 32. Find the coefficient of a^2b^3c *in the expansion of* $(a+b+c)^6$.

If $b+c = x$, the term containing a^2 in the expansion of $(a+x)^6$ is $15a^2x^4$; i.e. $15a^2(b+c)^4$.

In the expansion of $(b+c)^4$, the term containing b^3c is $4b^3c$.

So the term containing a^2b^3c in the expansion of $(a+b+c)^6$ is $60a^2b^3c$ and the required coefficient is 60.

(A) EXAMPLES 7

1. Expand: (i) $(x+2y)^5$; (ii) $(3a+b)^4$; (iii) $(2r-s)^6$; (iv) $(x+1/x)^3$.
2. Find the coefficient of each of the following terms in the given expansions: (i) a^9b^4 in $(a+b)^{13}$; (ii) r^4s^5 in $(2r+3s)^9$; (iii) x^4 in $(x^2+1/x)^5$.
3. Expand $(x+y-z)^3$.
4. Find the term independent of a in the expansion of $(2a-1/a^3)^8$.
5. Express $(1+\sqrt{2})^5$ in the form $a+b\sqrt{2}$.
6. Expand $(x-y)^6$ and hence evaluate $(19.75)^6$ correct to the nearest thousand.
7. Find the term independent of x in the expansion of $(x+1/x)^4\,(x-1/x)^6$.
8. Find the coefficient of $a^4b^3c^2$ in the expansion of $(a+b+c)^9$.
9. Find the value of the positive integer n if in the expansion of $(2+x)^n$ the coefficient of x^4 is five times the coefficient of x^5.
10. Expand $(1+x+x^2)^n$, n a positive integer, in ascending powers of x as far as the term in x^3.
11. Evaluate exactly $(2+\sqrt{3})^7+(2-\sqrt{3})^7$.
12. Find the coefficient of $a^3b^2c^2$ in the expansion of $(a+2b+3c)^7$.
13. In the expansion of $(1+x+px^2)^7$ the coefficient of x^2 is zero. Find the value of p.
14. Show that the coefficient of x in the expansion of $(x-1)^{2n}$ is $-2n$.
15. Given that $(1+ax+bx^2)^{10} = 1-30x+410x^2\ldots$, find the values of the constants a, b.
16. Given that $(1-2x+5x^2-10x^3)(1+x)^n = 1+a_1x+a_2x^2+\ldots$ and that $a_1^2 = 2a_2$, find the value of the positive integer n.

SERIES. ARITHMETIC AND GEOMETRIC SERIES

Notation

First term u_1, second term u_2, third term $u_3, \ldots$, rth term $u_r, \ldots$, nth term u_n.

Sum to n terms,

$$S_n = u_1 + u_2 + u_3 + \ldots + u_r + \ldots + u_n = \sum_{r=1}^{n} u_r.$$

Note

(i) If u_r is given as a function of r, then the values of successive terms $u_1, u_2, u_3 \ldots$ are obtained by substituting $r = 1, 2, 3 \ldots$, e.g. if $u_r = r^2(2r-1)$,

$$u_1 = 1(1) = 1;\ u_2 = 4(3) = 12;\ u_3 = 9(5) = 45.$$

(ii) If S_n is given as a function of n, then successive terms $u_1, u_2, u_3 \ldots u_r \ldots u_n$ are obtained by noting that $u_1 = S_1$; $u_2 = S_2 - S_1$; $u_3 = S_3 - S_2$; $u_r = S_r - S_{r-1}$; $u_n = S_n - S_{n-1}$, e.g. if $S_n = n^2 + n$,

$$u_1 = S_1 = 2;\ u_2 = S_2 - S_1 = 6 - 2 = 4;\ u_3 = S_3 - S_2 = 12 - 6 = 6;$$

$$u_r = S_r - S_{r-1} = r^2 + r - [(r-1)^2 + (r-1)] = 2r;\ S_n = S_n - S_{n-1} = 2n.$$

Infinite series

If $S_n = \sum_{r=1}^{n} u_r$, approaches a limiting value S as $n \to \infty$, the series is said to be *convergent*. The limiting value S is called the sum to infinity or simply the sum of the infinite series.

Use of the method of induction

The method of induction can be used to verify the stated sum of a given finite series.

Example 33. Use the method of induction to prove:
(i) $2 + 3.2 + 4.2^2 + 5.2^3 + \ldots + n$ *terms* $= n2^n$; *(ii)* $\sum_{r=1}^{n} 1/[(r+1)(r+2)] = n/[2(n+2)]$

(i) When $n = 1$, series $= 2$, stated sum $= 2$; so the result is true for $n = 1$. Noting that $u_r = (r+1)2^{r-1}$, assume the result is true for $n = r$; i.e. that

$$S_r = 2 + 3.2 + 4.2^2 + 5.2^3 + \ldots + (r+1)2^{r-1} = r2^r,$$

then $$S_{r+1} = S_r + u_{r+1} = r2^r + (r+2)2^r = (r+1)2^{r+1},$$

establishing that if the result is true for $n = r$ it is also true for $n = r+1$. As the result is true for $n = 1$, it is also true for $n = 2$; as the result is true for $n = 2$, it is also true for $n = 3$ and so on for all positive integral values of n.

(ii) When $n = 1$, series $= 1/6$, stated sum $= 1/6$; so the result is true for $n = 1$. Assume the result is true for $n = r$, i.e. that

$$S_r = \sum_{r=1}^{r} \frac{1}{(r+1)(r+2)} = \frac{r}{2(r+2)},$$

then

$$S_{r+1} = S_r + u_{r+1} = \frac{r}{2(r+2)} + \frac{1}{(r+2)(r+3)} = \frac{r^2 + 3r + 2}{2(r+2)(r+3)} = \frac{r+1}{2(r+3)}.$$

establishing that if the result is true for $n = r$ it is also true for $n = r+1$. The statement of the proof then follows as in (i).

Powers of natural numbers

$$\sum_{r=1}^{n} r = \frac{1}{2}n(n+1);\ \sum_{r=1}^{n} r^2 = \frac{1}{6}n(n+1)(2n+1);\ \sum_{r=1}^{n} r^3 = \frac{1}{4}n^2(n+1)^2.$$

Example 34. Evaluate $\sum_{r=1}^{n}(r+2)(r+3)$.

$$\begin{aligned}\sum_{r=1}^{n}(r+2)(r+3) &= \sum_{r=1}^{n}(r^2+5r+6),\\ &= \sum_{r=1}^{n} r^2 + 5\sum_{r=1}^{n} r + 6\sum_{r=1}^{n} 1,\\ &= \frac{1}{6}n(n+1)(2n+1)+\frac{5}{2}n(n+1)+6n,\\ &= \frac{1}{3}n(n^2+9n+26).\end{aligned}$$

Arithmetic series

$$u_1 = a, u_2 = a+d, u_3 = a+2d, u_4 = a+3d, \ldots, u_n = a+(n-1)d,$$

where a is the first term and d the common difference.

Sum to n terms, $\quad S_n = \frac{n}{2}[2a+(n-1)d] = \frac{n}{2}[a+l]$, where $l = u_n$.

Geometric series

$$u_1 = a, u_2 = ar, u_3 = ar^2, u_4 = ar^3, \ldots, u_n = ar^{n-1},$$

where a is the first term and r the common ratio.

Sum to n terms,

$$S_n = \frac{a(1-r^n)}{1-r}, r \neq 1.$$

Infinite geometric series
If $|r| < 1$, the infinite geometric series

$$a+ar+ar^2+ar^3 \ldots \infty, \text{i.e.} \sum_{n=0}^{\infty} ar^n,$$

is convergent and has a *sum to infinity* $= a/(1-r)$.

Arithmetic and geometric means
a, x, b are successive terms of an arithmetic series if $2x = a+b$, $x = (a+b)/2$; a, x, b are successive terms of a geometric series if $x^2 = ab$, $x = \sqrt{(ab)}$, $a, b > 0$, or $x = -\sqrt{(ab)}$, $a, b > 0$.

Example 35. a, b, c three real and different numbers are successively the first three terms of an arithmetic series and a, c, b are the first three terms of a geometric series. Find the common ratio of the geometric series and its sum to infinity in terms of a.

We have $2b = a+c$ and $c = ar$, $b = ar^2$, where r is the common ratio of the geometric series.

Substituting in the first equation, $2ar^2 = a+ar$,

$$2r^2-r-1 = 0,$$

$$r = -\frac{1}{2}, 1,$$

and as the numbers are different, $r = -1/2$.

The geometric series can be summed to infinity as $|r| < 1$,

$$\text{sum to infinity} = \frac{a}{1-\left(-\frac{1}{2}\right)} = \frac{2}{3}a.$$

Example 36. The first and third terms of a geometric series of positive terms are 9 and 1 respectively. If the series is infinite, find the sum of all the terms after the nth.

$a = 9$, $ar^2 = 1$; so $r^2 = 1/9$, $r = 1/3$ as the terms are positive.

As $|r| < 1$, the series can be summed to infinity, sum to infinity $S = a/(1-r)$.

Sum of all terms after the nth

$$= S-S_n,$$

$$= \frac{a}{1-r}-\frac{a(1-r^n)}{1-r},$$

$$= \frac{ar^n}{1-r}, \quad \text{with } a = 9, r = \frac{1}{3},$$

$$= \frac{27}{2}\cdot\frac{1}{3^n} \quad \text{or} \quad \frac{1}{2.3^{n-3}},$$

Example 37. Evaluate $\sum_{r=1}^{r=n}(2^r+3r+1)$.

$$\text{Sum} = \sum_{r=1}^{n} 2^r+3\sum_{r=1}^{n} r+\sum_{r=1}^{n} 1.$$

$$\sum_{r=1}^{n} 2^r = 2+2^2+2^3+\ldots+2^n \text{ (a geometric series)} = \frac{2(1-2^n)}{1-2} = 2(2^n-1);$$

$$3\sum_{r=1}^{n} r = 3(1+2+3+\ldots+n) \text{ (an arithmetic series)} = \frac{3}{2}n(n+1);$$

$$\sum_{r=1}^{n} 1 = 1+1+1+\ldots+1 = n.$$

$$\text{Sum} = 2(2^n - 1) + \frac{3}{2}n(n+1) + n,$$

$$= 2(2^n - 1) + \frac{1}{2}n(3n+5).$$

(A) EXAMPLES 8

1. The nth term of an arithmetic series is $(3n-1)/6$. Write down the first three terms and prove that the sum to n terms is $n(3n+1)/12$.
2. Given $u_r = (r+2)/[r(r+1)]$, find u_1, u_2, u_3, u_{r+1} and u_{2n}.
3. The sum of n terms of a series is given by $S_n = n^2 + 3n$. Find the first three and the rth terms of the series and identify the series.
4. The first term of an arithmetic series is 2 and the fifth term is -2. Find the common difference and the sum of the first n terms.
5. The second term of a geometric series is 6 and the fourth term is 2/3. If the common ratio is positive find its value. Also find: (i) the first term; (ii) the sum to n terms; (iii) the sum to infinity.
6. Evaluate (i) $\sum_{r=1}^{10} (2r+1)$; (ii) $\sum_{r=1}^{n} 2^{r-1}$; (iii) $\sum_{r=1}^{\infty} 1/2^r$.
7. Prove by induction that for all positive integers n,

$$1.2 + 2.3 + 3.4 + \ldots + n(n+1) = \frac{1}{3}n(n+1)(n+2).$$

8. Given that the sum of the first n terms of a series is given by $S_n = 9(1 - 1/3^n)$, find the first three terms and the nth term and show that the series is geometric. State also: (i) the common ratio; (ii) the sum to infinity.
9. Find: (i) the number of terms; (ii) the sum of the arithmetic series $(m+1) + (m+3) + (m+5) + \ldots + 5m$, where $4m$ is an odd integer.
10. How many terms of the series $1/3 + 1/6 + 1/12 + 1/24 + \ldots$ must be taken for the sum to differ from the sum to infinity by less than 0.0001?
11. The sum of the first 10 terms of an arithmetic series is 80 and the twenty-eighth term is 83. Find the common difference and the sum of the first fifty terms.
12. Prove by induction: (i) $\sum_{r=1}^{n} r(3r-1) = n^2(n+1)$; (ii) $\sum_{r=1}^{n} 1/[r(r+1)] = n/(n+1)$.
13. If S_n is the sum to n terms of a geometric series with first term a and common ratio r, show that $S_{3n} - S_{2n} = r^{2n}S_n$.
14. The sum of the first n terms of an arithmetic series is equal to the sum of the first p terms where $n \neq p$. Prove that the sum of the first $(n+p)$ terms is zero.
15. An arithmetic series with first term 1 is such that the second, tenth and thirty-fourth terms are successive terms of a geometric series. Find: (i) the common difference of the arithmetic series; (ii) the common ratio of the geometric series.
16. A geometric series has common ratio $(a-b)/a$ where $a > 0$. Show that the series has a sum to infinity provided that $0 < b < 2a$. If the first term is $2a$, find the sum to infinity.
17. Find the sum to infinity of the series $0.23 + 0.0023 + 0.000023 + \ldots$ and hence express the continued decimal $0.232323\ldots$ as a fraction.
18. Prove by induction: (i) $\sum_{r=1}^{n} 1/[(2r-1)(2r+1)] = n/(2n+1)$; (ii) $\sum_{r=1}^{n} r \cdot r! = (n+1)! - 1$.
19. Prove by induction or otherwise that the sum of the squares of the first n natural numbers is $n(n+1)(2n+1)/6$. If $S_n = 1^2 + 3^2 + 5^2 + \ldots + (2n-1)^2$, find S_n and show that $6S_n$ is the product of three consecutive natural numbers.
20. In an infinite geometric series with common ratio numerically less than 1, prove that the ratio of the nth term to the sum of all terms which follow the nth term is independent of n.
21. Prove that $\sum_{r=1}^{n} r = n(n+1)/2$. The series $1 + 2 + 4 + 7 + 8 + 11 + 13 + 14 + 16 + \ldots + 299$ is formed by omitting from the sum of the first 300 positive integers all the multiples of 3 and 5. Find the sum of this series.
22. Find the set of values of x for which the series $\sum_{n=0}^{\infty} (2x-1)^n$ is convergent. Given that $x = 1/3$, find the value to which the series converges.

PARTIAL FRACTIONS

Expression of a compound algebraic fraction in partial fractions

Rule 1. *The first essential is that the compound fraction is either a proper fraction or is expressed in terms of a proper fraction.*

Rule 2. With this condition satisfied proceed as follows:

(i) *corresponding to each linear factor* $(ax+b)$ *in the denominator, assume a partial fraction of the form* $A/(ax+b)$, *where* A *is a constant;*

(ii) *corresponding to a repeated linear factor* $(ax+b)^2$ *in the denominator, assume two partial fractions of the forms* $A/(ax+b)$, $B/[(ax+b)^2]$, *where* A, B *are constants;*

(iii) *corresponding to a non-factorisable quadratic factor* (ax^2+bx+c) *in the denominator, assume a partial fraction of the form* $(Ax+B)/(ax^2+bx+c)$, *where* A, B *are constants.*

The methods of determining the different constants are illustrated in the following examples.

Example 38. Express $(x^2+1)/[x(x+1)]$ *in partial fractions.*

As the fraction is not proper, the process of division is used.

$$\frac{x^2+1}{x(x+1)} = 1+\frac{1-x}{x(x+1)}.$$

$$\begin{array}{r} 1 \\ x^2+x\,\overline{)\,x^2+1} \\ \underline{x^2+x} \\ -x+1 \end{array}$$

Assume $$\frac{1-x}{x(x+1)} = \frac{A}{x}+\frac{B}{x+1},$$

i.e. $$1-x = A(x+1)+Bx.$$

Let $x=0$, $\quad 1 = A; \quad A = 1.$

Let $x=-1$, $\quad 2 = -B; \quad B = -2.$

$$\therefore \quad \frac{x^2+1}{x(x+1)} = 1+\frac{1}{x}-\frac{2}{x+1}.$$

Example 39. Express $(3x^2+x-1)/[x(x+1)^2]$ *as the sum of 3 partial fractions.*

This is a proper fraction.

Assume $$\frac{3x^2+x-1}{x(x+1)^2} = \frac{A}{x}+\frac{B}{x+1}+\frac{C}{(x+1)^2},$$

i.e. $$3x^2+x-1 = A(x+1)^2+Bx(x+1)+Cx.$$

Let $x=0$, $\quad -1 = A; \quad A = -1.$

let $x=-1$, $\quad 1 = -C; \quad C = -1;$

equating coefficients of x^2, $\quad 3 = A+B; \; B = 4.$

$$\therefore \quad \frac{3x^2+x-1}{x(x+1)^2} = -\frac{1}{x}+\frac{4}{x+1}-\frac{1}{(x+1)^2}.$$

Example 40. *If a is a constant, express* $(2x^2-ax-a^2)/[(x+a)(x^2+a^2)]$ *in partial fractions.*

This is a proper fraction.

Assume $$\frac{2x^2-ax-a^2}{(x+a)(x^2+a^2)} = \frac{A}{x+a}+\frac{Bx+C}{x^2+a^2},$$

i.e. $$2x^2-ax-a^2 = A(x^2+a^2)+(Bx+C)(x+a).$$

Let $x = -a$, $\quad 2a^2 = A(2a^2); \qquad A = 1;$

equating coefficients of x^2, $\quad 2 = A+B; \qquad B = 1;$

equating coefficients of x, $\quad -a = aB+C; \qquad C = -2a.$

$$\therefore \qquad \frac{2x^2-ax-a^2}{(x+a)(x^2+a^2)} = \frac{1}{x+a}+\frac{x-2a}{x^2+a^2}.$$

Uses of partial fractions

The main applications of the method of partial fractions are (i) in the expansion of a compound algebraic fraction as a power series using the Binomial expansion and (ii) the integration of such a fraction. These applications are illustrated in subsequent sections.

(A) EXAMPLES 9

Express in partial fractions:

1. $\dfrac{2x-1}{(2x+1)(x-3)}$ 2. $\dfrac{x^2+3x}{(x-2)(x+1)}$ 3. $\dfrac{3}{x(x-2)^2}$

4. $\dfrac{x^2+1}{x(x-1)(x+2)}$ 5. $\dfrac{3x^2-4}{x(1+x^2)}$ 6. $\dfrac{x^2}{(x-1)^2}$

7. $\dfrac{x^2+x}{x^2+3x-4}$ 8. $\dfrac{3x+4}{(x-1)(x+2)^2}$ 9. $\dfrac{1}{x(x^2+4)}$

10. $\dfrac{x^2+1}{x(x^2-1)}$ 11. $\dfrac{x^3+1}{x^2(x^2+4)}$ 12. $\dfrac{x^3}{(x+1)(x^2-x+1)}$.

If a, b are constants, express the following in partial fractions:

13. $\dfrac{2a}{(x-a)(x+a)}$ 14. $\dfrac{2a^2}{x(x^2+a^2)}$ 15. $\dfrac{a^2-b^2}{(x+a)(x-b)^2}$.

BINOMIAL EXPANSION

Binomial expansion

If $|x| < 1$ *and n is not a positive integer,*

$$(1+x)^n = 1+nx+\frac{n(n-1)}{2!}x^2+\frac{n(n-1)(n-2)}{3!}x^3+\ldots\infty$$

Note

(i) an expression of the form $(a+b)^n$ where $|b/a|<1$, is expanded by first expressing it in the form $a^n(1+b/a)^n$;

(ii) *if x is large* so that $|1/x|<1$, $(1+x)^n$ is expressed in the form $x^n(1+1/x)^n$ and expanded in descending powers of x;

(iii) a trinomial term such as $(1+x+x^2)^n$, where x is small, is expanded by first expressing it in the form $(1+X)^n$, where $X=x+x^2$.

Example 41. If x is small, find the first 3 terms in the expansions of: (i) $\sqrt{(4+x)}$; *(ii)* $1/[(x-2)^2]$ *in ascending powers of x. State the restriction on x in each case.*

(i) $$\sqrt{(4+x)}=2\sqrt{\left(1+\frac{x}{4}\right)}=2\left(1+\frac{x}{4}\right)^{1/2}.$$

$$2\left(1+\frac{x}{4}\right)^{1/2}=2\left[1+\frac{1}{2}\left(\frac{x}{4}\right)+\frac{\left(\frac{1}{2}\right)\left(-\frac{1}{2}\right)}{2}\left(\frac{x}{4}\right)^2+\ldots\right].$$

$$\therefore\ \sqrt{(4+x)}=2+\frac{1}{4}x-\frac{1}{64}x^2\ldots.$$

The result is true if $|x|<4$.

(ii) $$\frac{1}{(x-2)^2}=\frac{1}{(2-x)^2}=\frac{1}{4\left(1-\frac{x}{2}\right)^2}=\frac{1}{4}\left(1-\frac{x}{2}\right)^{-2}.$$

$$\frac{1}{4}\left(1-\frac{x}{2}\right)^{-2}=\frac{1}{4}\left[1+(-2)\left(-\frac{x}{2}\right)+\frac{(-2)(-3)}{2}\left(-\frac{x}{2}\right)^2+\ldots\right].$$

$$\therefore\quad \frac{1}{(x-2)^2}=\frac{1}{4}+\frac{1}{4}x+\frac{3}{16}x^2+\ldots.$$

The result is true if $|x|<2$.

Expansions of compound algebraic fractions

First express the compound fraction in partial fractions and then use one or more of the following binomial expansions:

$$\frac{1}{1+x}=(1+x)^{-1}=1-x+x^2-x^3+\ldots+(-1)^r x^r+\ldots;$$

$$\frac{1}{1-x}=(1-x)^{-1}=1+x+x^2+x^3+\ldots+x^r+\ldots;$$

$$\frac{1}{(1+x)^2}=(1+x)^{-2}=1-2x+3x^2-4x^3+\ldots+(-1)^r(r+1)x^r+\ldots;$$

$$\frac{1}{(1-x)^2}=(1-x)^{-2}=1+2x+3x^2+4x^3+\ldots+(r+1)x^r+\ldots.$$

Example 42. Assuming x is small, find the coefficient of x^r in the expansion in ascending powers of x of $(6+9x-14x^2)/[(1-2x)^2(3+x)]$.

Using the method of partial fractions,

$$\text{given fraction} = \frac{1}{1-2x} + \frac{2}{(1-2x)^2} - \frac{3}{3+x},$$

$$= (1-2x)^{-1} + 2(1-2x)^{-2} - \left(1+\frac{x}{3}\right)^{-1}.$$

$$(1-2x)^{-1} = 1+2x+(2x)^2+\ldots+(2x)^r+\ldots;$$

$$(1-2x)^{-2} = 1+2(2x)+3(2x)^2+\ldots+(r+1)(2x)^r+\ldots;$$

$$\left(1+\frac{x}{3}\right)^{-1} = 1-\frac{x}{3}+\left(\frac{x}{3}\right)^2-\ldots.+(-1)^r\left(\frac{x}{3}\right)^r\ldots.$$

So the coefficient of x^r in the expansion of the given fraction

$$= 2^r+2(r+1)2^r-(-1)^r\left(\frac{1}{3}\right)^r \quad \text{or} \quad (2r+3)2^r+(-1)^{r+1}\left(\frac{1}{3}\right)^r.$$

(A) EXAMPLES 10

1. Find the first 3 terms in the expansion of each of the following functions in ascending powers of x and in each case give the restriction on the value of x:
(i) $(1+2x)^{1/2}$; (ii) $(1-2x)^{-1}$; (iii) $(1+x)^{-2}$;
(iv) $1/(2-x)$; (v) $1/(x-2)$; (vi) $1/\surd(4+x)$.
2. Find the expansion in ascending powers of x as far as the term in x^3 of each of the following expressions: (i) $(1+x)(1-x)^{1/2}$; (ii) $(1-x)(1+x)^{-1}$; (iii) $(1-2x)/(1-x)$; (iv) $(1+x)/(1-x)^2$; (v) $(1+x+x^2)/(1+x)$; (vi) $(1+3x^2)/[\surd(1+2x^2)]$; (vii) $x/[\surd(4+x^2)]$; (viii) $(1+x)^2\surd(1+2x)$; (ix) $[(1+x)^{3/2}]/(1-x)$.
3. By writing $\surd 98$ in the form $\surd(100-2)$ and expanding, obtain the value of $\surd 2$ correct to 5 places of decimals.
4. State the coefficients of x^r in the expansions of $(1-x)^{-1}$, $(1+x)^{-1}$, $(1+x)^{-2}$ in ascending powers of x. Use these results to write down the coefficients of x^r in the expansions in ascending power of x of the functions: (i) $(1-2x)^{-1}$; (ii) $(1+3x)^{-1}$; (iii) $(1-2x)^{-2}$; (iv) $1/(x+2)^2$.
5. Write down the first three terms in the binomial expansion of $[1-1/(1000)]^{1/3}$. Show that the given expression is equal to $3\sqrt[3]{37}/10$ and hence evaluate $\sqrt[3]{37}$ correct to six decimal places.
6. By first expressing in partial fractions, obtain the first three terms in the expansion of each of the following functions in ascending powers of x and state the restriction on the values of x: (i) $1/[(1-x)(1-2x)]$; (ii) $x/[(1+x)(1-x)^2]$; (iii) $2/[(2-x)(1+2x)]$; (iv) $4x/[(x-1)(x+1)^2]$.
7. Expand $(1-x+x^2)^{1/2}$ in ascending powers of x as far as the term in x^3.
8. If x is so small that x^3 and higher powers of x can be ignored, show that $\surd[(1+x)/(1-x)] \approx 1+x+(x^2/2)$. Obtain the same result by first expressing the function as $(1+x)(1-x^2)^{-1/2}$.
9. If x is *large*, obtain the expansions of the following functions in descending powers of x as far as the term in $1/x^3$: (i) $(x^2+1)^{1/2}$; (ii) $(x+2)^{-1}$; (iii) $(4+x^2)^{-1/2}$.
10. Expand the following functions in ascending powers of x as far as the term in x^3: (i) $1/(1+x+2x^2)$; (ii) $(1+x)/(1+x+x^2)$; (iii) $1/[\surd(1+x+x^2)]$; (iv) $1/[\surd(2+2x+x^2)]$.
11. If x is *large*, show that $\surd(x^2+2x) \approx x+1$ and $1/(x^2+2x) \approx 1/x^2-2/x^3$.
12. Find the constants a, b in the approximate result $(1-x-2x^2)^{1/2} \approx 1+ax+bx^2$.
13. Express $(x-2)/[(x+1)^2(x-1)]$ in partial fractions and find the coefficient of x^n in the expansion of the function in ascending powers of x.

14. If x is small, obtain the first three terms in the expansions of $\sqrt[5]{(1+x)}$ and $(1+ax)(1+bx)^{-1}$. Show that if $a = 3/5$, $b = 2/5$ the expansions are approximately equal.

(B) MISCELLANEOUS EXAMPLES

1. The sum to n terms of a series is given by $S_n = 6-2^{n+1} \cdot 3^{1-n}$. Show that the series is geometric and find: (i) the common ratio; (ii) the sum to infinity.
2. If $(1+x^2)^2(1+x)^n = a_0+a_1x+a_2x^2+\ldots$, where n is a positive integer and the coefficients a_0, a_1, a_2, are successive terms of an arithmetic series, find the possible values of n.
3. Express in partial fractions $y = 5/[(x-2)(x^2+1)]$ and hence find y as a power series in x as far as the term in x^4.
4. Prove by induction, or otherwise, that $\sum_{r=1}^{n}(2r-1)^3 = n^2(2n^2-1)$.
5. By expressing each term in terms of $\log_3 x$, show that the series $(\log_3 x)^{-1}+(\log_9 x)^{-1}+(\log_{27} x)^{-1}+\ldots$ is arithmetic and find an expression for the sum of the first n terms.
6. If x is small, obtain the expansion of $(1-x+x^2)/(1+x+x^2)$ in ascending powers of x as far as the term in x^4.
7. An infinite geometric series is such that the sum of all terms after the nth is three times the nth term. Find the common ratio and show that the sum to infinity of the series is four times the first term.
8. Express $7x/[(3x-1)(x+1)^2]$ in partial fractions. Hence find the coefficient of x^n in the expansion of the expression in ascending powers of x. Also state the range of value of x for which the expansion is valid.
9. If m is a positive integer, show that the sum of the series $m+(m+3)+(m+6)+\ldots+4m$ is five times the sum of the series $1+2+3+\ldots+\text{m}$.
10. If the coefficients of x and x^2 in the expansion of $(1+x+ax^2)(1+bx)^{10}$ are both zero, find the values of the constants a and b.
11. Express $(3x-1)/[(x^2+1)(x-2)]$ in the form $(Ax+B)/(x^2+1)+C/(x-2)$. If $|x|<1$, find the coefficient of x^6 in the expansion of the expression in ascending powers of x.
12. Prove by induction that $\sum_{r=1}^{n} 1/[r(r+1)(r+2)] = 1/4-1/[2(n+1)(n+2)]$.
13. Two positive numbers a, b are such that $a = b-1$. If n is a positive integer, express the expression $a^{2n}+2nb-1$ in ascending powers of b and show that it is exactly divisible by b^2. Choosing suitable values of a and n, deduce that $2^{40}+119$ is divisible by 9.
14. Write down the roots of the equation $x^2-px-1 = 0$. If p is small, show that the roots are approximately equal to $[p \pm 2(1+p^2/8)]/2$.
15. Prove by induction, or otherwise, that $\sum_{r=1}^{n} r^3 = n^2(n+1)^2/4$. Hence show that the sum of the cubes of all numbers between 100 and 200 which are divisible by 3 is $27.33^2 \cdot 4200$.
16. Prove that if E denotes the expression $x^2/[2-x+2\sqrt{(1-x)}]$, then $E = 2-x-2\sqrt{(1-x)}$ and deduce that if x is small, then $E \approx x^2/4$.
17. Find the range of values of x for which the series $\sum_{n=0}^{\infty}[x/(1+x)]^n$ is convergent. Also find: (i) the limit to which the sum approaches when $x = 1/2$; (ii) the value of x when this limit is 3.
18. Obtain the expansion in ascending powers of x of $\sqrt[4]{(1+8x)}$ as far as the term in x^3 and show that when x is small, $\sqrt[4]{(1+8x)} \approx (1+5x)/(1+3x)$. Hence obtain in the form of a rational number an approximation to $\sqrt[4]{1.16}$.
19. State the range of values of x for which each of the following geometric series has a sum to infinity and find this sum: (i) $1+2x+4x^2+\ldots$; (ii) $1-e^x+e^{2x}-\ldots$; (iii) $\sum_{n=0}^{\infty}(3-4x)^n$.
20. If $S_n = \sum_{n=0}^{n} ar^n$, show that $S_{3n}-S_{2n} = r^{2n}S_n$. Given that $r = 1/3$, evaluate $\sum_{r=1}^{\infty}(S_{3n}-S_{2n})/S_n$.
21. Find the expansion of the expression $1/[(x+2)^2(2x+1)]$ in ascending powers of x giving the first four terms and the coefficient of x^n. Show that if x is so small that x^4 can be neglected, the given expression can be represented by $1/[(3x+2)^2]+kx^3$, where k is a constant to be found.
22. Express in partial fractions $[(b-c)(c-a)(a-b)]/[(1-ax)(1-bx)(1-cx)]$, where a, b, c are unequal constants.
23. Prove: (i) $\sum_{r=1}^{n} r = [n(n+1)]/2$; (ii) $\sum_{r=0}^{n}\log_a(2a^r) = [(n+1)(n+\log_a 4)]/2$.
24. The first term of an arithmetic series is a and the common difference is d; the sum to n terms is S_n. A new series is formed with nth term, $u_n = (S_1+S_2+S_3+\ldots+S_n)/n(n+1)$, find u_1, u_2, u_3, u_4 and show that the new series is also arithmetic.

25. Show that the rth term of the series $1+(1+2)+(1+2+2^2)+(1+2+2^2+2^3)+\ldots$ is 2^r-1. Hence find the sum of the first n terms of the series.

26. Find the set of values of x for which the series $\sum_{n=0}^{\infty}[2x/(x+1)]^n$ is convergent. Given that the series converges to the value 3, find the value of x.

27. A sequence of numbers $u_1, u_2, u_3, \ldots$ is such that $u_1 = 1$, $u_2 = 1+2$, $u_3 = 1+2+3, \ldots$. Find a concise expression for u_r. Use this result to obtain the coefficient of x^r in the expansion of $(1-x)^{-3}$ in ascending powers of x.

28. If $|x| < 1$, write down the expansion of $(1-x)^{-2}$ as far as the term in x^4. Hence sum to infinity the series $3+4x+5x^2+\ldots+(r+3)x^r+\ldots$.

29. In each of a set of n arithmetic series the first term is 1; the common difference of the first series is 1, of the second series, 2, of the third, 2^2 and so on. Find in its simplest form an expression for the sum of the nth terms of the series.

30. Write down the sum of the series $\sum_{r=1}^{r+1} 3^{r-1}$ and show that $\sum_{r=1}^{n}(3^r+3^{r-1}+3^{r-2}+\ldots+1) = (3^{n+2}-2n-9)/4$.

Trigonometry

FUNDAMENTAL RESULTS, IDENTITIES AND THEOREMS

Important results

$$180° = \pi \text{ rad}; \ 90° = \frac{\pi}{2}\text{rad}; \ 60° = \frac{\pi}{3}\text{rad}; \ 45° = \frac{\pi}{4}\text{rad}; \ 30° = \frac{\pi}{6}\text{rad}.$$

sin θ Maximum value $= 1$ for $\theta = \pi/2, 5\pi/2\ldots$ or generally $\theta = (4r+1)\pi/2$.
Minimum value $= -1$ for $\theta = 3\pi/2, 7\pi/2\ldots$ or generally $\theta = (4r-1)\pi/2$.
$\sin(0) = 0$ and generally $\sin(r\pi) = 0$.
$\sin(\pi/6) = 1/2$; $\sin(\pi/4) = (\sqrt{2})/2$; $\sin(\pi/3) = \sqrt{3}/2$.

cos θ Maximum value $= 1$ for $\theta = 0, 2\pi, \ldots$ or generally $\theta = 2r\pi$.
Minimum value $= -1$ for $\theta = \pi, 3\pi, \ldots$ or generally $\theta = (2r-1)\pi$.
$\cos(\pi/2) = 0$ and generally $\cos(2r-1)\pi/2 = 0$.
$\cos(\pi/6) = \sqrt{3}/2$; $\cos(\pi/4) = (\sqrt{2})/2$; $\cos(\pi/3) = 1/2$.

tan θ Values of $\tan\theta$ range from $-\infty$ to $+\infty$.
For values of θ which are odd multiples of $\pi/2$, i.e. $\theta = (2r+1)\pi/2$, $\tan\theta$ is not defined, it $\to +\infty$ as $x \to (2r+1)\pi/2$ from below and $\to -\infty$ as $x \to (2r+1)\pi/2$ from above.
$\tan(0) = 0$ and generally $\tan(r\pi) = 0$.
$\tan(\pi/6) = 1/\sqrt{3}$; $\tan(\pi/4) = 1$; $\tan(\pi/3) = \sqrt{3}$.

Note $\tan\theta = \dfrac{\sin\theta}{\cos\theta}$.

Graphs

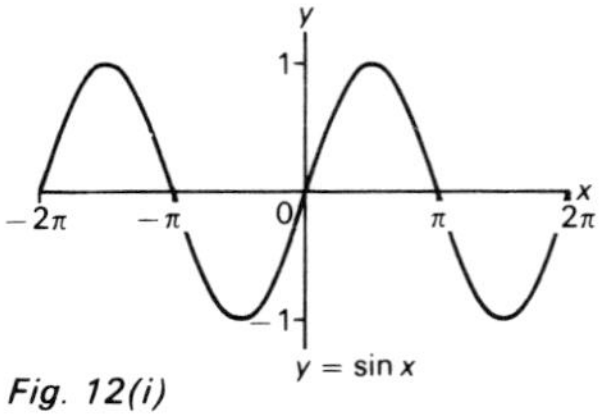

Fig. 12(i)

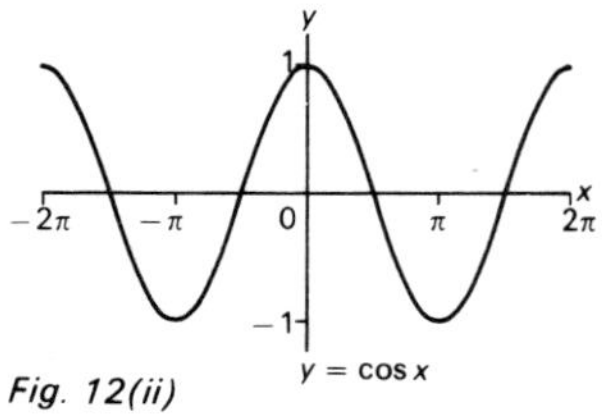

Fig. 12(ii)

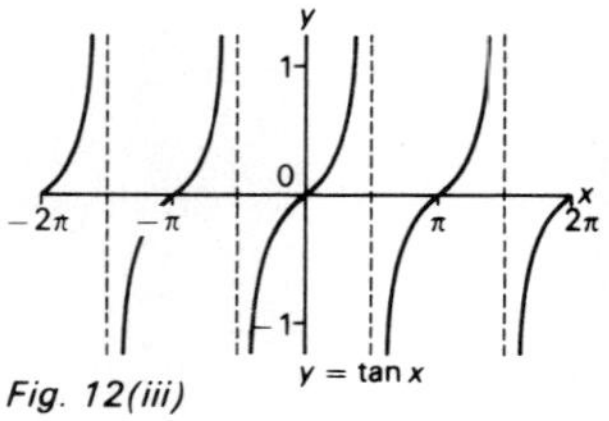

Fig. 12(iii)

Other trigonometrical ratios

$$\cot\theta = \frac{1}{\tan\theta} = \frac{\cos\theta}{\sin\theta};\ \sec\theta = \frac{1}{\cos\theta};\ \operatorname{cosec}\theta = \frac{1}{\sin\theta}.$$

Fundamental identities

$$\sin^2\theta + \cos^2\theta = 1;\ \sec^2\theta = 1 + \tan^2\theta;\ \operatorname{cosec}^2\theta = 1 + \cot^2\theta.$$

Addition theorems

$$\sin(A+B) = \sin A\cos B + \cos A\sin B \qquad \sin(A-B) = \sin A\cos B - \cos A\sin B;$$

$$\cos(A+B) = \cos A\cos B - \sin A\sin B \qquad \cos(A-B) = \cos A\cos B + \sin A\sin B;$$

$$\tan(A+B) = \frac{\tan A + \tan B}{1 - \tan A\tan B} \qquad \tan(A-B) = \frac{\tan A - \tan B}{1 + \tan A\tan B}.$$

Double and half-angle results

$$\sin 2\theta = 2\sin\theta\cos\theta;\ \cos 2\theta = \cos^2\theta - \sin^2\theta = 2\cos^2\theta - 1 \text{ or } 1 - 2\sin^2\theta;$$

$$\tan 2\theta = \frac{2\tan\theta}{1-\tan^2\theta}.$$

Note

$$\sin^2\theta = \frac{(1-\cos 2\theta)}{2} \qquad \cos^2\theta = \frac{(1+\cos 2\theta)}{2}.$$

$$\sin\theta = 2\sin\frac{\theta}{2}\cos\frac{\theta}{2} \qquad \cos\theta = \cos^2\frac{\theta}{2} - \sin^2\frac{\theta}{2} = 2\cos^2\frac{\theta}{2} - 1 \text{ or } 1 - 2\sin^2\frac{\theta}{2};$$

$$\tan\theta = \frac{2\tan\frac{\theta}{2}}{1-\tan^2\frac{\theta}{2}}.$$

If $t = \tan\theta/2$,

$$\tan\theta = \frac{2t}{1-t^2} \qquad \sin\theta = \frac{2t}{1+t^2} \qquad \cos\theta = \frac{1-t^2}{1+t^2}$$

Factors

$$\sin A + \sin B = 2\sin\frac{(A+B)}{2}\cos\frac{(A-B)}{2}$$

$$\sin A - \sin B = 2\cos\frac{(A+B)}{2}\sin\frac{(A-B)}{2}$$

$$\cos A + \cos B = 2\cos\frac{(A+B)}{2}\cos\frac{(A-B)}{2}$$

$$\cos A - \cos B = -2\sin\frac{(A+B)}{2}\sin\frac{(A-B)}{2}$$

Note These factors results are often used in reverse to express products of the sines and/or cosines of multiple angles as sums or differences.

Example 1. Express $\cos(\pi/2+\theta)\cos\theta$ *in the form of a sum and hence determine its maximum value.*

$$\cos\left(\frac{\pi}{2}+\theta\right)\cos\theta=\frac{1}{2}\left[\cos\theta\left(\frac{\pi}{2}+\theta+\theta\right)+\cos\left(\frac{\pi}{2}+\theta-\theta\right)\right]=\frac{1}{2}\left[\cos\left(\frac{\pi}{2}+2\theta\right)+\cos\frac{\pi}{2}\right]$$

$$=\frac{1}{2}\cos\left(\frac{\pi}{2}+2\theta\right).$$

$$\text{Maximum value}=\frac{1}{2}$$

The function $a\cos\theta+b\sin\theta$

Functions of this type can be expressed as a multiple of a single sine or a single cosine by expressing them in the form:

$$a\cos\theta+b\sin\theta=\sqrt{(a^2+b^2)}\left[\frac{a}{\sqrt{(a^2+b^2)}}\cos\theta+\frac{b}{\sqrt{(a^2+b^2)}}\sin\theta\right],$$

and writing $a/[\sqrt{(a^2+b^2)}]$, $b/[\sqrt{(a^2+b^2)}]$ as $\sin\alpha$, $\cos\alpha$ or $\cos\alpha$, $\sin\alpha$ and determining the value of the angle α from the value of its tangent.

Example 2. Express $\sqrt{3}\sin 2\theta-\cos 2\theta$ *in the form* $R\sin(2\theta-\alpha)$.

Here $\sqrt{(a^2+b^2)}=\sqrt{(3+1)}=2$,

so
$$\sqrt{3}\sin 2\theta-\cos 2\theta=2\left[\frac{\sqrt{3}}{2}\sin 2\theta-\frac{1}{2}\cos 2\theta\right],$$

$$=2\left[\cos\alpha\sin 2\theta-\sin\alpha\cos 2\theta\right],$$

$$\text{where }\tan\alpha=\frac{1}{\sqrt{3}};\text{ i.e. }\alpha=\frac{\pi}{6},$$

$$=2\sin\left(2\theta-\frac{\pi}{6}\right).$$

Example 3. Find the turning points on the curve $y=1+\cos x+\sin x$ *for* $0\leqslant x\leqslant 2\pi$.

$$\cos x+\sin x=\sqrt{2}\left[\frac{1}{\sqrt{2}}\cos x+\frac{1}{\sqrt{2}}\sin x\right]=\sqrt{2}\left[\sin\alpha\cos x+\cos\alpha\sin x\right]$$

$$=\sqrt{2}\sin(x+\alpha),\text{ where }\tan\alpha=1,\text{ i.e. }\alpha=\frac{\pi}{4}.$$

So
$$y=1+\sqrt{2}\sin\left(x+\frac{\pi}{4}\right).$$

$\therefore$ the curve $y=1+\cos x+\sin x$ has a maximum point $(\pi/4,\ 1+\sqrt{2})$ and a minimum point $(5\pi/4,\ 1-\sqrt{2})$.

(A) EXAMPLES 11

1. State the values of: (i) $\sin \pi$; (ii) $\cos \pi$; (iii) $\tan 3\pi/4$; (iv) $\cos 2\pi$; (v) $\sin 7\pi/6$; (vi) $\cos(-\pi)$; (vii) $\tan \pi$; (viii) $\sin 3\pi/4$; (ix) $\cos 3\pi/2$.
2. Simplify: (i) $\sin^2 2\theta + \cos^2 2\theta$; (ii) $\sin^2 \theta + 2\cos^2 \theta$; (iii) $2 + 2\tan^2 \theta$; (iv) $(1+\sin\theta)^2 + \cos^2\theta$; (v) $\sec^2\theta - \tan^2\theta$.
3. Express the following in terms of the angle $\theta/2$: (i) $\sin\theta$; (ii) $1+\cos\theta$; (iii) $1-\cos\theta$; (iv) $\tan\theta$; (v) $(1+\cos\theta)/(1-\cos\theta)$; (vi) $(1-\cos\theta)/\sin\theta$.
4. Express $\sin(-\theta)$, $\cos(-\theta)$ and $\tan(-\theta)$ in terms of $\sin\theta$, $\cos\theta$, $\tan\theta$ respectively.
5. State the maximum and minimum values of: (i) $3\cos(x+\pi/3)$; (ii) $\sqrt{5}\sin(2x-\pi/4)$; (iii) $1+2\sin x$; (iv) $2-\sqrt{3}\cos(x-\pi/3)$.
6. Using known values for the sine, cosine and tangent of 30°, 45° and 60°, find in surd form the values of: (i) $\sin 75°$; (ii) $\cos 15°$; (iii) $\tan 75°$; (iv) $\sin 105°$.
7. Express: (i) $\sin^2 x$ in terms of $\cos 2x$; (ii) $\sin^4 x$ in terms of $\cos 2x$ and $\cos 4x$.
8. Express as sums or differences: (i) $\sin 3x \sin x$; (ii) $\cos 5x \cos 2x$; (iii) $\sin 4x \cos 3x$; (iv) $\cos 5x \sin x$; (v) $\sin(\pi+x)\cos x$.
9. Express: (i) $4\sin x + 3\cos x$ in the form $R\sin(x+\alpha)$; (ii) $\sqrt{3}\sin 2\theta - \cos 2\theta$ in the form $R\sin(2\theta-\alpha)$; (iii) $2\cos x/2 + \sqrt{5}\sin x/2$ in terms of a single cosine.
10. Using the expression for $\tan(45°+\theta)$ in terms of $\tan\theta$, find the value of $\tan 75°$ in the form $a+b\sqrt{3}$, where a, b are integers.
11. Write down the values of: (i) $\sin^2 15° + \cos^2 15°$; (ii) $2\sin 15° \cos 15°$ and deduce that $\sin^4 15° + \cos^4 15° = 7/8$.
12. If $x = \sin 3A - \sin A$, $y = \cos 3A + \cos A$, show that $x/y = \tan A$.
13. Prove that $\sin 105° = \sqrt{2}(\sqrt{3}+1)/4$ and obtain a similar expression for $\cos 105°$.
14. Express each of the following functions as a sum or a difference and hence write down its maximum value: (i) $\sin(\theta+\pi/6)\cos\theta$; (ii) $\cos(\theta+\pi/4)\cos\theta$; (iii) $\sin(\theta+\pi/2)\sin\theta$.
15. Establish the results: (i) $\cos 3\theta = 4\cos^3\theta - 3\cos\theta$; (ii) $\sin 3\theta = 3\sin\theta - 4\sin^3\theta$.
16. Show that: (i) $(1-\tan\theta)(1+\tan\theta) = \cos 2\theta/\cos^2\theta$; (ii) $(1+\tan\theta)^2 + (1-\tan\theta)^2 = 2\sec^2\theta$.
17. Using the value of $\tan 45°$, show that $\tan 22.5° = \sqrt{2}-1$.
18. Establish the results $\cos 15° = \sqrt{2}(\sqrt{3}+1)/4$, $\sin 15° = \sqrt{2}(\sqrt{3}-1)/4$ and deduce that $\operatorname{cosec} 15° - \sec 15° = 2\sqrt{2}$.
19. Prove that $\cos\theta + \cos(\theta+2\pi/3) + \cos(\theta+4\pi/3) = 0$ and find the value of $\sin\theta + \sin(\theta+2\pi/3) + \sin(\theta+4\pi/3)$.
20. Find the maximum and minimum values of each of the following functions: (i) $\cos x - \sin x$; (ii) $3\sin x + 4\cos x$; (iii) $\sqrt{3}\sin 2x + \cos 2x$.
21. If $t = \tan\theta/2$, show that $(3+\cos\theta)/\sin\theta = (2+t^2)/t$.
22. Given that $\sin(150°-\theta) = p\sin\theta$, show that $\cot\theta = 2p - \sqrt{3}$ and by choosing a suitable value of θ show that $\cot 75° = 2-\sqrt{3}$.

EQUATIONS

General solutions of equations

If $x = \alpha$ is a solution of the equation $\sin x = c$, the general solution is

$$x = n\pi + (-1)^n\alpha, \text{ where } n \text{ is an integer;}$$

if $x = \alpha$ is a solution of the equation $\cos x = c$, the general solution is

$$x = 2n\pi \pm \alpha, \text{ where } n \text{ is an integer;}$$

if $x = \alpha$ is a solution of the equation $\tan x = c$, the general solution is

$$x = n\pi + \alpha, \text{ where } n \text{ is an integer.}$$

Example 4. If x is measured in degrees, find the general solutions of the equations: (i) $\sin 2x = 0.5$; *(ii)* $\tan x/2 = \tan 25°$.

(i) An angle whose sine is 0.5 is 30°, so the general solution is $2x = n\,180° + (-1)^n 30°$ leading to $x = n\,90° + (-1)^n 15°$;

(ii) one value of $x/2$ is 25°, so the general solution is $x/2 = n180° + 25°$, leading to $x = n360° + 50°$.

Types of trigonometrical equations

(i) Equations solvable by factorisation; (ii) equations reducible to a quadratic form; (iii) equations of the type $a \sin x + b \cos x = c$.

The different methods of solution are illustrated in the following worked examples.

Example 5. Solve: (i) $\sin 2x + \cos x = 0$; (ii) $\cos 3x = \cos 2x$; (iii) $\sin 2x + \sin x = \cos x/2$, *giving values of x in the interval* $0 \leqslant x \leqslant 2\pi$.

(i) $$2 \sin x \cos x + \cos x = 0,$$

$$\cos x\,(2 \sin x + 1) = 0.$$

$\therefore$ $$\cos x = 0;\ x = \frac{\pi}{2}, \frac{3\pi}{2};$$

or $$\sin x = -\frac{1}{2};\ x = \frac{7\pi}{6}, \frac{11\pi}{6}.$$

(ii) $$\cos 3x - \cos 2x = 0,$$

factorising, $$-2 \sin\frac{5x}{2} \sin\frac{x}{2} = 0.$$

$$\sin\frac{5x}{2} = 0;\ \frac{5x}{2} = 0, \pi, 2\pi, 3\pi, 4\pi, 5\pi,$$

$$x = 0, \frac{2\pi}{5}, \frac{4\pi}{5}, \frac{6\pi}{5}, \frac{8\pi}{5}\ 2\pi;$$

or $$\sin\frac{x}{2} = 0;\ \frac{x}{2} = 0, \pi;\ x = 0, 2\pi.$$

So the required solutions are $x = 0, 2\pi/5, 4\pi/5, 6\pi/5, 8\pi/5, 2\pi$.

(iii) $$\sin 2x + \sin x = \cos\frac{x}{2},$$

factorising, $$2 \sin\frac{3x}{2} \cos\frac{x}{2} = \cos\frac{x}{2},$$

$$\cos\frac{x}{2}\left(2 \sin\frac{3x}{2} - 1\right) = 0.$$

$\therefore$ $$\cos\frac{x}{2} = 0;\ \frac{x}{2} = \frac{\pi}{2};\ x = \pi;$$

or $$\sin\frac{3x}{2} = \frac{1}{2};\ \frac{3x}{2} = \frac{\pi}{6}, \frac{5\pi}{6}, \frac{13\pi}{6}, \frac{17\pi}{6};$$

$$x = \frac{\pi}{9}, \frac{5\pi}{9}, \frac{13\pi}{9}, \frac{17\pi}{9}.$$

So the required solutions are $x = \pi/9, 5\pi/9, \pi, 13\pi/9, 17\pi/9$.

Example 6. Find the general solutions of the equations: (i) $\cos 2\theta = 7\cos\theta + 3$; (ii) $3\sec^2\theta = 5(\tan\theta + 1)$.

(i) Writing $\cos 2\theta = 2\cos^2\theta - 1$, the equation becomes

$$2\cos^2\theta - 7\cos\theta - 4 = 0,$$

$$(2\cos\theta + 1)(\cos\theta - 4) = 0.$$

As $\cos\theta \leqslant 1$, the only solution here is $\cos\theta = -1/2$, leading to the general solution

$$\theta = 2n\pi \pm \frac{2\pi}{3}.$$

(ii) Writing $\sec^2\theta = 1 + \tan^2\theta$, the equation becomes

$$3\tan^2\theta - 5\tan\theta - 2 = 0,$$

$$(3\tan\theta + 1)(\tan\theta - 2) = 0.$$

$\therefore$ $\quad \tan\theta = -\frac{1}{3};\ \theta = 2.820\,\text{rad};$ general solution $\theta = n\pi + 2.820\,\text{rad}$;

or $\quad \tan\theta = 2;\quad 0 = 1.107\,\text{rad};$ general solution $\theta = n\pi + 1.107\,\text{rad}$.

Example 7. Solve the equation $12\sin x - 5\cos x + 6.5 = 0$, *for* $0 \leqslant x \leqslant 360°$.

First express the function $12\sin x - 5\cos x$ as a single sine

$$12\sin x - 5\cos x = 13\left[\frac{12}{13}\sin x - \frac{5}{13}\cos x\right],$$

$$= 13\sin(x - \alpha), \text{ where } \tan\alpha = \frac{5}{12},\ \alpha = 22°37'.$$

So $$13\sin(x - 22°37') = -6.5,$$

$$\sin(x - 22°37') = -0.5.$$

$$x - 22°37' = 210°, 330°,$$

$$x = 232°37', 352°37'.$$

(A) EXAMPLES 12

1. Write down the general solutions of the equations: (i) $\tan x = \tan 35°$; (ii) $\cos x = 0.5$; (iii) $\sin 2x = -1$; (iv) $\tan 3x/2 = 1$.
2. By first determining the values of $\tan x$, find the solutions of the following equations in the interval $0 \leqslant x \leqslant 360°$: (i) $2\sin x + \cos x = 0$; (ii) $3\sin x = 4\cos x$; (iii) $\cos(30° - x) = 2\cos x$.

3. Solve the following equations for x in the interval $0 \geqslant x \geqslant 2\pi$: (i) $\sin^2 x = 1/4$; (ii) $2\sin^2 x - \sin x = 0$; (iii) $\sin 2x = \cos x$; (iv) $2\sin 2x = 3\sin x$.
4. By noting that $\cos x = \sin(\pi/2 - x)$ and $\sin x = \cos(\pi/2 - x)$, find the general solutions of the equations: (i) $\sin x = \cos(0.2)$; (ii) $\cos 2x = \sin(0.2)$.
5. Solve the equation $\cos 2x - \sin 2x = \sqrt{2}$, for $0 \leqslant x \leqslant 2\pi$.
6. For x in the interval $0 \leqslant x \leqslant 360°$, solve the equations: (i) $2\sin^2 x = 1 - \cos x$; (ii) $2\cos 2x = 1 + 4\cos x$; (iii) $\tan 2x = 3\tan x$.
7. If $\tan x = \cot y$, where both x and y are acute angles, what is the relationship between x and y? Use this result to find a solution of the equation $\tan(\pi/4 + x) = \cot 2x$ in the interval $0 \leqslant x \leqslant \pi/2$.
8. Find the solutions of the equation $4\sin x/2 - 2\cos x = 1$ which lie in the interval $0 \leqslant x \leqslant 180°$.
9. Solve the equation $3\cos 2\theta - \sin 2\theta = 2$ for values of θ between 0° and 180°.
10. Find the values of θ between $-180°$ and $+180°$ which satisfy the equation $5\cos\theta + 12\sin\theta = 3.25$.
11. Solve the equation $\cos 2\theta + \cos\theta = \cos\theta/2$ for values of θ in the interval $0° \leqslant \theta \leqslant 180°$.
12. Solve the equation $\cos(90° - x) + \cos x = 1$ for values of x in the interval $-180° \leqslant x \leqslant 180°$.
13. Find the solution of the equation $\cot 2x = \tan(60° - x)$ in the interval $0 < x < 90°$.
14. Find the general solution of the equation $\sin 7\theta - \sin\theta = \sin 3\theta$, expressing the result in radians.
15. For what values of k has the equation $\sqrt{5}\cos 2x - 2\sin 2x = k$ real solutions? Solve the equation in the case where $k = 1.5$ for x in the interval $0 \leqslant x \leqslant 360°$.

APPROXIMATIONS; THE TRIANGLE AND THE CIRCLE

Approximations

If θ, *measured in radians*, is small such that its third and higher powers can be ignored, then

$$\sin\theta \approx \theta;\ \cos\theta \approx 1 - \frac{\theta^2}{2};\ \tan\theta \approx \theta.$$

Example 8. If θ is so small that θ^3 and higher powers can be ignored, obtain an approximate value for $(1 - \cos 2\theta)/2$.

$$\frac{(1-\cos 2\theta)}{2} \approx \frac{\left[1 - \left(1 - \frac{(2\theta)^2}{2}\right)\right]}{2},$$

i.e.

$$\frac{(1-\cos 2\theta)}{2} \approx \theta^2.$$

Example 9. If x is small, show that the approximate value of $\sin(\pi/4 + x)$ is $\sqrt{2}(2 + 2x - x^2)/4$.

$$\sin\left(\frac{\pi}{4} + x\right) = \sin\frac{\pi}{4}\cos x + \cos\frac{\pi}{4}\sin x,$$

$$= \frac{\sqrt{2}(\cos x + \sin x)}{2};$$

$$\sin\left(\frac{\pi}{4} + x\right) \approx \frac{\sqrt{2}\left(1 - \frac{x^2}{2} + x\right)}{2},$$

$$\approx \frac{\sqrt{2}(2 + 2x - x^2)}{4}.$$

The Triangle

Sine Rule $$\frac{a}{\sin A} = \frac{b}{\sin B} = \frac{c}{\sin C} = 2R,$$ where R is the radius of the circumcircle.

Cosine Rule $$a^2 = b^2 + c^2 - 2bc\cos A;$$

$$\cos A = \frac{(b^2 + c^2 - a^2)}{2bc}.$$

Area of triangle $$\text{Area} = \frac{bc}{2}\sin A.$$

Example 10. In triangle ABC, angle BAC = θ rad where θ is small enough for θ^3 and higher powers to be ignored, use the Cosine Rule to show that $\theta^2 \approx [a^2 - (b-c)^2]/bc$.

$$a^2 = b^2 + c^2 - 2bc\cos A = b^2 + c^2 - 2bc\cos\theta;$$

As θ is small, $$\cos\theta \approx 1 - \frac{\theta^2}{2},$$

so $$a^2 \approx b^2 + c^2 - 2bc\left(1 - \frac{\theta^2}{2}\right),$$

$$-bc\theta^2 \approx b^2 + c^2 - 2bc - a^2 \text{ or } (b-c)^2 - a^2,$$

$$\theta^2 \approx \frac{a^2 - (b-c)^2}{bc}.$$

Example 11. In triangle ABC, $\angle A = 105°$, $\angle B = 30°$, $\angle C = 45°$; P is the mid-point of BC and $\angle BAP = \theta°$. Prove that $\sqrt{2}\sin\theta = \sin(105° - \theta)$.

Using the Sine Rule, in $\triangle$ABP, (Fig. 13)

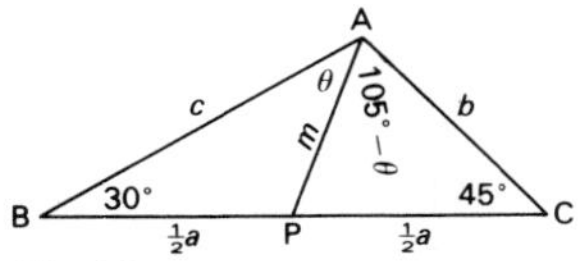

Fig. 13

$$\frac{\frac{a}{2}}{\sin\theta} = \frac{m}{\sin 30°};$$

so $$a = 4m\sin\theta.$$

In $\triangle$APC,

$$\frac{\frac{a}{2}}{\sin(105° - \theta)} = \frac{m}{\sin 45°};$$

so $$a = 2\sqrt{2}m\sin(105° - \theta).$$

$\therefore$ $$4m\sin\theta = 2\sqrt{2}m\sin(105° - \theta),$$

or $$\sqrt{2}\sin\theta = \sin(105° - \theta).$$

The Circle

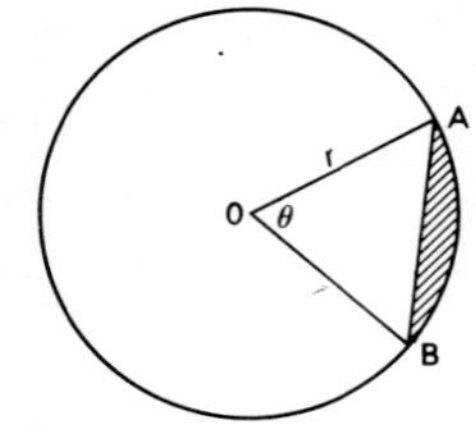

Fig. 14

In Fig. 14 where the angle at the centre, $\angle AOB = \theta$ rad,

length of arc AB $= r\theta$;
area of sector AOB $= r^2\theta/2$;
area of minor segment $= r^2(\theta - \sin\theta)/2$.

Example 12. A chord PQ of a circle radius r subtends an angle θ rad at the centre O. A second chord RS, parallel to and on the same side of the centre as PQ, subtends an angle $(\theta+\pi/3)$ *at O. Show that the area enclosed between the chords is* $r^2[\pi/6 - \cos(\theta+\pi/6)/2]$.

In Fig. 15, shaded area = area of segment RTS − area of segment PTQ,

$$= \frac{r^2}{2}\left[\left(\theta+\frac{\pi}{3}\right)-\sin\left(\theta+\frac{\pi}{3}\right)\right]-\frac{r^2}{2}(\theta-\sin\theta)$$

$$= \frac{\pi r^2}{6}-\frac{r^2}{2}\left[\sin\left(\theta+\frac{\pi}{3}\right)-\sin\theta\right],$$

$$= \frac{\pi r^2}{6}-\frac{r^2}{2}\cdot 2\cos\left(\theta+\frac{\pi}{6}\right)\sin\frac{\pi}{6},$$

$$= r^2\left[\frac{\pi}{6}-\frac{1}{2}\cos\left(\theta+\frac{\pi}{6}\right)\right].$$

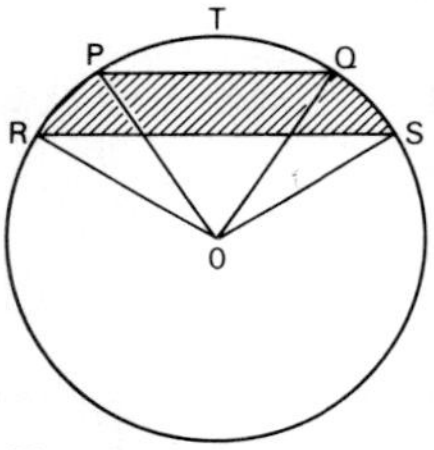

Fig. 15

(A) EXAMPLES 13

1. If θ is small such that powers above the second can be ignored find the approximate values of: (i) $\cos 2\theta$; (ii) $(1+2\sin\theta)^2$; (iii) $1-\tan 3\theta$; (iv) $\cos 2\theta - 2\cos\theta$; (v) $(1+\sin 2\theta)^2$; (vi) $(1+\tan\theta)(1+\cos\theta)$; (vii) $\cos^3\theta$.
2. In triangle ABC, $a = 2$, $b = 48$ and $\angle A = 1/25$ rad. Show that $\sin B$ is approximately equal to 24/25.
3. If A, B, C are the angles of a triangle show that: (i) $\sin(B+C) = \sin A$; (ii) $\cos(B+C) = -\cos A$; (iii) $\sin(B+C)/2 = \cos A/2$; (iv) $b = c \sin B \operatorname{cosec}(A+B)$.
4. The sides of a triangle are in the ratios 3:5:7, find the largest angle. If the area of the triangle is $15\sqrt{3}$ cm^2, find also the length of the shortest side.
5. The area of triangle ABC $= \sqrt{[s(s-a)(s-b)(s-c)]}$ where $s = (a+b+c)/2$. If $a = 6$, $s = 9$ and the area $= 12$, show that $3bc = 97$ and deduce the value of sin A as a fraction.
6. If θ is small, show that $(2-\tan\theta)(1+\sin 2\theta)-2 \approx 3\theta$.
7. In triangle ABC, D is the mid-point of BC and angle ADC $= \theta$. Obtain expressions for b^2 and c^2 in terms of θ and deduce the result $AB^2+AC^2 = 2AD^2+2BD^2$.
8. If $\theta = 0.05$ rad, find the approximate values of: (i) $\sin(\pi/2+\theta)$; (ii) $\cos(\pi/4-\theta)$; (iii) $\tan(\pi/4+\theta)$.
9. In ΔABC, $\angle A$ is acute and $c = a\sqrt{2}$; express b^2 in terms of a and A and deduce that there are two possible triangles if A < 45°.
10. In △ABC, AB $= 3k$ and AC $= 4k$; P is the mid-point of AB and Q is a point on AC such that AQ $= x$. If the area of △APQ = 1/3 area △ABC, find x in terms of k.
11. In △ABC, AB = AC = 1 unit and $\angle A = \theta$ rad where θ is small. Show that BC $\approx \theta$ and by using the Cosine Rule deduce the result $\cos\theta \approx 1-\theta^2/2$.

12. In $\triangle$ABC, show that the length of the perpendicular from A to BC is $bc \sin A/a$. Find the length of this perpendicular in the case where $b = 4$ cm, $c = 5$ cm, A = 150°.
13. A, B, C, D are points on a semicircle such that chords AD, BC are parallel; arcs AB, BD subtend angles α, β radians at the centre. Show that the area of the part of the semicircle between the parallel chords is $r^2(\alpha - \sin\alpha \cos\beta)$, where r is the radius of the semicircle.
14. In $\triangle$ABC, AB > AC, M is the mid-point of BC and angle AMC = θ. Using the perpendicular from A to BC, prove that $2 \cot\theta = \cot B - \cot C$.
15. If θ is so small that θ^3 and higher powers can be ignored show that $\sec\theta \approx 1 + \theta^2/2$.
16. Square OABC has side a; a circle centre O, is drawn cutting AB at P and BC at Q. If $\angle$POQ = 2θ and the area of sector OPQ is equal to one half the area of the square, show that $\sin 2\theta = 4\theta - 1$. Verify that $\theta \approx 0.445$ rad.
17. The sides a, b and the angle A of $\triangle$ABC are given and there are two possible values c_1, c_2 of the length of the side AB. Write down a quadratic equation using the Cosine Rule whose roots are c_1 and c_2 and deduce the results: (i) $c_1 + c_2 = 2b \cos A$; (ii) $c_1 c_2 = b^2 - a^2$. Show also, if C_1, C_2 are the possible values of angle ACB, that $a(\sin C_1 + \sin C_2) = b \sin 2A$.
18. ABCD is a trapezium in which AB is parallel to DC. If AB = a, BC = b, CD = c, AD = d, BD = x, using the Cosine Rule show that $x^2 = ac + (ab^2 - cd^2)/(a - c)$.
19. A circle radius r, centre O, is inscribed in $\triangle$ABC touching the sides BC, CA, AB at D, E, F respectively. Given OA = $2r$, OB = $r\sqrt{2}$, show that the area of ΔABC = $(3 + 2\sqrt{3})r^2$ and find the area bounded by AE, AF and the minor arc EF.
20. If the length of the sides AB, BC, CD, DA of a cyclic quadrilateral ABCD are a, b, c, d respectively, by using the Cosine Rule in triangles ABC, ACD show that $AC^2 = (ac + bd)(ad + bc)/(ab + cd)$.
21. AB is an arc of a circle centre C, radius d and O is the centre of the circle through A, B, C. If angle AOB = $2\pi/7$, show the area bounded by OA, OB and arc AB = $d^2[\pi - 7 \tan(\pi/14)]/14$ and that this area is approximately equal to $\pi d^2/28$.

TRIGONOMETRIC FUNCTIONS

Odd and even functions

As $\sin(-x) = -\sin x$, $\sin x$ is an odd function of x;

as $\cos(-x) = \cos x$, $\cos x$ is an even function of x;

as $\tan(-x) = \tan x$, $\tan x$ is an odd function of x.

and similarly for $\sin mx$, $\cos mx$, $\tan mx$.

Combinations of even or odd functions

Sums and differences. $f \pm g$ will be even if both functions are even, odd if both functions are odd and neither if one function is even and the other odd; e.g. $\sin 2x + 2x$ is an odd function; $\sin 2x + x^2$ is neither even nor odd.

Products and quotients. $f \cdot g$ and f/g will be even if both functions are even or both functions are odd and odd if one function is even and the other odd; e.g. $x \sin x$ is an even function; $\cos x/x$ is an odd function.

Composite functions. $g_0 f$ and $f_0 g$ will be even if at least one of the separate functions is even and odd if both functions are odd; e.g. $\sin(\cos 2x)$ is even; $\tan(x^3)$ is odd.

Periodic functions

The basic trigonometric functions $\sin mx$, $\cos mx$ are periodic with a period of $2\pi/m$

as are the allied functions cosec mx and sec mx. The functions tan mx, cot mx are periodic with period π/m.

Combinations of periodic functions

Let f, g be periodic functions with periods p_f, p_g respectively.

Sums and differences. $f \pm g$ will be periodic with period p where $p = mp_f = np_g$ and m, n are the least positive integers for which $mp_f = np_g$; e.g. $\sin 3x + 2\cos 2x$ where the separate functions have periods of $2\pi/3$ and π respectively, is periodic with a period $p = 3(2\pi/3)$ or $2(\pi)$, i.e. 2π.

Products and quotients. $f \cdot g$ and f/g will be periodic with period $p/2$ or p, where p is defined as above. The ambiguity can be resolved by determining whether or not the period is $p/2$ or alternatively it can be eliminated by expressing the combined function in terms of a sum or a difference if this is possible. E.g. for the function $F(x) = \sin 3x \cos 2x$, $p = 3(2\pi/3) = 2(\pi)$, so $p/2 = \pi$; $F(x+\pi) = \sin 3(x+\pi)\cos 2(x+\pi) = -\sin 3x \cdot \cos 2x = -F(x)$ and hence the period is not $p/2$ and consequently it is p or 2π as can be readily verified.

Alternatively, $F(x) = (\sin 5x + \sin x)/2$ and the period $p = 5(2\pi/5) = 1(2\pi) = 2\pi$ as before.

Composite functions. $g_0 f$ will be periodic with period p_f; $f_0 g$ will be periodic with period p_g; e.g. cos (sin $2x$) is periodic with period π.

Note The composite function $g_0 f$ will be periodic even when g is non-periodic. Usually the period will be p_f but in some cases it will be $p_f/2$ as for example when $g(x) = x^2$, $f(x) = \sin x$; similarly for $f_0 g$.

Example 13. For the functions $f(x) = x - \pi \cos(x/3)$, $g(x) = 2x + \pi \sin(x/2)$, (i) determine whether each function is even, odd or neither; (ii) find constants a, b such that $F = af + bg$ is periodic and find the period.

(i) $f(-x) = -x - \pi\cos(-x/3) = -x - \pi\cos(x/3)$; so $f(x)$ is neither even nor odd.
 $g(-x) = -2x + \pi\sin(-x/2) = -2x - \pi\sin(x/2) = -g(x)$; so $g(x)$ is odd.

(ii) Neither function is periodic because of the linear term, so to make the function $af + bg$ periodic it is necessary to choose values for the constants a, b so that the term in x is eliminated.

$$\therefore \qquad a = -2, b = 1 \text{ and } F(x) = 2\pi\cos\left(\frac{x}{3}\right) + \pi\sin\left(\frac{x}{2}\right).$$

The separate functions have periods 6π and 4π and F is periodic with period $2(6\pi)$ or $3(4\pi)$, i.e. 12π.

Inverse circular functions

If $x = \sin y$ where $-\pi/2 \leqslant y \leqslant \pi/2$, then y is the *inverse sine of* x and is written as *sin*^{-1}x or *arcsin* x.

If $x = \cos y$ where $0 \leqslant y \leqslant \pi$, then y is the *inverse cosine of* x and is written as *cos*$^{-1}\,x$ or *arc cos* x.

If $x = \tan y$ where $-\pi/2 < y < \pi/2$, then y is the *inverse tangent of* x and is written as $\tan^{-1} x$ or *arc tan* x.

Alternatively, the function $f(x) = \sin x$ when defined in the restricted domain $-\pi/2 \leqslant x \leqslant \pi/2$, has an inverse function $f^{-1}(x)$ written as $\sin^{-1} x$ or $\arcsin x$ which has a domain $-1 \leqslant x \leqslant 1$ and a range $-\pi/2 \leqslant \sin^{-1} x \leqslant \pi/2$. Similarly for $\cos^{-1} x$ with a domain $-1 \leqslant x \leqslant 1$ and a range $0 \leqslant \cos^{-1} x \leqslant \pi$ and $\tan^{-1} x$ with a domain $-\infty < x < +\infty$ and a range $-\pi/2 < \tan^{-1} x < \pi/2$.

Graphs

The graphs of $y = \sin^{-1} x$, $y = \cos^{-1} x$, $y = \tan^{-1} x$ are shown in Fig. 16.

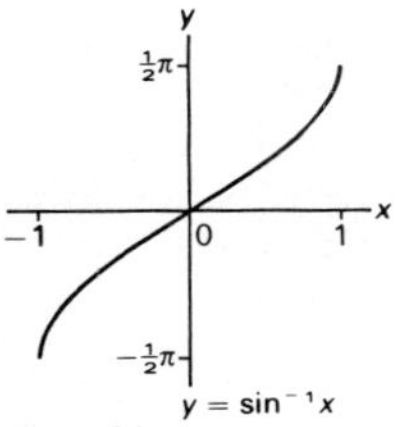

Fig. 16(i)

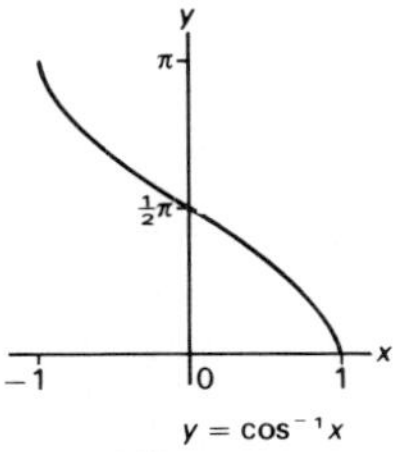

Fig. 16(ii)

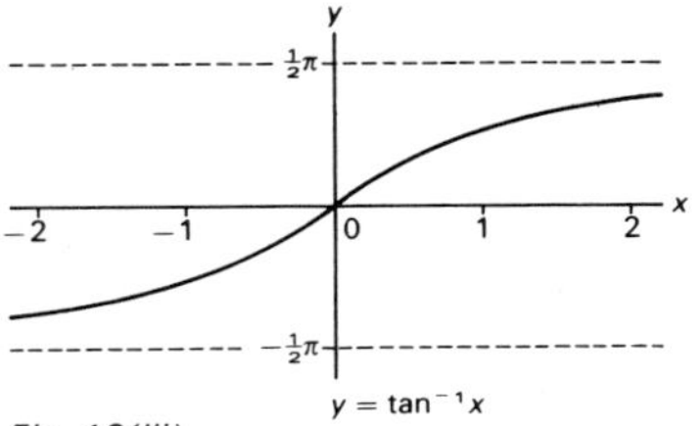

Fig. 16(iii)

Example 14. Evaluate: (i) $\sin^{-1} 0.5$; (ii) $\cos^{-1} 0$; (iii) $\tan^{-1}(-\sqrt{3})$.

(i) $\sin^{-1} 0.5 = \pi/6$; (ii) $\cos^{-1} 0 = \pi/2$; (iii) $\tan^{-1}(-\sqrt{3}) = -\pi/3$.

Example 15. If $0 \leqslant x < 1$, *show that* $\tan^{-1}[(1+x)/(1-x)] = \pi/4 + \tan^{-1} x$.

The restriction on the value of x ensures that $0 \leqslant \tan^{-1}x < \pi/4$ and that $\pi/4 \leqslant \tan^{-1}[(1+x)/(1-x)] < \pi/2$.

We have
$$\tan\left(\frac{\pi}{4}+\tan^{-1} x\right) = \frac{\tan\frac{\pi}{4}+\tan(\tan^{-1} x)}{1-\tan\frac{\pi}{4}\tan(\tan^{-1} x)},$$
$$= \frac{1+x}{1-x}, \text{ as } \tan(\tan^{-1} x) = x.$$

$$\therefore \qquad \tan^{-1}\left(\frac{1+x}{1-x}\right) = \frac{\pi}{4}+\tan^{-1} x.$$

Example 16. Given $f(x) = \cos x - \sin x$, $-\pi/4 \leqslant x \leqslant 3\pi/4$, *find* f^{-1} *and state its domain and range.*

$$y = f(x) = \cos x - \sin x,$$
$$= \sqrt{2}\cos\left(x+\frac{\pi}{4}\right),\ 0 \leqslant x+\frac{\pi}{4} \leqslant \pi.$$

Interchanging x and y, $$x=\sqrt{2}\cos\left(y+\frac{\pi}{4}\right),$$

i.e. $$y+\frac{\pi}{4}=\cos^{-1}\left(\frac{x}{\sqrt{2}}\right),$$

$$y=f^{-1}(x)=\cos^{-1}\left(\frac{x}{\sqrt{2}}\right)-\frac{\pi}{4}.$$

The domain of f^{-1} is $-\sqrt{2}\leqslant x\leqslant\sqrt{2}$ and the range is $-\pi/4\leqslant f^{-1}(x)\leqslant 3\pi/4$.

(A) EXAMPLES 14

1. State whether the following functions are even, odd or neither: (i) $\sin 2x$; (ii) $\cos 3x$; (iii) $\tan x/2$; (iv) $1+\sin x$; (v) $x\cos x$; (vi) $x^3\sin x$; (vii) $x^2\cos x$; (viii) $x+\sin x$; (ix) $x-\cos x$; (x) $2x-\tan x$; (xi) $\sin x/x$; (xii) $\sin^2 x$; (xiii) $\tan^3 x$; (xiv) $\sin(\sin x)$; (xv) $\cos(\sin 2x)$; (xvi) $\cos(\pi\cos x)$.
2. In each of the following cases state whether or not the given function is periodic and if so give the period: (i) $\sin(3x/2)$; (ii) $\tan(x/2)$; (iii) $\cos(x+\pi/4)$; (iv) $x+\sin x$; (v) $\sin x+\cos x$; (vi) $1+\sin 2x$; (vii) $2+\cos(2x/3)$; (viii) $x\cos x$; (ix) $\sin 3x-\sin x$; (x) $\cos 5x+\cos 3x$; (xi) $\tan(3x-\pi/2)$.
3. Evaluate: (i) $\tan^{-1}1$; (ii) $\cos^{-1}0.5$; (iii) $\arcsin(1/\sqrt{2})$; (iv) $\tan^{-1}(-1/\sqrt{3})$; (v) $\arccos(-\sqrt{3}/2)$; (vi) $\sin^{-1}(-1/2)$; (vii) $\arctan(\tan 1)$; (viii) $\sin(\tan^{-1}3/4)$.
4. Show that $\tan^{-1}(5/12)=\sin^{-1}(5/13)=\cos^{-1}(12/13)$.
5. Evaluate: (i) $\sin(\pi/4+\theta)$ where $\theta=\arctan(3/4)$; (ii) $\cos(\pi/2-\theta)$ where $\theta=\arcsin(3/5)$.
6. If the angles are acute, show that $\sin^{-1}x+\cos^{-1}x=\pi/2$ and find x if $2\sin^{-1}x=\cos^{-1}x$.
7. For each of the functions $f(x)=1+\cos x$, $g(x)=2-\sin(x/2)$, state: (i) the period; (ii) whether the function is odd, even or neither. Find the period of the function F defined by $F=2f-g$.
8. If $x\geqslant 0$, show that: (i) $\sin(\tan^{-1}x)=x/\sqrt{(1+x^2)}$; (ii) $\cos(\tan^{-1}x)=1/\sqrt{(1+x^2)}$.
9. State the period of each of the following functions: (i) $\sin(\sin x)$; (ii) $\cos(\sin 2x)$; (iii) $\sin(\cos 3x/2)$; (iv) $\tan(2\tan x)$; (v) $e^{\sin 2x}$; (vi) $\cos^2 2x$.
10. Given $\tan x=1/2$, $0\leqslant x<\pi/4$, find the value of $\tan 2x$ and deduce the result $2\tan^{-1}(1/2)=\tan^{-1}(4/3)$.
11. Using the expression for $\tan(A+B)$ in terms of $\tan A$ and $\tan B$ where $A=\tan^{-1}a$, $B=\tan^{-1}b$ and the angles A, B, A+B are all acute, establish the result $\tan^{-1}a+\tan^{-1}b=\tan^{-1}[(a+b)/(1-ab)]$.
12. Use the result in the previous example to show that $2\tan^{-1}(1/3)+\tan^{-1}(1/7)=\pi/4$.
13. Find the periods of the following functions: (i) $1+\cos(x/2)$; (ii) $\pi-2\tan 2x$; (iii) $\sin 2x+\sin x$; (iv) $2\cos 3x-\sin 2x$; (v) $\tan(x/2)+\tan x$; (vi) $\sin(2x/3)+\pi\sin x/2$; (vii) $2\cos(3x/2)-\cos(5x/2)$; (viii) $\sin x\cos x$; (ix) $\sin 4x\cos 2x$; (x) $\cos 5x\sin x$; (xi) $\cos 5x/2\cos x/2$; (xii) $\sin^2 x$; (xiii) $\sin 5x\cos x$; (xiv) $\cos^3 2x$; (xv) $\sin^2 x\cos^2 x$; (xvi) $\sin^2 2x\cos 2x$.
14. In each of the following examples where a function f is defined over a stated domain, find the inverse function f^{-1} and also the value of $f^{-1}(1)$: (i) $f(x)=\sin 2x$, $-\pi/4\leqslant x\leqslant\pi/4$; (ii) $f(x)=2\cos x$, $0\leqslant x\leqslant\pi$; (iii) $f(x)=(1/\pi)\tan(x/2)$, $-\pi<x<\pi$; (iv) $f(x)=2\sin(x+\pi/4)$, $-3\pi/4\leqslant x\leqslant 5\pi/4$.
15. By first expressing $f(x)=\sin x+\cos x$, $-3\pi/4\leqslant x\leqslant\pi/4$, in the form $R\sin(x+\alpha)$, find the inverse function f^{-1}.

(B) MISCELLANEOUS EXAMPLES

1. Given that $(x+y)=\sin(\theta+75°)$, $x-y=\sin(\theta+15°)$, express x and y in terms of $\sin(\theta+45°)$ and $\cos(\theta+45°)$. Hence obtain the relationship between x, y and constants.
2. Prove that $\sin 3\theta/\sin\theta-\cos 3\theta/\cos\theta=2$ and by substituting a suitable value for θ, show that $\operatorname{cosec}15°-\sec 15°=2\sqrt{2}$.

3. Express $\cos x+2\sin x$ in the form $R\sin(x+\alpha)$ and hence solve the following equations for values of x in the interval $0 \leqslant x \leqslant 360°$: (i) $2\cos x+4\sin x = 1$; (ii) $\cos x(\cos x+2\sin x) = 1$.
4. Prove that $\sin 3x = 3\sin x-4\sin^3 x$ and solve the equation $\sin 3x = \sin^2 x$ for values of x in the interval $0 \leqslant x \leqslant 2\pi$.
5. In $\triangle ABC$, P is the mid-point of AB and $\angle APC = \theta$. Prove that $2c\cos\theta/(a^2-b^2) = 1/CP = c\sin\theta/2\triangle$ where $\triangle$ = area $\triangle ABC$.
6. If θ is small and powers of θ above the second can be ignored, show that $\cos 2\theta/\cos\theta \approx 1-3\theta^2/2$.
7. If $0 \leqslant x \leqslant 2\pi$, find the coordinates of the turning points on the curves with equations: (i) $y = \sqrt{3}\cos x-\sin x$; (ii) $y = 1-\sqrt{3}\cos x+\sin x$; (iii) $y = 1/(2+\sqrt{3}\cos x-\sin x)$.
8. Find the general solution of the equation $\cos 3x+2\cos 5x+\cos 7x = 0$.
9. Show that $\sin 7\theta+\sin\theta = 8\sin\theta\cos\theta\cos 2\theta\cos 3\theta$. Hence solve the equation $\cos\theta\cos 2\theta\cos 3\theta = 1/4$ for values of θ given by $0 \leqslant \theta \leqslant 180°$.
10. If $\cos(30°-\theta) = \lambda\cos\theta$, show that $\tan\theta = 2\lambda-\sqrt{3}$ and deduce the value of $\tan 15°$.
11. Show that $2\sin\theta(\cos 2\theta+\cos 4\theta+\cos 6\theta) = \sin 7\theta-\sin\theta$. By writing $\theta = \pi/7$, deduce that $\cos 2\pi/7+\cos 4\pi/7+\cos 6\pi/7 = -1/2$.
12. Functions f and g are defined for real values of x by $f(x) = 2-\cos x$, $g(x) = 2+\sin(2x/3)$. For each function state: (i) the period; (ii) whether the function is even, odd or neither. Sketch the graphs of the functions for $-3\pi/2 < x < 3\pi/2$. Is the function F defined by $F(x) = g(x)-f(x)$ periodic? If so state the period.
13. Any point P is taken on the circumference of a circle radius $5r$. With P as centre an arc of a circle of radius $8r$ is drawn to cut the first circle. Show that the smaller of the two areas into which the given circle is divided by the arc is $2r^2(12-7\theta)$, where $\theta = \tan^{-1}3/4$.
14. Solve the equations: (i) $2\tan^2 x = 3(11+\sec x)$; (ii) $2\sin 3x+3\sin 2x = 0$ for values of x given by $0° \leqslant x \leqslant 180°$.
15. In $\triangle ABC$, $BC = a$ and angle $CAB = \theta$; AC is produced to D and angle $BCD = 4\theta$. Prove: (i) $AB = 4a\cos\theta\cos 2\theta$; (ii) $AC = a(1+2\cos 2\theta)$.
16. For what values of the constant c has the equation $\cos(x+60°)+\cos x = c$ real solutions? When $c = 1$, find the solutions in the interval $0 \leqslant x \leqslant 360°$. Sketch the graph of $y = \cos(x+60°)+\cos x$ for $0 \leqslant x \leqslant 360°$.
17. Express $\tan\theta$ and $\sec\theta$ in terms of t, where $t = \tan\theta/2$ and show that $\sec\theta+\tan\theta = \tan(45°+\theta/2)$. Find the solution in the interval $0 < \theta < 90°$ of the equation $\sec\theta+\tan\theta = \cot 2\theta$.
18. A point P is taken on the circumference of a circle C, radius r, and with P as centre an arc of a circle of radius $r\sqrt{2}$ is drawn to cut C at points A, B. Prove that the two regions into which the circle C is divided by the arc have equal perimeters and find the ratio of the areas of the two regions.
19. Given that, for real values of x, $f(x) = \sin 2x-2x$; $g(x) = \cos 2x+x^2$; $h(x) = \sin(\sin x)$, find whether each of these functions is even, odd or neither. The function F is defined for real values of x by $F(x) = \sin[f(x/2)+x]+4g(x/2)-h(x)-x^2$. Simplify $F(x)$ and determine whether it is even, odd or neither. Show also that F is a periodic function and state its period.
20. If $\tan\theta = t$, express the equation $a\cos 2\theta+b\sin 2\theta = c$ as a quadratic equation in t. Writing the roots of this equation as $\tan\alpha$, $\tan\beta$, show: (i) $\tan\alpha+\tan\beta = 2b/(a+c)$; (ii) $\tan\alpha\tan\beta = (c-a)/(a+c)$.
21. Show that $\cos 3\theta = 4\cos^3\theta-3\cos\theta$. If $x = 1+2\cos\theta$, express the function x^3-3x^2+1 in terms of $\cos 3\theta$ and hence find the solutions of the equation $x^3-3x^2+1 = 0$.
22. In $\triangle ABC$, D, E, F are the mid-points of the sides BC, CA, AB respectively. Using the Cosine Rule in triangles BDA, CDA establish the result $b^2+c^2 = a^2/2+2AD^2$ and write down similar results involving BE^2 and CF^2. Hence prove that $AD^2+BE^2+CF^2 = 3(a^2+b^2+c^2)/4$.
23. Show that $\tan 3\theta = (3t-t^3)/(1-3t^2)$, where $t = \tan\theta$. If $\tan\theta = 1/3$, find the value of $\tan(3\theta-\pi/4)$.
24. If the inverse tangents refer to positive acute angles, show that $\tan^{-1}a+\tan^{-1}b = \tan^{-1}(a+b)/(1-ab)$ and solve the equation $\tan^{-1}3x+\tan^{-1}x = \tan^{-1}(1/2)$.
25. Show that $\cos(\alpha-\beta)+\sin(\alpha+\beta) = (\cos\alpha+\sin\alpha)(\cos\beta+\sin\beta)$ and hence prove the result $(\cos 4\theta+\sin 6\theta)/(\cos 5\theta+\sin 5\theta) = (\cos 2\theta+\sin 4\theta)/(\cos 3\theta+\sin 3\theta)$.
26. For values of x given by $0 \leqslant x \leqslant 180°$, solve the equations: (i) $3\tan 2x+8\cot x = 0$; (ii) $6\sin^2 x+7\sin x\cos x-3\cos^2 x = 0$.
27. A function f is defined for real values of x by: (i) $f(x) = \sin 2x$, $0 \leqslant x \leqslant \pi/4$; (ii) $f(x) = 2-4x/\pi$, $\pi/4 < x \leqslant \pi/2$; (iii) f is an odd function; (iv) f is periodic with period π. Sketch the graph of $y = f(x)$ for $-\pi \leqslant x \leqslant \pi$. Find two intervals each of length $\pi/2$, such that f when restricted to either interval, will have an inverse and in each case find an expression for this inverse function.

Complex Numbers

ALGEBRAIC FORM OF A COMPLEX NUMBER

Definitions
Complex number $\quad z = x + iy$, where x, y are real numbers and $i = \sqrt{-1}$.

Conjugate complex number $\quad z^* = x - iy$.

Fundamental processes
The definitions of the processes of addition, subtraction, multiplication and division as applied to complex numbers are such that the results of these processes can be achieved by the use of the ordinary rules and methods of real algebra together with the results $i^2 = -1, i^3 = i, i^4 = 1 \ldots$. The method used for division is the same as that used in the case of surds* and should be carefully noted.

Example 1. If $z_1 = 4-3i$, $z_2 = 2+i$, find in the algebraic form the value of each of the following complex numbers: (i) $z_1^2 - z_1 z_2$; (ii) z_1/z_2; (iii) z_2^5.

(i) $z_1^2 - z_1 z_2 = (4-3i)^2 - (4-3i)(2+i) = 16 - 24i - 9 - (8 - 2i + 3),$

$$= -4 - 22i.$$

(ii) $$\frac{z_1}{z_2} = \frac{4-3i}{2+i} = \frac{(4-3i)(2-i)}{(2+i)(2-i)} = \frac{5-10i}{5} = 1-2i.$$

(iii) $$z_2^5 = (2+i)^5 = 2^5 + 5(2^4)i + 10(2^3)i^2 + 10(2^2)i^3 + 5(2)i^4 + i^5,$$

$$= 32 + 80i - 80 - 40i + 10 + i,$$

$$= -38 + 41i.$$

Equality
Complex numbers $z_1 = x_1 + iy_1$, $z_2 = x_2 + iy_2$ are equal if, and only if, $x_1 = x_2$ and $y_1 = y_2$.

---

* *See p. 2.*

This result is the basis of the principle of equating real (Re) and imaginary (Im) parts in a complex equation as illustrated in the following examples.

Example 2. *If $x(1+i)+y(2-i) = 1+4i$ find the values of x and y.*

Equating real and imaginary parts, $x+2y = 1$,

and $x-y = 4$.

Solving these equations, $x = 3, y = -1$.

Example 3. *Given $z = x+iy = \sqrt{(8+6i)}$, find the values of x and y and write down the square roots of $8+6i$.*

We have $(x+iy)^2 = 8+6i$,

$$x^2-y^2+2ixy = 8+6i.$$

Equating real and imaginary parts, $x^2-y^2 = 8$

and $xy = 3$.

Solving these equations, $x = 3$, $y = 1$ and $x = -3$, $y = -1$.

$\therefore$ the square roots of $8+6i$ are $\pm(3+i)$.

Example 4. *The equation $z+a+i(z-2) = 0$, where a is real, has a real solution for z. Find this solution and the value of a.*

As z is real it can be taken equal to x where x is real.

So $x+a+i(x-2) = 0$.

Equating real and imaginary parts, $x+a = 0$

and $x-2 = 0$.

$\therefore$ $z = x = 2;\ a = -2$.

Example 5. *The equation $z^4+2z^3+az^2-8z+4 = 0$ has a solution for z which is wholly imaginary. Find the value of the real constant a.*

$z = iy$, where y is real.

Substituting for z and simplifying,

$$y^4+2iy^3-ay^2-8iy+4 = 0.$$

Equating real and imaginary parts, $y^4-ay^2+4 = 0$

and $2y^3-8y = 0$.

Solving the second equation gives $y = \pm 2$, as clearly $y \neq 0$.

$\therefore$ $16-4a+4 = 0$,

$$a = 5.$$

(A) EXAMPLES 15

1. Express in the form $a+ib$: (i) $(1+2\mathrm{i})(1-\mathrm{i})$; (ii) $(2+\mathrm{i})^2$; (iii) $1/(1-\mathrm{i})$; (iv) $(1-\mathrm{i})/(3+2\mathrm{i})$; (v) $1/[(1+2\mathrm{i})^2]$; (vi) $(1-\mathrm{i})^3$; (vii) $(2-\mathrm{i})^4$.
2. If $z = 1+2\mathrm{i}$, express z^2+1/z^2 in the algebraic form.
3. Simplify $(1+\mathrm{i}\sqrt{3})^3-(1-\mathrm{i}\sqrt{3})^3$.
4. If $(x+\mathrm{i}y)(2+\mathrm{i}) = 3-\mathrm{i}$, find the values of x and y.
5. If $z = 3+2\mathrm{i}$, find the value of $(1+z)(1+z^{-1})$ in the form $a+ib$.
6. Solve for z each of the equations: (i) $(2+\mathrm{i})z = 1-\mathrm{i}$; (ii) $(1+\mathrm{i})z+3\mathrm{i} = (-1+2\mathrm{i})z$.
7. If $(z-2)(1+\mathrm{i}) = z+2$, where $z = x+\mathrm{i}y$, find the values of x and y.
8. Find the roots of the following equations in the form $a \pm ib$: (i) $(z-1)^2+3 = 0$; (ii) $z^2-z+1 = 0$; (iii) $2z^2-z+4 = 0$.
9. Given $\omega = (-1+\mathrm{i}\sqrt{3})/2$, show that: (i) $1+\omega+\omega^2 = 0$; (ii) $\omega^3 = 1$.
10. If $z_1 = 3+4\mathrm{i}_1 z_2 = 2-3\mathrm{i}$, find the values of real numbers p, q such that $pz_1+qz_2 = 4-\mathrm{i}$.
11. Expand $(1+\mathrm{i}a)^5$, where a is real, in powers of a and find the values of a for which the function is real.
12. Express: (i) $(1-\mathrm{i})/(3-\mathrm{i})^2$; (ii) $(c+\mathrm{i})^4$ where c is real, in the form $a+ib$.
13. Given $\sqrt{(x+\mathrm{i}y)} = a+ib$ where a, b are real, show that $x = a^2-b^2$, $y = 2ab$. Find the values of a, b when $x = 3$, $y = 4$.
14. Given $z = x+\mathrm{i}y$ and $z+2 = \lambda\mathrm{i}(z+8)$, where λ is a real parameter, show that $x+\lambda y+2 = 0$, $y = \lambda(x+8)$ and eliminate λ from these two equations.
15. If $z = (-1-\mathrm{i}\sqrt{3})/2$, show that the real part of $(1+z)^{-1}$ is 1/2.
16. If $z = x+\mathrm{i}y$ and z^* is its conjugate, show that $zz^*+2z+2z^*$ is real.
17. The complex number $z = x+\mathrm{i}y$ is such that $(z+2)(z-\mathrm{i}) = \lambda\mathrm{i}$, where λ is real. Show that $x(x+2) = y(1-y)$.
18. Solve the equation $zz^*-2z+2z^* = 5-4\mathrm{i}$ for $z(=x+\mathrm{i}y)$, where z^* is the conjugate of z.
19. Obtain the values of the ratio z_2/z_1, in the form $a+ib$, if $z_2^2-z_1z_2+z_1^2 = 0$.
20. Determine all pairs of values of the real numbers p, q for which $z = 1+\mathrm{i}$ is a root of the equation $z^3+pz^2+qz-pq = 0$.
21. Complex numbers $z_1 = a/(1-\mathrm{i})$, $z_2 = b/(2+\mathrm{i})$, where a, b are real are such that $z_1-z_2 = 1$. Find the values of a and b.
22. Find the values of the complex numbers z and t which satisfy the simultaneous equations $z-\mathrm{i}t = -2$, $2z-t = 7\mathrm{i}$, expressing the results in the form $a+ib$.

GEOMETRICAL REPRESENTATION

The complex number $z = x+\mathrm{i}y$ is represented in *an Argand diagram* by the point with Cartesian coordinates (x, y).

Example 6. Show that the points representing the complex numbers 1, $(-1 \pm \mathrm{i}\sqrt{3})/2$ in an Argand diagram are the vertices of an equilateral triangle whose circumcircle has centre the origin and radius unity.

The Argand diagram is shown in Fig. 17 where A, B, C are the points with coordinates $(1,0)$, $(-1/2, \sqrt{3}/2)$ and $(-1/2, -\sqrt{3}/2)$ respectively.

Using elementary coordinate geometry, $AB = BC = CA = \sqrt{3}$, so ABC is an equilateral triangle of side $\sqrt{3}$. Also $OA = OB = OC = 1$ and so O is the centre of the circumcircle whose radius is 1.

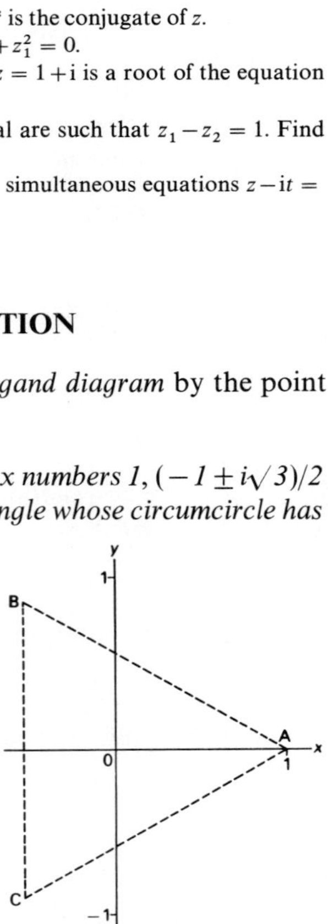

Fig. 17

Example 7. *Given $(z-1)/(z+1) = \lambda i$, where λ is a real parameter and $z = x+iy$, find the Cartesian equation of the locus of the point P which represents z in an Argand diagram as λ varies.*

We have
$$z-1 = \lambda \mathrm{i}(z+1),$$
$$x+\mathrm{i}y-1 = \lambda \mathrm{i}(x+\mathrm{i}y+1)$$

and equating real and imaginary parts,

$$x-1 = -\lambda y \text{ and } y = \lambda x+\lambda.$$

Eliminating λ by substituting $\lambda = (1-x)/y$ in the second equation, gives $x^2+y^2 = 1$ – the equation of the locus of $P(x, y)$ as λ varies.

The locus is a circle, centre the origin and radius 1.

(A) EXAMPLES 16

1. If $z = 3+4\mathrm{i}$, express the complex numbers: (i) z^*+1; (ii) $1/z$; (iii) $z/(z+1)$ in the algebraic form and represent them by points in an Argand diagram.
2. Represent the complex numbers $3-2\mathrm{i}$ and $-1+4\mathrm{i}$ by points P and Q respectively in an Argand diagram. What complex numbers are represented by: (i) the mid-point M of PQ; (ii) the reflection of M in the y-axis?
3. Show that the points representing the complex numbers $1+2\mathrm{i}$, $3+4\mathrm{i}$, $-1+6\mathrm{i}$ in an Argand diagram are the vertices of an isosceles triangle.
4. The complex number $z = \lambda(2-\mathrm{i})$ where λ is real, is represented by a point P in an Argand diagram. Show that P lies on the line $2y+x = 0$.
5. The complex numbers $2+\mathrm{i}$, $2+3\mathrm{i}$, $5+6\mathrm{i}$ are represented by the points P, Q, R respectively in an Argand diagram. Find the complex number which is represented by: (i) the point S where PQRS is a parallelogram; (ii) the point of intersection of the diagonals of this parallelogram.
6. If P represents the complex number $3+2\mathrm{i}$ in an Argand diagram, what complex numbers are represented by: (i) the reflection of P in the x-axis; (ii) the reflection of P in the line $x = 1$; (iii) the reflection of P in the line $y = x$?
7. Show that the points representing the complex numbers $1+3\mathrm{i}$, $3+4\mathrm{i}$, $4-3\mathrm{i}$, in an Argand diagram are three vertices of a rectangle and find the complex number which is represented by the fourth vertex.
8. Express the complex number $(4-3\mathrm{i})/(2+\mathrm{i})$ in the form $a+\mathrm{i}b$. If, in an Argand diagram, this complex number is represented by the point A and the complex number $4+\mathrm{i}$ is represented by the point B, find the distance AB.
9. In an Argand diagram, P represents the complex number $\lambda\mathrm{i}(2-3\mathrm{i})$ where λ is a real parameter. Write down the coordinates (x, y) of P in terms of λ and hence find the Cartesian equation of the locus of P as λ varies.
10. The complex numbers $z_1 = a/(1+\mathrm{i})$, $z_2 = b/(1+2\mathrm{i})$ where a, b are real, are such that $z_1+z_2 = 1$. Find: (i) the values of a and b; (ii) the distance between the points representing z_1, z_2 in an Argand diagram.
11. If $z = 1+\mathrm{i}\sqrt{2}$, express the complex numbers $z_1 = z+z^{-1}$, $z_2 = z-z^{-1}$ in the algebraic form. In an Argand diagram, points P, Q represent z_1, z_2 respectively. If O is the origin, M the mid-point of PQ and G the point on OM such that OG = 2OM/3 show that angle PGQ = 90°.
12. In an Argand diagram, the point P represents the complex number $z = x+\mathrm{i}y$. If $z+1 = \lambda\mathrm{i}(z+6)$, where λ is a real parameter, find the Cartesian equation of the locus P as λ varies.

In Fig. 18, the complex number $z = x + iy$ is represented by $P(x, y)$;

the modulus of z, $|z| = r$, the length OP;

the argument of z, $\arg z = \theta$, the angle OP makes with Ox.

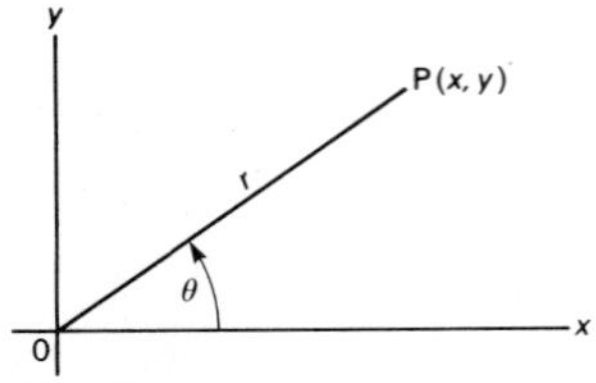

Fig. 18

Note

(i) $|z| = \sqrt{(x^2 + y^2)}$ is always taken as positive;

(ii) $\arg z$ or θ is measured with the usual sign convention and is taken to be in the interval $-\pi < \theta \leqslant \pi$. Although $\tan\theta = y/x$, $\arg z$ cannot always be expressed as $\tan^{-1} y/z$ as the inverse tangent only takes values between $-\pi/2$ and $\pi/2$;

(iii) the use of a diagram is valuable when expressing a complex number in the trigonometrical or (r, θ) form.

Example 8. Find the modulus and argument of each of the complex numbers: (i) $-3+4i$*; (ii)* $2/(1+i)$*; (iii)* $5(1-i)/(1+2i)$*.*

(i) In Fig. 19, the complex number $-3+4i$ is represented by the point $P(-3, 4)$.

$$|-3+4i| = r_1 = \sqrt{(3^2+4^2)} = 5;$$

$$\arg(-3+4i) = \theta_1 = \pi - \tan^{-1}\frac{4}{3} = 2.214 \text{ rad.}$$

(ii) $$\frac{2}{1+i} = \frac{2(1-i)}{(1+i)(1-i)} = 1 - i.$$

In Fig. 19, the complex number $1-i$ is represented by the point $Q(1, -1)$.

$$|1-i| = r_2 = \sqrt{(1^2+1^2)} = \sqrt{2};$$

$$\arg(1-i) = \theta_2 = \tan^{-1}(-1) = -\frac{\pi}{4}.$$

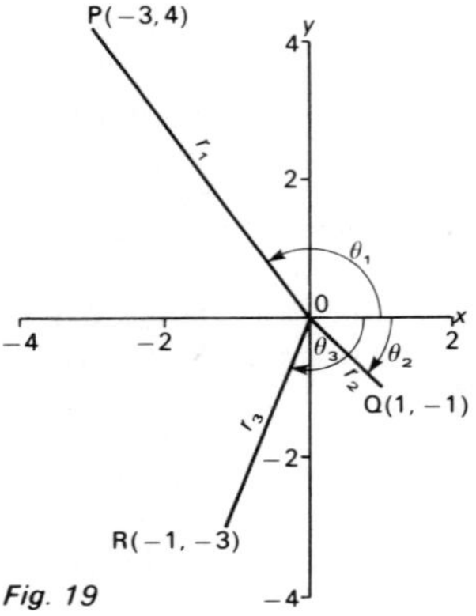

Fig. 19

(iii) $$\frac{5(1-i)}{1+2i} = \frac{5(1-i)(1-2i)}{(1+2i)(1-2i)} = -1-3i.$$

In Fig. 19, the complex number $-1-3i$ is represented by the point $R(-1, -3)$.

$$|-1-3i| = r_3 = \sqrt{(1^2+3^2)} = \sqrt{10};$$

$$\arg(-1-3i) = \theta_3 = -(\pi - \tan^{-1} 3) = -1.892 \text{ rad.}$$

Example 9. Find the argument of each of the following complex numbers: (i) $\cos 5\pi/3 + i\sin 5\pi/3$*; (ii)* $\cos 2\pi/3 - i\sin 2\pi/3$*; (iii)* $\sin\theta + i\cos\theta$ *where* $0 < \theta < \pi$*.*

(i) $\cos 5\pi/3 + i\sin 5\pi/3 = \cos(-\pi/3) + i\sin(-\pi/3)$, so the argument is $-\pi/3$;

(ii) $\cos 2\pi/3 - i\sin 2\pi/3 = \cos(-2\pi/3) + i\sin(-2\pi/3)$, so the argument is $-2\pi/3$;
(iii) $\sin\theta + i\cos\theta = \cos(\pi/2-\theta) + i\sin(\pi/2-\theta)$, so the argument is $\pi/2-\theta$.

Products and quotients

If $$z_1 = r_1(\cos\theta_1 + i\sin\theta_1),\ z_2 = r_2(\cos\theta_2 + i\sin\theta_2)$$

then $$z_1 z_2 = r_1 r_2[\cos(\theta_1+\theta_2) + i\sin(\theta_1+\theta_2)]$$

and $$z_1/z_2 = r_1/r_2[\cos(\theta_1-\theta_2) + i\sin(\theta_1-\theta_2)].$$

When multiplying two complex numbers expressed in the (r,θ) form, multiply the moduli and add the arguments and when dividing, divide the moduli and subtract the arguments.

Clearly the product rule can be extended to any number of complex numbers with the important special case, if n is a positive integer,

$$(\cos\theta + i\sin\theta)^n = \cos n\theta + i\sin n\theta \qquad \text{(De Moivre's theorem.)}$$

Example 10. *Given $z_1 = 2(\cos\pi/5 + i\sin\pi/5)$, $z_2 = \cos 2\pi/5 + i\sin 2\pi/5$, express in the (r,θ) form: (i) z_1z_2; (ii) z_1^2; (iii) z_1/z_2; (iv) $1/z_1$; (v) z_2^5; (vi) z_1^3/z_2^2.*

(i) $z_1z_2 = 2[\cos(\pi/5+2\pi/5) + i\sin(\pi/5+2\pi/5)] = 2(\cos 3\pi/5 + i\sin 3\pi/5)$;
(ii) $z_1^2 = 2^2[\cos(\pi/5+\pi/5) + i\sin(\pi/5+\pi/5)] = 4(\cos 2\pi/5 + i\sin 2\pi/5)$;
(iii) $z_1/z_2 = 2[\cos(\pi/5-2\pi/5) + i\sin(\pi/5-2\pi/5)]$
$= 2[\cos(-\pi/5) + i\sin(-\pi/5)]$;
(iv) $1/z_1 = (\cos 0 + i\sin 0)/2(\cos\pi/5 + i\sin\pi/5)$,
$= [\cos(-\pi/5) + i\sin(-\pi/5)]/2$;
(v) $z_2^5 = \cos(5\text{x}2\pi/5) + i\sin(5\text{x}2\pi/5) = \cos 2\pi + i\sin 2\pi$,
$= \cos 0 + i\sin 0$;
(vi) $z_1^3/z_2^2 = 8(\cos 3\pi/5 + i\sin 3\pi/5)/(\cos 4\pi/5 + i\sin 4\pi/5)$,
$= 8[\cos(-\pi/5) + i\sin(-\pi/5)]$.

(A) EXAMPLES 17

1. Express the following complex numbers in the (r,θ) form: (i) $1+i$; (ii) $i-1$; (iii) $2i$; (iv) 1; (v) -1; (vi) i^{-1}; (vii) $4-3i$; (viii) $-\sqrt{3}-1$.
2. Find the modulus and argument of each of the following complex numbers: (i) $(1-i)(1+3i)$; (ii) $(2-i)^2$; (iii) $1/(1-i)$; (iv) $(1+2i)/(1+i)$; (v) $(1-i)^2/(1-2i)$.
3. Find the argument θ where $-\pi < \theta \leqslant \pi$, of each of the complex numbers: (i) $\cos 5\pi/3 + i\sin 5\pi/3$; (ii) $\cos 2\pi + i\sin 2\pi$; (iii) $\cos\pi/3 - i\sin\pi/3$; (iv) $\sin 2\pi/7 + i\cos 2\pi/7$; (v) $\sin 2\pi/5 - i\cos 2\pi/5$.
4. Express in the (r,θ) form: (i) $(\cos\theta + i\sin\theta)^3$; (ii) $(\cos 2\theta + i\sin 2\theta)(\cos 3\theta + i\sin 3\theta)$; (iii) $(\cos\theta + i\sin\theta)^{-1}$; (iv) $(\cos\theta - i\sin\theta)^2$.
5. If $z = 3(\cos\pi/5 + i\sin\pi/5)$, find the modulus and argument of: (i) z^2; (ii) z^3; (iii) z^{-1}.
6. Given $z_1 = 4(\cos\pi/3 + i\sin\pi/3)$, $z_2 = 2(\cos\pi/6 + i\sin\pi/6)$, find the values of: (i) z_1^2; (ii) z_2^{-1}; (iii) z_2^3; (iv) z_1^2/z_2 in the (r,θ) form.
7. If $z = \cos\theta + i\sin\theta$, show that: (i) $z^{-1} = \cos\theta - i\sin\theta$; (ii) $z^2 + z^{-2} = 2\cos 2\theta$.
8. By first expressing the complete number $1+i$ in the (r,θ) form, obtain the value of $(1+i)^6$ in the algebraic form.
9. Express the complex number $(\sqrt{3}-i)^5$ in: (i) the (r,θ) form; (ii) the $a+ib$ form.
10. Express in the algebraic form the complex numbers: (i) $(1-i)^8$; (ii) $(1+i\sqrt{3})^6$; (iii) $(\sqrt{3}+i)^{-4}$.

11. By using the result $\cos 2\theta + i \sin 2\theta = (\cos\theta + i \sin\theta)^2$ and expanding the power term, establish the results $\cos 2\theta = \cos^2\theta - \sin^2\theta$, $\sin 2\theta = 2\sin\theta\cos\theta$.
12. Use the method of the previous example to obtain the results $\cos 3\theta = 4\cos^3\theta - 3\cos\theta$, $\sin 3\theta = 3\sin\theta - 4\sin^3\theta$.
13. Express $(1+i\sqrt{3})^6(\sqrt{3}-i)^4$ in: (i) the trigonometric; (ii) the algebraic form.
14. By expressing $1+\cos\theta$ and $\sin\theta$ in terms of $\theta/2$, find the modulus and argument of the complex number $1+\cos\theta + i\sin\theta$.
15. Find the modulus and argument of $1-\cos\theta+i\sin\theta$ and express $(1-\cos\theta+i\sin\theta)^3$ in the (r, θ) form.
16. If $z = \cos\theta + i\sin\theta$, find the values of: (i) $z+z^{-1}$; (ii) $z^n + z^{-n}$; where n is a positive integer.

DE MOIVRE'S THEOREM AND APPLICATIONS

De Moivre's theorem

If n is a positive integer,

$$(\cos\theta + i\sin\theta)^n = \cos n\theta + i \sin n\theta.$$

As $\cos\theta - i\sin\theta = \cos(-\theta) + i\sin(-\theta)$, it follows also that

$$(\cos\theta - i\sin\theta)^n = \cos n\theta - i \sin n\theta.$$

Applications of De Moivre's theorem

(i) In the expression of $\cos n\theta$ and $\sin n\theta$ in terms of powers of $\cos\theta$ and $\sin\theta$;
(ii) in the expression of $\cos^n\theta$ and $\sin^n\theta$ in terms of the cosine and sine of multiple angles;
(iii) in the solution of equations of the form $z^n = k^n$, where k is a real constant.

The applications are illustrated in the following examples.

Example 11. Express $\cos 5\theta$ in terms of powers of $\cos\theta$.

Let $\quad z = \cos\theta + i\sin\theta \quad$ so $\quad z^5 = \cos 5\theta + i\sin 5\theta.$

Expanding,

$$\begin{aligned}(\cos\theta + i\sin\theta)^5 &= \cos^5\theta + 5\cos^4\theta\,(i\sin\theta) + 10\cos^3\theta\,(i\sin\theta)^2 \\ &\quad + 10\cos^2\theta\,(i\sin\theta)^3 + 5\cos\theta\,(i\sin\theta)^4 + (i\sin\theta)^5, \\ &= \cos^5\theta + 5i\cos^4\theta\sin\theta - 10\cos^3\theta\sin^2\theta \\ &\quad - 10i\cos^2\theta\sin^3\theta + 5\cos\theta\sin^4\theta + i\sin^5\theta.\end{aligned}$$

Equating real parts,

$$\begin{aligned}\cos 5\theta &= \cos^5\theta - 10\cos^3\theta\sin^2\theta + 5\cos\theta\sin^4\theta, \\ &= \cos^5\theta - 10\cos^3\theta\,(1-\cos^2\theta) + 5\cos\theta\,(1-\cos^2\theta)^2, \\ &= 16\cos^5\theta - 20\cos^3\theta + 5\cos\theta.\end{aligned}$$

By equating imaginary parts, an expression for $\sin 5\theta$ is obtained.

Example 12. Obtain an expression for $\sin^5\theta$ in terms of multiple angles.

Let $\quad z = \cos\theta + \mathrm{i}\sin\theta \quad \text{so} \quad z^{-1} = \cos\theta - \mathrm{i}\sin\theta$

and $\quad z^n = \cos n\theta + \mathrm{i}\sin n\theta \quad z^{-n} = \cos n\theta - \mathrm{i}\sin n\theta$

$\therefore \quad z - z^{-1} = 2\mathrm{i}\sin\theta \quad \text{and} \quad z^n - z^{-n} = 2\mathrm{i}\sin n\theta.$

$$\begin{aligned}(2\mathrm{i}\sin\theta)^5 &= (z-z^{-1})^5,\\ &= z^5 - 5z^3 + 10z - 10z^{-1} + 5z^{-3} - z^{-5},\\ &= (z^5 - z^{-5}) - 5(z^3 - z^{-3}) + 10(z - z^{-1}),\\ &= 2\mathrm{i}\sin 5\theta - 10\mathrm{i}\sin 3\theta + 20\mathrm{i}\sin\theta.\end{aligned}$$

$\therefore$
$$2^5\sin^5\theta = 2\sin 5\theta - 10\sin 3\theta + 20\sin\theta,$$

$$\sin^5\theta = \frac{1}{2^4}(\sin 5\theta - 5\sin 3\theta + 10\sin\theta).$$

A similar result for $\cos^5\theta$ is obtained by using $z + z^{-1} = 2\cos\theta$, $z^n + z^{-n} = 2\cos n\theta$.

Example 13. Solve the equations: (i) $z^3 = 1$; (ii) $z^6 + 2^6 = 0$.

(i) Let $z = r(\cos\theta + \mathrm{i}\sin\theta)$ so $z^3 = r^3(\cos 3\theta + \mathrm{i}\sin 3\theta)$,

$$r^3(\cos 3\theta + \mathrm{i}\sin 3\theta) = 1,$$

i.e. $\quad r^3\cos 3\theta = 1;\ r^3\sin 3\theta = 0.$

$\therefore \quad r = 1,\ 3\theta = 0, 2\pi, 4\pi, 6\pi, \ldots,$

$$\theta = 0, \frac{2\pi}{3}, \frac{4\pi}{3}, 2\pi, \ldots.$$

After the first three values of θ, the values of $\cos\theta$ and $\sin\theta$ repeat themselves and the different solutions are

$$z = \cos 0 + \mathrm{i}\sin 0,\ \cos\frac{2\pi}{3} + \mathrm{i}\sin\frac{2\pi}{3},\ \cos\frac{4\pi}{3} + \mathrm{i}\sin\frac{4\pi}{3},$$

$$= 1, \frac{(-1+\sqrt{3}\mathrm{i})}{2}, \frac{(-1-\sqrt{3}\mathrm{i})}{2}.$$

(ii) Let $\quad z = r(\cos\theta + \mathrm{i}\sin\theta) \quad \text{so} \quad z^6 = r^6(\cos 6\theta + \mathrm{i}\sin 6\theta),$

$$r^6(\cos 6\theta + \mathrm{i}\sin 6\theta) = -2^6,$$

i.e. $\quad r^6\cos 6\theta = -2^6;\ r^6\sin 6\theta = 0.$

$\therefore \quad r = 2,\ \cos 6\theta = -1;\ \sin 6\theta = 0.$

$$6\theta = \pi, 3\pi, 5\pi, 7\pi, 9\pi, 11\pi, \ldots,$$

$$\theta = \frac{\pi}{6}, \frac{\pi}{2}, \frac{5\pi}{6}, \frac{7\pi}{6}, \frac{3\pi}{2}, \frac{11\pi}{6}, \ldots.$$

After the first six values of θ, the values of $\cos\theta$ and $\sin\theta$ repeat themselves and the different solutions are:

$$z = 2\left(\cos\frac{\pi}{6}+\mathrm{i}\sin\frac{\pi}{6}\right), 2\left(\cos\frac{\pi}{2}+\mathrm{i}\sin\frac{\pi}{2}\right), 2\left(\cos\frac{5\pi}{6}+\mathrm{i}\sin\frac{5\pi}{6}\right),$$

$$2\left(\cos\frac{7\pi}{6}+\mathrm{i}\sin\frac{7\pi}{6}\right), 2\left(\cos\frac{3\pi}{2}+\mathrm{i}\sin\frac{3\pi}{2}\right), 2\left(\cos\frac{11\pi}{6}+\mathrm{i}\sin\frac{11\pi}{6}\right),$$

$$= \sqrt{3}+\mathrm{i}, 2\mathrm{i}, -\sqrt{3}+\mathrm{i}, -\sqrt{3}-\mathrm{i}, -2\mathrm{i}, \sqrt{3}-\mathrm{i}.$$

(A) EXAMPLES 18

1. Simplify: (i) $(\cos\theta+\mathrm{i}\sin\theta)^5$; (ii) $(\cos\pi/3+\mathrm{i}\sin\pi/3)^6$; (iii) $(\cos\theta+\mathrm{i}\sin\theta)^3(\cos 2\theta+\mathrm{i}\sin 2\theta)$.
2. Show that $(\cos\theta-\mathrm{i}\sin\theta)^{-1} = \cos\theta+\mathrm{i}\sin\theta$ and simplify $(\cos 3\theta+\mathrm{i}\sin 3\theta)/(\cos\theta-\mathrm{i}\sin\theta)$.
3. If $z = \cos\theta+\mathrm{i}\sin\theta$ find the values of: (i) z^{-1}; (ii) $z+z^{-1}$; (iii) z^3+z^{-3}; (iv) z^3-z^{-3}; (v) $z^3+z^2+z+z^{-1}+z^{-2}+z^{-3}$ in terms of θ.
4. Given $z = \cos\theta+\mathrm{i}\sin\theta$ show that $(1+2z)(1+2z^{-1}) = 3+4\cos\theta$.
5. Express: (i) $\cos 3\theta$; (ii) $\cos 4\theta$; (iii) $\cos 5\theta$; (iv) $\sin 6\theta/\sin\theta$ in terms of $\cos\theta$.
6. Express: (i) $\sin 3\theta$; (ii) $\cos 4\theta$; (iii) $\sin 5\theta$; (iv) $\cos 5\theta/\cos\theta$ in terms of $\sin\theta$.
7. Express in terms of multiple angles: (i) $\cos^3\theta$; (ii) $\sin^4\theta$: (iii) $\cos^5\theta$; (iv) $\sin^3\theta\cos\theta$; (v) $\cos^4\theta\sin 3\theta$.
8. Solve the equations: (i) $z^4-1 = 0$; (ii) $8z^3+27 = 0$; (iii) $z^5+1 = 0$.
9. Solve the equation $z^8 = 1$ and show that one root is $\alpha = \cos\pi/4+\mathrm{i}\sin\pi/4$. Prove that the roots can be expressed as $z = 1, \alpha, a^2, \ldots, \alpha^7$.
10. Express $\cos 5\theta$ and $\sin 5\theta$ in terms of $\cos\theta$ and $\sin\theta$. Hence prove that $\tan 5\theta = (5t-10t^3+5t)/(1-10t^2+5t^4)$, where $t = \tan\theta$.
11. Solve the equation $w^6 = 1$ and hence by writing $(z-1)/2 = w$, solve the equation $(z-1)^6 = 64$.
12. Evaluate $(\sqrt{3}+\mathrm{i})^8+(\sqrt{3}-\mathrm{i})^8$ by first expressing the complex numbers in the (r, θ) form.

GEOMETRICAL PROPERTIES OF THE ARGAND DIAGRAM

In the following section, P_1 P_2 are fixed points in an Argand diagram, not collinear with O, representing given complex numbers z_1, z_2 and P is a variable point representing a variable complex number z.

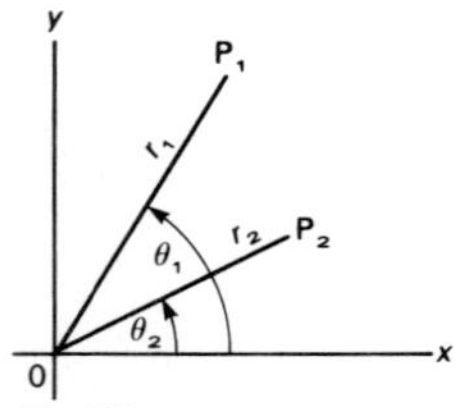

Fig. 20

(i) $|z_1| = r_1 = OP_1$; $|z_2| = r_2 = OP_2$;

$$\arg z_1 = \theta_1 = \angle P_1Ox; \arg z_2 = \theta_2 = \angle P_2Ox.$$

$$\arg\frac{z_1}{z_2} = \theta_1-\theta_2 = \angle P_1OP_2 \text{ (Fig. 20)}.$$

This result is true for $-\pi < \theta_1-\theta_2 \leqslant \pi$.

(ii) OP_1SP_2 is a parallelogram (Fig. 21).

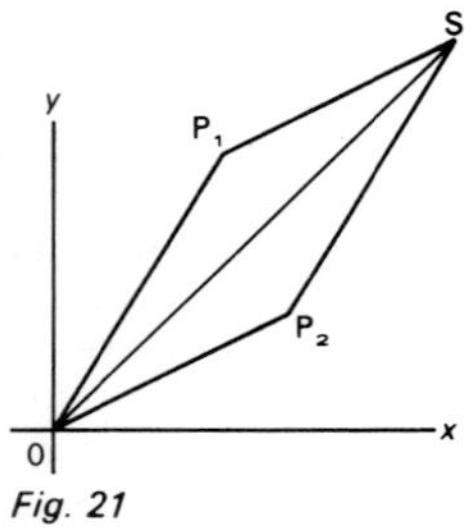

Fig. 21

S represents the complex number z_1+z_2.

$$|z_1+z_2| = OS; \arg(z_1+z_2) = \angle SOX.$$

As $OS < OP_1+P_1S$ or OP_1+OP_2,

$$|z_1+z_2| < |z_1|+|z_2|.$$

(iii) OP_2P_1D is a parallelogram (Fig. 22).

D represents the complex number $z_1 - z_2$ and D′ represents the complex number $z_2 - z_1$. (OP_1P_2D' is a parallelogram.)

$$|z_1 - z_2| = |z_2 - z_1| = P_1P_2; \; \arg(z_1 - z_2) = \phi$$
$$\arg(z_2 - z_1) = \phi'.$$

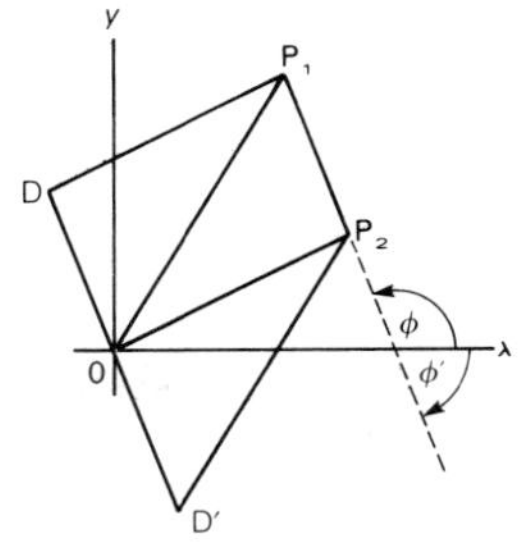

Fig. 22

Important special cases

(iv) Given $|z - z_1| = k$, a constant.

As $|z - z_1| = PP_1$, it follows that $PP_1 = k$.

∴ P lies on the circle centre P_1, radius k.

Note To interpret $|z + z_1|$ geometrically write it as $|z - (-z_1)|$.

(v) Given arg $(z - z_1) = \alpha$, a constant.

As $\arg(z - z_1)$ = angle between the direction P_1P and the positive direction of the x-axis, P lies on the line drawn from P, making an angle α with Ox.

Note To interpret $\arg(z + z_1)$ geometrically write it as $\arg(z - (-z_1))$.

Example 14. The complex number z is represented in the Argand diagram by the point P. Describe geometrically the locus of P in each of the following cases: (i) $|z| = |4 - 3i|$; (ii) $|z + 2| = |4 - 3i|$; (iii) $\arg(z - 4 + 3i) = \pi/3$.

(i) $$|z| = |4 - 3\text{i}| = 5;$$

∴ P lies on the circle centre O, radius 5.

(ii) $|z + 2| = |z - (-2)| = AP$ where A is the point $(-2, 0)$.
As $AP = 5$, P lies on the circle centre $A(-2, 0)$, radius 5.

(iii) $\arg(z - (4 - 3\text{i}))$ = angle P_1P makes with Ox where P_1 is the point (4, −3).
So the line joining $P_1(4, -3)$ to P is inclined at an angle of $\pi/3$ to Ox and P lies on the line drawn from P_1, inclined at an angle of $\pi/3$ to Ox.

(A) EXAMPLES 19

1. In an Argand diagram plot the points P_1, P_2 which represent the complex numbers $z_1 = 2 + 3\text{i}$, $z_2 = 1 + \text{i}$. Indicate on the diagram: (i) lengths representing $|z_1 + z_2|$ and $|z_1 - z_2|$; (ii) angles representing $\arg(z_1 - z_2)$ and $\arg z_1/z_2$.
2. Show in an Argand diagram, the locus of the point P which represents the variable complex number z in each of the cases: (i) $|z| = 2$; (ii) $|z| = |3 + 4\text{i}|$; (iii) $\arg z = \pi/4$; (iv) $\arg z = \arg(1 + \text{i}\sqrt{3})$.
3. Find the modulus and argument of the complex numbers $z = 2\text{i}$, $w = 1 + \text{i}\sqrt{3}$. Show in an Argand diagram the points which represent z, w, $z + w$ and $z - w$.
4. If P represents the complex number z in an Argand diagram indicate the lengths which represent: (i) $2|z|$; (ii) $|3z|$; (iii) $|z^*|$; (iv) $|z - 2|$; (v) $|z + 2|$; (vi) $|z - (1 - \text{i})|$; (vii) $|z + 1 - 2\text{i}|$; (viii) $|z^* - \text{i}|$.
5. If $|z - 1| = 1$, show that the point representing z in an Argand diagram lies on a circle of unit radius which passes through the origin.

6. Indicate in separate Argand diagrams the line on which the point representing z lies in each of the cases: (i) $\arg z = \pi/2$; (ii) $\arg(z-1) = \pi/4$; (iii) $\arg(z-1-\mathrm{i}) = \pi/3$.
7. If $|z+2| = |z-1|$, show that the point representing z in an Argand diagram lies on the line $x = -1/2$.
8. Indicate in separate Argand diagrams the regions in which the point representing the complex number z must lie if: (i) $|z| \leqslant 1$; (ii) $0 \leqslant \arg z \leqslant \pi/4$; (iii) $|z-1| \leqslant 2$; (iv) $\arg(z-1) \leqslant \pi/4$.
9. If $|(z-2)/(z+1)| = 1$, show that the point P representing z in an Argand diagram is equidistant from two fixed points. State the coordinates of these points and the Cartesian equation of the locus of P.
10. Represent in an Argand diagram the locus of the point representing the complex number z when $|z-1| = 1$. If $\arg z = \pi/4$ show that $|z| = \sqrt{2}$.

(B) MISCELLANEOUS EXAMPLES

1. Given that $z_1 = 2-\mathrm{i}$, $z_2 = -1+2\mathrm{i}$, find in the algebraic form the complex number z which is such that $z^{-1} = z_1^{-1}+z_2^{-1}$. Also find the modulus and argument of z.
2. A and C are points in an Argand diagram representing the complex numbers $1+\mathrm{i}$ and $5+3\mathrm{i}$ respectively. If AC is a diagonal of the square ABCD, find the complex numbers represented by the vertices B and D.
3. The roots of the equation $2\mathrm{i}z^2+z(1-\mathrm{i})+1 = 0$ are z_1, z_2. Write down the values of: (i) z_1+z_2; (ii) z_1z_2 and express them in the form $a+ib$. Express in a similar form the value of $z_1^{-2}+z_2^{-2}$
4. Express the complex number $z_1 = (11+2\mathrm{i})/(3-4\mathrm{i})$ in the algebraic form. If $z_2 = 2-5\mathrm{i}$, find the distance between the points representing z_1, z_2 in an Argand diagram. Also find the real numbers a, b such that $az_1+bz_2 = -4+\mathrm{i}$.
5. Solve the equation $z^3 = 1$ and use the result to find the roots of the equation $(z-1)^3 = 8$.
6. Sketch the regions in an Argand diagram in which the point representing the complex number z must lie if: (i) $0 < \arg(z+\mathrm{i}) < \pi/4$; (ii) $|z-1| < |z|$.
7. Simplify $(1+\mathrm{i}\sqrt{3})^8+(1-1\sqrt{3})^8$.
8. The sum of the squares of the roots of the equation $z^2+(p+\mathrm{i}q)z+3\mathrm{i} = 0$, where p, q are real, is 8. Find the possible values of p and q.
9. In an Argand diagram, P represents the complex number $\lambda(2-\mathrm{i})$, where λ is a real parameter. Sketch the locus of P as λ varies. The point Q represents the complex number $1/\lambda(2-\mathrm{i})$, where $\lambda \neq 0$, and R is the mid-point of PQ. If R represents the number $x+\mathrm{i}y$, find x and y in terms of λ.
10. Find the Cartesian equation of the locus of the point P representing the complex number z where: (i) $|z-1| = |z+3|$; (ii) $|z-1| = 2|z+1|$.
11. Sketch in an Argand diagram the locus of the point representing the complex number z where $|z-\sqrt{2}| = 1$. If $\arg z = \pi/4$ show that $|z| = 1$.
12. If $w = 2+z$ where $z = 2(\cos\theta+\mathrm{i}\sin\theta)$, find $|w|$ and $\arg w$. Show that the point P representing w in an Argand diagram lies on a circle centre $(2, 0)$, radius 2.
13. Show that the argument of the complex number $z = 1+\sin\phi+\mathrm{i}\cos\phi$ $(0 < \phi < \pi/2)$ is $\pi/4-\phi/2$ and find its modulus. Prove that $(1+\sin\phi+\mathrm{i}\cos\phi)/(1+\sin\phi-\mathrm{i}\cos\phi) = \sin\phi+\mathrm{i}\cos\phi$.
14. Taking $z = r(\cos\theta+\mathrm{i}\sin\theta)$, find the roots of the equation $z^3 = 2+2\mathrm{i}$ in the (r, θ) form.
15. The complex number $z = x+\mathrm{i}y$ is such that $(z+3)/(z-4\mathrm{i}) = \lambda\mathrm{i}$, where λ is real. Show that $x(x+3)+y(y-4) = 0$. If z is represented by P in an Argand diagram, deduce that as λ varies, P moves on a circle and find the complex number represented by the centre of the circle.
16. Find the Cartesian equations of the loci of the points representing the complex number z which satisfy: (i) $|z-3| = 4$; (ii) $\arg(z-1) = \pi/4$; (iii) $|z| = 2|z-2|$.
17. The complex number z satisfies the equation $(2-\mathrm{i})z = \lambda+\mathrm{i}\mu$, where λ, μ are real. If the point P representing z in an Argand diagram moves on a unit circle centre the origin, prove that $\lambda^2+\mu^2 = 5$.
18. Given that $|z-1| = 1$ and $\arg z = \pi/6$, show in an Argand diagram the position of the point which represents z and deduce that: (i) $|z| = \sqrt{3}$; (ii) $|z-2| = 1$.
19. Solve the equation $z^4 = \sqrt{3}-\mathrm{i}$, expressing the roots in the (r, θ) form.
20. Express the function $\sin^3 2\theta \sin\theta$ in the form $\mathrm{A}\cos\theta+\mathrm{B}\cos 3\theta+\mathrm{C}\cos 5\theta+\mathrm{D}\cos 7\theta$, where A, B, C, D are constants.

21. If $z = 2i$, $w = 1+i/3$, plot in an Argand diagram the points which represent z, w, $(z+w)$ and $(z-w)$. Deduce the *exact* values of $\arg(z+w)$ and $\arg(z-w)$.
22. The complex number z is such that $|z-2| = 2$ and $\arg z = \theta$, where $0 < \theta < \pi/2$. Prove that $z-4 = iz\tan\theta$.
23. Find z in the form $a+ib$ when z satisfies the relations $|z+i| = |z|$ and $\arg(z+i) - \arg z = \pi/3$.
24. With the help of a diagram, find the complex number z, of argument $\pi/4$, such that $|z-1-6i| = |z-5-8i|$. Show that no complex number of argument $3\pi/4$ will satisfy this equation.
25. If $|z+2-i| \leqslant 2$ use an Argand diagram to show that $\sqrt{5}-2 \leqslant |z| \leqslant \sqrt{5}+2$.
26. Express $z_1 = (7+4i)/(3-2i)$ in the algebraic form. Sketch in an Argand diagram the locus of the point representing the complex number z where $|z-z_1| = \sqrt{5}$ and find the greatest value of $|z|$ subject to this condition.

Analysis and Numerical Analysis

DIFFERENTIATION

Standard results

$$\frac{d}{dx}(x^n) = nx^{n-1}, \text{ for all values of } n; \ \frac{d}{dx}(\sin x) = \cos x;$$

$$\frac{d}{dx}(\ln x) = \frac{1}{x}, x > 0; \ \frac{d}{dx}(\cos x) = -\sin x;$$

$$\frac{d}{dx}(e^x) = e^x; \ \frac{d}{dx}(\tan x) = \sec^2 x;$$

$$\frac{d}{dx}(\sin^{-1} x) = \frac{1}{\sqrt{(1-x^2)}}, -\frac{\pi}{2} \leqslant x \leqslant \frac{\pi}{2}; \ \frac{d}{dx}(\cot x) = -\text{cosec}^2 x;$$

$$\frac{d}{dx}(\cos^{-1} x) = -\frac{1}{\sqrt{(1-x^2)}}, 0 \leqslant x \leqslant \pi; \ \frac{d}{dx}(\sec x) = \sec x \tan x;$$

$$\frac{d}{dx}(\tan^{-1} x) = \frac{1}{1+x^2}, -\frac{\pi}{2} < x < \frac{\pi}{2}; \ \frac{d}{dx}(\text{cosec } x) = -\text{cosec } x \cot x.$$

Methods of differentiation

(*a*) *Function of a function rule* $\quad \dfrac{dy}{dx} = \dfrac{dy}{du} \times \dfrac{du}{dx}.$

Note

(i) Used in the differentiation of composite functions such as $\sin 5x$, $\sin^5 x$, $e^{\sin x}$;

(ii) also used in the differentiation of a function of one variable with respect to a second variable, as for example $d/dx(y^3) = 3y^2\, dy/dx$; $d/dt(\sin x) = \cos x\, dx/dt$;

(iii) note the special case $\mathrm{d}x/\mathrm{d}y = 1/(\mathrm{d}y/\mathrm{d}x)$.

(*b*) *Product rule* $$\frac{\mathrm{d}}{\mathrm{d}x}(uv) = \frac{\mathrm{d}u}{\mathrm{d}x}v + u\frac{\mathrm{d}y}{\mathrm{d}x}.$$

Note

(i) The result can be extended to products of more than two functions;

(ii) note particularly products such as xy^3, $y\,\mathrm{d}y/\mathrm{d}x$; $\mathrm{d}/\mathrm{d}x\,(xy^3) = y^3 + 3xy^2\,\mathrm{d}y/\mathrm{d}x$, $\mathrm{d}/\mathrm{d}x\,(y\,\mathrm{d}y/\mathrm{d}x) = (\mathrm{d}y/\mathrm{d}x)^2 + y\,\mathrm{d}^2y/\mathrm{d}x^2$.

(*c*) *Quotient rule* $$\frac{\mathrm{d}}{\mathrm{d}x}\left(\frac{u}{v}\right) = \frac{\left(\dfrac{\mathrm{d}u}{\mathrm{d}x}v - u\dfrac{\mathrm{d}v}{\mathrm{d}x}\right)}{v^2}.$$

(*d*) *Implicit relations* $f(x, y) = c$.

To find $\mathrm{d}y/\mathrm{d}x$ in terms of x and y, differentiate term by term with respect to x, e.g. if $y^2x + x^2y^3 = 1$, then $2xy\,\mathrm{d}y/\mathrm{d}x + y^2 + 2xy^3 + 3x^2y^2\,\mathrm{d}y/\mathrm{d}x = 0$ and hence $\mathrm{d}y/\mathrm{d}x$.

(*e*) *Parametric functions* $x = f(t)$, $y = g(t)$.

$$\frac{\mathrm{d}y}{\mathrm{d}x} = \frac{\mathrm{d}y}{\mathrm{d}t} \times \frac{\mathrm{d}t}{\mathrm{d}x} = \frac{\dfrac{\mathrm{d}y}{\mathrm{d}t}}{\dfrac{\mathrm{d}x}{\mathrm{d}t}} = \frac{g'(t)}{f'(t)} = \mathrm{F}(t) \text{ say;}$$

$$\frac{\mathrm{d}^2y}{\mathrm{d}x^2} = \frac{\mathrm{d}}{\mathrm{d}x}(\mathrm{F}(t)) = \frac{\mathrm{d}}{\mathrm{d}t}(\mathrm{F}(t))\frac{\mathrm{d}t}{\mathrm{d}x} = \frac{\mathrm{F}'(t)}{\dfrac{\mathrm{d}x}{\mathrm{d}t}} = \frac{\mathrm{F}'(t)}{f'(t)}.$$

Example 1. Differentiate with respect to x: (i) $e^{-2x}\cos 3x$*; (ii)* $\ln[(1+\tan x)/(1-\tan x)]$*; (iii)* $\tan^{-1}(\sin x)$.

(i) Here the product rule and the function of a function rule are used noting that $\mathrm{d}/\mathrm{d}x\,(e^{-2x}) = -2e^{-2x}$ and $\mathrm{d}/\mathrm{d}x\cos 3x = -3\sin 3x$.

$$\frac{\mathrm{d}}{\mathrm{d}x}(e^{-2x}\cos 3x) = -2e^{-2x}\cos 3x + e^{-2x}(-3\sin 3x)$$
$$= -e^{-2x}(2\cos 3x + 3\sin 3x).$$

(ii) In this example it is important to simplify the logarithmic function before differentiating, then the terms $\ln(1+\tan x)$, $\ln(1-\tan x)$ are differentiated by using the function of a function rule.

$$\frac{\mathrm{d}}{\mathrm{d}x}\ln\left(\frac{1+\tan x}{1-\tan x}\right) = \frac{\mathrm{d}}{\mathrm{d}x}\ln(1+\tan x) - \frac{\mathrm{d}}{\mathrm{d}x}\ln(1-\tan x),$$
$$= \frac{\sec^2 x}{1+\tan x} - \frac{-\sec^2 x}{1-\tan x},$$
$$= \frac{2\sec^2 x}{1-\tan^2 x}.$$

(iii) Using the standard result for the derivative of $\tan^{-1} u$ with respect to u and the function of a function rule,

$$\frac{d}{dx}\tan^{-1}(\sin x) = \frac{1}{1+\sin^2 x}\cos x = \frac{\cos x}{1+\sin^2 x}.$$

Example 2. Given that $\sin^{-1} 3x + \cos^{-1} 2y + \sin^{-1}(xy) = \pi/2$, find the value of dy/dx when $x = y = 0$.

Using the function of a function rule,

$$\frac{d}{dx}\sin^{-1} 3x = \frac{1}{\sqrt{(1-(3x)^2)}}\cdot 3 = \frac{3}{\sqrt{(1-9x^2)}};$$

$$\frac{d}{dx}\cos^{-1} 2y = -\frac{1}{\sqrt{(1-(2y)^2)}}\cdot 2\frac{dy}{dx} = -\frac{2}{\sqrt{(1-4y^2)}}\frac{dy}{dx};$$

$$\frac{d}{dx}\sin^{-1}(xy) = \frac{1}{\sqrt{(1-(xy)^2)}}\cdot\frac{d}{dx}(xy) = \frac{1}{\sqrt{(1-x^2y^2)}}\cdot\left(y+x\frac{dy}{dx}\right).$$

So differentiating the given relation with respect to x,

$$\frac{3}{\sqrt{(1-9x^2)}} - \frac{2}{\sqrt{(1-4y^2)}}\frac{dy}{dx} + \frac{1}{\sqrt{(1-x^2y^2)}}\left(y+x\frac{dy}{dx}\right) = 0,$$

when $x = y = 0$,

$$3-2\frac{dy}{dx} = 0,$$

$$\frac{dy}{dx} = \frac{3}{2}.$$

Example 3. Given that $x = 4\cos\theta - \cos 2\theta$, $y = \cos 2\theta$, where θ is a parameter, find expressions for dy/dx and d^2y/dx^2 in terms of θ.

Here $$\frac{dx}{d\theta} = -4\sin\theta + 2\sin 2\theta;\quad \frac{dy}{d\theta} = -2\sin 2\theta.$$

$$\therefore\quad \frac{dy}{dx} = \frac{\dfrac{dy}{d\theta}}{\dfrac{dx}{d\theta}} = \frac{-2\sin 2\theta}{-4\sin\theta + 2\sin 2\theta},$$

$$= \frac{-4\sin\theta\cos\theta}{-4\sin\theta(1-\cos\theta)},$$

$$\frac{dy}{dx} = \frac{\cos\theta}{1-\cos\theta}.$$

In finding d^2y/dx^2, care must be taken to differentiate both sides of this relationship *with respect to x,*

giving
$$\frac{d^2y}{dx^2} = \frac{d}{dx}\left(\frac{\cos\theta}{1-\cos\theta}\right),$$

$$= \frac{d}{d\theta}\left(\frac{\cos\theta}{1-\cos\theta}\right)\cdot\frac{d\theta}{dx},$$

$$= \frac{-\sin\theta(1-\cos\theta)-\cos\theta(\sin\theta)}{(1-\cos\theta)^2}\cdot\frac{1}{\dfrac{dx}{d\theta}},$$

$$= \frac{-\sin\theta}{(1-\cos\theta)^2}\cdot\frac{1}{-4\sin\theta(1-\cos\theta)},$$

$$= \frac{1}{4(1-\cos\theta)^3}.$$

(A) EXAMPLES 20

Differentiate with respect to x:

1. $2x^2+x^{-2}$.
2. $(2x-1)^3$.
3. $1/(x+1)$.
4. $\sqrt{(x^2+1)}$.
5. $\sin 3x$.
6. $\sin^3 x$.
7. $x/(x-1)$.
8. e^{-4x}.
9. $\tan x/2$.
10. $x(1-x)^4$.
11. $x\cos x$.
12. x^2e^x.
13. $\ln(2x+1)$.
14. $\sin^{-1} 2x$.
15. $\cos^{-1} 3x$.
16. $\tan^{-1}(x^2)$.
17. $\ln(x^2+1)$.
18. xe^{-2x}.
19. $x\ln x - x$.
20. $(1-x^2)^{-1/2}$.
21. $\sin x/x$.
22. $\tan^{-1}\sqrt{x}$.
23. $\ln\sqrt{(x^2+1)}$.
24. $e^{2x}\sin 3x$.
25. $\sec 2x$.
26. $\cot x/2$.
27. $x\tan^{-1} x$.
28. $\cos^2 3x$.
29. $x^2e^{-x^2}$.
30. $\ln\cot x$.
31. $\sin x/(1-\cos x)$.
32. $\sin^2 x\cos^3 x$.
33. $x\cos^{-1} x$.
34. $\ln(1+\sin x)$.
35. $e^{\sin x}$.
36. $\sqrt{[(1+x)/(1-x)]}$.
37. $\lg x$.
38. $\tan^{-1}(\sin x)$.
39. $\sin^{-1}\sqrt{x}$.
40. $\ln(1+x^4)^{1/2}$.
41. Find dy/dx in terms of x and y if (i) $x^2+y^2=1$; (ii) $x^3+y^3=4x$; (iii) $xy=1$; (iv) $(x+1)y^2=2$; (v) $x\ln y = x^2+1$; (vi) $xy^2+yx^2=6x$; (vii) $ye^x-xe^y=1$; (viii) $x\sin 2y+y\sin x=\pi/2$; (ix) $e^{xy}+2e^x=e^y$.
42. Find dy/dx and d^2y/dx^2 in terms of the parameter t if: (i) $x=t^2$, $y=2t$; (ii) $x=3t^2$, $y=2t^3$; (iii) $x=4\cos t$, $y=3\sin t$; (iv) $x=2(t+t^{-1})$, $y=t-t^{-1}$.
43. Show that $2^x = e^{x\ln 2}$ and hence find $d/dx\, 2^x$.
44. Differentiate with respect to x: (i) xe^y+ye^x; (ii) $\cos(xy)$; (iii) e^{x^2y}; (iv) $\sin^{-1}(xy)$.
45. Differentiate $e^{\sqrt{3}x}\sin x$ with respect to x and express the result in the form $Re^{\sqrt{3}x}\sin(x+\alpha)$, stating the values of R and α.
46. Differentiate with respect to x the function $\ln[(1+2x^2)^{1/2}(1+x^2)^{-1/2}]$ and use the result to find $d/dx[(1+2x^2)^{1/2}(1+x^2)^{-1/2}]$.
47. If $x=\ln(1+y)$, show that $d^2y/dx^2 = 1+y$.
48. Show that $d/dx\ln(\sec x+\tan x)=\sec x$ and find the value of $d/dx\ln(\operatorname{cosec} x+\cot x)$.
49. Given that $12x^3-4xy^2-y^3+3=0$, find the values of x and y for which $dy/dx=0$.
50. Differentiate with respect to t: (i) $2x+y$; (ii) xy; (iii) x/y; (iv) x^2+y^2; (v) $\tan^{-1}(y/x)$.
51. Given $y=1-\cos\theta$, $x=\theta+\sin\theta$, show that: (i) $dy/dx=\sin\theta/(1+\cos\theta)=\tan\theta/2$; (ii) $d^2y/dx^2=\sec^4/4\,\theta/2$.
52. Find: (i) $d/dx\,(x^2y)$; (ii) $d/dx\,(x\,dy/dx)$; (iii) $d/dx\,(dy/dx)^2$.

APPLICATIONS OF DIFFERENTIATION

(a) Rates of change

$$\frac{dy}{dx} = \text{the rate of increase of } y \text{ with respect to } x;$$

$$\frac{dV}{dt} = \text{the rate of increase of } V \text{ with respect to } t\text{, and so on.}$$

(i) If a point P moves in a straight line such that at time t after the start its displacement from a fixed origin in the line is s, then

$$\text{velocity of P, } v = \frac{ds}{dt}; \text{ acceleration of P} = \frac{dv}{dt} \text{ or } v\frac{dv}{ds}.$$

(ii) If a line OP is rotating and at time t its angular displacement from a fixed direction OX is θ rad, then

$$\text{angular velocity of OP} = \frac{d\theta}{dt}.$$

Example 4. The point $P(x, y)$ *moves on the curve* $y^3 = 2(x+1)^2$ *such that the rate of increase of* x *is constant and equal to 2 units/s. When P is at the point (1,2), find: (i) the rate of increase of* y*; (ii) the angular velocity of the line OP, where O is the origin.*

(i) Differentiating with respect to t,

$$\frac{d}{dt}y^3 = \frac{d}{dt}2(x+1)^2,$$

$$3y^2\frac{dy}{dt} = 4(x+1)\frac{dx}{dt}.$$

But $dx/dt = 2$ and $x = 1$, $y = 2$,

so $$12\frac{dy}{dt} = 8.2; \quad \frac{dy}{dt} = \frac{4}{3}\text{ units/s.}$$

i.e. the rate of increase of $y = 4/3$ units/s.

(ii) At the variable point (x, y) on the curve, the inclination θ of OP to the positive direction of the x-axis, is given by $\tan\theta = y/x$.

Differentiating with respect to t, $$\sec^2\theta\frac{d\theta}{dt} = \frac{\left(x\frac{dy}{dt} - y\frac{dx}{dt}\right)}{x^2}.$$

At the point (1,2), $$\sec^2\theta = 1+\tan^2\theta = 5; \frac{dx}{dt} = 2; \frac{dy}{dt} = \frac{4}{3};$$

$$\therefore \quad \text{angular velocity of OP} = \frac{d\theta}{dt} = -\frac{8}{15}\text{rad/s.}$$

(b) Increasing and decreasing functions

$f(x)$ increases with x if $f'(x)$ is positive;

$f(x)$ decreases with x if $f'(x)$ is negative.

(c) Gradient of a curve

The gradient of a (x, y) curve at any point or of the tangent to the curve is given by the value of dy/dx.

(d) Turning points on a curve

To determine maximum and minimum points on (x, y) curves proceed as follows:

(i) find dy/dx and solve the equation $dy/dx = 0$; let the roots be $x_1, x_2, \ldots$;

(ii) find d^2y/dx^2 if this is readily obtainable and substitute successively the values $x = x_1, x_2 \ldots$; if d^2y/dx^2 is positive, the value of x concerned gives a minimum value for y and if negative, a maximum value for y;

(iii) if d^2y/dx^2 is difficult to obtain or if $d^2y/dx^2 = 0$ for some particular value of x, use the signs of dy/dx for values of x on either side of the values $x_1, x_2, \ldots$. If in the direction of x increasing, there is a sign change from $+$ to $-$, the point is a maximum point; if the sign change is $-$ to $+$, the point is a minimum point; if there is no sign change, the point is a special sort of inflexion point.

(e) Inflexion points

To determine inflexion points on (x, y) curves proceed as follows:

(i) find d^2y/dx^2 and solve the equation $d^2y/dx^2 = 0$; let the roots be $x_1, x_2, \ldots$;

(ii) for an inflexion point, d^2y/dx^2 changes sign in passing through the point; this can be established as in the case of turning points or, in most cases, more simply by showing that $d^3y/dx^3 \neq 0$ at the point concerned.

(f) Stationary points

These are all the points on a curve where $dy/dx = 0$; the procedure in (d) is followed to find whether a particular value for x corresponds to a maximum, minimum or inflexion point.

Example 5. Find the stationary points on the curve $y = x^2(x-3)^3$ and distinguish between them.

Differentiating with respect to x,

$$\frac{dy}{dx} = 2x(x-3)^3 + 3x^2(x-3)^2,$$

$$= x(x-3)^2(5x-6).$$

For stationary points, $\quad x(x-3)^2(5x-6) = 0,$

$$x = 0, 3, \frac{6}{5}.$$

In this case and in all cases involving repeated factors in dy/dx, it is better to use the dy/dx sign change method to distinguish between maximum, minimum and inflexion points.

For x slightly < 0, $\frac{dy}{dx} = (-)(+)(-) = +$;

for x slightly > 0, $\frac{dy}{dx} = (+)(+)(-) = -$

so $x = 0$ makes y a maximum and $(0,0)$ is a maximum point.

For x slightly $< 3, \frac{dy}{dx} = (+)(+)(+) = +$;

for x slightly $> 3, \frac{dy}{dx} = (+)(+)(+) = +$

so $x = 3$ gives an inflexion and (3,0) is an inflexion point.

For x slightly $< \frac{6}{5}, \frac{dy}{dx} = (+)(+)(-) = -$;

for x slightly $> \frac{6}{5}, \frac{dy}{dx} = (+)(+)(+) = +$

so $x = 6/5$ makes y a minimum and $(6/5, -4.3^8/5^5)$ is a minimum point.

(g) Problems involving maximum and minimum values

Problems of a more practical nature involving the determination of maximum and minimum values are dealt with by a procedure identical with that used for the location of turning points on a curve. The first essential is to obtain a relationship between the quantity to be maximised or minimised in terms of one other variable.

Example 6. Show that the maximum volume of a circular cylinder which can be cut from a solid right circular cone of height h and semi-vertical angle α, where the axis of the cylinder lies along the axis of the cone is $(4\pi/27)h^3 \tan^2 \alpha$.

The diagram Fig. 23 shows the cone and cylinder in section.

In order to find the maximum value of the volume V of the cylinder, it is necessary to express V in terms of one other variable; in this case x, the height of the cylinder, is a convenient one to use as it readily follows that the radius of the cylinder $r = (h-x)\tan\alpha$.

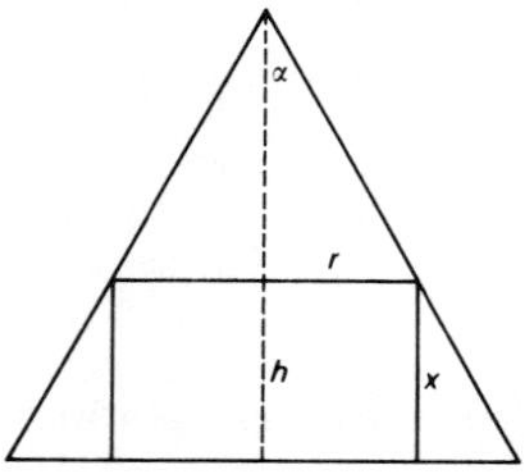

Fig. 23

So $$V = \pi(h-x)^2 \tan^2 \alpha x,$$
$$= \pi \tan^2 \alpha(h^2x - 2hx^2 + x^3).$$

For maximum or minimum values of V, $dV/dx = 0$,

$$\therefore \quad \pi \tan^2 \alpha(h^2 - 4hx + 3x^2) = 0,$$
$$3x^2 - 4hx + h^2 = 0,$$
$$(3x-h)(x-h) = 0,$$
$$x = \frac{1}{3}h, h.$$

$$\frac{d^2V}{dx^2} = \pi \tan^2 \alpha(-4h + 6x)$$

and when $x = h/3$, $\frac{d^2V}{dx^2} = \pi \tan^2 \alpha(-2h)$ which is negative.

$\therefore \quad x = h/3$ makes V a maximum and the maximum value of $V = \frac{4\pi}{27}h^3 \tan^2 \alpha$.

(h) Small changes

To obtain the approximate value of a small increase δy in y arising from a small increase δx in x, find dy/dx and replace it by the approximate value $\delta y/\delta x$.

So if $y = f(x)$, $\qquad \delta y \approx f'(x)\delta x.$

Example 7. Given $y = \sin x/x$, find the approximate change in y when x increases from $\pi/2$ to $\pi/2+\varepsilon$, where ε is small.

$$\frac{dy}{dx} = \frac{x\cos x - \sin x}{x^2},$$

so

$$\delta y \approx \frac{x\cos x - \sin x}{x^2}\cdot\delta x;$$

when $x = \pi/2$ and $\delta x = \varepsilon$,

$$\delta y \approx \frac{-1}{\pi^2/4}\varepsilon \quad\text{or}\quad \frac{-4\varepsilon}{\pi^2}.$$

So the change in y is a decrease of approximately $4\varepsilon/\pi^2$.

(A) EXAMPLES 21

1. The volume V ml of water in a vessel at time t sec is given by $V = 200+5t+t^3$. Find the rates at which water is: (i) running into the vessel at time $t = 0$; (ii) running out of the vessel at time $t = 2$.
2. Find the equation of the tangent to the curve $y = x(x-1)^2$ at the point (4,36).
3. If $y = x^5$, find the approximate increase in y when x increased from 2 to 2.001.
4. Show that the function $f(x) = x-\sin x\cos x$ increases for all values of x except $x = r\pi$. Write down the values of $f(0)$ and $f(\pi/2)$ and prove graphically that $0 < f(x) < \pi/2$ for $0 < x < \pi/2$.
5. Find the stationary points on the curve $y = 2x^3-3x^2-12x+8$, distinguishing between maximum, minimum and inflexion points.
6. A point P(x, y) moves on the curve $y^2 = x^3$. If u, v are the rates of increase of x, y respectively with respect to the time t, show that $2yv = 3x^2u$ and find the coordinates of P at the instant when the rates of increase of y and x with respect to time are in the ratio 3:2.
7. Find the gradient of the curve with parametric equations $x = t^3$, $y = 3t^2$ at the point where $t = 2$. Also find the equation of the tangent to the curve at this point.
8. A point P moves in a straight line; at time t its displacement from a fixed origin in the line is x and its velocity is v. Show that the acceleration of P is $v\,dv/dx$ and find the acceleration in terms of x in the case where $v^2 = 10-x^2$.
9. If $y = \sin x$, find the approximate increase in y when x increases from θ to $\theta+\alpha$ radians, where α is small. Use the result to find the approximate values of: (i) $\sin(\pi/3+0.001)$; (ii) $\sin 30°1'$.
10. Find the maximum and minimum points on the curve $y = x^2(1-x^2)$.
11. A curve whose equation has the form $y = x(x-2)(ax+b)$ touches the x-axis at the point where $x = 2$ and touches the line $y = 2x$ at the origin. Find the values of the constants a and b.
12. An open rectangular box made of thin material has a square base, side x cm, and a capacity of 4000 cm^3. If A cm^2 is the area of material used to make the box show that $A = x^2+16\,000x^{-1}$ and find the value of x which makes the amount of material used a minimum.
13. Sketch the curve $x = a\cos\theta$, $y = b\sin\theta$ where $a > b > 0$ and $0 \leqslant \theta < 2\pi$. Also find the equation of the tangent to the curve at the point parameter ϕ.
14. Given that $f(x) = \ln(1+x)-x+x^2/2$, $x > -1$, show that: (i) $f(x)$ is an increasing function; (ii) $f(0) = 0$; (iii) $f(x) > 0$ for $x > 0$.
15. If δy, δx are corresponding small increases in y and x, express δy in terms of x, y and δx in each of the cases: (i) $y = e^{2x}$; (ii) $y = x\sin x$; (iii) $y = x/\cos x$; (iv) $(y+1)^2 = 4(x+2)^3$; (v) $\ln y = x^2$.
16. Find the coordinates of the point of inflexion on the curve $y = xe^{-x}$ and the gradient of the tangent to the curve at this point.

17. Find the equations of the tangent and the normal at the point $(a\sec\theta, a\tan\theta)$ on the curve with parametric equations, $x = a\sec\theta$, $y = a\tan\theta$.
18. Find the minimum point on the curve $y = 4\cos\theta+\sec\theta$, $0 < \theta < \pi/2$ and deduce that $4\cos\theta+\sec\theta \geqslant 4$ for $0 < \theta < \pi/2$.
19. The base of a right circular cone is a plane section of a sphere centre O, and of unit radius. The vertex of the cone is on the sphere and O is within the cone. If the distance of O from the base of the cone is x, prove that V, the volume of the cone is given by $V = \pi/3(1-x)(1+x)^2$. Hence find the maximum value of V.
20. For what range of values of x does the function $e^{2x}/(1-x)$ increase as x increases?
21. Given $dy/dx = (1+y)^2$, find d^2y/dx^2 in terms of y and show that all turning and inflexion points on the corresponding (x, y) curve lie on the line $y = -1$.
22. Variables u and v are connected by the relation $1/u+1/v = 1/f$ where f is constant. Given $f = 12$ and that u is decreasing at a constant rate of 3 units/s, find the rate of increase of v when $u = 48$.
23. Find the minimum value of the function $x^2 \ln x$, $x > 0$.
24. A point $P(x, y)$ moves on the curve with equations $x = 4\lambda^3$, $y = 3\lambda^4$, where λ is a parameter, such that x increases at a constant rate of 2 units/s. At the instant when $x = 1/2$, find: (i) $d\lambda/dt$; (ii) the rate of increase of y; (iii) the rate of increase of r, where $r = OP$, O being the origin; (iv) the angular velocity of the line OP.
25. Show that the volume V of a right circular cone of slant height l and semi-vertical angle θ is given by $V = (\pi/3)l^3\sin^2\theta\cos\theta$. Find the maximum value of V for a fixed value of l and $0 < \theta < \pi/2$.
26. Find the coordinates of all the points of inflexion on the curve $y = x-\sin x$, $0 \leqslant x \leqslant 4\pi$.
27. Show that the curve $y = xe^{-x^2/2}$ has two stationary points and determine their natures.
28. In $\triangle ABC$, the length a is determined by the Sine Rule for the values $b = 5$, $A = 30°$, $B = 45°$. If there is an error of 0.1 % in the value of A, use a calculus method to find the approximate percentage error in the calculated value of a.
29. The area between two concentric circles of radii x and y $(x > y)$ is denoted by A. Given x is increasing at the rate of 2 cm/s, y is increasing at the rate of 3 cm/s and that initially $x = 4$ cm, $y = 1$ cm, find: (i) the rate of increase of A when $t = 0$; (ii) the ratio of $x:y$ when A begins to decrease; (iii) the time when A is zero.
30. A right circular cylinder of height $2h$ is inscribed in a sphere of radius $\sqrt{3}R$. Show that the maximum value of the volume of the cylinder is $4\pi R^3$.

EXPANSIONS AND APPROXIMATIONS

Maclaurin's series

If, in some particular domain, a function $f(x)$ can be expressed as a convergent power series. then in this domain

$$f(x) = f(0)+xf'(0)+\frac{x^2}{2!}f''(0)+\frac{x^3}{3!}f'''(0)+\ldots+\frac{x^r}{r!}f^r(0)\ldots\infty,$$

where $f(0), f'(0), f''(0), \ldots, f^r(0), \ldots$ are the values of the function and its successive derivatives when $x = 0$.

Using this series, expansions such as the following are obtained.

Binomial expansion

If n is not a positive integer and $|x| < 1$,

$$(1+x)^n = 1+nx+\frac{n(n-1)}{2!}x^2+\frac{n(n-1)(n-2)}{3!}x^3+\ldots\infty;$$

this expansion has been dealt with in a previous section.

Exponential expansion

For all values of x,

$$e^x = 1+x+\frac{x^2}{2!}+\frac{x^3}{3!}+\ldots+\frac{x^r}{r!}\ldots\infty.$$

Note

(i) $e^{2x} = 1+(2x)+(2x)^2/2!\ldots$; $1/e^x = e^{-x} = 1+(-x)+(-x)^2/2!\ldots$;

(ii) to expand e^{a+bx}, express the function as $e^a \cdot e^{bx}$ and similarly for $e^{a+bx+cx^2}$;

(iii) if x is so small that powers above, say, the second can be neglected, functions such as $1/(1+e^x)$, $\sqrt{(e^x+e^{-x})}$ can be approximated to by writing $e^x \approx 1+x+x^2/2$, $e^{-x} \approx 1-x+x^2/2$ and then using the binomial expansion.

Logarithmic expansions

$$\ln(1+x) = x-\frac{x^2}{2}+\frac{x^3}{3}-\frac{x^4}{4}+\ldots+(-1)^{r+1}\frac{x^r}{r}\ldots\infty, \textit{ valid for } -1<x\leqslant 1;$$

this is the basic logarithmic expansion but the following expansions which can be derived from it are important;

$$\ln(1-x) = -\left(x+\frac{x^2}{2}+\frac{x^3}{3}+\frac{x^4}{4}+\ldots+\frac{x^r}{r}\ldots\infty\right), \textit{ valid for } -1\leqslant x<1;$$

$$\ln\left(\frac{1+x}{1-x}\right) = 2\left(x+\frac{x^3}{3}+\frac{x^5}{5}+\frac{x^7}{7}+\ldots+\frac{x^{2r-1}}{2r-1}\ldots\infty\right), \textit{ valid for } -1<x<1.$$

Note

(i) A function of the form $\ln(a+b)$, where $-1 < b/a \leqslant 1$, is expanded by expressing it in the form $\ln a+\ln(1+b/a)$;

(ii) if x is *large*, $\ln(1+x)$ is expressed as $\ln x+\ln(1+1/x)$ and the latter term is expanded in descending powers of x;

(iii) $\ln(a+bx+cx^2)$ is expanded by factorising the trinomial term and expressing the function as the sum of the logarithms of two linear terms or, if factorisation is not possible, by expanding it in the form $\ln a+\ln(1+X)$, where $X = (1/a)(bx+cx^2)$.

Trigonometric expansions

For all values of x,

$$\sin x = x-\frac{x^3}{3!}+\frac{x^5}{5!}-\frac{x^7}{7!}+\ldots+(-1)^{r+1}\frac{x^{2r-1}}{(2r-1)!}\ldots\infty;$$

$$\cos x = 1-\frac{x^2}{2!}+\frac{x^4}{4!}-\frac{x^6}{6!}+\ldots+(-1)^{r+1}\frac{x^{2r-2}}{(2r-2)!}\ldots\infty.$$

Note

(i) The first few terms in the expansion of $\tan x$, $-\pi/2 < x < \pi/2$, can be obtained by writing $\tan x = \sin x/\cos x$ and using approximations for $\sin x$ and $\cos x$, or by using Maclaurin's series. It is found that $\tan x = x+x^3/3+2x^5/15\ldots$;

(ii) the expansion of a function of the form $\sin(\pi/4+x)$ is obtained by first expressing the function in terms of $\sin x$ and $\cos x$.

Example 8. If x is small enough for powers above the second to be neglected, find the approximate value of $1/\sqrt{(e^x+e^{-x})}$.

$$e^x+e^{-x} \approx 1+x+\frac{x^2}{2}+1-x+\frac{x^2}{2} \text{ or } 2+x^2;$$

$$\therefore \qquad \frac{1}{\sqrt{(e^x+e^{-x})}} = (e^x+e^{-x})^{-1/2},$$

$$\approx (2+x^2)^{-1/2} \text{ or } \frac{1}{\sqrt{2}}\left(1+\frac{x^2}{2}\right)^{-1/2},$$

$$\approx \frac{1}{\sqrt{2}}\left(1-\frac{x^2}{4}\right), \text{ using the binomial expansion.}$$

Example 9. Find an expression for the coefficient of x^r, $r > 0$, *in the expansion of* $\ln(1+x)+3\ln(3+x)-3\ln(3+2x)$ *and state the range of values of x for which the expansion is valid.*

$$\ln(1+x) = x-\frac{x^2}{2}+\frac{x^3}{3}+\ldots+(-1)^{r+1}\frac{x^r}{r}\ldots, \text{ valid for } 1 < x \leqslant 1;$$

$$3\ln(3+x) = 3\ln 3+3\ln\left(1+\frac{x}{3}\right) = 3\ln 3+3\left[\frac{x}{3}-\frac{1}{2}\left(\frac{x}{3}\right)^2+\frac{1}{3}\left(\frac{x}{3}\right)^3+\ldots\right.$$

$$\left.+\frac{(-1)^{r+1}}{r}\left(\frac{x}{3}\right)^r\ldots\right], \text{ valid for } -3 < x \leqslant 3;$$

$$3\ln(3+2x) = 3\ln 3+3\ln\left(1+\frac{2x}{3}\right) = 3\ln 3+3\left[\frac{2x}{3}-\frac{1}{2}\left(\frac{2x}{3}\right)^2+\frac{1}{3}\left(\frac{2x}{3}\right)^3+\ldots\right.$$

$$\left.+\frac{(-1)^{r+1}}{r}\left(\frac{2x}{3}\right)^r\ldots\right], \text{ valid for } -\frac{3}{2} < x \leqslant \frac{3}{2}.$$

$$\therefore \quad \text{coefficient of } x^r \textit{ in the expansion} = \frac{(-1)^{r+1}}{r}\left[1+3\cdot\frac{1}{3^r}-3\cdot\frac{2^r}{3^r}\right].$$

From the three separate conditions, it follows that the expansion is valid for $-1 < x \leqslant 1$.

Example 10. Find the expansion of $e^{\sin x}$ *as far as the term in* x^4.

$$\sin x \approx x-\frac{x^3}{3!} \quad \text{or} \quad x-\frac{x^3}{6}.$$

$$\therefore \qquad e^{\sin x} \approx e^{x-x^3/6} \quad \text{or} \quad e^x\cdot e^{-x^3/6},$$

$$\approx \left(1+x+\frac{x^2}{2}+\frac{x^3}{6}+\frac{x^4}{24}\right)\left(1-\frac{x^3}{6}\right),$$

$$\approx 1+x+\frac{x^2}{2}-\frac{x^4}{8}.$$

(A) EXAMPLES 22

1. Obtain the first three terms in the expansion of each of the following functions in ascending powers of x and state the values of x for which the expansion is valid: (i) e^{3x}; (ii) e^{x^2}; (iii) $1/e^{2x}$; (iv) $\ln(1+2x)$; (v) $\ln(1-x/2)$; (vi) $\ln(1+x^2)$; (vii) $\sin 2x$; (viii) $1-\cos 2x$; (ix) $\cos^2 x$—express in terms of $\cos 2x$.
2. Write down the first four terms of the infinite series whose sums are: (i) e; (ii) $1/e$; (iii) $\sqrt{e}$; (iv) e^2+e^{-2}; (v) $(e-e^{-1})^2$.
3. Show that $\sin(\pi/4+x) \approx \sqrt{2}(1+x-x^2/2-x^3/6)/2$ and obtain a corresponding approximation to $\cos(\pi/4+x)$, x being assumed small.
4. Obtain the expansions of the following functions in ascending powers of x as far as the term in x^3: (i) $(x-2)e^x$; (ii) $(x+1)\ln(1+2x)$; (iii) $(x^2+1)\sin x$; (iv) $(x+3)/e^x$.
5. If x is small, show that $\ln(1+x^2)-\ln(1+x)-\ln(1-x) \approx 2x^2+2x^6/3$.
6. Find the first three terms in the expansions of the following functions in ascending powers of x and in each case state any restriction on the values of x: (i) $\ln(2+x)$; (ii) $\ln(3-x)$; (iii) $\ln[(1+x)(1-x)]$; (iv) $\ln[(2-x)(1+x)]$; (v) $\ln(1-2x-3x^2)$; (vi) $\ln[(1+x)/(1-x)]^{1/2}$.
7. What are the coefficients of x^3 in the expansions of: (i) $(e^x)^2$; (ii) $\sqrt{e^x}$; (iii) e^{x+1}?
8. Show that $\cos 3x = 4\cos^3 x - 3\cos x$ and use this result to obtain the expansion of $\cos^3 x$ in ascending powers of x as far as the term in x^4.
9. If x is *large*, show that $\ln(x^2+x) \approx 2\ln x + 1/x - 1/2x^2$.
10. Expand in ascending powers of x as far as the term in x^3: (i) $e^{3x}-2e^x+e^{-x}$; (ii) $\ln[(1+2x)/(1-2x)]-\ln[(1+x)/(1-x)]^2$.
11. Obtain the first three terms in the expansions of: (i) $e^x \sin x$; (ii) $e^{-x}\cos x$ in ascending powers of x.
12. Find the coefficients of x^r in the expansions in ascending powers of x of: (i) e^{2x}; (ii) e^{-x}; (iii) $\ln(1+2x)$; (iv) $\ln(1-3x)$; (v) $(x+1)e^x$; (vi) $(1-x)\ln(1-x)$; (vii) $(1+2x)/e^x$.
13. Show that $2\sin(\pi/4+x)\cos x = \sin(\pi/4+2x)+\sin \pi/4$ and use this result to obtain the expansion of $\sin(\pi/4+x)\cos x$ in ascending powers of x as far as the term in x^6.
14. By writing down the expansions of e^{-2x} and e^{x^2} in ascending powers of x as far as the terms in x^4, show that when x is small, $e^{-2x+x^2} \approx 1-2x+3x^2-10x^3/3$.
15. If $|x|<1$, expand $\ln\{[(1+x)^2]/(1+x^2)\}$ in ascending powers of x giving the first three terms and the term in x^{2r}.
16. Expand as far as the term in x^3: (i) $\ln(1+x+x^2)$; (ii) $\ln(1+x+x^2)^{1/2}$, $|x|<1$.
17. Obtain the first three terms in the expansions in ascending powers of x of: (i) $1/(1+e^x)$; (ii) $\ln(1+e^x)$; (iii) $\ln(1+\sin x)$; (iv) $e^{\cos x}$, stating any restrictions on the values of x.

APPROXIMATE SOLUTIONS OF EQUATIONS

Numerical methods for the approximate solutions of equations depend on (a) locating the roots and finding rough approximations to their values and (b) improving these approximations to a required degree of accuracy.

Location of roots

The real roots of an equation $f(x) = 0$ can be located and their approximate values determined by sketching the graph of $y = f(x)$ and noting the approximate positions of the points where this graph meets the x-axis. It is often better to express the equation in the form $f_1(x) = f_2(x)$, where $f_1(x)$, $f_2(x)$ are functions of a standard type, the roots of $f(x) = 0$ being given by the x-coordinates of the common points of the graphs of $y = f_1(x)$ and $y = f_2(x)$.

Alternatively, the sign change method can be used. This method requires that $f(x)$ is a continuous function for the range of values of x under consideration; it states that if $f(a)$ and $f(b)$ are of opposite signs, then there is at least one real root of the equation $f(x) = 0$ in the interval $a < x < b$. To establish there is just one root in the interval it is sufficient to show that the curve $y = f(x)$ has no turning point for $a < x < b$.

Example 11. Find graphically, the number of real roots and their approximate values for each of the equations: (i) $x^3+x-3 = 0$; (ii) $e^x-2x-1 = 0$.

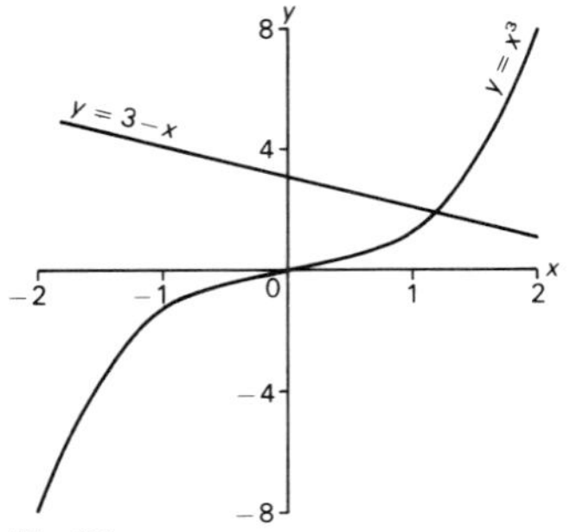

Fig. 24

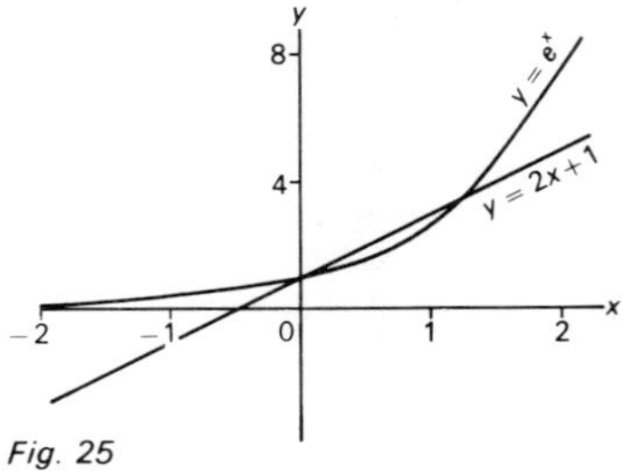

Fig. 25

(i) Using a sketch of the graphs of $y = x^3$ and $y = 3-x$ (Fig. 24), it is seen that the equation $x^3 = 3-x$, i.e. $x^3+x-3 = 0$, has just one real root whose approximate value is $x = 1.2$.

(ii) Using a sketch of the graphs of $y = e^x$ and $y = 2x+1$ (Fig. 25), it is seen that the equation $e^x = 2x+1$, i.e. $e^x-2x-1 = 0$, has two real roots one of which is zero and the other has the approximate value $x = 1.3$.

Example 12. Show that the equation $x^3-4x-1 = 0$ *has a real root in the interval* $2 < x < 3$.

Writing $\quad f(x) = x^3-4x-1,\ f(2) = -1;\ f(3) = +14.$

Because of the sign change, there is at least one real root of the equation $f(x) = 0$ in the interval $2 < x < 3$. Also as $f'(x) = 3x^2-4$ does not vanish in this interval, it follows that there is one root of the equation in the interval.

Linear interpolation

If $a, b\ (> a)$ are two values of x between which a root of the equation $f(x) = 0$ lies and if $f(a) = A, f(b) = -B$, where A, B have the same sign, then the approximate value of the root is given by

$$x = a+\frac{A}{A+B}(b-a).$$

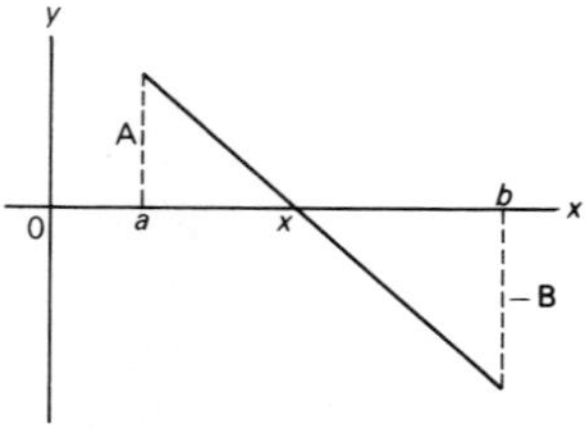

Fig. 26

This result is obtained by taking the graph of $y = f(x)$ for $a \leqslant x \leqslant b$ as a straight line (Fig. 26).

Iterative methods

Having obtained a rough approximation to the value of a particular root of a given equation there are various methods of obtaining the root to a higher degree of accuracy. The most common methods are given here.

Interval bisection

Suppose the equation $f(x) = 0$ has a root in the interval $a < x < b$, i.e. $f(a)$, $f(b)$ are of opposite signs. Find the value of $f[(a+b)/2]$ and determine by the sign change method in which of the two intervals $a < x < (a+b)/2$ or $(a+b)/2 < x < b$ the root lies. Repeat this process of interval bisection until the necessary degree of accuracy is achieved and use interpolation for the final approximation.

Example 13. Obtain the root of the equation $x^3 - 4x - 1 = 0$ between 2 and 3, correct to one decimal place.

Writing $f(x) = x^3 - 4x - 1$, then $f(2) = -1$ and $f(3) = 14$.

As $f[(2+3)/2]$, i.e. $f(2.5) \approx 4.6$, the root lies in the interval $2 < x < 2.5$.
As $f[(2+2.5)/2]$, i.e. $f(2.25) \approx 1.4$, the root lies in the interval $2 < x < 2.25$.

By interpolation,
$$\text{root} \approx 2 + \frac{1}{1+1.4} \cdot 0.25,$$
$$\approx 2.1.$$

Newton–Raphson

If $x = a$ is an approximate root of the equation $f(x) = 0$, then a better approximation is usually given by

$$x = a - \frac{f(a)}{f'(a)}.$$

Note

(i) This method can be used repeatedly until a desired degree of accuracy is obtained;
(ii) the method fails when the root under consideration is close to another root. Consequently before this method is used it is advisable to consider the problem graphically.

Example 14. Given that $x = 1.3$ is a rough approximation to the non-zero root of the equation $f(x) = e^x - 2x - 1 = 0$, find the root correct to two decimal places.

$$f(x) = e^x - 2x - 1 \qquad f'(x) = e^x - 2.$$
$$f(1.3) = 0.069 \qquad f'(1.3) = 1.669$$

and
$$\frac{f(1.3)}{f'(1.3)} \approx 0.041.$$

So a closer approximation to the root $= 1.3 - 0.041$ or 1.26 correct to two decimal places.

Iteration

This method requires that the given equation $f(x) = 0$ is expressible in the form

$$x = \mathrm{F}(x);$$

in the case of polynomial equations this can be done in two or even three or more ways, e.g. if

$$f(x) = x^3 - 2x + 3 = 0, \text{ we can write } x = \frac{x^3 + 3}{2} \text{ or } x = \sqrt[3]{(2x - 3)}.$$

If $x = x_1$ is an approximation to a root $x = \alpha$ of the given equation, then successively closer approximations $x_2, x_3, x_4, \ldots, x_n, x_{n+1}$, are in general, obtained using the relationships

$$x_2 = F(x_1);\ x_3 = F(x_2);\ x_4 = F(x_3); \ldots x_{n+1} = F(x_n).$$

The process is best illustrated graphically. In Fig. 27, the graphs $y = x$, $y = F(x)$ intersect at the point P whose x-coordinate is α.

The approximation $x = x_1$ corresponds to the point P_1 on the curve $y = F(x)$ and the point R_1 on the line $y = x$. So the error in taking x_1 as the root of the given equation is represented by P_1R_1.

We have $P_1Q_1 = F(x_1)$; $R_2Q_2 = P_1Q_1 = F(x_1) = x_2$; $OQ_2 = x_2$; $P_2Q_2 = F(x_2) = x_3$ and so on.

Clearly in the case illustrated the successive values $x_1, x_2, x_3, \ldots$ converge to the value α.

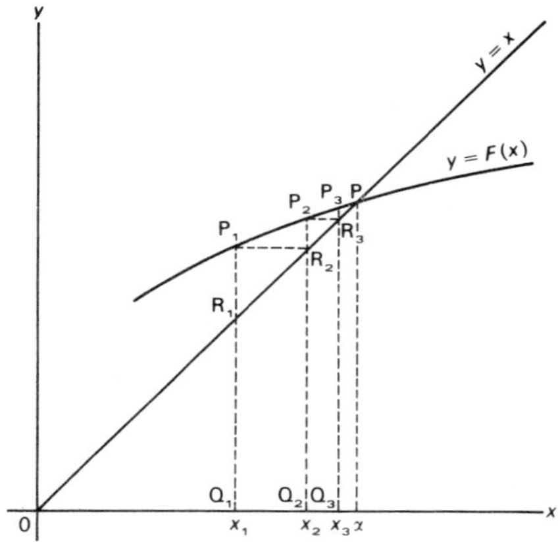

Fig. 27

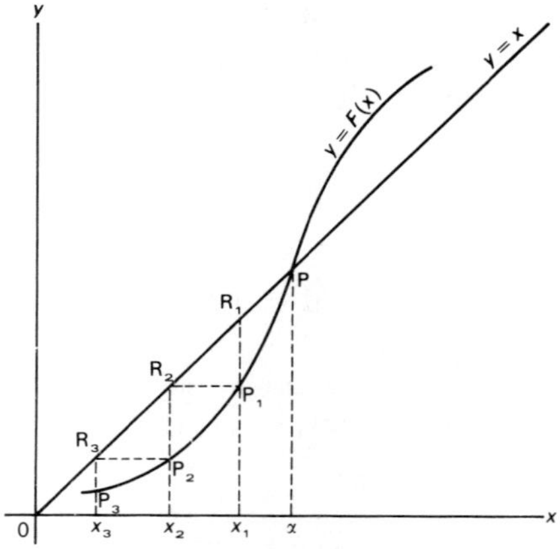

Fig. 28

Cases of failure

The iteration process fails in cases similar to that illustrated graphically in Fig. 28. Clearly the successive values $x_1, x_2, x_3, \ldots$ diverge away from α.

Analytical criterion

The procedure defined by the sequence

$$x_{n+1} = F(x_n)$$

will produce successive values $x_1, x_2, x_3, \ldots$ which converge to the root of the equation $x = F(x)$ if for values of x in the neighbourhood of $x = \alpha$, $|F'(x)| < 1$. If $|F'(x)| > 1$, the successive values will diverge from α.

Example 15. Verify that the equation $x^3-4x^2+6=0$ has a root α between 3 and 4. Show that for this equation there are three possible iterations in the form $x_{n+1}=F(x_n)$ and establish graphically which of these starting from $x_1=3$ converges to the root α. Using a suitable iteration obtain the value of α correct to two decimal places.

The given equation can be expressed in the form $x = F(x)$ in the following ways:

$$\text{(i)}\ x=\sqrt[3]{(4x^2-6)};\quad \text{(ii)}\ x=\frac{\sqrt{(x^3+6)}}{2};\quad \text{(iii)}\ x=4-\frac{6}{x^2}.$$

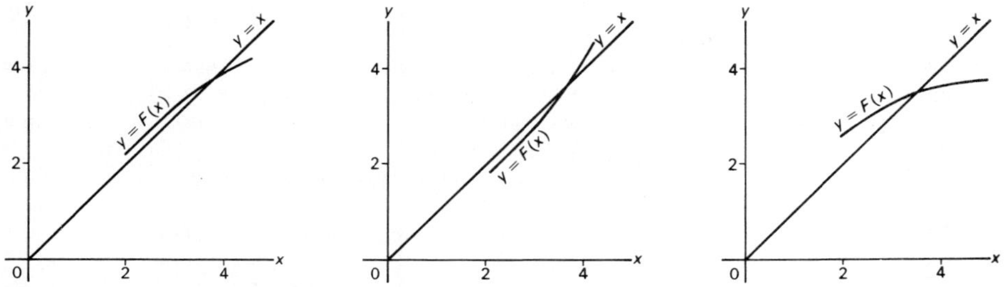

Fig. 29(i) *Fig. 29(ii)* *Fig. 29(iii)*

Sketch graphs of $y = x$ and $y = F(x)$ for the three cases are shown in Fig. 29. The sketches show that cases (i) and (iii) will give iterations which converge to the root α.

Using case (iii), the corresponding sequence is given by $x_{n+1} = 4-6/x_n^2$.

Taking $x_1 = 3$,

$$x_2 = 4-\frac{6}{x_1^2} = 3.333;$$

$$x_3 = 4-\frac{6}{x_2^2} = 3.459;$$

$$x_4 = 4-\frac{6}{x_3^2} = 3.498;$$

$$x_5 = 4-\frac{6}{x_4^2} = 3.510;$$

$$x_6 = 4-\frac{6}{x_5^2} = 3.513;$$

$$x_7 = 4-\frac{6}{x_6^2} = 3.514.$$

The approximate value of $\alpha = 3.51$.

(A) EXAMPLES 23

1. Without solving, show that the roots of the equation $2x^2+5x-4=0$ lie one in each of the intervals -4 to -3 and 0 to 1.
2. If $f(x)=x^3-3x+1$, find the signs of $f(-2)$, $f(-1)$, $f(0)$, $f(1)$ and $f(2)$. Hence find the pairs of successive integers between which the three roots of the equation $x^3-3x+1=0$ lie.
3. Sketch the graph of $y=x^3$ and using this graph and those of suitable straight lines, determine the

number of real roots of each of the equations: (i) $x^3 = 2-x$; (ii) $x^3 = x+1$; (iii) $x^3+2x-1 = 0$; (iv) $x^3-2x+1 = 0$.

4. Use linear interpolation to estimate the value of a root of the equation $f(x) = 0$ given that $f(2) = -7.65$ and $f(3) = 2.35$.
5. Show that the equation $x^3-27x-36 = 0$ has a real root in each of the intervals -5 to -4, -2 to -1, 5 to 6.
6. Draw the graph of $y = e^x$ for $-3 \leqslant x \leqslant 2$. Using this graph and those of suitable straight lines find (a) the number of real roots, (b) an approximate value of the positive root of each of the equations: (i) $e^x = x+2$; (ii) $e^x+x-2 = 0$; (iii) $2e^x+x-3 = 0$.
7. Show that the equation $x^3-2x^2-1 = 0$ has just one root in the interval 2 to 3.
8. Sketch the graphs of $y = 2x^3$ and $y = 1-x^2$ and deduce that the equation $2x^3+x^2-1 = 0$ has only one real root which lies between 0 and 1.
9. Sketch the graphs of $y = 2\sin x$ and $y = x$ for $0 < x \leqslant \pi$ and show that the equation $x = 2\sin x$ has one root in this interval. Verify that $x = 1.9$ rad is a close approximation to this root.
10. Prove graphically or otherwise that the equation $x^3+x-3 = 0$ has a root between 1 and 2 and using the method of interval bisection find the value of this root correct to one decimal place.
11. Use the method of linear interpolation to obtain an approximation to the root of the equation $e^x+x-3 = 0$ which lies between 0.7 and 0.9.
12. Prove that the equation $x^3-4x-1 = 0$ has three real roots and state the pairs of successive integers between which each of them lies.
13. Show graphically that the equation $x^3 = 2x^2+1$ has a root close to 2 and use the Newton–Raphson procedure to show that an approximate value of the root is 2.25.
14. The equation $\sin x = x/2$ has a root close to 2. Use one iteration of the Newton–Raphson method to find a more accurate approximation to the root.
15. The equation $x^3+2x-2 = 0$ has a root approximately equal to 0.8. Find a more accurate approximation by performing two iterations using the sequence $x_{n+1} = (2-x_n^3)/2$, starting with $x_1 = 0.8$. Illustrate by sketching the graphs of $y = x$ and $y = (2-x^3)/2$ for $0 \leqslant x \leqslant 1$.
16. Show that the equation $e^x+x-10 = 0$ has a root approximately equal to 2. Working to two decimal places, use the Newton–Raphson method to obtain a better approximation.
17. Draw the graphs of $y = x$ and $y = \sqrt[3]{(3x+8)}$ for $0 \leqslant x \leqslant 3$. Starting with the value of $x, x_1 = 2$ show on your diagram the successive values x_2, x_3, x_4 determined by using the relationship $x_{n+1} = \sqrt[3]{(3x_n+8)}$. Hence show that the sequence $x_1, x_2, x_3, x_4 \ldots$ will converge to a value α which is the root of the equation $x^3 = 3x+8$ in the interval 2 to 3.
18. Show graphically that the equation $\sin x = 1/x$ has two roots in the interval $0 < x < \pi$ and verify that $x = 1.1$ rad is an approximation to one of these roots. Use the Newton–Raphson method to find the root correct to two decimal places.
19. Prove graphically or otherwise that the equation $x^3+x-5 = 0$ has just one real root and that the root lies between 1 and 2. Show that the root can be found by the iteration $x_{n+1} = \sqrt[3]{(5-x_n)}$, and find the value obtained after four iterations starting with $x_1 = 1$.
20. Sketch the graphs of $y = \ln x$ and $y = 1-x/2$ for $1/2 \leqslant x \leqslant 4$. Show that the equation $2\ln x+x-2 = 0$ has one real root which is approximately equal to 1.4 and use the Newton–Raphson method to find the root correct to three decimal places.
21. Show that the equation $x^3 = x^2+1$ has a root between 1 and 2. By sketching the graphs of $y = x$ and $y = 1+1/x^2$ on the same diagram show that the root can be found by using the iteration $x_{n+1} = 1+1/x_n^2$ starting with $x_1 = 1$. Obtain the values of the iterates $x_2, x_3, x_4, \ldots$, until successive iterates differ by less than 0.05.
22. Show graphically that the root of the equation $x^3 = x^2+1$ between 1 and 2, cannot be found by using the iteration $x_{n+1} = \sqrt{(x_n^3-1)}$.

(B) MISCELLANEOUS EXAMPLES

1. Find the equation of the tangent to the curve with equations $x = a(t+t^{-1})$, $y = a(t-t^{-1})$, where t is a parameter and a a constant, at the point where $t = 2$.
2. Given $y = (\sec x+\tan x)^n$, show that $\cos x\, dy/dx = ny$.
3. Expand in ascending powers of x as far as the term in x^4: (i) $\ln(e^x+e^{-x})$; (ii) $e^x \sin x$; (iii) $e^{x^2}\cos 2x$; (iv) $\sec x$, $-\pi/2 < x < \pi/2$.

4. Given that $x = \sec\theta + \tan\theta$, $y = \operatorname{cosec}\theta + \cot\theta$, show that $(1+x^2)\,dy/dx + 1 + y^2 = 0$.
5. Show graphically that the equation $e^x + x - 3 = 0$ has just one real root and that the root lies between 0.7 and 0.9. Obtain approximations to the root by: (i) linear interpolation between $x = 0.7$ and $x = 0.9$; (ii) one application of the Newton–Raphson method commencing with $x = 0.8$.
6. The curve $y = x^3 + ax^2 + bx + c$ has stationary points where $x = -1$ and $x = 3$ and passes through the point $(1, -2)$. Find the values of the constants a, b, c. Identify the stationary points and find the coordinates of the point of inflexion. Sketch the curve.
7. Find the equation of the tangent to the curve $3ay^2 = x^2(x+a)$, where a is a constant, at the point $(2a, 2a)$.
8. For a point moving in a straight line the displacement s from a fixed point in the line at time t is given by $s = ae^{pt} + be^{-pt}$, where a, b, p are constants. If the initial displacement is zero and the initial velocity is u, show that $v^2 = u^2 + p^2s^2$ where v is the velocity at time t.
9. Find the coordinates of the turning point on the curve $y = x(1 - \ln x)$, $x > 0$, and determine its nature. Make a rough sketch of the curve.
10. If $e^y(1-x) = 1 + 2x$, expand y in ascending powers of x as far as the term in x^4. State also: (i) the range of values of x for which the expansion is valid; (ii) the coefficient of x^r in the expansion.
11. Show that the equation $x^3 = 2 - 2x$ has only one real root and this lies between 0.7 and 1. Working to three decimal places obtain an approximation to this root by three iterations using the procedure defined by $x_{n+1} = (2 - x_n^3)/2$ and starting with $x_1 = 0.8$.
12. Differentiate with respect to x: (i) $\ln(\sin x - \cos x)^2$; (ii) $(1-x^2)^{1/2} \arcsin x$; (iii) $(1-x^2)/(1+x^2)^2$.
13. The coordinates of a point on a curve are given in terms of the parameter θ by the equations $x = a\sec\theta$, $y = a\tan\theta$. Find the equations of the tangent and normal at the point $P(a\sec\theta, a\tan\theta)$. The tangent and normal at P meet the x-axis at T and N; show that $OT \cdot ON = 2a^2$ where O is the origin.
14. Obtain the expansion of $\sin^2 x$ in ascending powers of x as far as the term in x^4 and hence obtain the expansion of $e^{\sin^2 x}$ as far as the term in x^4.
15. An open cylindrical waste-paper basket is to be made with a capacity of $1000\pi\,\text{cm}^3$. Show that a base radius of 10 cm will make the total surface area a minimum.
16. Find the coordinates of the turning point on the curve with equation $y = ax^{-1} + \ln x$, where a is a positive constant and $x > 0$. Show that the point is a minimum point and deduce the range of values of a for which $y \geqslant 0$ for $x > 0$.
17. Show graphically that the equation $e^x = 10 - x$ has just one real root. Taking $x = 2$ as an initial approximation to this root and working to 3 decimal places use two applications of the Newton–Raphson procedure to obtain a closer approximation to the root.
18. Given $x^3 + 3xy^2 + y^3 = 5$, find the values of dy/dx and d^2y/dx^2 at the point $(1, 1)$.
19. Find the coefficient of x^r in the expansion of each of the following functions in ascending powers of x: (i) $(1-x)/e^x$; (ii) e^{2+x}; (iii) $1/(2-x)^2$; (iv) $(1+x)\ln(1-2x)$.
20. For a point moving along the x-axis, $x = 16(e^{-t} - e^{-2t})$ at time t. Find the acceleration of the point at the instant when it is at its maximum distance from the origin.
21. Find the coordinates of the stationary points on the curve $y = x(x-1)^4$ and determine whether these points are maxima, minima or points of inflexion. Make a rough sketch of the curve.
22. Given that $\ln y = x - y\ln x$, find dy/dx in terms of x and y. Also find the approximate value of y when $x = 1 + \varepsilon$, where ε is small.
23. Find the expansion of $\ln[\sqrt{(1+x)/(1-x)}]$, $|x| < 1$, in ascending powers of x as far as the term in x^3. Given that $\ln[\sqrt{(1+x)(1-x)}]/(1-ax) \approx 3x/2 + kx^3$, find the values of the constants a and k.
24. In triangle ABC, a is constant and as A varies, b and c change so that $b + c =$ constant. Show that $db/dA = -dc/dA$ and by using the Cosine Rule establish that $db/dA = bc\sin A/[(c-b)(1+\cos A)]$.
25. Prove that the equation $x^3 + x - 5 = 0$ has only one real root and that this root lies between 1 and 2. Show that the root cannot be found by the iteration $x_{n+1} = 5 - x_n^3$ and find another iteration in the form $x_{n+1} = F(x_n)$ which can be used to give successive approximations to the root. Starting with $x_1 = 1$, find the root correct to two decimal places.
26. In the interval $-\pi \leqslant x \leqslant \pi$, find the values of x for which $y = x\sin x + \cos x$ is stationary and determine in each case whether the point is a maximum, minimum or an inflexion.
27. Find $d/dx[x/(1+x)]$ and use the result in finding the equation of the tangent to the curve $y/(1+y) + x/(1+x) - x^2y^3 = 0$ at the point $(1, 1)$.
28. The fixed point A has coordinates $(a, 0)$ and initially the moving point P has coordinates $(3a, 0)$, a

being a positive constant. The line OP, of fixed length, rotates in a counterclockwise direction about the origin O with angular velocity 2 rad/s. At the instant when OP has rotated through an angle of $\pi/3$ find: (i) the rate of increase of the distance AP; (ii) the angular velocity of the line AP.

29. Given that $x = a(\theta - \sin\theta)$, $y = a(1 - \cos\theta)$, where a is a constant show that: (i) $\mathrm{d}y/\mathrm{d}x = \cot(\theta/2)$; (ii) $y^2(\mathrm{d}^2y/\mathrm{d}x^2) + a = 0$.
30. Show that the equation $x^3 - 3x - 8 = 0$ has only one real root α and establish that the root lies between 2 and 3. Sketch on the same axes the graphs of $y = x$ and $y = \sqrt[3]{(3x+8)}$ for $0 \leqslant x \leqslant 3$. Use your diagram to show that the sequence defined by $x_{n+1} = \sqrt[3]{(3x_n+8)}$, $x_1 = 2$ is convergent to the root α and calculate α correct to two decimal places. Use a sketch graph of $y = (x^3 - 8)/3$, together with that of $y = x$ for $x \geqslant 0$ to investigate the convergence or otherwise of the sequence defined by $x_{n+1} = (x_n^3 - 8)/3$, $x_1 = 2.2$.

INTEGRATION

Indefinite integration

$$\int f(x)\,\mathrm{d}x = \mathrm{F}(x) + c, \textit{ where } \frac{\mathrm{d}}{\mathrm{d}x}\mathrm{F}(x) = f(x).$$

Definite integration

$$\int_a^b f(x)\,\mathrm{d}x = \mathrm{F}(b) - \mathrm{F}(a), \textit{ where } \frac{\mathrm{d}}{\mathrm{d}x}\mathrm{F}(x) = f(x);$$

alternatively,

$$\int_a^b f(x)\,\mathrm{d}x = \lim_{\delta x \to 0} \sum_{x=a}^{x=b} f(x)\,\delta x.$$

Standard integrals

$$\int x^n\,\mathrm{d}x = \frac{x^{n+1}}{n+1} + c,\ n \neq -1$$

$$\int \frac{\mathrm{d}x}{x} = \ln x + c,\ x > 0$$

$$= \ln(-x) + c,\ x < 0$$

$$\int e^x\,\mathrm{d}x = e^x + c$$

$$\int \frac{\mathrm{d}x}{\sqrt{(a^2 - x^2)}} = \sin^{-1}\frac{x}{a} + c$$

$$\int \frac{\mathrm{d}x}{a^2 + x^2} = \frac{1}{a}\tan^{-1}\frac{x}{a} + c$$

$$\int \sin x\,\mathrm{d}x = -\cos x + c$$

$$\int \cos x\,\mathrm{d}x = \sin x + c$$

$$\int \sec^2 x\,\mathrm{d}x = \tan x + c$$

$$\int \operatorname{cosec}^2 x\,\mathrm{d}x = -\cot x + c$$

$$\int \sin^2 x\,\mathrm{d}x = \left(\frac{x - \dfrac{\sin 2x}{2}}{2}\right) + c$$

$$\int \cos^2 x\,\mathrm{d}x = \left(\frac{x + \dfrac{\sin 2x}{2}}{2}\right) + c.$$

More general standard integrals

The above results are readily extended by replacing x by the *linear* function $(ax+b)$, e.g.

$$\int (ax+b)^n\,dx = \frac{1}{a}\cdot\frac{(ax+b)^{n+1}}{n+1}+c,\ n \neq -1$$

$$\int \frac{dx}{ax+b} = \frac{1}{a}\ln(ax+b)+c,\ ax+b > 0$$

$$\int e^{ax+b}\,dx = \frac{1}{a}e^{ax+b}+c \qquad \int \sin(ax+b)\,dx = -\frac{1}{a}\cos(ax+b)+c$$

$$\int \cos(ax+b)\,dx = \frac{1}{a}\sin(ax+b)+c \qquad \int \sec^2(ax+b)\,dx = \frac{1}{a}\tan(ax+b)+c$$

Example 16. *Find:* (i) $\int dx/[\surd(4x+3)]$; (ii) $\int dx/(4x+3)$; (iii) $\int dx/e^{2x}$; (iv) $\int_0^1 \sin^2(\pi t/4)\,dt$.

(i) $$\int \frac{dx}{\surd(4x+3)} = \int (4x+3)^{-1/2}\,dx = \frac{2(4x+3)^{1/2}}{4}+c = \frac{\surd(4x+3)}{2}+c;$$

(ii) $$\int \frac{dx}{4x+3} = \frac{\ln(4x+3)}{4}+c;$$

(iii) $$\int \frac{dx}{e^{2x}} = \int e^{-2x}\,dx = -\frac{e^{-2x}}{2}+c;$$

(iv) $$\int_0^1 \sin^2\frac{\pi t}{4}\,dt = \frac{1}{2}\int_0^1\left(1-\cos\frac{\pi t}{2}\right)dt = \frac{1}{2}\left[t-\frac{2}{\pi}\sin\frac{\pi t}{2}\right]_0^1 = 1-\frac{2}{\pi}.$$

Example 17. *Find:* (i) $\int dx/[\surd(4-3x^2)]$; (ii) $\int_0^2 dx/(4+3x^2)$.

(i) $$\int \frac{dx}{\surd(4-3x^2)} = \frac{1}{\surd 3}\int \frac{dx}{\sqrt{\left(\frac{4}{3}-x^2\right)}} = \frac{1}{\surd 3}\sin^{-1}\frac{\surd 3x}{2}+c;$$

(ii) $$\int_0^2 \frac{dx}{4+3x^2} = \frac{1}{3}\int_0^2 \frac{dx}{\frac{4}{3}+x^2} = \left[\frac{1}{3}\frac{\surd 3}{2}\tan^{-1}\frac{\surd 3x}{2}\right]_0^2 = \frac{1}{2\surd 3}\cdot\frac{\pi}{3} = \frac{\pi}{6\surd 3}.$$

Reverse function of a function rule

If u is a function of x, $(d/dx)f(u) = f'(u)\,du/dx$ and consequently

$$\int f'(u)\frac{du}{dx}\,dx = f(u)+c.$$

So, for example,

$$\int (1+x^2)^5 x\,dx = \frac{1}{2}\int (1+x^2)^5 2x\,dx = \frac{1}{2}\cdot\frac{1}{6}(1+x^2)^6 + c = \frac{1}{12}(1+x^2)^6 + c;$$

$$\int \sin^3 x \cos x\,dx = \frac{\sin^4 x}{4} + c; \quad \int \tan^2 x \sec^2 x\,dx = \frac{\tan^3 x}{3} + c.$$

Note Important special case

$$\int \frac{f'(x)}{f(x)}\,dx = \ln f(x) + c,\ f(x) > 0.$$

So, for example, $\displaystyle\int \frac{x^2\,dx}{1+x^3} = \frac{1}{3}\int \frac{3x^2\,dx}{1+x^3} = \frac{\ln(1+x^3)}{3} + c;$

$$\int \frac{\cos x\,dx}{1+\sin x} = \ln(1+\sin x) + c; \quad \int \frac{e^{2x}\,dx}{1+e^{2x}} = \frac{\ln(1+e^{2x})}{2} + c.$$

Example 18. Find: (i) $\int (3x-1)/(x^2+4)\,dx$; *(ii)* $\int_0^{\pi/6} \tan 2x\,dx$.

(i) $$\int \frac{3x+1}{x^2+4}\,dx = \int \frac{3x\,dx}{x^2+4} + \int \frac{dx}{x^2+4} = \frac{3\ln(x^2+4)}{2} + \frac{\tan^{-1}\dfrac{x}{2}}{2} + c;$$

(ii) $$\int_0^{\pi/6} \tan 2x\,dx = \int_0^{\pi/6} \frac{\sin 2x}{\cos 2x}\,dx = \left[-\frac{\ln\cos 2x}{2}\right]_0^{\pi/6} = \frac{\ln 2}{2}.$$

(A) EXAMPLES 24

Find the integrals:

1. $\displaystyle\int \frac{dx}{\surd(2x+3)}$; 2. $\displaystyle\int \frac{dx}{2x+1}$; 3. $\displaystyle\int (1-x)^6\,dx$; 4. $\displaystyle\int \sin 5x\,dx$;

5. $\displaystyle\int \frac{dx}{(1-2x)^2}$; 6. $\displaystyle\int \left(\sec^2\frac{x}{2} - 1\right)dx$; 7. $\displaystyle\int \frac{(e^{2x}-e^{-2x})}{2}\,dx$; 8. $\displaystyle\int \frac{dx}{\surd(4-x^2)}$;

9. $\displaystyle\int \frac{dx}{9+x^2}$; 10. $\displaystyle\int \cos^3 x \sin x\,dx$; 11. $\displaystyle\int \surd(\tan x)\sec^2 x\,dx$; 12. $\displaystyle\int \frac{x\,dx}{1+x^2}$;

13. $\displaystyle\int \cot x\,dx$; 14. $\displaystyle\int (1+x^2)^4 x\,dx$; 15. $\displaystyle\int e^{-x^2} x\,dx$; 16. $\displaystyle\int \frac{\sin x}{1-\cos x}\,dx$;

17. $\displaystyle\int \frac{1+x}{1+x^2}\,dx$; 18. $\displaystyle\int \frac{dx}{\surd(9-4x^2)}$; 19. $\displaystyle\int \frac{dx}{9+4x^2}$; 20. $\displaystyle\int \frac{x\,dx}{9-x^2}, |x| < 3.$

Evaluate the definite integrals:

21. $\displaystyle\int_0^1 (x+2)^5\,dx$; 22. $\displaystyle\int_0^{\pi/2} \sin^5 x \cos x\,dx$; 23. $\displaystyle\int_0^1 \frac{x^3\,dx}{1+x^4}$;

24. $\displaystyle\int_0^{1/2} \frac{dx}{\surd(1-2x^2)}$; 25. $\displaystyle\int_0^2 \frac{x\,dx}{\surd(1+x^2)}$; 26. $\displaystyle\int_0^1 (2x^3+3x+1)(2x^2+1)\,dx$;

27. $\displaystyle\int_0^{\pi/3} \frac{\sin x}{\cos^2 x}\,dx$; 28. $\displaystyle\int_0^1 \frac{e^x}{1+e^x}\,dx$.

29. Find the following integrals by expressing each of them as a sum or difference of two integrals:

(i) $\displaystyle\int \frac{x-2}{\sqrt{(1-x^2)}}\,dx$; (ii) $\displaystyle\int \frac{4-x}{4+x^2}\,dx$; (iii) $\displaystyle\int \frac{3-2x}{\sqrt{(9-x^2)}}\,dx$.

30. Find the following integrals by first expressing the integrands in terms of proper fractions:

(i) $\displaystyle\int \frac{x\,dx}{x-1}, x>1$; (ii) $\displaystyle\int \frac{x^2\,dx}{x-1}, x>1$; (iii) $\displaystyle\int \frac{x+1}{x-1}\,dx, x>1$; (iv) $\displaystyle\int \frac{x^2}{x^2+2}\,dx$.

METHODS OF INTEGRATION

Products of sines and cosines of multiple angles

Integration of such a product is achieved by first expressing the product as the sum or difference of two sines or two cosines., e.g.

$$\int \sin 5x \cos 2x\,dx = \frac{1}{2}\int (\sin 7x + \sin 3x)\,dx = -\frac{\left(\dfrac{\cos 7x}{7}+\dfrac{\cos 3x}{3}\right)}{2} + c.$$

Powers of sine and cosine

If the integrand includes an *odd* power of sine or cosine, proceed as in the following examples:

$$\int \sin^5 x\,dx = \int \sin^4 x \sin x\,dx = \int (1-\cos^2 x)^2 \sin x\,dx = \int \sin x\,dx$$

$$-2\int \cos^2 x \sin x\,dx + \int \cos^4 x \sin x\,dx,$$

$$= -\cos x + \frac{2\cos^3 x}{3} - \frac{\cos^5 x}{5} + c;$$

$$\int \cos^3 x \sin^2 x\,dx = \int \cos^2 x \sin^2 x \cos x\,dx = \int (1-\sin^2 x)\sin^2 x \cos x\,dx$$

$$= \int \sin^2 x \cos x\,dx - \int \sin^4 x \cos x\,dx,$$

$$= \frac{\sin^3 x}{3} - \frac{\sin^5 x}{5} + c.$$

If the powers concerned are *even*, the integrand must be expressed in terms of multiple angles, e.g.

$$\int \sin^2 x\, dx = \frac{1}{2}\int (1-\cos 2x)\, dx = \frac{1}{2}\left(x - \frac{\sin 2x}{2}\right) + c;$$

$$\int \cos^4 x\, dx = \int (\cos^2 x)^2\, dx = \frac{1}{4}\int (1+\cos 2x)^2\, dx$$

$$= \frac{1}{4}\int \left[1 + 2\cos 2x + \frac{(1+\cos 4x)}{2}\right] dx,$$

$$= \frac{3x}{8} + \frac{\sin 2x}{4} + \frac{\sin 4x}{32} + c.$$

Powers of tangent and cotangent

$$\int \tan x\, dx = \int \frac{\sin x}{\cos x}\, dx = -\ln \cos x + c;$$

$$\int \cot x\, dx = \int \frac{\cos x}{\sin x}\, dx = \ln \sin x + c.$$

$$\int \tan^2 x\, dx = \int (\sec^2 x - 1)\, dx = \tan x - x + c;$$

$$\int \cot^2 x\, dx = \int (\operatorname{cosec}^2 x - 1)\, dx = -\cot x - x + c.$$

The method of dealing with higher powers is illustrated in the case of $\int \tan^4 x\, dx$.

$$\int \tan^4 x\, dx = \int \tan^2 x \tan^2 x\, dx = \int \tan^2 x(\sec^2 x - 1)\, dx = \int \tan^2 x \sec^2 x\, dx$$

$$- \int \tan^2 x\, dx,$$

$$= \frac{\tan^3 x}{3} - (\tan x - x) + c.$$

(A) EXAMPLES 25

Integrate with respect to x:

1. $\sin x \cos x$.
2. $\sin 3x \cos x$.
3. $\cos x \cos 2x$.
4. $\cos 5x \sin 2x$.
5. $\sin 2x \sin 3x$.
6. $\sin^3 x$.
7. $\cos^5 x$.
8. $\tan^3 x$.
9. $\sin^3 x \cos^2 x$.
10. $\cos^2 2x$.
11. $\cot x/2$.
12. $\sin^2 x \cos^2 x$.
13. $\tan^2 2x$.
14. $\cos^3 x \sin^3 x$.
15. $\sin 2x \cos 2x$.
16. $\sin^3 x/2$.

Evaluate the integrals:

17. $\int_0^{\pi/4} \sin^2 2x\, dx$.
18. $\int_0^{\pi/2} \cos 3x \sin x\, dx$.
19. $\int_{-\pi/2}^{\pi/2} \cos^3 x\, dx$.
20. $\int_{\pi/4}^{\pi/2} \cot^2 x\, dx$.
21. $\int_0^{\pi/3} \sin x \sin 2x\, dx$.
22. $\int_0^{\pi/8} \sin 2x \cos 2x\, dx$.

23. $\int_{-\pi/4}^{0} \tan^4 x\,dx$. 24. $\int_{0}^{\pi/4} \sin^3 2x\,dx$.

25. By expressing the integrand in terms of the angle $x/2$, find the integrals:

(i) $\int \frac{dx}{1+\cos x}$; (ii) $\int \frac{dx}{1-\cos x}$; (iii) $\int \frac{1-\cos x}{1+\cos x}\,dx$.

Integration by partial fractions

The integration of a quotient of two polynomials is effected by first expressing the quotient in terms of a proper fraction and then using the methods of partial fractions. The integrals involved will be of the types $\int dx/(ax+b)$; $\int dx/[(ax+b)^2]$; $\int (cx+d)dx/(ax^2+b)$, a and $b > 0$; these have already been dealt with.

Example 19. Evaluate (i) $\int_3^5 (x^2+3x-8)/[(x-2)(x-1)^2]\,dx$; *(ii)* $\int_1^3 (x^2+x+3)/[x(x^2+3)]\,dx$.

(i) Using the method of partial fractions,

$$\frac{x^2+3x-8}{(x-2)(x-1)^2} = \frac{2}{x-2} - \frac{1}{x-1} + \frac{4}{(x-1)^2}.$$

$$\therefore \quad \int_3^5 \frac{x^2+3x-8}{(x-2)(x-1)^2}\,dx = 2\int_3^5 \frac{dx}{x-2} - \int_3^5 \frac{dx}{x-1} + 4\int_3^5 \frac{dx}{(x-1)^2},$$

$$= 2[\ln(x-2)]_3^5 - [\ln(x-1)]_3^5 + 4\left[-\frac{1}{(x-1)}\right]_3^5,$$

$$= 2\ln 3 - (\ln 4 - \ln 2) + 4\left(-\frac{1}{4}+\frac{1}{2}\right),$$

$$= 1 + \ln\frac{9}{2}.$$

(ii) Using the method of partial fractions:

$$\frac{x^2+x-3}{x(x^2+3)} = -\frac{1}{x} + \frac{2x+1}{x^2+3}.$$

$$\therefore \quad \int_1^3 \frac{x^2+x-3}{x(x^2+3)}\,dx = -\int_1^3 \frac{dx}{x} + \int_1^3 \frac{2x+1}{x^2+3}\,dx,$$

$$= -\int_1^3 \frac{dx}{x} + \int_1^3 \frac{2x\,dx}{x^2+3} + \int_1^3 \frac{dx}{x^2+3},$$

$$= -[\ln x]_1^3 + [\ln(x^2+3)]_1^3 + \left[\frac{1}{\sqrt{3}}\tan^{-1}\frac{x}{\sqrt{3}}\right]_1^3,$$

$$= -\ln 3 + (\ln 12 - \ln 4) + \left(\frac{1}{\sqrt{3}}\tan^{-1}\sqrt{3} - \frac{1}{\sqrt{3}}\tan^{-1}\frac{1}{\sqrt{3}}\right),$$

$$= -\ln 3 + \ln 3 + \frac{1}{\sqrt{3}}\cdot\frac{\pi}{3} - \frac{1}{\sqrt{3}}\cdot\frac{\pi}{6},$$

$$= \frac{\pi\sqrt{3}}{18}.$$

Integration by parts

If u, v are functions of x,

$$\int uv\,\mathrm{d}x = u\int v\,\mathrm{d}x - \int (\textstyle\int v\,\mathrm{d}x)\frac{\mathrm{d}u}{\mathrm{d}x}\mathrm{d}x.$$

Note

(i) In many products it is only possible to integrate, as a standard form, one of the functions and clearly this must be chosen as v; in cases where both functions are standard integral forms it is usual to choose, if possible, the function u as one which simplifies on differentiation;

(ii) the method is used in the integration of (a) products of different types of functions such as $x^3 \sin x$, $x^2 e^{2x}$, $\sqrt{x} \ln x$, $e^x \sin 2x$, $x \tan^{-1} x$; (b) logarithmic and inverse circular functions such as $\ln x$, $\ln(1+x^2)$, $\sin^{-1} x$, $\tan^{-1} x$, where the second function is taken as unity.

Example 20. Find the integrals: (i) $\int x \cos x\,dx$; *(ii)* $\int x^2 e^{-x}\,dx$; *(iii)* $\int 1/x^2 \ln x\,dx$, $x > 0$; *(iv)* $\int \sin^{-1} x\,dx$.

(i) $$\int x\cos x\,\mathrm{d}x = x(\sin x) - \int (\sin x)\cdot 1\,\mathrm{d}x = x\sin x + \cos x + c;$$

(ii) $$\int x^2 e^{-x}\,\mathrm{d}x = x^2(-e^{-x}) - \int (-e^{-x})\cdot 2x\,\mathrm{d}x = -x^2e^{-x} + 2\int xe^{-x}\,\mathrm{d}x,$$

$$= -x^2e^{-x} + 2\left[x(-e^{-x}) - \int (-e^{-x})\cdot 1\,\mathrm{d}x\right],$$

$$= -e^{-x}(x^2+2x+2) + c;$$

(iii) $$\int \frac{1}{x^2}\ln x\,\mathrm{d}x = \ln x\left(-\frac{1}{x}\right) - \int\left(-\frac{1}{x}\right)\cdot\frac{1}{x}\mathrm{d}x = -\frac{1}{x}\ln x + \int\frac{\mathrm{d}x}{x^2},$$

$$= -\frac{1}{x}(\ln x + 1) + c;$$

(iv) $$\int \sin^{-1} x\,\mathrm{d}x = \int 1\cdot\sin^{-1} x\,\mathrm{d}x,$$

$$= \sin^{-1} x(x) - \int (x)\frac{1}{\sqrt{(1-x^2)}}\mathrm{d}x,$$

$$= x\sin^{-1} x + \sqrt{(1-x^2)} + c.$$

Integration by substitution

The method of substitution, or change of variable, is used in the cases of non-standard integrals. It involves change of integrand, change of differential and in a definite integral, change of limits.

Types of substitution

The form of substitution used depends on that of the integrand. Generally, a change of variable which simplifies a 'difficult term' will suffice as in the following cases:

(i) $\int \frac{dx}{2+\sqrt{x}}$ — let $x = u^2$; (ii) $\int \frac{x^2}{(x+1)^3}\,dx$ — let $x+1 = u$;

(iii) $\int \frac{dx}{e^x+e^{-x}}$ — let $e^x = u$; (iv) $\int (e^x+1)^5\,dx$ — let $e^x+1 = u$;

(v) $\int \frac{x-1}{\sqrt{(x+1)}}\,dx$ — let $x+1 = u^2$; (vi) $\int x^2(1-x)^8\,dx$ — let $1-x = u$.

There are however less obvious substitutions and it is useful to remember that:

(i) an integral involving the function $\sqrt{(a^2-x^2)}$ is usually best dealt with by using the substitution $x = a\sin\theta$;

(ii) an integral involving some function of x, $f(x)$ and the term $f'(x)\,dx$ can usually be evaluated by using the substitution $f(x) = u$, e.g.

$$\int \sqrt{(1+\sin x)}\cos x\,dx \text{ — let } 1+\sin x = u; \quad \int (1+x^3)^4 x^2\,dx \text{ — let } 1+x^3 = u;$$

$$\int \frac{x\,dx}{1+x^4} \text{ — let } x^2 = u.$$

Example 21. Evaluate: (i) $\int_0^1 \sqrt{(e^x-1)}\,dx$; (ii) $\int_0^1 x^2\,dx/[\sqrt{(4-x^2)}]$; (iii) $\int_0^{1/\sqrt{2}} x\,dx/[\sqrt{(1-x^4)}]$.

(i) Let $e^x - 1 = u^2$, so $e^x\,dx = 2u\,du$, $dx = 2u/(u^2+1)\,du$.
When $x = 0$, $u = 0$ and when $x = 1$, $u = \sqrt{(e-1)}$.

$$\therefore \int_0^1 \sqrt{(e^x-1)}\,dx = \int_0^{\sqrt{(e-1)}} u\cdot\frac{2u}{u^2+1}\,du = 2\int_0^{\sqrt{(e-1)}} \frac{u^2}{u^2+1}\,du,$$

$$= 2\int_0^{\sqrt{(e-1)}} \left(1-\frac{1}{u^2+1}\right)du,$$

$$= 2[u-\tan^{-1}u]_0^{\sqrt{(e-1)}},$$

$$= 2(\sqrt{(e-1)}-\tan^{-1}\sqrt{(e-1)}).$$

(ii) Let $x = 2\sin\theta$, so $dx = 2\cos\theta\,d\theta$ and $\sqrt{(4-x^2)} = 2\cos\theta$.
When $x = 0$, $\theta = 0$ and when $x = 1$, $\theta = \pi/6$.

$$\therefore \int_0^1 \frac{x^2\,dx}{\sqrt{(4-x^2)}} = \int_0^{\pi/6} \frac{4\sin^2\theta}{2\cos\theta}\cdot 2\cos\theta\,\theta = \int_0^{\pi/6} 4\sin^2\theta\,d\theta,$$

$$= 2\int_0^{\pi/6} (1-\cos 2\theta)\,d\theta,$$

$$= 2\left[\theta-\frac{\sin 2\theta}{2}\right]_0^{\pi/6},$$

$$= \frac{\pi}{3}-\frac{\sqrt{3}}{2}.$$

(iii) Let $x^2 = u$, so $2x\,dx = du$, $x\,dx = du/2$.

When $x = 0$, $u = 0$ and when $x = 1/\sqrt{2}$, $u = 1/2$.

$$\int_0^{1/\sqrt{2}} \frac{x\,dx}{\sqrt{(1-x^4)}} = \frac{1}{2}\int_0^{1/2} \frac{du}{\sqrt{(1-u^2)}},$$

$$= \frac{1}{2}[\sin^{-1} u]_0^{1/2},$$

$$= \frac{\pi}{12}.$$

(A) EXAMPLES 26

Integrate with respect to x:

1. $\dfrac{1}{(x+1)(x+2)}$.
2. $x\cos x$.
3. $\dfrac{1}{x^2(x-1)}$.
4. $(e^x+1)^3$.
5. xe^x.
6. $\ln x$.
7. $\dfrac{2x^2}{(x-1)(1+x^2)}$.
8. $x^3 \ln x$.
9. $x(1-x)^4$.
10. $x\sin 2x$.
11. $\dfrac{x^2}{x^2-1}$.
12. $x\sec^2 x$.
13. $\dfrac{3x+4}{\sqrt{(x+1)}}$.
14. x^2e^{2x}.
15. $\dfrac{1+3x^2}{(1-x)^2(1+x)}$.
16. $\dfrac{x}{\sqrt{(1-x^2)}}$.

Evaluate the following integrals:

17. $\displaystyle\int_2^5 \frac{2(x+1)\,dx}{(x-1)(2x-1)}$.
18. $\displaystyle\int_0^{\pi/2} x\cos\frac{x}{2}\,dx$.
19. $\displaystyle\int_0^1 \frac{x^2\,dx}{(x+1)^2}$.
20. $\displaystyle\int_1^2 \frac{dx}{x^2+3x+2}$.
21. $\displaystyle\int_0^2 \sqrt{(4-x^2)}\,dx$.
22. $\displaystyle\int_0^1 \tan^{-1} x\,dx$.
23. $\displaystyle\int_0^1 x\tan^{-1} x\,dx$.
24. $\displaystyle\int_0^1 \frac{x\,dx}{1+x^4}$.
25. $\displaystyle\int_{-1}^0 \frac{x^2\,dx}{(x-2)^2}$.
26. $\displaystyle\int_0^2 \ln(1+x)\,dx$.
27. $\displaystyle\int_{1/2}^1 \frac{dx}{x^2\sqrt{(1-x^2)}}$.
28. $\displaystyle\int_1^4 \frac{dx}{(1+x)\sqrt{x}}$.
29. Use the substitution $x^4+1 = u$, to evaluate $\int_1^2 dx/[x(x^4+1)]$.
30. Use the method of integration by parts to find: (i) $\int \sin^{-1} 2x\,dx$; (ii) $\ln(1+x^2)\,dx$.
31. Evaluate the integral $\int_0^1 dx/[(1+x^2)^{3/2}]$ by using the substitution $x = \tan\theta$.
32. If $I = \int e^x \sin x\,dx$, $I' = \int e^x \cos x\,dx$, show that $I = e^x \sin x - I'$ and $I' = e^x \cos x + I$. Hence by solving these simultaneous equations find $\int e^x \sin x\,dx$ and $\int e^x \cos x\,dx$.
33. Express $(1-3x)/[(2-x)(1+x^2)]$ in partial fractions and evaluate $\int_0^1 (1-3x)/[(2-x)(1+x^2)]\,dx$.
34. By using the substitution $e^x+1 = u$, evaluate $\int_0^1 e^{2x}/[(e^x+1)^2]\,dx$.
35. Evaluate the integral $\int_0^1 \sqrt{[(1-x)/x]}\,dx$ by using the substitution $x = \sin^2\theta$.

Area under a curve

In Fig. 30 *area* $A = \int_a^b y\,dx = \int_a^b f(x)\,dx.$

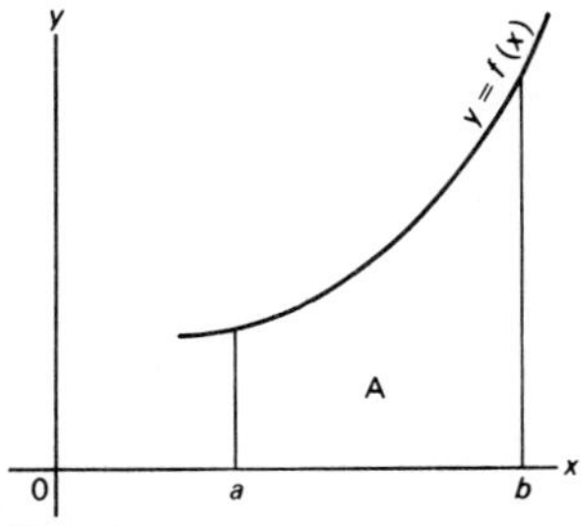

Fig. 30

Note
(i) A is positive for areas above the x-axis and negative for areas below the x-axis;
(ii) the area bounded by the arc of the curve from $y = c$ to $y = d$ and the y-axis is $\int_c^d x\,dy$.

Volume of revolution

The volume of revolution V formed when area A is rotated completely about the x-axis is given by

$$V = \pi \int_a^b y^2\,dx = \pi \int_a^b [f(x)]^2\,dx.$$

Note
(i) There is a corresponding result when the rotation is about the y-axis;
(ii) for a rotation about an axis parallel to the x-axis, say $y = k$, express the equation of the curve with this line as the x-axis.

Mean value

The mean value of y with respect to x in the interval $x = a$ to $x = b$,

$$= \frac{1}{b-a}\int_a^b y\,dx = \frac{1}{b-a}\int_a^b f(x)\,dx, b > a.$$

Centroid

If $(\bar{x}, \bar{y})$ are the coordinates of the centroid of area A,

$$\bar{x} = \frac{1}{A}\int_a^b xy\,dx = \frac{1}{A}\int_a^b xf(x)\,dx;$$

$$\bar{y} = \frac{1}{A}\int_a^b \frac{y^2}{2}\,dx = \frac{1}{2A}\int_a^b [f(x)]^2\,dx.$$

Example 22. Sketch the graph of $y = x/(2+x)$ for positive values of x and find: (i) the area bounded by the curve and the lines $x = 0$, $x = 1$, $y = 1$; (ii) the volume obtained when this area is rotated completely about the line $y = 1$.

(i) Area $A = 1 - \int_0^1 \frac{x\,dx}{2+x} = 1 - \int_0^1 \left(1 - \frac{2}{2+x}\right)dx,$

$= 1 - [x - 2\ln(2+x)]_0^1,$

$= 1 - 1 + 2\ln\frac{3}{2} = 2\ln\frac{3}{2}.$

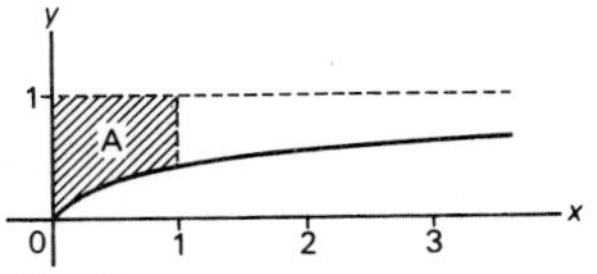

Fig. 31

(ii) Changing the x-axis to the line $y = 1$, the equation of the curve becomes $y+1 = x/(2+x)$, i.e. $y = -2/(2+x)$.

$$\text{Volume of revolution} = \pi \int_0^1 \left(-\frac{2}{2+x}\right)^2 \mathrm{d}x = 4\pi \int_0^1 \frac{\mathrm{d}x}{(2+x)^2},$$

$$= 4\pi\left[-\frac{1}{2+x}\right]_0^1,$$

$$= \frac{2\pi}{3}.$$

Parametric equations

When a curve is defined by parametric equations $x = f(t)$, $y = g(t)$, the corresponding results for area, volume of revolution and centroid for the arc of the curve between $t = t_1$ and $t = t_2$, are obtained by replacing x by $f(t)$, y by $g(t)$ and $\mathrm{d}x$ by $f'(t)\,\mathrm{d}t$ in the previous results.

$$\text{Area } A = \int_{t_1}^{t_2} g(t)f'(t)\,\mathrm{d}t;$$

$$\text{Volume } V = \pi \int_{t_1}^{t_2} [g(t)]^2 f'(t)\,\mathrm{d}t;$$

$$\text{Centroid of } A: \quad \bar{x} = \frac{1}{A}\int_{t_1}^{t_2} f(t)g(t)f'(t)\,\mathrm{d}t;\ \bar{y} = \frac{1}{2A}\int_{t_1}^{t_2} [g(t)]^2 f'(t)\,\mathrm{d}t.$$

Example 23. For the curve with parametric equations $x = 2t^3$, $y = 2+t-t^2$ find: (i) the area contained between the curve and the x-axis; (ii) the x-coordinate of the centroid of this area.

The curve cuts the x-axis where $y = 0$, i.e. $2+t-t^2 = 0$, $t = -1$ and 2.

(i) Area between curve and x-axis, $A = \int_{-1}^{2} (2+t-t^2)6t^2\,\mathrm{d}t,$

$$= \int_{-1}^{2} (12t^2+6t^3-6t^4)\,\mathrm{d}t,$$

$$= \left[4t^3 + \frac{3t^4}{2} - \frac{6t^5}{5}\right]_{-1}^{2},$$

$$= 18.9.$$

(ii) x-coordinate of centroid $= \frac{1}{A}\int_{-1}^{2} 2t^3(2+t-t^2)6t^2\,\mathrm{d}t,$

$$= \frac{1}{A}\int_{-1}^{2} (24t^5+12t^6-12t^7)\,\mathrm{d}t,$$

$$= \frac{1}{A}\left[4t^6 + \frac{12t^7}{7} - \frac{3t^8}{2}\right]_{-1}^{2},$$

$$= \frac{1}{18.9}\cdot 90.6$$

$$= 4.79.$$

(A) EXAMPLES 27

1. Find the area of the region enclosed by the curve $y = e^x - 1$, the line $x = 1$ and the x-axis. Also determine: (i) the volume generated when this area is rotated completely about the x-axis; (ii) the x-coordinate of the centroid of this region.
2. Find the mean value with respect to t of the function $2\sin 2t$ in the interval $t = \pi/8$ to $t = \pi/4$.
3. The curves $y^2 = 2x$, $x^3 = 4y$ intersect at the points (0,0) and (2,2). Find: (i) the area enclosed between the curves; (ii) the volume generated by rotating this area about the x-axis.
4. If O is the origin and P the point (p^2, p^3) on the curve with parametric equations $x = t^2$, $y = t^3$, show that the area bounded by the arc of the curve OP and the x-axis is $2p^5/5$ and find the volume of revolution of this area about the x-axis.
5. Find the mean value of $(1+\sin x)^2$ with respect to x in the interval $x = 0$ to $\pi/2$.
6. Show that the curves $y = 1+x^3$, $y = 3(x^2-1)$ intersect at the points $(-1,0)$, $(2,9)$ and find the area enclosed by the curves.
7. The region bounded by the x-axis, the line $x = \pi/2$ and the arc of the curve $y = \tan(x/2)$ from $x = 0$ to $x = \pi/2$ is rotated completely about the x-axis, show that the volume generated is $\pi(4-\pi)/2$.
8. Show that the curve with parametric equations $x = 2\cos t$, $y = \cos 2t$ cuts the x-axis at the points where $t = \pi/4$ and $3\pi/4$. Evaluate the area bounded by this portion of the curve and the x-axis.
9. Find the mean value of the function $x\cos x$ in the interval $x = 0$ to $x = \pi/2$.
10. Find the area bounded by the curve $y = \ln x/\sqrt{x}$, the x-axis between $x = 1$ and $x = e$ and the line $x = e$.
11. The portion of the curve $y = (e^x + e^{-x})/2$ between $x = 0$ and $x = a$ is rotated completely about the x-axis. Find the volume of the solid of revolution formed.
12. Find the area of the region bounded by the curve $y = x(x-3)^4$ and the part of the x-axis between $x = 0$ and $x = 3$. Also find the x-coordinate of the centroid of this area.
13. The area bounded by the curve $y = (2x+1)/(x+1)$ and the lines $x = 0$, $x = 2$, $y = 2$ is rotated completely about the line $y = 2$. Find the volume generated.
14. Find the area bounded by the arc of the curve $y = x\sin x$ between $x = 0$ and $x = \pi$ and the x-axis. Also find the mean values of xy with respect to x in this interval.
15. The region bounded by the curve $y = 2\sqrt{x}/(1+2x^2)$, the x-axis and the lines $x = 0$, $x = 1$ is rotated about the x-axis. Find the volume swept out.
16. Prove that the area bounded by the curve $y = x(1-\ln x)$, the line $x = e^{-1}$ and the part of the x-axis between $x = e^{-1}$ and $x = e$ is $(e^2 - 5e^{-2})/4$.
17. Find the volume generated by the rotation through one revolution about the x-axis of the region between the x-axis and that part of the curve $y = 2\cos x - 1$ for which $|x| < \pi$ and $y > 0$.
18. Sketch the curves $y = xe^{-x}$, $y = xe^x$ and calculate the area bounded by the curves and the line $x = 1$.
19. Find the coordinates of the points of intersection of the curve $y^2 = x^3$ and the line $y = mx$ where $m > 0$. The area enclosed between the curve and the line is rotated about the x-axis, show that the volume generated is $\pi m^8/12$.
20. Find the area bounded by the curve $y = 10/(3x-2)$, the x-axis and the lines $x = 7/3$, $x = 22/3$. Also find the value of a for which the line $x = a$ bisects this area.
21. Find the area bounded by the curve with parametric equations $x = t^3$, $y = 1-t^2$ and the x-axis. Also find the coordinates of the centroid of this area.
22. Sketch the curves $y = \sin x$, $y = \sin 2x$ for $0 \leqslant x \leqslant \pi$ and show that they intersect at the origin O and the point P $(\pi/3, \sqrt{3}/2)$. Show that the area enclosed between the curves from O to P is 1/4.
23. If $x^2 + 4y^2 = 4$, find the mean value of: (i) xy^2; (ii) xy with respect to x in the interval $0 \leqslant x \leqslant 2$.

APPROXIMATE NUMERICAL INTEGRATION

$$\int_a^b f(x)\,dx = \textit{area under curve } y = f(x) \textit{ between } x = a \textit{ and } x = b.$$

An approximate value of a definite integral is obtained by estimating the numerical value of this area; there are two recognised methods of doing this using (i) the trapezoid rule; (ii) Simpson's rule.

Trapezoid rule

The area under the curve $y = f(x)$ is split up into a number of areas by ordinates drawn at equal intervals. In the case shown in Fig. 32, there are 6 areas and the interval $h = (b-a)/6$.

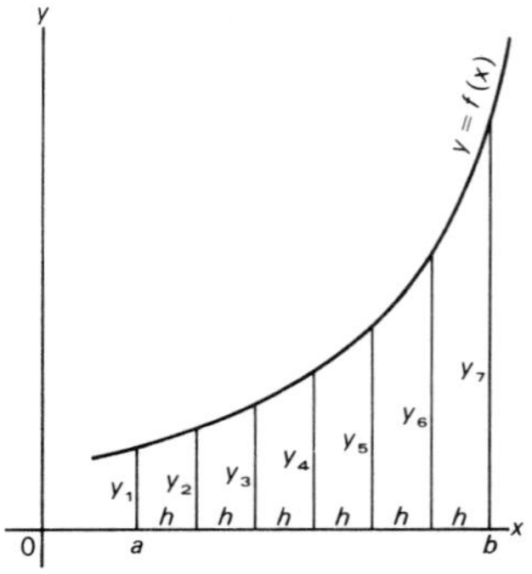

Fig. 32

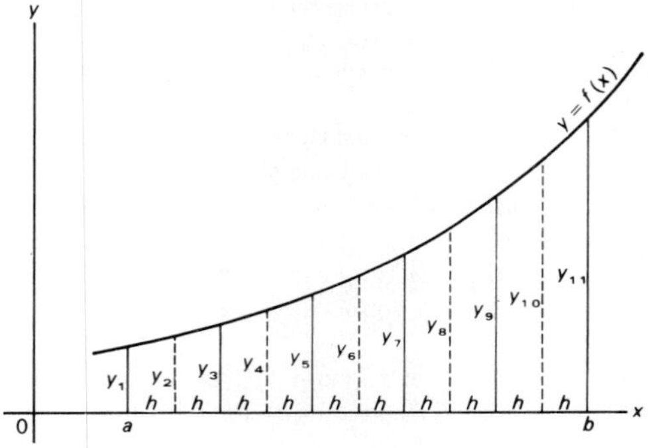

Fig. 33

Each sub-area is treated as a trapezium leading to the result in the case shown,

$$\int_a^b f(x)\,dx \approx \frac{1}{2}(y_1+y_2)h+\frac{1}{2}(y_2+y_3)h+\ldots+\frac{1}{2}(y_6+y_7)h,$$

$$\approx \frac{1}{2}h\,[y_1+y_7+2(y_2+y_3+y_4+y_5+y_6)].$$

Generally,

$$\int_a^b f(x)\,dx \approx \frac{1}{2}(\textit{interval between ordinates})\,[\textit{first ordinate} + \textit{last ordinate} + \textit{twice the sum of the other ordinates}].$$

Example 24. Tabulate values of $\sqrt{(1+x^2)}$ *at unit intervals from* $x = 1$ *to* $x = 6$ *and use these values to estimate by the trapezoid rule, the mean value of* $\sqrt{(1+x^2)}$ *in this interval.*

x	1	2	3	4	5	6
$\sqrt{(1+x^2)}$	1.414	2.236	3.162	4.123	5.099	6.083

Using the trapezoid rule

$$\int_1^6 \sqrt{(1+x^2)}\,dx \approx \frac{1}{2}[1.414+6.083+2(2.236+3.162+4.123+5.099)],$$

$$\approx 18.37.$$

Mean value of $\sqrt{(1+x^2)}$ in the interval $1 \leqslant x \leqslant 6$

$$\approx \frac{18.37}{5} = 3.67.$$

Simpson's rule

In Fig. 33, the area under the curve $y = f(x)$ is split up into 5 sub-areas by the ordinates y_1, y_3, y_5, y_7, y_9, y_{11}, the other ordinates, shown dotted, are the mid-ordinates of the sub-areas.

Simpson's rule states that the area of a sub-area $\approx$ 1/6(width of sub-area) [first ordinate + last ordinate + 4 (mid-ordinate)].

So in this case

$$\int_a^b f(x)\,dx \approx \frac{h}{3}(y_1+y_3+4y_2)+\frac{h}{3}(y_3+y_5+4y_4)+\frac{h}{3}(y_5+y_7+4y_6)$$

$$+\frac{h}{3}(y_7+y_9+4y_8)+\frac{h}{3}(y_9+y_{11}+4y_{10}),$$

$$\approx \frac{h}{3}[y_1+y_{11}+2(y_3+y_5+y_7+y_9)+4(y_2+y_4+y_6+y_8+y_{10})].$$

Generally

$$\int_a^b f(x)\,dx \approx \frac{1}{3}(\textit{interval between ordinates})\,[\textit{first ordinate}$$

$$+\textit{last ordinate}$$

$$+2(\textit{remaining odd ordinates})+4(\textit{even ordinates})].$$

Note Remember that the use of Simpson's Rule requires an odd number of ordinates.

Example 25. Calculate the approximate value of $\int_1^3 x(x-1)^{1/2}\,dx$ using Simpson's rule with five ordinates.

x	1	1.5	2	2.5	3
$x(x-1)^{1/2}$	0	1.06	2	3.08	4.24
	y_1	y_2	y_3	y_4	y_5

By Simpson's rule,

$$\int_1^3 x(x-1)^{1/2}\,dx \approx \frac{(0.5)}{3}[0+4.24+2(2)+4(1.06+3.08)],$$

$$\approx 4.13.$$

The integral can be evaluated by using the substitution $u^2 = x-1$; correct to 3 significant figures its value is 4.15.

(A) EXAMPLES 28

Using the trapezoid rule with the number of ordinates stated, obtain approximations to the values of the following integrals:

1. $\int_0^2 \sqrt{(1+x^2)}\,dx$, using ordinates at intervals of 0.2.
2. $\int_0^1 \frac{dx}{\sqrt{(1+x^2)}}$, using ordinates at intervals of 0.1.
3. $\int_0^2 2^x\,dx$, using 11 ordinates.
4. $\int_1^3 (1+x^2)^{1/3}\,dx$, using 5 ordinates.
5. $\int_0^{\pi/2} e^{\sin x}\,dx$, using 5 ordinates.
6. $\int_2^3 (x^3-4)^{1/2}\,dx$, using 6 ordinates.

Using Simpson's rule with the number of ordinates stated, obtain approximations to the values of the following integrals:

7. $\int_0^3 \sqrt{(1+x^2)}\,dx$, using 7 ordinates.
8. $\int_0^2 \ln(1+x^2)\,dx$, using 5 ordinates.
9. $\int_1^3 2^x\,dx$, using 9 ordinates.
10. $\int_0^\pi \sqrt{\sin x}\,dx$, using 5 ordinates.
11. Use the trapezoid rule to obtain the approximate value of $\int_0^1 dx/(1+x^2)$ taking ordinates at intervals of 0.1 and use the result to obtain an approximate value of π.
12. Evaluate $\int_0^2 x^2(2-x^2)\,dx$ exactly and also obtain an approximate value of the integral by using Simpson's rule with 5 ordinates.
13. Approximate to the integral $\int_0^1 \sqrt{(1-x^3)}\,dx$ using the trapezoid rule with 5 ordinates.
14. Evaluate $\int_0^{1/2} (1-x^2)^{-1/2}\,dx$: (i) by using the trapezoid rule with 6 ordinates and working to 4 significant figures; (ii) exactly in terms of π. Hence estimate the value of π.
15. Show that $\int_0^{\pi/3} \tan x\,dx = \ln 2$. Using Simpson's rule with 5 ordinates, obtain an approximate value of the integral and hence of ln 2.

FIRST ORDER DIFFERENTIAL EQUATIONS

Standard forms of equations with variables separable

(i) $f(x)+g(y)\frac{dy}{dx} = 0$; solution $\int f(x)\,dx + \int g(y)\,dy = c$;

(ii) $f(x)\frac{dy}{dx} + g(y) = 0$; solution $\int \frac{dy}{g(y)} + \int \frac{dx}{f(x)} = c$.

Example 26. Find the solution of the equation $dy/dx = xy/(x^2+1)$ for which $y = 2\sqrt{2}$ when $x = 1$.

Separating the variables $$\int \frac{dy}{y} = \int \frac{x\,dx}{x^2+1},$$

integrating $$\ln y = \frac{\ln(x^2+1)}{2} + c;$$

but $y = 2\sqrt{2}$, when $x = 1$, so $$\ln 2\sqrt{2} = \frac{\ln 2}{2} + c,$$

$$c = \ln 2\sqrt{2} - \ln\sqrt{2} = \ln 2.$$

$\therefore$ $$\ln y = \ln\sqrt{(x^2+1)} + \ln 2$$

i.e. $$y = 2\sqrt{(x^2+1)}.$$

Example 27. The rate of decrease of temperature of a hot body is proportional to the temperature difference of the body and the surrounding medium. If the temperature of a hot body at time t min after the body was put into a large room at temperature α°C, assumed constant, is θ°C, show that $\theta - \alpha = Ae^{-kt}$ where k is a positive constant and A an arbitrary constant. Given α = 20°C and that the time taken for the body to cool from 60°C to 50°C is 5 mins, find the temperature after a further 5 minutes.

We have $d\theta/dt = -k(\theta - \alpha)$, where k is a positive constant,

separating the variables $$\int \frac{d\theta}{\theta - \alpha} = -k\,dt,\ \theta > \alpha,$$

integrating $$\ln(\theta - \alpha) = -kt + c,$$

$$\theta - \alpha = e^{-kt+c}$$
$$= e^c e^{-kt},$$
$$\theta - \alpha = Ae^{-kt}, \quad \text{writing } e^c = A.$$

Initially when $t = 0$, $\theta = 60°$ and $\alpha = 20°$,

so $$40 = Ae^{\circ};\ A = 40;$$

also when $t = 5$, $\theta = 50°$,

so $$30 = 40e^{-5k};\ e^{-5k} = \frac{3}{4}.$$

$\therefore$ when $t = 10$, $$\theta - 20 = 40e^{-10k},$$
$$= 40(e^{-5k})^2,$$
$$= 22.5.$$

After 10 minutes the temperature of the body is 42.5°C.

Example 28. A particle moving in a straight line passes through a point O with velocity u. When displaced from O a distance x the retardation of the particle is x^2v^3, where v is the velocity at that instant. Show that $1/v = x^3/3 + 1/u$ and find the time taken for the particle to travel a distance b from O.

Acceleration $= v\dfrac{dv}{dx} = -x^2v^3,$

separating the variables $-\displaystyle\int \frac{dv}{v^2} = \int x^2\,dx,$

integrating $\dfrac{1}{v} = \dfrac{x^3}{3}+c;$

but $v = u$ when $x = 0$, $c = \dfrac{1}{u},$

$\therefore$ $\dfrac{1}{v} = \dfrac{x^3}{3}+\dfrac{1}{u}.$

To find t in terms of x, write $v = \dfrac{dx}{dt};$

$$\frac{dt}{dx} = \frac{x^3}{3}+\frac{1}{u}$$

separating the variables $\displaystyle\int dt = \int\left(\frac{x^3}{3}+\frac{1}{u}\right)dx,$

integrating $t = \dfrac{x^4}{12}+\dfrac{x}{u}+c;$

but $x = 0$ when $t = 0$, $c = 0,$

$\therefore$ $t = \dfrac{x^4}{12}+\dfrac{x}{u},$

and when $x = b$, $t = \dfrac{b^4}{12}+\dfrac{b}{u}.$

(A) EXAMPLES 29

Find the general solutions of the differential equations:

1. $\dfrac{dy}{dx} = 4x.$
2. $\dfrac{dy}{dx}+\dfrac{1}{x^2} = 0.$
3. $\dfrac{dy}{dx} = y.$
4. $\dfrac{dy}{dx} = \dfrac{x}{y}$
5. $y\dfrac{dy}{dx} = x^2.$
6. $y^2\dfrac{dy}{dx} = 2x+1.$
7. $x\dfrac{dy}{dx} = y^2.$
8. $xy\dfrac{dy}{dx} = 1.$
9. $(x+1)\dfrac{dy}{dx} = y.$
10. $(x-2)\dfrac{dy}{dx} = x(y+1).$
11. $x^2y\dfrac{dy}{dx} = y^2-1.$
12. $(1+x^2)\dfrac{dy}{dx} = x(1+y^2).$
13. Obtain the solution of the equation $x^2\,dy/dx+y = 1$ for which $y = 1+e$ when $x = 1$.
14. Solve the equation $dv/dt+kv = g$ where k, g are constants, given that $v = 0$ when $t = 0$.
15. Find the general solution of the equation $x\,dy/dx+y(1+x^2) = 0$, giving the result in the form $y = f(x)$.

16. Find y in terms of x given that $dy/dx = y(1-y)$ and that $y = 1/2$ when $x = 0$.
17. The rate of increase of p is proportional to p^2. Given that $p = 1$ when $t = 0$ and $p = 2$ when $t = 1$, find p in terms of t, the time.
18. The rate of decrease of q is $k(q+1)$, where k is a constant. Given that $q = 2$ when the time, $t = 0$, find the relationship between q, t and k.
19. A radioactive substance disintegrates at a rate km, where k is a positive constant and m the mass remaining at time t. If m_0 is the initial mass, show that $m = m_0 e^{-kt}$.
20. The daily price £y of an article is decreasing at the rate $k\sqrt{y}$ where k is a positive constant. Given $y = C$ when $t = 0$, find y in terms of k, C and the time t.
21. Given that $p+1 = k/q$ and that the rate of decrease of q is constant and equal to k, express p in terms of the time t if it is also given that $p = 0$ when $t = 0$.
22. A particle is projected vertically upwards with speed u. If the particle experiences a retardation equal to $g+kv$, where g, k are positive constants and v the velocity after time t, show that the particle attains its greatest height after a time $\ln[(g+ku)/g]k$.

(B) MISCELLANEOUS EXAMPLES

1. Evaluate: (i) $\int_0^1 (x^2+4x-1)/[(2+x)(1+x^2)]\,dx$; (ii) $\int_0^{\pi/3} \sin^3 x\,dx$; (iii) $\int_0^2 dx/[\sqrt{(32-2x^2)}]$.
2. Show on a diagram the region defined by the inequalities $y \geqslant 0$, $y \leqslant x^2$, $y \leqslant 2x-x^2$ and calculate the area of this region.
3. (i) Solve the equation $dy/dx = (1+y^2)/(1+x^2)$ given that $y = 2$ when $x = 1$; (ii) find the general solution of the equation $x\,dy/dx = y[(1+y)/(y-1)]-y$.
4. Evaluate: (i) $\int_{-1}^1 (x^2+6x+7)/[(x+2)(x+3)]\,dx$; (ii) $\int_0^1 dx/(4-x^2)$.
5. Use the substitution $x = a\sin\theta$ to evaluate the integral $\int_0^{a/2} dx/[(a^2-x^2)^{3/2}]$.
6. Prove that the area bounded by the two parabolas $ay = 2x^2$, $y^2 = 4ax$ is $2a^2/3$.
7. Find the volume generated when the region bounded by the curve $y = x\sin x$ for $0 \leqslant x \leqslant \pi/2$, the ordinate $x = \pi/2$ and the x-axis is rotated completely about the x-axis.
8. Evaluate: (i) $\int_0^1 x^2(1-x)^8\,dx$; (ii) $\int_0^1 (e^x+1)^4\,dx$; (iii) $\int_0^3 x\ln(1+x)\,dx$.
9. Evaluate $\int_2^4 \ln x/x\,dx$, $x > 0$: (i) by using the substitution $u = \ln x$; (ii) by using the trapezoid rule with 4 strips, i.e. 5 ordinates. Give each answer correct to three significant figures.
10. Given $y = \ln x$ and that the rate of increase of y at time t is $k(x-a)$, where k, a are constants, show that $(x-a)/x = Ae^{akt}$, where A is an arbitrary constant.
11. Evaluate: (i) $\int_1^2 (x^2+2)\,dx/(x+1)$ correct to 2 decimal places; (ii) $\int_0^{\pi/6} \cos x\,dx/(1+\cos 2x)$ using the substitution $u = \sin x$.
12. Sketch the curve $27y^2 = x^3$ and find the equation of the tangent to the curve at the point P(12,8). Verify that this tangent cuts the curve again at the point Q(3, −1). If O is the origin, find the area enclosed by the arcs OP, OQ of the curve and the line PQ.
13. Differentiate $(\ln x)^2$ with respect to x and hence evaluate $\int_1^e x(\ln x)^2\,dx$.
14. By applying Simpson's rule to the integral $\int_{n-1}^{n+1} dx/x$, $n > 1$, obtain the approximation $\ln[(n+1)/(n-1)] \approx [1/(n-1)+1/(n+1)+4/n]/3$.
15. Given that $t = \tan(\theta/2)$, show that $\int_0^{\pi/2} d\theta/(1+5\cos\theta+5\sin\theta) = \int_0^1 dt/[(3-t)(1+2t)]$ and hence evaluate this integral.
16. The rate of increase of the number of bacteria in a colony at time t is proportional to n, the number present at that time. Show that $n = Ae^{kt}$, where A, k are constants. If the original number of bacteria was n_0 and the number increased to $5n_0$ in 2 sec, find the constants A and k.
17. Evaluate: (i) $\int_{-1}^1 x^2\,dx/(4-x^2)$; (ii) $\int_0^{\pi/4} \tan x(1+\cos^2 x)\,dx$; (iii) $\int_0^1 x^2/[\sqrt{(4-x^2)}]\,dx$.
18. If $y = e^x+e^{-x}$, find the mean values of: (i) y^2; (ii) xy with respect to x in the interval $x = 0$ to $x = 1$.
19. Find: (i) the area; (ii) the volume of revolution about the x-axis; (iii) the x-coordinate of the centroid of the region bounded by the ellipse $x = a\cos\theta$, $y = b\sin\theta$ and the positive x- and y-axes.
20. Estimate the value of the integral $\int_1^9 dx/[(2+\sqrt{x})^2]$ using Simpson's rule with nine ordinates and compare the result with the exact value obtained by using a suitable substitution.
21. At the instant when its radius is r, the volume of a sphere is increasing at the rate $\pi(R^3-r^3)$, where R is a constant. Express the rate of increase of the volume in terms of the rate of increase of the radius r and show that $4r^2\,dr/dt = R^3-r^3$. If initially the volume is zero, find the value of the time t when the volume is $\pi R^3/6$.

22. Prove that: (i) $\int_0^1 x^2\,dx/[(x+1)^2] = 3/2 - 2\ln 2$; (ii) $\int_0^{2\pi} |\sin x|\,dx = 2$.
23. For the curve $y = (x+1)/(x+2)$, find: (i) the area bounded by the curve, the x-axis and the ordinates $x = 0$, $x = 2$; (ii) the volume obtained when this area is rotated about the line $y = 1$.
24. Obtain approximate values of the integral $\int_0^1 \sqrt{(4-x^4)}\,dx$ by: (i) using the trapezoid rule with 6 ordinates; (ii) by expanding the integrand as a power series as far as the term in x^{12}.
25. Find the constants A, B, C if $(3x^2 - ax)/[(x-2a)(x^2+a^2)] \equiv A/(x-2a) + (Bx+C)/(x^2+a^2)$, where a is a constant. Hence show that $\int_0^a (3x^2 - ax)\,dx/[(x-2a)(x^2+a^2)] = \pi/4 - 3\ln 2/2$.
26. Evaluate: (i) $\int_0^{\pi/2} \cos^4 x \sin^3 x\,dx$; (ii) $\int_0^1 x\tan^{-1} x\,dx$; (iii) $\int_0^1 e^{2x}\,dx/(1+e^x)$.
27. The rate of decay of a radioactive substance at any instant is proportional to the amount of the substance remaining at that instant. If the initial amount is A gm, and the amount remaining after time t hr is x gm, show that $x = Ae^{-kt}$ where k is a positive constant. If the amount remaining is reduced from $A/2$ to $A/3$ in 8 hrs, prove that the initial amount was halved in about 13.7 hrs.
28. (i) Find the value of a if $\int_0^1 (x-a)\,dx/[(x+1)(3x+1)] = 0$; (ii) using the substitution $x = 1/u$ prove that $\int_{1/c}^{c} \ln x\,dx/(x^2+1) = 0$.

Coordinate Geometry

THE STRAIGHT LINE

The straight line

(*i*) *An equation of the first degree in x and y represents a straight line and conversely;*

(*ii*) *the equation* $y = mx + c$ *represents a straight line with gradient m;*

(*iii*) *the equation of the straight line passing through the point* (h, k) *and having gradient m is* $(y - k) = m(x - h)$;

(*iv*) *the equation of the straight line joining the points* (x_1, y_1), $(x_2\ y_2)$, *is* $(y - y_1)/(y_2 - y_1) = (x - x_1)/(x_2 - x_1)$;

(*v*) *if* m_1, m_2 *are the gradients of perpendicular lines, then* $m_1 m_2 = -1$;

(*vi*) *if* $P(x', y')$ *divides the line joining the points* (x_1, y_1), (x_2, y_2) *in the ratio* $m:n$, *then* $x' = (mx_2 + nx_1)/(m+n)$; $y' = (my_2 + ny_1)/(m+n)$.

Note

(a) If P is the mid-point of the line its coordinates are $(x_1 + x_2)/2$, $(y_1 + y_2)/2$;

(b) for internal division, *m* and *m* are both positive and for external division, either *m* or *n* is taken as negative.

(*vii*) *The length of the perpendicular from the point* (h,k) *to the line* $ax + by + c = 0$ *is* $\pm(ah + bk + c)/[\sqrt{(a^2 + b^2)}]$, *the sign being chosen to make the perpendicular from the origin positive;*

(*viii*) *an angle* θ *between lines with gradients* m_1, m_2 *is given by* $\tan\theta = (m_1 - m_2)/(1 + m_1 m_2)$;

(*ix*) *the equation of any line passing through the point of intersection of two given lines with equations* $L_1 \equiv a_1x + b_1y + c_1 = 0$, $L_2 \equiv a_2x + b_2y + c_2 = 0$ *is* $L_1 + \lambda L_2 = 0$, *where* λ *is a parameter.*

Example 1. Find the equations of the lines through the point $(-2, -1)$ *each inclined at* $45°$ *to the line* $y = 2x + 3$.

If *m* is the gradient of one of the required lines,

$$\tan 45° = \frac{m-2}{1+2m},$$

$$1+2m = m-2,$$

$$m = -3.$$

As the required lines are perpendicular, the gradient of the second line is 1/3 and the equation of the lines are $y+1 = -3(x+2)$, $y+1 = (x+2)/3$, i.e.

$$y+3x+7 = 0 \quad \text{and} \quad 3y-x+1 = 0.$$

Example 2. *Find the equation of the chord joining the points (p^2, p^3), (q^2, q^3), $p \neq q$.*

$$\text{Gradient of chord} = \frac{p^3-q^3}{p^2-q^2} = \frac{(p-q)(p^2+pq+q^2)}{(p-q)(p+q)} = \frac{p^2+pq+q^2}{p+q}, \text{ as } p \neq q;$$

equation of chord is $$y-p^3 = \frac{p^2+pq+q^2}{p+q}(x-p^2),$$

i.e. $$x(p^2+pq+q^2)-y(p+q) = p^2q^2.$$

Example 3. *Find the equation of the line with gradient 2/3 which passes through the point of intersection of the lines $y-x = 2$, $2y+x = 1$.*

Any line passing through the point of intersection of the given lines has an equation of the form:

$$y-x-2+\lambda(2y+x-1) = 0;$$

gradient of this line, $$\frac{1-\lambda}{1+2\lambda} = \frac{2}{3}; \text{ i.e. } \lambda = \frac{1}{7}.$$

So the required equation is $y-x-2+\frac{1}{7}(2y+x-1) = 0$,

or $$3y-2x-5 = 0.$$

(A) EXAMPLES 30

1. Find the length of the perpendicular from the point $(2, -3)$ to the line joining the points $(-1, 0)$, $(1, 2)$.
2. Find the tangent of the acute angle between the lines $y-x+1 = 0$, $2y+x-3 = 0$.
3. Find: (i) the gradient; (ii) the equation, of the line joining the points $(ap^2, 2ap)$, $(aq^2, 2aq)$.
4. Find the equation of the line passing through the common point of the lines $y = x+1$, $2y = 3x-2$ and through the origin.
5. P divides the line joining the origin to the point $(cp, c/p)$ in the ratio 2:1. Find the coordinates of P when: (i) the division is internal; (ii) the division is external.
6. Find the coordinates of the foot of the perpendicular drawn from the point $(a, 0)$ to the line with equation $y = mx + a/m$.
7. Find: (i) the equation of the perpendicular bisector of the line joining the points $(a, 0)$, $(0, b)$; (ii) the coordinates of the point where this line meets the x-axis.
8. Points P, Q divide the line joining the points $(-3, 1)$, $(1, 4)$ internally and externally in the ratio 3:5. Find the coordinates of the mid-point of PQ.

9. What are the perpendicular distances of the origin from: (i) the line $3y-4x+10=0$; (ii) the line $3y-4x-5=0$? Use the results to find the perpendicular distance between these parallel lines.
10. The vertices of a triangle are A$(-1,2)$, B$(1,5)$, C$(3,2)$. If A$'$ is the mid-point of BC, find the coordinates of G, the point dividing AA$'$ internally in the ratio 2:1.
11. Find angle AOB, where O is the origin and A, B the points $(1,4)$, $(4,1)$.
12. Find the equation of the line through the origin which divides the line joining the points $(-1,2)$, $(3,4)$ internally in the ratio 3:2.
13. A line AB is produced to C such that λBC = AB. Given that the coordinates of A, B respectively are $(-2,0)$, $(3,2)$, find the coordinates of C in terms of λ.
14. A line of gradient m is inclined to the line $2y-x+1=0$ at an angle of $\tan^{-1}(1/2)$. Find the possible values of m.
15. Find the distance between the parallel lines $y=mx+c$, $y=mx+d$.
16. Find the equation of the line passing through the point of intersection of the lines $3x-y+1=0$, $2x+3y=4$ which is perpendicular to the first of these lines.
17. Find the coordinates of the reflection of the point $(2,5)$ in the line $y=x-1$.
18. A line of gradient m is drawn through the point $(2,3)$ and meets the x- and y-axes at the points P, Q respectively. Find, in terms of m, the coordinates of the point which divides PQ internally in the ratio 2:3.
19. The equations of the lines AB, AD are $x-y=2$, $2x+3y=4$ respectively and C is the point $(4,5)$. Find: (i) the equation of AC; (ii) the acute angles CAB, CAD.
20. Show that for all values of m, the line $x(5m+1)+y(2m-3)+2-3m=0$, passes through the point of intersection of two fixed lines and state the equations of these lines.
21. A line L is drawn through the point A$(0,2)$ and cuts the line $y=3x-5$ at P and the line $x+y=8$ at Q. If AQ = 2AP, find the equation of L.
22. A line parallel to the line $2x+y=0$ cuts the x-axis at A and the y-axis at B. The perpendicular bisector of AB meets the y-axis at C. Show that the gradient of AC $=-3/4$ and find the tangent of the acute angle between AC and the bisector of angle AOB, where O is the origin.
23. The points A$(-8,9)$, C$(1,2)$ are opposite vertices of a parallelogram ABCD; the sides BC, CD have equations $x+7y-15=0$, $x-y+1=0$ respectively. Calculate: (i) the coordinates of D; (ii) the tangent of the acute angle between the diagonals; (iii) the length of the perpendicular from A to the side CD; (iv) the area of the parallelogram.
24. The coordinates of opposite vertices of a square are $(1,1)$, $(4,7)$. Find the coordinates of the other vertices.
25. Points A, B, C have coordinates $(0,6)$, $(1,-1)$, $(9,3)$ respectively. Find: (i) the coordinates of the point D which is such that angles BAD, BCD are each 90°; (ii) the angle ABC.

THE CIRCLE

The circle

(i) *The equation of the circle, centre (a,b), radius r is $(x-a)^2+(y-b)^2=r^2$;*

(ii) *the general equation of a circle is $x^2+y^2+2gx+2fy+c=0$; where $g^2+f^2-c>0$.*

Note

(a) An equation of the 2nd degree in x and y having equal coefficients of x^2 and y^2 and no term in xy, usually represents a circle;

(b) the coordinates of the centre of a circle whose equation is expressed in the general form and its radius are determined by expressing the equation in the form (i).

For the circle with equation (ii), the centre is the point $(-g, -f)$ and the radius is $\sqrt{(g^2+f^2-c)}$.

(*iii*) *The equation of the tangent at the point* (x_1, y_1) *on the circle with the general equation (ii) is* $xx_1+yy_1+g(x+x_1)+f(y+y_1)+c = 0$;

(*iv*) *the square of the lengths of the tangents from the point* (h,k) *to the circle with equation (ii) is* $h^2+k^2+2gh+2fk+c$;

(*v*) *the equation of any circle passing through the common points of the circles* $S_1 \equiv x^2+y^2+2g_1x+2f_1y+c_1 = 0$, $S_2 \equiv x^2+y^2+2g_2x+2f_2y+c_2 = 0$ *is* $S_1+\lambda S_2 = 0$, *where* λ *is a parameter.*

Note The equation of the common chord of the two circles is $S_1-S_2 = 0$.

(*vi*) *The equation of any circle passing through the points of intersection of the circle* $S_1 = 0$ *and the line* $L \equiv ax+by+c = 0$ *is* $S_1+\lambda L = 0$, *where* λ *is a parameter.*

In dealing with problems involving circles which touch each other or which cut orthogonally, think of the relationships between radii and the distance between the centres.

Example 4. Find the equation of the circle which passes through the points $A(2,5)$, $B(4,3)$ *and has its centre C on the line* $x+y = 3$.

C is the point of intersection of the line $x+y = 3$ and the perpendicular bisector of AB.

Mid-point of AB has coordinates $(3,4)$; gradient of perpendicular bisector of AB $= 1$; equation of perpendicular bisector of AB is

$$y-4 = 1(x-3),$$

i.e.

$$y-x = 1.$$

Solving this equation with the equation $x+y = 3$, gives $x = 1$, $y = 2$.

So the centre C is $(1,2)$ and the radius $(CA) = \sqrt{10}$.

Equation of the circle is $(x-1)^2+(y-2)^2 = 10$,

i.e.

$$x^2+y^2-2x-4y-5 = 0.$$

Example 5. Prove that the circles $S_1 \equiv x^2+y^2+2g_1x+2f_1y+c_1 = 0$, $S_2 \equiv x^2+y^2+2g_2x+2f_2y+c_2 = 0$ *cut orthogonally if* $2g_1g_2+2f_1f_1f_2 = c_1+c_2$.

The centres of the circles are $C_1(-g_1, -f_1)$, $C_2(-g_2, -f_2)$; if A is a point of intersection the circles cut orthogonally when angle $C_1AC_2 = 90°$.

By Pythagoras,

$$(C_1C_2)^2 = (AC_1)^2+(AC_2)^2$$

where

$$(C_1C_2)^2 = (g_1-g_2)^2+(f_1-f_2)^2,$$
$$AC_1^2 = (\text{radius of } S_1)^2 = g_1^2+f_1^2-c_1,$$
$$(AC_2)^2 = (\text{radius of } S_2)^2 = g_2^2+f_2^2-c_2.$$

Substituting in these values and simplifying leads to the required result.

Example 6. Find the condition that the circle $S \equiv x^2+y^2+2gx+2fy+c = 0$ *should cut the circle* $S' \equiv x^2+y^2+2g'x+2f'y+c' = 0$ *at the ends of a diameter of the circle* S'.

The condition is satisfied if the centre $C'(-g', -f')$ of the circle S' lies on the common chord of the two circles.

Equation of common chord is

$$x(2g-2g')+y(2f-2f')+c-c' = 0,$$

and the required condition is

$$(-g')(2g-2g')+(-f')(2f-2f')+c-c' = 0,$$

i.e.
$$2g'^2+2f'^2-2gg'-2ff'+c-c' = 0.$$

(A) EXAMPLES 31

1. Find the coordinates of the centre and the radius of the circle $2x^2+2y^2-4x+6y-3 = 0$.
2. Find the equation of the tangent to the circle $x^2+y^2-6x+4y+3 = 0$ at the point $(0, -1)$.
3. Prove that the length of the tangents to the circle $2x^2+2y^2+6x-7y+1 = 0$ from the point $(2,3)$ is 3.
4. Find the coordinates of the points where the common chord of the circles $x^2+y^2-5x-y-7 = 0$, $x^2+y^2-3x-4y-5 = 0$ meets the axes of x and y.
5. Show that the circles $x^2+y^2+6y+8 = 0$, $x^2+y^2-12x-10y-60 = 0$ touch each other and find the equation of the tangent to the circles at the common point.
6. Find the equation of the circle which passes through the origin and the common points of the circles $x^2+y^2-4x+8y-30 = 0$, $x^2+y^2+8x-16y+30 = 0$.
7. Find the equation of the diameter of the circle $x^2+y^2+6x-4y-23 = 0$ which passes through the point $(5, -2)$. Also find the equation of the perpendicular diameter.
8. Using the fact that an angle in a semicircle is a right angle, show that the equation of the circle having the points (x_1, y_1), (x_2, y_2) at the ends of a diameter is $(x-x_1)(x-x_2)+(y-y_1)(y-y_2) = 0$.
9. Show that the circles $x^2+y^2-16x-10y+8 = 0$, $x^2+y^2+6x-4y-36 = 0$ intersect at right angles.
10. Find the coordinates of the centres of the circles which can be drawn to pass through the points $(1,1)$, $(2,0)$ and touch the line $x = 0$.
11. Find the equation of the circle which passes through the points $(1,0)$, $(4,0)$ and $(0,2)$. Show that the circle touches both the y-axis and the line $3x+4y = 3$.
12. Find the equation of the circle with centre on the line $x+y = 4$ which passes through the points $(1,0)$, $(0,2)$.
13. Show that the equation of the locus of the centre of a circle of radius 5 which touches the circle $S \equiv x^2+y^2-4x-60 = 0$ externally is the circle $x^2+y^2-4x-165 = 0$. Hence find the centre, in the positive quadrant, of the circle of radius 5 which touches the circle S externally and also touches the x-axis.
14. Find the equation of the circle passing through the point $(1,1)$ which meets the circle $x^2+y^2-4x-6y-10 = 0$ at the ends of the chord $x+y = 6$.
15. Find the equations of the circles which touch both axes and pass through the point $(6,3)$. Also find: (i) the equations of the tangents to the circles at the point $(6,3)$; (ii) the tangent of the acute angle at which the circles intersect at the point $(6,3)$.
16. Show that the locus of the point whose coordinates are given by $x = 3\cos\theta+2$, $y = 3\sin\theta-4$ is a circle. Show the circle on a diagram and indicate the points on it corresponding to $\theta = \pi/4$ and $\theta = \pi$.
17. The tangents from the point P, coordinates (X, Y), to the circles $x^2+y^2+6x = 0$, $x^2+y^2+4x-2y-4 = 0$ are equal in length. Find the equation relating X and Y and deduce that P lies on the common chord of the two circles.
18. The line $3x+4y-8 = 0$ is a common tangent to circles with centres $(0,1)$ and $(3,2)$. Find the equations of these circles and show that another common tangent is parallel to the x-axis.
19. Show that the line $y = mx$ meets the circle $x^2+y^2-4x-3y+4 = 0$ at the points whose x-coordinates are the roots of the equation $x^2(1+m^2)-x(4+3m)+4 = 0$. Hence find the values of m for which the line is a tangent to the circle.

20. Find the centre and radius of the circle $S \equiv 5x^2+5y^2-4x-22y+20 = 0$ and show that the tangent to the circle at the point P(6/5, 8/5) passes through the origin O. Also find the coordinates of the centre of the circle S′ which is the reflection of S in the tangent OP.

LOCI

Loci

The methods used in the determination of the Cartesian equation of a locus are illustrated in the following examples:

Example 7. Find the Cartesian equation of the locus of a point P which moves such that its distance from the point A(1, −4) is twice its distance from the line x = −1.

Let P have coordinates (x, y); distance PA $= \sqrt{[(x-1)^2+(y+4)^2]}$; distance of P from the line $x = -1$ is $x+1$.

$$\therefore \qquad \sqrt{[(x-1)^2+(y+4)^2]} = 2(x+1),$$

squaring and simplifying, $3x^2-y^2+10x-8y-13 = 0$, the equation of the locus of P.

Example 8. Find the (x, y) equation of the curve traced out by the point P (1 + sin t, 2 cos 2t) as the parameter t varies.

If P is the point (x, y),

$$x = 1+\sin t,\ y = 2\cos 2t = 2(1-2\sin^2 t);$$

eliminating $\sin t$,

$$y = 2-4(x-1)^2,$$

i.e.

$$y = -2(2x^2-4x+1), \text{ the required equation.}$$

Because of the limitations on the value of $\sin t$, P describes only that part of this curve for which $0 \leqslant x \leqslant 2$.

Example 9. The line y = t(x − t) where t is a parameter, meets the axes of x and y at the points L, M respectively. Find: (i) the coordinates of the point P which divides LM internally in the ratio 1:2; (ii) the (x, y) equation of the locus of P as t varies.

L is the point $(t, 0)$ and M the point $(0, -t^2)$;

$$\therefore \qquad P \text{ is the point } \left(\frac{2t}{3}, -\frac{t^2}{3}\right).$$

So if P has coordinates (x, y),

$$x = \frac{2t}{3};\ y = -\frac{t^2}{3}$$

and eliminating t, $4y+3x^2 = 0$, the equation of the locus of P.

(A) EXAMPLES 32

In each of the examples 1–6, find the (x, y) equation of the locus of the variable point P.

1. The distance of P from the origin is twice its distance from the point $(-3, 0)$.
2. The distance of P from the line $y = 2$ is equal to its distance from the point $(0, -3)$.
3. The distances of P from the points $(-2, 1)$, $(2, 0)$ are in the ratio $2:3$.
4. The distance of P from the line $x = -a$ is equal to its distance from the point $(a, 0)$.
5. The sum of the distances of P from the points $(-2, 0)$, $(2, 0)$ is constant and equal to 6.
6. The sum of the squares of the distances of P from the points $(\pm a, 0)$ is $2k^2$, $k > a$.
7. Find the (x, y) equations of the loci of the following points as the parameter t varies: (i) $(4t, 4/t)$; (ii) $(2t-1, t^2)$; (iii) $(3t+2, t+1)$; (iv) (t^2, t^3); (v) $(t+t^{-1}, t-t^{-1})$; (vi) $3\cos t, 3\sin t)$; (vii) $(4\cos t, \sin t)$; (viii) $(2\cos t, \cos 2t)$; (ix) $(1-4\cos t, 2+3\sin t)$; (x) $(t/(1+t), 1/(1+t))$; (xi) $(\tan t, \tan 2t)$; (xii) $(t/(1+t^3), t^2/(1+t^3))$.
8. A line of gradient m passing through the point $(2, 1)$ meets the coordinate axes at the points L, M; find the Cartesian equation of the locus of the mid-point of LM as m varies.
9. Find the (x, y) equation of the locus of the point (p^2+q^2, pq) when p, q vary such that $p-q = 1$.
10. Find the equation of the locus of the centre of a circle which passes through the origin and touches the line $x+y = 2a$, where a is a constant.
11. A line of gradient m passing through the point $(1, 2)$ meets the axes of x and y at the points H, K respectively and the parallelogram OHKL, where O is the origin, is completed. Find the (x, y) equation of the locus of L for varying values of m.
12. Find the Cartesian equation of the locus of the point $[p^2+pq+q^2, pq(p+q)]$ when p, q vary such that $pq = -1$.
13. Find the $(x\,y)$ equation of the locus of the mid-point of the line joining the fixed point $(a, 0)$ to the variable point $(a\cos\theta, b\sin\theta)$, where θ is a parameter.
14. The coordinates of points A, B, C are $(-a, 0)$, $(-a, 4a)$, $(3a, 4a)$ respectively. The point P is taken on BC such that $BP = tBC$ and the point Q is taken on AP such that $AQ = tAP$. Find the equation of the locus of Q as the parameter t varies.
15. Obtain the equation of the locus of the mid-point of the line joining the point A$(7, 8)$ to the variable point P$(2t+3, t-9)$ and find the value of t when AP is perpendicular to this locus.
16. T is a variable point with coordinates $(t, 0)$ and R is the point $(3, 1)$. The perpendicular to TR at T meets the y-axis at Q and P is the mid-point of TQ. Find the (x, y) equation of the locus of P as t varies.

THE PARABOLA

The parabola

Cartesian equation $y^2 = 4ax$ in Fig. 34, $a > 0$.

Focus S is the point $(a, 0)$.

Parametric equations $x = at^2$, $y = 2at$.

Gradient $\dfrac{dy}{dx} = \dfrac{2a}{y} = \dfrac{1}{t}$.

Equations of tangent and normal at the point $(at^2, 2at)$

tangent $yt - x = at^2$;

normal $y + tx = 2at + at^3$.

Chord joining the points $P(ap^2, 2ap)$ *and* $Q(aq^2, 2aq)$

gradient of chord $= \dfrac{2}{p+q}$;

equation of chord $(p+q)y - 2x = 2apq$.

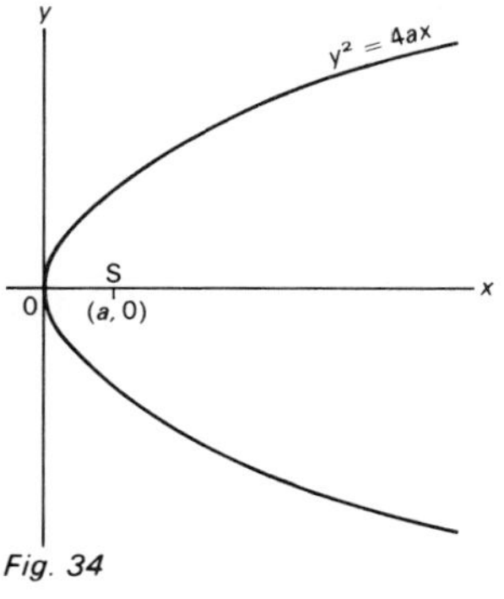

Fig. 34

Connections between the parameters of related points

Let P, Q be points on the parabola $y^2 = 4ax$ with coordinates $(ap^2, 2ap)$, $(aq^2, 2ap)$. To find the relationship between p and q when:

(i) chord PQ has a specified gradient m—equate the gradient of PQ to m;

(ii) chord PQ passes through a specified point $A(h, k)$—either express the fact that (h, k) satisfies the equation of chord PQ or equate the gradient of the chord to the gradient of PA or QA;

(iii) chord PQ is normal to the curve at P—equate the gradient of the chord to the gradient of the normal to the curve at P;

(iv) the lines joining P and Q to some specified point $A(h, k)$ are perpendicular—express the fact that the product of the gradients of lines AP, AQ is -1;

(v) the tangents at P and Q to the curve are perpendicular—express the fact that the products of the gradients of these tangents is -1;

(vi) chord PQ is divided by a given line in a specified ratio $\lambda:1$—write down the coordinates of the point dividing PQ in the ratio $\lambda:1$ and express the fact that these coordinates satisfy the equation of the given line.

Example 10. The normal at the point $P(p^2, 2p)$ to the parabola $y^2 = 4x$ meets the curve again at the point $Q(q^2, 2q)$. Find the relationship between p and q.

At P,
$$\frac{dy}{dx} = \frac{2}{y} = \frac{1}{p};$$

so the gradient of the normal at P $= -p$.

$$\therefore \qquad -p = \text{gradient of chord PQ} = \frac{2}{p+q},$$

i.e.
$$p(p+q) = -2.$$

Example 11. Find the coordinates of R, the point of intersection of the tangents to the parabola $y^2 = 4ax$ at the points $P(ap^2, 2ap)$, $Q(aq^2, 2aq)$ and show that the join of R to the mid-point M of PQ is parallel to the axis of the curve.

Tangent at P, $\qquad yp - x = ap^2;$

tangent at Q $\qquad yq - x = aq^2.$

Solving these equations, the coordinates of R are $x = apq$, $y = a(p+q)$. As M is the point $[a(p^2+q^2)/2, a(p+q)]$, R and M have the same y-coordinate and hence RM is parallel to the x-axis which is the axis of the parabola.

Example 12. Variable points $P(ap^2, 2ap)$, $Q(aq^2, 2aq)$ on the parabola $y^2 = 4ax$ are such that the chord PQ passes through the fixed point $A(0, a)$. Find the Cartesian equation of the locus of M, the mid-point of PQ.

Equation of chord PQ,
$$(p+q)y - 2x = 2apq;$$
as the chord passes through $A(0, a)$
$$p+q = 2pq. \qquad (1)$$

Taking M as the point (x, y)

$$x = \frac{a}{2}(p^2+q^2),\ y = a(p+q). \qquad (2)$$

From equations (1) and (2),
$p+q = y/a$; $pq = y/2a$ and writing $p^2+q^2 = (p+q)^2-2pq$,

we have $$x = \frac{a}{2}\left(\frac{y^2}{a^2}-\frac{y}{a}\right),$$

i.e. $$y^2-ay = 2ax.$$

(A) EXAMPLES 33

1. Sketch the parabolas: (i) $y^2 = 4x$; (ii) $y^2+4x = 0$; (iii) $x^2 = 4y$.
2. Sketch the curves with the parametric equations: (i) $x = 2t^2, y = 4t$; (ii) $x = -t^2, y = 2t$; (iii) $x = 8t, y = 4t^2$.
3. Find the equation of the tangent to the curve $y^2 = 8x$ at the point $(2p^2, 4p)$ and write down the equation of the tangent at the point $(2/p^2, 4/p)$.
4. What is the gradient of the tangent to the curve $y^2 = 4x$ at the point $(t^2, 2t)$? Deduce the coordinates of the point of contact of the tangent to the curve of gradient m.
5. Find the equations of the tangent and normal to the curve $x^2 = 4y$ at the point $(2t, t^2)$.
6. Find the equation of the normal to the parabola $y^2 = 4ax$ at the point $P(ap^2, 2ap)$. This normal meets the x-axis at G and N is the foot of the perpendicular from P to the x-axis; show that the length NG is constant and equal to $2a$.
7. Points $P(ap^2, 2ap)$, $Q(aq^2, 2aq)$ lie on the parabola $x = at^2, y = 2at$. Find: (i) the equation of the chord PQ; (ii) the relationship between p and q if the chord passes through the focus $(a, 0)$.
8. Write down, or find, the equation of the tangent to the curve $x = t^2, y = 2t$ at the point parameter t. Find the values of t for which the tangent passes through the point A(2, 3) and hence find the equations of the tangents drawn from A to the curve.
9. Find the equations of the tangent and normal to the parabola $y^2 = 4ax$ at the point $P(at^2, 2at)$. The tangent and normal meet the x-axis at T and N respectively, show that $PT^2+PN^2 = 4a^2(1+t^2)^2$.
10. Show that the line $y = mx+2/m$ is a tangent to the parabola $y^2 = 8x$ for all values of m and state the coordinates of the point of contact.
11. Find the coordinates of R the point of intersection of the tangents to the curve $y^2 = 4x$ at the points $P(p^2, 2p)$, $Q(q^2, 2q)$. If the gradient of the chord PQ is equal to k, a constant, show that R lies on the line $y = 2/k$.
12. Find the equation of the tangent to the parabola $y^2 = 4ax$ at the point $(at^2, 2at)$. Show that the foot of the perpendicular from the point $(a, 0)$ on to this tangent lies on the y-axis.
13. Show that the normals to the curve $y^2 = 4x$ at the points $P(p^2, 2p)$, $Q(q^2, 2q)$ meet at the point (α, β) where $\alpha = 2+p^2+pq+q^2$, $\beta = -pq(p+q)$.
14. A line of gradient m drawn through the point $(2a, 0)$ meets the parabola $y^2 = 4ax$ at the points P and Q. Show that the y-coordinate of the mid-point of PQ is $2a/m$.
15. The chord joining the points $P(ap^2, 2ap)$, $Q(aq^2, 2aq)$ on the parabola $y^2 = 4ax$ passes through the focus $(a, 0)$. Prove: (i) $pq = -1$; (ii) the tangents at P and Q to the curve are perpendicular.
16. Write down the equation of the tangent at the point $(t^2, 2t)$ on the curve $y^2 = 4x$. Show that when $t = -2$, this tangent touches the curve $xy = 2$ and deduce the equation of the common tangent to the two curves.
17. The points $P(2ap, ap^2)$, $Q(2aq, aq^2)$ move on the parabola $x^2 = 4ay$ such that $p+q = 2$. Show that the gradient of the chord PQ is constant and find the (x, y) equation of the locus of the mid-point of PQ.
18. Find the equation of the normal to the curve $y^2 = 8x$ at the point $P(2p^2, 4p)$; this normal meets the x-axis at L and Q is the point on PL produced such that $PQ = 3PL/2$. Find: (i) the coordinates of Q in terms of p; (ii) the equation of the locus of Q as p varies.

19. The points $P(ap^2, 2ap)$, $Q(aq^2, 2aq)$ on the parabola $y^2 = 4ax$ are such that the tangent at P to the curve is parallel to the chord OQ where O is the origin. Show that $q = 2p$ and find the coordinates of R, the point of intersection of the tangents to the curve at P and Q in terms of p. Deduce the (x, y) equation of the locus of R as p varies.
20. Show that the normal to the parabola $y^2 = 4x$ at the point $P(p^2, 2p)$ cuts the curve again at the point $Q(q^2, 2q)$ where $(p-q)^2 = 4p^2+8+4/p^2$.
21. The chord PQ, where P, Q are the points $(ap^2, 2ap)$, $(aq^2, 2aq)$ on the parabola $y^2 = 4ax$, subtends a right angle at the origin O. Prove that the equation of the locus of the mid-point of PQ is the parabola $y^2 = 2a(x-4a)$.

THE RECTANGULAR HYPERBOLA

The rectangular hyperbola

Cartesian equation $\quad xy = c^2$. (Fig. 35).

The axes 0x, 0y are asymptotes to the curve.

Parametric equations $\quad x = ct,\ y = \dfrac{c}{t}$.

Gradient $$\frac{dy}{dx} = -\frac{c^2}{x^2} = -\frac{1}{t^2}.$$

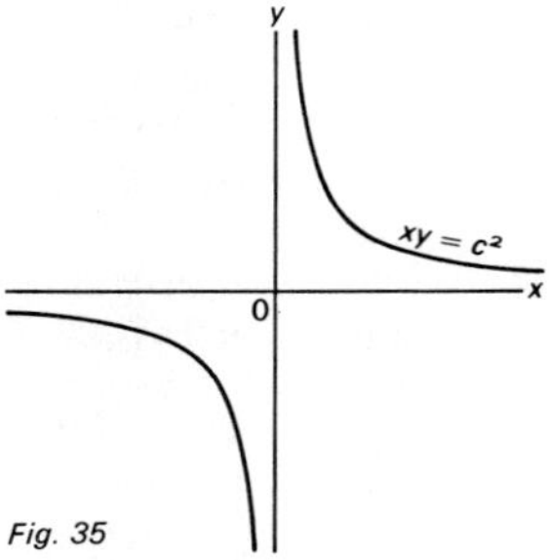

Fig. 35

Equations of tangent and normal at the point $(ct, c/t)$

tangent $\quad t^2y+x = 2ct;$

normal $\quad ty-t^3x = c(1-t^4).$

Chord joining the points $P(cp, c/p)$, $Q(cq, c/q)$

gradient of chord $= -\dfrac{1}{pq}$;

equation of chord $\quad ypq+x = c(p+q).$

Connections between the parameters of related points.

These are dealt with as in the case of the parabola.

Example 13. Find the equations of the tangents which can be drawn from the point $A(-3, 1)$ to the rectangular hyperbola $xy = 1$.

Let $P(t, 1/t)$ be any point on the curve. Then the tangent at P has the equation
$$t^2y+x = 2t;$$
this tangent passes through A if
$$t^2-2t-3 = 0,$$
i.e.
$$t = 3, -1.$$
So the required equations are $9y+x-6 = 0$ and $y+x+2 = 0$.

Example 14. Find the coordinates of T, the point of intersection of the tangents to the curve $xy = c^2$ at the points $P(cp, cp^{-1})$, $Q(cq, cq^{-1})$. If T lies on the curve $xy = k^2$ for all positions of P and Q, prove that $4c^2pq = k^2(p+q)^2$.

Equations of the tangents at P and Q are:

$$p^2y+x = 2cp,$$

$$q^2y+x = 2cq.$$

Subtracting $\quad y(p^2-q^2) = 2c(p-q),$

$$y = \frac{2c}{p+q};\ x = \frac{2cpq}{p+q}.$$

T is the point $\quad \left(\frac{2cpq}{p+q}, \frac{2c}{p+q}\right).$

As T lies on the curve $xy = k^2$,

$$\frac{2cpq}{p+q}\cdot\frac{2c}{p+q} = k^2,$$

i.e. $\quad 4c^2pq = k^2(p+q)^2.$

Example 15. The line $y = t(x-2t)$ meets the rectangular hyperbola $xy = 4$ at the points P, Q. Find: (i) the coordinates of M, the mid-point of PQ, in terms of t; (ii) the equation of the locus of M as t varies.

Solving the equations $y = t(x-2t)$, $xy = 4$ by substituting for y;

$$xt(x-2t) = 4,$$

$$x^2t-2t^2x-4 = 0.$$

The roots x_1, x_2 of this equation are the x coordinates of P and Q.

$$\therefore \quad x \text{ coordinate of M} = \frac{(x_1+x_2)}{2},$$

$$= \frac{1}{2}\cdot\frac{2t^2}{t} = t;$$

as M lies on the line $y = t(x-2t)$,

$$y \text{ coordinate of M} = -t^2.$$

Taking M as the point (x, y),

$$x = t,\ y = -t^2,$$

and eliminating t,

$$y+x^2 = 0,$$

the equation of the locus of M.

(A) EXAMPLES 34

1. Sketch the curves: (i) $xy = 4$; (ii) $xy = -4$; (iii) $(x-1)y = 1$.
2. Sketch the curves with the parametric equations: (i) $x = 3t,\ y = 3t^{-1}$; (ii) $x = t,\ y = -t^{-1}$; (iii) $x+1 = 2t, y = 2t^{-1}$.
3. The tangent at the point $P(2t, 2t^{-1})$ on the rectangular hyperbola $xy = 4$ meets the coordinate axes at the points Q and R. Show that P is the mid-point of QR.
4. Write down, or find, the equation of the tangent at the point $P(t, t^{-1})$ to the curve $xy = 1$ and find the coordinates of the points on the curve where the tangent is parallel to the line $4y+x = 0$.

5. Find the coordinates of the points of contact of the tangents which can be drawn from the point $(-5, 1)$ to the rectangular hyperbola $xy = 4$.
6. A line gradient m is drawn through the point $(4, 6)$ to meet the curve $xy = 8$ at the points P and Q. Find the coordinates of the mid-point of PQ in terms of m.
7. The normal at the point $P(cp, c/p)$ to the rectangular hyperbola $xy = c^2$ meets the curve again at the point $Q(cq, c/q)$, show that $q = -1/p^3$.
8. Prove that it is not possible to find two points on the curve $xy = c^2$ at which the tangents to the curve are perpendicular.
9. The tangents at the points $P(p, p^{-1})$, $Q(q, q^{-1})$ to the curve $xy = 1$ meet the x-axis at the points P′, Q′ respectively and the chord PQ meets this axis at K. Show that K is the mid-point of P′Q′.
10. Find the equation of the tangent to the rectangular hyperbola $xy = 4$ at the point $(2t, 2t^{-1})$. This tangent meets the x-axis at A and the y-axis at B; C is the point dividing AB internally in the ratio 3:2. Find: (i) the coordinates of C in terms of t; (ii) the (x, y) equation of the locus of C as t varies.
11. The tangent to the curve $xy = 16$ at the point $P(4t, 4t^{-1})$ cuts the x-axis at Q and the y-axis at R. The line through Q parallel to the y-axis meets the curve at T and the line through R parallel to the x-axis meets the curve at S. Show that TS is parallel to RQ.
12. If the normal to the curve $xy = c^2$ at the point $P(cp, c/p)$ meets the curve again at $Q(cq, c/q)$, show that $c^2PQ = OP^3$.
13. Find the non-zero value of t for which the line $yt - x = t^2$ is a tangent to the rectangular hyperbola $xy = 16$. Deduce the equation of the common tangent to the rectangular hyperbola and the parabola $y^2 = 4x$.
14. The points $P(cp, cp^{-1})$, $Q(cq, cq^{-1})$, $R(cr, cr^{-1})$ on the curve $xy = c^2$ are such that QR subtends a right angle at P. Show that: (i) $p^2 = -1/qr$; (ii) QR is parallel to the normal at P.
15. Find the equation of the chord joining the points $P(cp, c/p)$, $Q(cq, c/q)$ on the rectangular hyperbola $xy = c^2$. If PQ produced meets the asymptotes of the curve at the points P′, Q′, prove that PP′ = QQ′.
16. P is the point $(cp, c/p)$ on the curve $xy = c^2$ and N is the foot of the perpendicular from P to the x-axis. The tangent to the curve at P meets the y-axis at M and the line through M parallel to the x-axis meets the curve at Q. Find the coordinates of Q and show that NQ is the tangent at Q.
17. The tangent at the point $P(p, p^{-1})$ to the curve $xy = 1$ meets the asymptotes of the curve at the points A and B and the normal at P meets the lines $y = \pm x$ at the points C and D. Show that A, B, C, D are the vertices of a square.

THE ELLIPSE

The ellipse

Cartesian equation $\dfrac{x^2}{a^2}+\dfrac{y^2}{b^2} = 1.$ (Fig. 36).

In the case shown in Fig. 36, A′A is the major axis and B′B the minor axis.

Parametric equations $x = a\cos\theta,\ y = b\sin\theta.$

Gradient $\dfrac{dy}{dx} = -\dfrac{b^2x}{a^2y} = -\dfrac{b\cos\theta}{a\sin\theta}.$

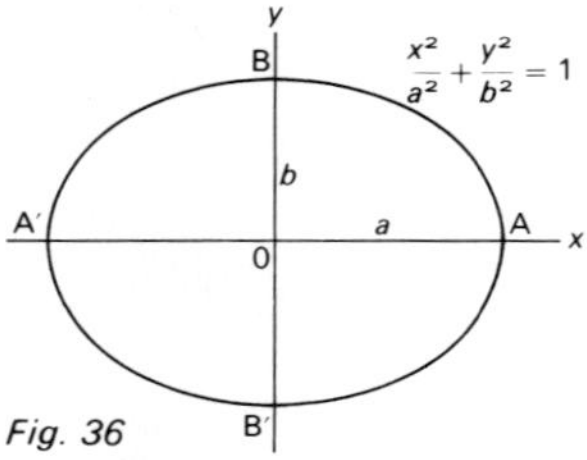

Fig. 36

Equations of the tangent and normal at the point $(a\cos\theta, b\sin\theta)$

tangent $$\frac{x\cos\theta}{a}+\frac{y\sin\theta}{b} = 1;$$

normal $$\frac{ax}{\cos\theta}-\frac{by}{\sin\theta} = a^2-b^2.$$

Example 16. *Show that the locus of the point $P(4+5\cos\theta, 2-3\sin\theta)$ as θ varies, is an ellipse and state the coordinates of the centre and the lengths of the axes.*

Let P be the point (x, y), so $x = 4+5\cos\theta$, $y = 2-3\sin\theta$;

$$\cos\theta = \frac{x-4}{5},\ \sin\theta = \frac{2-y}{3}.$$

The equation of the locus P is

$$\left(\frac{x-4}{5}\right)^2+\left(\frac{2-y}{3}\right)^2 = 1.$$

i.e.

$$\frac{(x-4)^2}{25}+\frac{(y-2)^2}{9} = 1.$$

The locus is an ellipse with centre $(4, 2)$ and axes of lengths 10 and 6 units.

Example 17. *Find the coordinates of the points of contact of the tangents to the ellipse $x^2/4+y^2/3 = 1$ which can be drawn from the point $A(2, 1)$.*

Let $P(2\cos\theta, \sqrt{3}\sin\theta)$ be a point of contact; so the tangent at P to the ellipse passes through A.

The equation of the tangent at P is

$$\frac{x\cos\theta}{2}+\frac{y\sin\theta}{\sqrt{3}} = 1,$$

as $(2, 1)$ satisfies this equation,

$$\cos\theta+\frac{\sin\theta}{\sqrt{3}} = 1,$$

$$\sqrt{3}\cos\theta+\sin\theta = \sqrt{3}.$$

This equation is solved by expressing $\sqrt{3}\cos\theta+\sin\theta$ as $2\sin(\theta+\pi/3)$;

we have

$$\sin\left(\theta+\frac{\pi}{3}\right) = \frac{\sqrt{3}}{2},$$

$$\theta = 0, \frac{\pi}{3}.$$

The coordinates of the points of contact are $(2, 0)$ and $(1, 3/2)$.

Example 18. *The tangent and normal at the point $P(a\cos\phi, b\sin\phi)$ on the ellipse $b^2x^2+a^2y^2 = a^2b^2$ meet the x-axis at the points T, G respectively. If N is the foot of the perpendicular from P to the x-axis and O is the origin, prove that $OT\cdot NG = b^2$.*

Equation of tangent,

$$\frac{x\cos\phi}{a}+\frac{y\sin\phi}{b} = 1,$$

so T is the point

$$\left(\frac{a}{\cos\phi}, 0\right).$$

Equation of normal, $\frac{ax}{\cos\phi}-\frac{by}{\sin\phi}=a^2-b^2,$

So G is the point $\left(\frac{a^2-b^2}{a}\cos\phi, 0\right).$

As N is the point $(a\cos\phi, 0)$,

$$NG = a\cos\phi-\frac{a^2-b^2}{a}\cos\phi=\frac{b^2}{a}\cos\phi.$$

$$\therefore \qquad OT\cdot NG=\frac{a}{\cos\phi}\cdot\frac{b^2}{a}\cos\phi=b^2.$$

(A) EXAMPLES 35

1. Sketch the curves: (i) $x^2/9+y^2/4=1$; (ii) $x^2+4y^2=4$; (iii) $9x^2+4y^2=36$; (iv) $(x-1)^2/4+(y+1)^2/2=1$.
2. Find the (x, y) equations of the parametric curves: (i) $x=2\cos\theta$, $y=\sin\theta$; (ii) $x=\sqrt{2}\cos\theta$, $y=2\sin\theta$; (iii) $x=1+\sqrt{3}\cos\theta$, $y=\sin\theta$.
3. Find the equation of the tangent to the ellipse $x=2\cos\theta$, $y=\sin\theta$ at the point where $\theta=3\tan^{-1}/4$. If this tangent meets the axes of the curve at A and B, find the area of triangle AOB, where O is the centre of the ellipse.
4. The locus $x=4\cos\theta$, $y=3\sin\theta$ meets the positive x and y-axes at A and B. Find: (i) the equation of the perpendicular bisector of AB; (ii) the coordinates of the points where this line meets the axes.
5. The chord joining the points $(a\cos\theta, b\sin\theta)$, $(a\cos\phi, b\sin\phi)$ on the ellipse $b^2x^2+a^2y^2=a^2b^2$ passes through the origin. Find the relationship between the angles θ and ϕ.
6. Find the equation of the tangent to the locus $x=3\cos\theta$, $y=2\sin\theta$ at the point $(3\cos\phi, 2\sin\phi)$. State the value of the parameter θ at the point $(3\sin\phi, 2\cos\phi)$ and write down the equation of the tangent at this point.
7. Show that the equation of the tangent to the ellipse $b^2x^2+a^2y^2=a^2b^2$ at the point (x_1, y_1) can be expressed in the form $b^2xx_1+a^2yy_1=a^2b^2$.
8. P is the point $(3\cos\theta, 2\sin\theta)$ on the ellipse $4x^2+9y^2=36$ and N is the foot of the perpendicular from P to the major axis of the curve; NP is produced to Q such that PQ = PN. Write down the coordinates of Q and find the (x, y) equation of its locus as θ varies.
9. The tangent to the locus $x=\sqrt{3}\cos\theta$, $y=\sin\theta$ at the point $(\sqrt{3}\cos\phi, \sin\phi)$ is parallel to the line $3y+x=0$. Find the two values of ϕ in the range $0\leqslant\phi\leqslant 2\pi$.
10. The tangent at the point $P(a\cos\theta, b\sin\theta)$ on the ellipse $b^2x^2+a^2y^2=a^2b^2$ meets the tangent at the point $(a, 0)$ at Q. Show that the line joining the origin to Q is parallel to the line joining the point $(-a, 0)$ to P.
11. Find the equation of the normal to the curve $x^2+3y^2=3a^2$ at the point $(\sqrt{3}a\cos\theta, a\sin\theta)$. If this normal passes through the negative end of the minor axis of the curve find the value of θ in the range $0<0<\pi/2$.
12. P and Q are points on the ellipse $x=a\cos\theta$, $y=b\sin\theta$ where the parameter θ is equal to ϕ and $\pi/2+\phi$. Show that $OP^2+OQ^2=a^2+b^2$, where O is the origin.
13. Find the four values of θ in the range $0\leqslant\theta\leqslant 2\pi$ for which the point $(a\cos\theta, b\sin\theta)$ lies on the rectangular hyperbola $4xy=ab$ and deduce the coordinates of the common points of this hyperbola and the ellipse $x^2/a^2+y^2/b^2=1$.
14. The ellipse $x=a\cos\theta$, $y=b\sin\theta$ cuts the positive x-axis at A and the positive y-axis at B. If the perpendicular bisector of AB meets the x-axis at P and M is the mid-point of AB, prove that the area of $\triangle$PMA is $b(a^2+b^2)/8a$.
15. Find the equation of the tangent to the ellipse $x^2/2+y^2=1$ at the point $(\sqrt{2}\cos\theta, \sin\theta)$. Show that the two tangents to the curve from the point $(0, \sqrt{3})$ are perpendicular and find the coordinates of the points of contact of these tangents.

16. Show that the points $(a\cos\theta, b\sin\theta)$, $(a\cos(\theta+\pi/2), b\sin(\theta+\pi/2))$ on the ellipse $x^2/a^2+y^2/b^2 = 1$ are such that the tangent to the curve at one is parallel to the line joining the origin to the other.
17. The normal at the point parameter ϕ on the locus $x = \sqrt{2}a\cos\theta$, $y = a\sin\theta$ meets the axes at the points M and N. Express the coordinates of the mid-point of MN in terms of ϕ and hence find the (x, y) equation of the locus of this point as ϕ varies.
18. Show that the equation of the chord joining the points with parameters $\alpha+\beta$ and $\alpha-\beta$ on the ellipse $x = a\cos\theta$, $y = b\sin\theta$ is $x\cos\alpha/a+y\sin\alpha/b = \cos\beta$.
19. P is the point $(a\cos\theta, a\sin\theta)$ on the circle $x^2+y^2 = a^2$ and PN is the perpendicular from P to the x-axis. Show that the locus of the point Q which divides PN internally in the ratio 2:3 is an ellipse and state the lengths of its semi-major and semi-minor axes.
20. The tangent to the ellipse $x = a\cos\theta$, $y = b\sin\theta$ at the point $P(a\cos\phi, b\sin\phi)$ meets the x-axis at T and the y-axis at U and the normal at P meets these axes at M, N respectively. Prove: (i) that NT is perpendicular to MU; (ii) that the locus of the mid-point of MN as ϕ varies is an ellipse.

(B) MISCELLANEOUS EXAMPLES

1. A, B are the fixed points $(a, 0)$, $(-a, 0)$ respectively. Show that the locus of a point P which moves such that its distances from A, B are in the ratio $\lambda:1$, where $\lambda > 0$, is a circle of radius $2a\lambda/(\lambda^2-1)$.
2. Show that for all values of m, the line $x(2m-3)+y(3-m)+1-2m = 0$ passes through a fixed point and determine the coordinates of this point.
3. Show that for all values of c, the equation $x(x-1)+y(y-1) = c(x+y-1)$ represents a circle passing through the points $(1, 0)$, $(0, 1)$. Find: (i) the equation of such a circle with its centre on the line $x+2y = 6$; (ii) the value of c which gives a circle touching the x-axis.
4. The lines joining a variable point P to the fixed points $(6a, 0)$, $(-2a, 0)$ meet the y-axis at the points $(0, y_1)$, $(0, y_2)$ respectively. If P moves in such a way that $y_1y_2 = 9a^2$, show that its locus has the equation $3x^2+4y^2-12ax-36a^2 = 0$.
5. Show that the equation of the tangent at the origin to the circle $x^2+y^2 = ax+by$ is $ax+by = 0$ The circle $x^2+y^2 = 15x-10y$ cuts a circle S at right angles at the origin. If S passes through the point $(2, 0)$, find its equation.
6. The tangents to the parabola $x = t^2$, $y = t$ at the points $P(p^2, p)$, $Q(q^2, q)$ meet at N. If M is the mid-point of PQ show that $MN = (p-q)^2/2$. Given also that the tangents are perpendicular: (i) show that the locus of N is a straight line; (ii) find the (x, y) equation of the locus of M.
7. Show that the coordinates of the point of intersection, T, of the tangents to the ellipse $x^2/a^2+y^2/b^2 = 1$ at the points $(a\cos\theta, b\sin\theta)$, $(-a\sin\theta, b\cos\theta)$ are $[a(\cos\theta-\sin\theta),\ b(\cos\theta+\sin\theta)]$. Deduce that the equation of the locus of T as θ varies is $x^2/a^2+y^2/b^2 = 2$.
8. A line with gradient m passing through the point $(1, 1)$ meets the x and y-axes at A, B respectively; P is the point dividing AB internally in the ratio 1:2. Show that as m varies, P moves on the curve with equation $3xy-x-2y = 0$. By expressing this equation in the form $(3x-2)(3y-1) = k$, identify the curve and state the coordinates of its centre.
9. The gradient of the side AB of rectangle ABCD is 2; the point $(2, 3)$ lies on AB and the point $(-1, 2)$ lies on AD. If the diagonals of the rectangle intersect at the point $(1/2, 5)$, find the equations of the sides of the rectangle.
10. The point A is the foot of the perpendicular from the origin O to the line with equation $x\cos\alpha+y\sin\alpha = p$. Find the coordinates of the point B which lies on OA produced and such that OA = AB.
11. Given circle $S \equiv x^2+y^2+2x-4y = 0$ and line $L \equiv x+y = 0$, identify the curves with equation $S+\lambda L = 0$, where λ is a constant. If $\lambda = 10$, show that S and the curve $S+\lambda L = 0$ intersect at right angles.
12. The points $P(ap^2, 2ap)$, $Q(aq^2, 2aq)$ on the parabola $x = at^2$, $y = 2at$ are such that the chord OQ, where O is the origin, is parallel to the tangent to the curve at P. Find the (x, y) equation of the locus of the point of intersection of the tangents at P and Q as p, q vary.
13. Show that the equation of the chord joining the points $P(cp, c/p)$, $Q(cq, c/q)$ on the rectangular hyperbola $xy = c^2$ is $x+pqy = c(p+q)$. A rectangle is formed by drawing lines parallel to the axes through P and Q; write down the coordinates of L, M the other two vertices of this rectangle. If the chord PQ passes through the fixed point $R(h, k)$, prove that L and M lie on the curve $xy-kx-hy+c^2 = 0$.

14. The tangent to the curve $x = t^2$, $y = t^3$ at the point $P(p^2, p^3)$ meets the curve again at the point $Q(q^2, q^3)$. Show that $p+2q = 0$ and find the (x, y) equation of the locus of R, the point which divides PQ internally in the ratio 1:2.
15. Find the equation of the tangent to the parabola $y^2 = 4ax$ at the point $(at^2, 2at)$. If P is the foot of the perpendicular from the origin to this tangent, show that as t varies, the locus of P is the curve $x(x^2+y^2) = ay^2$.
16. A, B, C are the points (3, 4), (9, 1), (7, 7) respectively. Find: (i) the coordinates of the point P which divides AB internally in the ratio $1:k$; (ii) the value of k when CP is perpendicular to AB. Hence find the coordinates of the foot of the perpendicular from C to AB.
17. Find the equation of the circle which passes through the common points of the circles $x^2+y^2-4x-8y-5 = 0$, $x^2+y^2-6x-10y+9 = 0$ whose centre lies on the line $x+y = 2$.
18. Eliminate θ between the equations $x\cos\theta+\sqrt{2}y\sin\theta = \sqrt{2}$, $\sqrt{2}x\sin\theta-y\cos\theta = 0$. Hence find the equation of the locus of the foot of the perpendicular from the origin to the tangent to the ellipse $x^2+2y^2 = 2$ at the point $(\sqrt{2}\cos\theta, \sin\theta)$ for varying values of θ.
19. P is the point $(a, 2a)$ on the parabola $y^2 = 4ax$. Find the equation of the normal to the curve at P and verify that it passes through the point $N(5a, -2a)$. If the chord joining the points $Q(aq^2, 2aq)$, $R(ar^2, 2ar)$ on the curve also passes through N, show that angle QPR $= 90°$.
20. The foot of the perpendicular from P to the line $x+y = \sqrt{2}$ is the point R and Q is the point $(\sqrt{2}, \sqrt{2})$. If P moves such that $PQ^2 = 2PR^2$, show that its locus is the rectangular hyperbola $xy = 1$. The tangent to this locus at the point $(t, 1/t)$ cuts the x-axis at A and the y-axis at B; C is the point dividing AB in the ratio $a:b$. Show that the locus of C as t varies is the rectangular hyperbola $xy = 4ab/(a+b)^2$.
21. Show that the equation of the tangent to the parabola $y^2 = 4ax$ at the point $(at^2, 2at)$ is $ty = x+at^2$. Using this result when $a = 1$, obtain the value of t for which this tangent also touches the parabola $x^2 = 32y$ and deduce the equation of the common tangent of the curves $y^2 = 4x$, $x^2 = 32y$.
22. In each of the following cases find the Cartesian equation of the locus of the point $P(x, y)$ as t varies and sketch the locus: (i) $x = 3+5\cos t$, $y = 4+5\sin t$, $0 \leqslant t \leqslant \pi$; (ii) $x = 3\cos t$, $y = 4\sin t$, $0 \leqslant t \leqslant \pi$; (iii) $x = 3+t\cos\pi/3$, $y = 4+t\sin\pi/3$, $-\infty < t < \infty$.
23. Show that the lines $y = 0$, $4x-3y+40 = 0$ are tangents to the circle C, $x^2+y^2-10y = 0$. Find the radii of the circles which touch both these lines and also cut circle C orthogonally.
24. The tangent and normal to the ellipse $x = a\cos\theta$, $y = b\sin\theta$ at the point $P(a\cos\phi, b\sin\phi)$ meet the axis of x at the points T, G respectively. If C is the centre of the ellipse and Y the foot of the perpendicular from C to the tangent at P, prove: (i) $CG \cdot CT = a^2-b^2$; (ii) $CY \cdot GP = b^2$.
25. Show that the normals to the parabola $y^2 = 4ax$ at the points $P(ap^2, 2ap)$, $Q(aq^2, 2aq)$ meet at the point $R(h, k)$ where $h = 2a+a(p^2+pq+q^2)$, $k = -apq(p+q)$. If the gradient of the chord PQ is m and it passes through the point $A(-2a, 0)$ show that p and q are the roots of the equation $mt^2-2t+2m = 0$ and deduce the values of $p+q$ and pq. Hence express h and k in terms of a and m and verify that R lies on the parabola.
26. Show that the equation of the tangent to the curve $x = 3t^2$, $y = 2t^3$ at the point $P(3p^2, 2p^3)$ is $px-y = p^3$. If Q is the point $(3q^2, 2q^3)$, find the coordinates of T, the point of intersection of the tangents to the curve at P and Q. If the tangents at P, Q make angles of θ and $\pi/2-\theta$ with the x-axis obtain a relationship between p and q and find the (x, y) equation of the locus of T for all values of θ.
27. Circles C_1, C_2 have equations $x^2+y^2-4x-8y-5 = 0$, $x^2+y^2-6x-10y+9 = 0$. Find the equations of the circles which pass through the common points of C_1 and C_2 and touch the line $y = 0$.
28. The tangent at the point $P(ct, c/t)$ to the rectangular hyperbola $xy = c^2$ meets the x-axis at Q and the y-axis at R. The line through Q parallel to the y-axis meets the curve at S and the line through R parallel to the x-axis meets the curve at T. Prove that as P varies, the locus of the mid-point of ST is the rectangular hyperbola $16xy = 25c^2$.
29. The normal at the point $P(ap^2, 2ap)$ to the parabola $y^2 = 4ax$ meets the curve again at the point $Q(aq^2, 2aq)$. Find q in terms of p and show that the tangents at P and Q intersect at the point $T(-2a-ap^2, -2a/p)$. Deduce the equation of the locus of T as p varies.
30. Prove that the equation of the tangent PT at the point $P(ct, c/t)$ on the rectangular hyperbola $xy = c^2$ is $x+t^2y = 2ct$. The perpendicular to PT from the origin O meets PT at Q and the normal at P meets the curve again at R. Prove: (i) that as P varies, the locus of Q is $(x^2+y^2)^2 = 4c^2xy$; (ii) $c^2PR = OP^3$.
31. The coordinates of the points P, Q, R on the parabola $x = at^2$, $y = 2at$ are $(ap^2, 2ap)$, $(aq^2, 2aq)$,

$(ar^2, 2ar)$ respectively. The tangents to the curve at P, Q meet the tangent at R at the points T, U respectively; the tangents at P and Q meet at V. Prove that, if U is the mid-point of RT, then $2q = p+r$. Show also that VU is parallel to PR.

32. Prove that the equation of the tangent to the curve $x = a\sec\theta$, $y = a\tan\theta$ at the point $P(a\sec\phi, a\tan\phi)$ is $x - y\sin\phi = a\cos\phi$ and find the equation of the normal at P. If the normal at P meets the coordinate axes at X and Y and O is the origin, prove that: (i) P is the mid-point of XY; (ii) OP is inversely proportional to the perpendicular distance of O from the tangent at P.

33. The points $P(ap^2, 2ap)$, $Q(aq^2, 2aq)$ lie on the parabola $x = at^2$, $y = 2at$ and the coordinates of the mid-point of PQ are (X, Y). Express $p+q$ and pq in terms of X and Y. If the chord PQ passes through the fixed point $(b, 0)$, show that the locus of the mid-point of the chord is a parabola.

Matrices

DEFINITIONS AND FUNDAMENTAL PROCESSES

A *matrix* is a rectangular or square array of numbers or elements; for example:

$$\begin{pmatrix} a_1 & b_1 \\ a_2 & b_2 \end{pmatrix}\text{—a } 2\times 2 \text{ matrix;} \quad \begin{pmatrix} a_1 & b_1 & c_1 \\ a_2 & b_2 & c_2 \end{pmatrix}\text{—a } 2\times 3 \text{ matrix.}$$

Matrices are denoted by capital letters in bold type, **A**, **B** and so on.

Special cases. Matrices with only one row or one column are called *vectors* and are usually denoted by small letters in bold type as is the practice for physical vectors;

e.g. $$\mathbf{a} = (a_1\,a_2)\text{—a row vector; } \mathbf{a} = \begin{pmatrix} a_1 \\ a_2 \\ a_3 \end{pmatrix}\text{—a column vector.}$$

Zero matrix

A matrix with all its elements zero is called a zero matrix and is denoted **0**.

Unit matrix

A unit matrix is a square matrix with the leading diagonal elements equal to unity and all other elements zero—it is denoted **I**.

Fundamental processes

Equality. Matrices **A**, **B** are equal if they have the same shape and identical elements.

Addition and subtraction

Matrices of the same shape are added or subtracted by adding or subtracting corresponding elements;

e.g. $$\begin{pmatrix} a_1 & b_1 & c_1 \\ a_2 & b_2 & c_2 \end{pmatrix} + \begin{pmatrix} p_1 & q_1 & r_1 \\ p_2 & q_2 & r_2 \end{pmatrix} = \begin{pmatrix} a_1+p_1 & b_1+q_1 & c_1+r_1 \\ a_2+p_2 & b_2+q_2 & c_2+r_2 \end{pmatrix}.$$

Multiplication by a number

The result of multiplying a matrix **A** by a number, or scalar, k is defined as the matrix **B** whose elements are those of **A** each multiplied by k;

e.g. $$3\begin{pmatrix}2 & -1\\ 1 & 3\end{pmatrix} = \begin{pmatrix}6 & -3\\ 3 & 9\end{pmatrix}.$$

Matrix multiplication

The products **AB**, **BA** exist only if the number of columns in the first matrix of the product is equal to the number of rows in the second;

if $$\mathbf{AB} = \mathbf{C},$$

a typical element of **C** is obtained by taking a row of **A** and a column of **B**, multiplying corresponding elements and then adding.

Example 1. Given $\mathbf{A} = \begin{pmatrix}3 & -1 & 2\\ 0 & 1 & -2\end{pmatrix}$, $\mathbf{B} = \begin{pmatrix}0 & 2\\ -1 & 1\\ 2 & 0\end{pmatrix}$, *find* **AB** *and* **BA**.

$$\mathbf{AB} = \begin{pmatrix}0+1+4 & 6-1+0\\ 0-1-4 & 0+1+0\end{pmatrix} = \begin{pmatrix}5 & 5\\ -5 & 1\end{pmatrix};$$

$$\mathbf{BA} = \begin{pmatrix}0+0 & 0+2 & 0-4\\ -3+0 & 1+1 & -2-2\\ 6+0 & -2+0 & 4+0\end{pmatrix} = \begin{pmatrix}0 & 2 & -4\\ -3 & 2 & -4\\ 6 & -2 & 4\end{pmatrix}.$$

Note

(i) Generally, even when both the products **AB**, **BA** exist they are quite different; in the cases where **AB** = **BA**, the matrices are said to *commute*;

(ii) if the product **AB** is zero, it is not necessarily true that **A** or **B** is zero;

(iii) the associative law **A(BC)** = **(AB)C** is true, provided that both sides are defined; the product can simply be written **ABC**;

(iv) in the case of a square matrix **A**, $\mathbf{A}^2 = \mathbf{AA}$; $\mathbf{A}^3 = \mathbf{AAA}$ and so on;

(v) if **A** is a square matrix and **I** the unit matrix of the same order,

$$\mathbf{IA} = \mathbf{AI} = \mathbf{A}.$$

Example 2. If $\mathbf{A} = \begin{pmatrix}3 & 1\\ -1 & 2\end{pmatrix}$, $\mathbf{B} = \begin{pmatrix}0 & 4\\ 1 & 5\end{pmatrix}$, $\mathbf{C} = \begin{pmatrix}1 & 1\\ 2 & 1\end{pmatrix}$, *verify that:* (*i*) $\mathbf{A}^2\mathbf{A} = \mathbf{AA}^2$; (*ii*) **A(BC)** = **(AB)C**.

(i) $$\mathbf{A}^2 = \begin{pmatrix}3 & 1\\ -1 & 2\end{pmatrix}\begin{pmatrix}3 & 1\\ -1 & 2\end{pmatrix} = \begin{pmatrix}8 & 5\\ -5 & 3\end{pmatrix};$$

so $$\mathbf{A}^2\mathbf{A} = \begin{pmatrix}8 & 5\\ -5 & 3\end{pmatrix}\begin{pmatrix}3 & 1\\ -1 & 2\end{pmatrix} = \begin{pmatrix}19 & 18\\ -18 & 1\end{pmatrix};$$

and $$\mathbf{AA}^2 = \begin{pmatrix}3 & 1\\ -1 & 2\end{pmatrix}\begin{pmatrix}8 & 5\\ -5 & 3\end{pmatrix} = \begin{pmatrix}19 & 18\\ -18 & 1\end{pmatrix}.$$

(ii) $$\mathbf{BC} = \begin{pmatrix} 0 & 4 \\ 1 & 5 \end{pmatrix}\begin{pmatrix} 1 & 1 \\ 2 & 1 \end{pmatrix} = \begin{pmatrix} 8 & 4 \\ 11 & 6 \end{pmatrix};$$

$$\mathbf{AB} = \begin{pmatrix} 3 & 1 \\ -1 & 2 \end{pmatrix}\begin{pmatrix} 0 & 4 \\ 1 & 5 \end{pmatrix} = \begin{pmatrix} 1 & 17 \\ 2 & 6 \end{pmatrix};$$

so $$\mathbf{A}(\mathbf{BC}) = \begin{pmatrix} 3 & 1 \\ -1 & 2 \end{pmatrix}\begin{pmatrix} 8 & 4 \\ 11 & 6 \end{pmatrix} = \begin{pmatrix} 35 & 18 \\ 14 & 8 \end{pmatrix};$$

and $$(\mathbf{AB})\mathbf{C} = \begin{pmatrix} 1 & 17 \\ 2 & 6 \end{pmatrix}\begin{pmatrix} 1 & 1 \\ 2 & 1 \end{pmatrix} = \begin{pmatrix} 35 & 18 \\ 14 & 8 \end{pmatrix}.$$

Transpose matrix

The transpose $\mathbf{A}^{\mathrm{T}}$ of a matrix $\mathbf{A}$ is the matrix obtained by interchanging the rows and columns of $\mathbf{A}$;

e.g. $$\text{if } \mathbf{A} = \begin{pmatrix} a_1 & b_1 & c_1 \\ a_2 & b_2 & c_2 \end{pmatrix}, \quad \mathbf{A}^{\mathrm{T}} = \begin{pmatrix} a_1 & a_2 \\ b_1 & b_2 \\ c_1 & c_2 \end{pmatrix}.$$

It can be established that:

$$(\mathbf{AB})^{\mathrm{T}} = \mathbf{B}^{\mathrm{T}}\mathbf{A}^{\mathrm{T}}.$$

Example 3. Verify the result $(\mathbf{AB})^{\mathrm{T}} = \mathbf{B}^{\mathrm{T}}\mathbf{A}^{\mathrm{T}}$ *in the case where* $\mathbf{A} = \begin{pmatrix} 0 & 1 \\ 2 & 3 \end{pmatrix}$, $\mathbf{B} = \begin{pmatrix} 3 & 6 & 1 \\ 1 & 4 & 8 \end{pmatrix}$.

$$\mathbf{AB} = \begin{pmatrix} 0 & 1 \\ 2 & 3 \end{pmatrix}\begin{pmatrix} 3 & 6 & 1 \\ 1 & 4 & 8 \end{pmatrix} = \begin{pmatrix} 1 & 4 & 8 \\ 9 & 24 & 26 \end{pmatrix};$$

so $$(\mathbf{AB})^{\mathrm{T}} = \begin{pmatrix} 1 & 9 \\ 4 & 24 \\ 8 & 26 \end{pmatrix}.$$

$$\mathbf{B}^{\mathrm{T}}\mathbf{A}^{\mathrm{T}} = \begin{pmatrix} 3 & 1 \\ 6 & 4 \\ 1 & 8 \end{pmatrix}\begin{pmatrix} 0 & 2 \\ 1 & 3 \end{pmatrix} = \begin{pmatrix} 1 & 9 \\ 4 & 24 \\ 8 & 26 \end{pmatrix},$$

verifying the result $(\mathbf{AB})^{\mathrm{T}} = \mathbf{B}^{\mathrm{T}}\mathbf{A}^{\mathrm{T}}$.

Orthogonal matrixes

A matrix $\mathbf{A}$ is **orthogonal** if $\mathbf{A}^{\mathrm{T}}\mathbf{A} = \mathbf{A}\mathbf{A}^{\mathrm{T}} = \mathbf{I}$.

e.g. the matrix $\mathbf{A} = \begin{pmatrix} \cos\alpha & -\sin\alpha \\ \sin\alpha & \cos\alpha \end{pmatrix}$ is orthogonal.

Determinants

The determinant, det **A** or $|\mathbf{A}|$, of matrix **A**, is only defined when **A** is a square matrix.

If
$$\mathbf{A} = \begin{pmatrix} a_1 & b_1 \\ a_2 & b_2 \end{pmatrix}, \quad \det \mathbf{A} = \begin{vmatrix} a_1 & b_1 \\ a_2 & b_2 \end{vmatrix},$$

where
$$\begin{vmatrix} a_1 & b_1 \\ a_2 & b_2 \end{vmatrix} = a_1 b_2 - b_1 a_2;$$

if
$$\mathbf{A} = \begin{pmatrix} a_1 & b_1 & c_1 \\ a_2 & b_2 & c_2 \\ a_3 & b_3 & c_3 \end{pmatrix}, \quad \det \mathbf{A} = \begin{vmatrix} a_1 & b_1 & c_1 \\ a_2 & b_2 & c_2 \\ a_3 & b_3 & c_3 \end{vmatrix},$$

where
$$\begin{vmatrix} a_1 & b_1 & c_1 \\ a_2 & b_2 & c_2 \\ a_3 & b_3 & c_3 \end{vmatrix} = a_1 \begin{vmatrix} b_2 & c_2 \\ b_3 & c_3 \end{vmatrix} - b_1 \begin{vmatrix} a_2 & c_2 \\ a_3 & c_3 \end{vmatrix} + c_1 \begin{vmatrix} a_2 & b_2 \\ a_3 & b_3 \end{vmatrix}.$$

Note If det $\mathbf{A} = 0$, **A** is said to be *singular*; if det $\mathbf{A} \neq 0$, **A** is *non-singular.*

Evaluation of determinants

The following laws are helpful in the evaluation of determinants:

(i) if any two parallel sets of elements, rows or columns, are interchanged the sign of the determinant is changed;

(ii) if any two parallel sets of elements, rows or columns, are identical the determinant is zero;

(iii) the value of the determinant is unchanged if rows and columns are interchanged; i.e. det $\mathbf{A} = \det \mathbf{A}^{\mathrm{T}}$.

(iv) if each element of a row or a column has a common factor k, then k is a factor of the determinant;

(v) the value of the determinant is unchanged when to the elements of any row are added or subtracted any multiple of the elements of one or more other rows, with a like result for columns.

Example 4. Evaluate: (*i*) $\begin{vmatrix} 15 & 13 & -8 \\ 12 & 17 & 6 \\ 0 & 1 & 0 \end{vmatrix}$; (*ii*) $\begin{vmatrix} 10 & 20 & 30 \\ 3 & 50 & -1 \\ 0 & 60 & 4 \end{vmatrix}$.

(i) Interchanging the first and third rows:

$$\text{determinant} = -\begin{vmatrix} 0 & 1 & 0 \\ 12 & 17 & 6 \\ 15 & 13 & -8 \end{vmatrix} = 1 \begin{vmatrix} 12 & 6 \\ 15 & -8 \end{vmatrix} = -186.$$

(ii) Taking out the factor 10 from the second column:

$$\text{determinant} = 10 \begin{vmatrix} 10 & 2 & 30 \\ 3 & 5 & -1 \\ 0 & 6 & 4 \end{vmatrix} = 10[10(26) - 2(12) + 30(18)],$$

$$= 7760.$$

Minors and cofactors

The *minor* of any particular element of a determinant is the determinant obtained when the row and column through the element are suppressed;

e.g. the minor of the element b_2 in the determinant

$$\begin{vmatrix} a_1 & b_1 & c_1 \\ a_2 & b_2 & c_2 \\ a_3 & b_3 & c_3 \end{vmatrix} \text{ is the determinant } \begin{vmatrix} a_1 & c_1 \\ a_3 & c_3 \end{vmatrix}.$$

The *cofactor* of any particular element of a determinant is equal to the minor of the element with a sign + or − prefixed; the sign being determined by moving from the top left-hand element by row or column to the position of the particular element and counting +, − alternately at each element. A capital letter in ordinary type can be used to represent a cofactor.

e.g. in the case above, the cofactor of b_2, $\mathrm{B}_2 = +\begin{vmatrix} a_1 & c_1 \\ a_3 & c_3 \end{vmatrix}$.

Adjoint matrix

If $\mathbf{A}$ is a square matrix, the *adjoint matrix*, adj $\mathbf{A}$, is the transpose of the matrix whose elements are the cofactors of the elements of det $\mathbf{A}$;

so if $\quad \mathbf{A} = \begin{pmatrix} a_1 & b_1 \\ a_2 & b_2 \end{pmatrix}, \qquad \operatorname{adj}\mathbf{A} = \begin{pmatrix} b_2 & -b_1 \\ -a_2 & a_1 \end{pmatrix};$

and if $\quad \mathbf{A} = \begin{pmatrix} a_1 & b_1 & c_1 \\ a_2 & b_2 & c_2 \\ a_3 & b_3 & c_3 \end{pmatrix}, \qquad \operatorname{adj}\mathbf{A} = \begin{pmatrix} \mathrm{A}_1 & \mathrm{A}_2 & \mathrm{A}_3 \\ \mathrm{B}_1 & \mathrm{B}_2 & \mathrm{B}_3 \\ \mathrm{C}_1 & \mathrm{C}_2 & \mathrm{C}_3 \end{pmatrix},$

where $\quad \mathrm{A}_1 = \begin{vmatrix} b_2 & c_2 \\ b_3 & c_3 \end{vmatrix}, \quad \mathrm{A}_2 = -\begin{vmatrix} b_1 & c_1 \\ b_3 & c_3 \end{vmatrix}, \quad \mathrm{A}_3 = \begin{vmatrix} b_1 & c_1 \\ b_2 & c_2 \end{vmatrix}$

and so on.

Inverse matrix

If $\mathbf{A}$ is a square *non-singular* matrix, the inverse matrix $\mathbf{A}^{-1}$ is given by

$$\mathbf{A}^{-1} = \frac{\operatorname{adj}\mathbf{A}}{\det\mathbf{A}};$$

it is such that $\mathbf{AA}^{-1} = \mathbf{A}^{-1}\mathbf{A} = \mathbf{I}$.

Note In the case of a 2×2 matrix

$$\mathbf{A} = \begin{pmatrix} a_1 & b_1 \\ a_2 & b_2 \end{pmatrix}, \quad \mathbf{A}^{-1} = \frac{1}{a_1 b_2 - a_2 b_1}\begin{pmatrix} b_2 & -b_1 \\ -a_2 & a_1 \end{pmatrix}.$$

Example 5. Given $\mathbf{A} = \begin{pmatrix} \cos\alpha & -\sin\alpha \\ \sin\alpha & \cos\alpha \end{pmatrix}$, *find* $\mathbf{A}^{-1}$ *and verify that* $\mathbf{AA}^{-1} = \mathbf{A}^{-1}\mathbf{A} = \mathbf{I}$.

The matrix of the cofactors of $\mathbf{A}$ is $\begin{pmatrix} \cos\alpha & -\sin\alpha \\ \sin\alpha & \cos\alpha \end{pmatrix}$,

so $$\operatorname{adj}\mathbf{A} = \begin{pmatrix} \cos\alpha & \sin\alpha \\ -\sin\alpha & \cos\alpha \end{pmatrix};$$

also $$\det\mathbf{A} = \begin{vmatrix} \cos\alpha & -\sin\alpha \\ \sin\alpha & \cos\alpha \end{vmatrix} = 1.$$

$\therefore$ $$\mathbf{A}^{-1} = \begin{pmatrix} \cos\alpha & \sin\alpha \\ -\sin\alpha & \cos\alpha \end{pmatrix},$$

$$\mathbf{AA}^{-1} = \begin{pmatrix} \cos\alpha & -\sin\alpha \\ \sin\alpha & \cos\alpha \end{pmatrix}\begin{pmatrix} \cos\alpha & \sin\alpha \\ -\sin\alpha & \cos\alpha \end{pmatrix},$$

$$= \begin{pmatrix} 1 & 0 \\ 0 & 1 \end{pmatrix} = \mathbf{I};$$

and similarly for $\mathbf{A}^{-1}\mathbf{A}$.

Example 6. *Verify the result* $(\mathbf{AB})^{-1} = \mathbf{B}^{-1}\mathbf{A}^{-1}$ *in the case where*

$$\mathbf{A} = \begin{pmatrix} 3 & 2 & 0 \\ 1 & 1 & 4 \\ -1 & 0 & 2 \end{pmatrix}, \quad \mathbf{B} = \begin{pmatrix} 1 & 1 & 0 \\ 2 & 1 & 3 \\ 0 & -4 & 1 \end{pmatrix}.$$

$$\mathbf{AB} = \begin{pmatrix} 7 & 5 & 6 \\ 3 & -14 & 7 \\ -1 & -9 & 2 \end{pmatrix};$$

$$\det(\mathbf{AB}) = 7(35) - 5(13) + 6(-41) = -66;$$

$$\operatorname{adj}(\mathbf{AB}) = \begin{pmatrix} 35 & -64 & 119 \\ -13 & 20 & -31 \\ -41 & 58 & -113 \end{pmatrix};$$

so $$(\mathbf{AB})^{-1} = -\frac{1}{66}\begin{pmatrix} 35 & -64 & 119 \\ -13 & 20 & -31 \\ -41 & 58 & -113 \end{pmatrix}.$$

Also $$\mathbf{A}^{-1} = -\frac{1}{6}\begin{pmatrix} 2 & -4 & 8 \\ -6 & 6 & -12 \\ 1 & -2 & 1 \end{pmatrix}; \quad \mathbf{B}^{-1} = \frac{1}{11}\begin{pmatrix} 13 & -1 & 3 \\ -2 & 1 & -3 \\ -8 & 4 & -1 \end{pmatrix},$$

so $$\mathbf{B}^{-1}\mathbf{A}^{-1} = -\frac{1}{66}\begin{pmatrix} 35 & -64 & 119 \\ -13 & 20 & -31 \\ -41 & 58 & -113 \end{pmatrix} = (\mathbf{AB})^{-1}.$$

(A) EXAMPLES 36

1. If $\mathbf{A}=\begin{pmatrix}-1 & 2\\ 3 & 1\end{pmatrix}$, $\mathbf{B}=\begin{pmatrix}0 & 4\\ -1 & 2\end{pmatrix}$ find: (i) $\mathbf{A}+\mathbf{B}$; (ii) $2\mathbf{A}-\mathbf{B}$; (iii) $\mathbf{AB}$; (iv) $\mathbf{BA}$.

2. Find the following products:

(i) $(-1\ \ 4\ \ 2)\begin{pmatrix}5\\ 1\\ 3\end{pmatrix}$; (ii) $\begin{pmatrix}2 & 1 & 4\\ 6 & -2 & 3\end{pmatrix}\begin{pmatrix}1\\ -2\\ 1\end{pmatrix}$; (iii) $\begin{pmatrix}4 & -1\\ 2 & 5\end{pmatrix}\begin{pmatrix}3 & -2\\ 1 & 6\end{pmatrix}$;

(iv) $\begin{pmatrix}3\\ 9\\ 2\end{pmatrix}(1\ \ -6\ \ 3)$; (v) $\begin{pmatrix}4 & -1 & 1\\ 2 & 3 & 0\end{pmatrix}\begin{pmatrix}7 & -3\\ 5 & 4\\ 1 & 2\end{pmatrix}$; (vi) $\begin{pmatrix}2 & 2 & 1\\ 1 & 0 & 2\\ 2 & 1 & 2\end{pmatrix}\begin{pmatrix}-2 & -3 & 4\\ 2 & 2 & -3\\ 1 & 2 & -2\end{pmatrix}$.

3. Given $\mathbf{A}=\begin{pmatrix}1 & -1\\ -1 & 1\end{pmatrix}$, $\mathbf{B}=\begin{pmatrix}1 & 1\\ 1 & 1\end{pmatrix}$, find: (i) $\mathbf{AB}$; (ii) $\mathbf{BA}$; (iii) $\mathbf{A}^2\mathbf{B}$.

4. Verify that $\mathbf{A}(\mathbf{BC})=(\mathbf{AB})\mathbf{C}$ in the case where $\mathbf{A}=\begin{pmatrix}3 & 1\\ -1 & 2\end{pmatrix}$, $\mathbf{B}=\begin{pmatrix}1 & 1\\ 2 & 5\end{pmatrix}$, $\mathbf{C}=\begin{pmatrix}0 & -1\\ 1 & 2\end{pmatrix}$.

5. Given $\mathbf{A}=\begin{pmatrix}\cos\pi/3 & -\sin\pi/3\\ \sin\pi/3 & \cos\pi/3\end{pmatrix}$, $\mathbf{B}=\begin{pmatrix}\cos\pi/6 & -\sin\pi/6\\ \sin\pi/6 & \cos\pi/6\end{pmatrix}$, show that $\mathbf{AB}=\mathbf{BA}$.

6. Verify the results: (i) $\mathbf{A}(\mathbf{B}+\mathbf{C})=\mathbf{AB}+\mathbf{AC}$; (ii) $(\mathbf{B}+\mathbf{C})\mathbf{A}=\mathbf{BA}+\mathbf{CA}$, in the case

$$\mathbf{A}=\begin{pmatrix}2 & -1 & 4\\ 4 & -3 & 1\\ 1 & 2 & 1\end{pmatrix}\ \mathbf{B}=\begin{pmatrix}3 & -1 & 5\\ 2 & 0 & 2\\ 1 & 1 & 1\end{pmatrix},\ \mathbf{C}=\begin{pmatrix}0 & 1 & 1\\ 3 & -1 & 2\\ 1 & 0 & 4\end{pmatrix}.$$

7. Given $\mathbf{A}=\begin{pmatrix}\cos\pi/4 & -\sin\pi/4\\ \sin\pi/4 & \cos\pi/4\end{pmatrix}$, find $\mathbf{A}^2$, $\mathbf{A}^3$, $\mathbf{A}^4$.

8. If $\mathbf{A}=\begin{pmatrix}1 & a\\ 0 & 1\end{pmatrix}$, find $\mathbf{A}^2$, $\mathbf{A}^3$, $\mathbf{A}^n$, where n is a positive integer.

9. Given $\mathbf{A}=\begin{pmatrix}0 & 1 & 0\\ 0 & 0 & 1\\ 0 & 0 & 0\end{pmatrix}$, find: (i) $\mathbf{AA}^{\mathrm{T}}$; (ii) $\mathbf{A}^{\mathrm{T}}\mathbf{A}$.

10. Find the value of det $\mathbf{A}$ in each of the following cases: (i) $\mathbf{A}=\begin{pmatrix}2 & -1\\ 1 & 2\end{pmatrix}$;

(ii) $\mathbf{A}=\begin{pmatrix}4 & 0\\ -1 & 2\end{pmatrix}$; (iii) $\mathbf{A}=\begin{pmatrix}\sin\alpha & \cos\alpha\\ -\cos\alpha & \sin\alpha\end{pmatrix}$; (iv) $\mathbf{A}=\begin{pmatrix}0 & a\\ 0 & a\end{pmatrix}$;

(v) $\mathbf{A}=\begin{pmatrix}1 & 0 & 1\\ 0 & 1 & 1\\ 1 & 1 & 0\end{pmatrix}$; (vi) $\mathbf{A}=\begin{pmatrix}1 & 2 & 3\\ 4 & 5 & 6\\ 7 & 8 & 9\end{pmatrix}$; (vii) $\mathbf{A}=\begin{pmatrix}1 & 0 & 0\\ 0 & \cos\alpha & -\sin\alpha\\ 0 & \sin\alpha & \cos\alpha\end{pmatrix}$.

11. Evaluate the determinants:

(i) $\begin{vmatrix}18 & 20\\ 19 & 21\end{vmatrix}$; (ii) $\begin{vmatrix}55 & 66\\ 50 & 60\end{vmatrix}$; (iii) $\begin{vmatrix}47 & 101\\ 47 & 116\end{vmatrix}$; (iv) $\begin{vmatrix}201 & 132\\ 100 & 66\end{vmatrix}$;

(v) $\begin{vmatrix}10 & 20 & 30\\ 1 & 0 & -2\\ 38 & 57 & -19\end{vmatrix}$; (vi) $\begin{vmatrix}1 & 1 & 1\\ 15 & 15 & 15\\ 21 & 23 & 25\end{vmatrix}$; (vii) $\begin{vmatrix}28 & 19 & 17\\ -9 & 25 & 3\\ 0 & 0 & 1\end{vmatrix}$; (viii) $\begin{vmatrix}10 & 11 & 12\\ 11 & 12 & 13\\ 12 & 13 & 14\end{vmatrix}$.

12. Verify that $(\mathbf{AB})^{\mathrm{T}} = \mathbf{B}^{\mathrm{T}}\mathbf{A}^{\mathrm{T}}$ in the following cases:

$$\text{(i) } \mathbf{A} = \begin{pmatrix} 2 & 1 \\ -1 & 0 \end{pmatrix};\ \mathbf{B} = \begin{pmatrix} 3 & 4 \\ 2 & -1 \end{pmatrix};\ \text{(ii) } \mathbf{A} = \begin{pmatrix} 0 & -1 \\ 1 & 0 \end{pmatrix};\ \mathbf{B} = \begin{pmatrix} \cos\alpha & -\sin\alpha \\ \sin\alpha & \cos\alpha \end{pmatrix};$$

$$\text{(iii) } \mathbf{A} = \begin{pmatrix} 0 & 1 & 0 \\ 1 & 0 & 0 \\ 0 & 0 & 1 \end{pmatrix},\ \mathbf{B} = \begin{pmatrix} 1 & 1 & 1 \\ 1 & 1 & 1 \\ 1 & 1 & 1 \end{pmatrix};\ \text{(iv) } \mathbf{A} = \begin{pmatrix} 2 & 1 & 2 \\ 3 & 5 & 7 \\ 1 & 0 & 1 \end{pmatrix};\ \mathbf{B} = \begin{pmatrix} -3 & 1 & 0 \\ 6 & 2 & 1 \\ 1 & -1 & 2 \end{pmatrix}.$$

13. Find $\mathbf{A}^{-1}$, the inverse matrix of $\mathbf{A}$, and verify that $\mathbf{AA}^{-1} = \mathbf{A}^{-1}\mathbf{A} = \mathbf{I}$ in each of the cases:

$$\text{(i) } \mathbf{A} = \begin{pmatrix} 2 & 3 \\ -1 & 4 \end{pmatrix};\ \text{(ii) } \mathbf{A} = \begin{pmatrix} 1/2 & -\sqrt{3}/2 \\ \sqrt{3}/2 & 1/2 \end{pmatrix};\ \text{(iii) } \mathbf{A} = \begin{pmatrix} \cos\alpha & \sin\alpha \\ -\sin\alpha & \cos\alpha \end{pmatrix};$$

$$\text{(iv) } \mathbf{A} = \begin{pmatrix} 2 & 3 & 1 \\ 3 & 1 & 2 \\ 1 & 2 & 3 \end{pmatrix};\ \text{(v) } \mathbf{A} = \begin{pmatrix} 1 & 0 & 0 \\ 0 & \cos\alpha & -\sin\alpha \\ 0 & \sin\alpha & \cos\alpha \end{pmatrix};\ \text{(vi) } \mathbf{A} = \begin{pmatrix} 0 & 0 & 1 \\ \cos 2\alpha & \sin 2\alpha & 0 \\ \sin 2\alpha & -\cos 2\alpha & 0 \end{pmatrix}.$$

14. Given $\mathbf{A}(\theta) = \begin{pmatrix} \cos\theta & \sin\theta \\ -\sin\theta & \cos\theta \end{pmatrix}$, show that $\mathbf{A}(\theta)\mathbf{A}(\phi) = \mathbf{A}(\theta+\phi)$.

15. Verify the results: (i) $\det(\mathbf{AB}) = \det\mathbf{A}\det\mathbf{B}$; (ii) $\det\mathbf{A}^{-1} = (\det\mathbf{A})^{-1}$ in the case where

$$\mathbf{A} = \begin{pmatrix} 0 & 1 & 0 \\ 1 & 2 & -1 \\ 0 & 1 & 3 \end{pmatrix},\ \mathbf{B} = \begin{pmatrix} 1 & 0 & 2 \\ 2 & 1 & 0 \\ -1 & 1 & -1 \end{pmatrix}.$$

16. Verify the expressions: (i) $(\mathbf{A}-\mathbf{B})^2 = (\mathbf{B}-\mathbf{A})^2$; (ii) $(\mathbf{A}-\mathbf{B})^2 = \mathbf{A}^2-\mathbf{AB}-\mathbf{BA}+\mathbf{B}^2$ when $\mathbf{A} = \begin{pmatrix} 0 & 3 \\ 4 & 5 \end{pmatrix}$, $\mathbf{B} = \begin{pmatrix} 2 & -1 \\ 3 & 2 \end{pmatrix}$.

17. Show that the matrix $\mathbf{A} = \begin{pmatrix} 6 & -4 \\ 9 & -6 \end{pmatrix}$ satisfies the equation $\mathbf{A}^2 = \mathbf{0}$ and find the relationship between a and b if the matrix $\begin{pmatrix} 1 & a \\ b & -1 \end{pmatrix}$ satisfies this equation.

18. Evaluate $\mathbf{A}^2$, where $\mathbf{A} = \begin{pmatrix} 2 & -5 \\ 3 & 1 \end{pmatrix}$, and find scalars α, β, such that $\mathbf{I}+\alpha\mathbf{A}+\beta\mathbf{A}^2 = \mathbf{0}$.

19. Find the 2×2 matrix $\mathbf{T}$ such that $\begin{pmatrix} 2 & 1 \\ 3 & 0 \end{pmatrix} = \mathbf{T}\begin{pmatrix} 1 & 0 \\ 2 & 2 \end{pmatrix}$.

20. Given $\mathbf{A} = \begin{pmatrix} 1 & a \\ 0 & 1 \end{pmatrix}$, $\mathbf{B} = \begin{pmatrix} 1 & b \\ 0 & 1 \end{pmatrix}$ show that $\mathbf{AB} = \mathbf{BA}$ and find b in terms of a if $\mathbf{B} = \mathbf{AB}^{-1}$.

21. If $\mathbf{A} = \begin{pmatrix} \cos\alpha & -\sin\alpha \\ \sin\alpha & \cos\alpha \end{pmatrix}$, $\mathbf{B} = \begin{pmatrix} 1 & 0 \\ 0 & -1 \end{pmatrix}$, show that $\mathbf{BAB} = \mathbf{A}^{-1}$.

22. Verify that $\mathbf{A} = \begin{pmatrix} \cos\alpha & -\sin\alpha \\ \sin\alpha & \cos\alpha \end{pmatrix}$ and $\mathbf{A} = \begin{pmatrix} \cos 2\alpha & \sin 2\alpha \\ \sin 2\alpha & -\cos 2\alpha \end{pmatrix}$ are orthogonal matrices, i.e. they both satisfy the equations $\mathbf{AA}^{\mathrm{T}} = \mathbf{A}^{\mathrm{T}}\mathbf{A} = \mathbf{I}$.

23. Verify the result $(\mathbf{AB})^{-1} = \mathbf{B}^{-1}\mathbf{A}^{-1}$ in the cases where: (i) $\mathbf{A} = \begin{pmatrix} 1 & 1 \\ 1 & 1 \end{pmatrix}$, $\mathbf{B} = \begin{pmatrix} 2 & 0 \\ 1 & 2 \end{pmatrix}$;

$$\text{(ii) } \mathbf{A} = \begin{pmatrix} 3 & -1 \\ 0 & 4 \end{pmatrix},\ \mathbf{B} = \begin{pmatrix} -2 & 1 \\ 3 & 0 \end{pmatrix};\ \text{(iii) } \mathbf{A} = \begin{pmatrix} \cos\alpha & -\sin\alpha \\ \sin\alpha & \cos\alpha \end{pmatrix},\ \mathbf{B} = \begin{pmatrix} \cos\alpha & \sin\alpha \\ -\sin\alpha & \cos\alpha \end{pmatrix}.$$

24. If $\mathbf{S} = \begin{pmatrix} \cos \pi/4 & -\sin \pi/4 \\ \sin \pi/4 & \cos \pi/4 \end{pmatrix}$, $\mathbf{P} = \begin{pmatrix} 1 & 3 \\ 3 & 1 \end{pmatrix}$, show that: (i) $\mathbf{SS}^{\mathrm{T}} = \mathbf{I}$; (ii) $\mathbf{SPS}^{\mathrm{T}}$ is a diagonal matrix—i.e. a square matrix with all elements zero except in the leading diagonal.

25. If $\mathbf{A} = \begin{pmatrix} 1 & 3 \\ 2 & 2 \end{pmatrix}$, $\mathbf{I} = \begin{pmatrix} 1 & 0 \\ 0 & 1 \end{pmatrix}$, show that the roots of the equation $\det(\mathbf{A} - \lambda\mathbf{I}) = 0$ are $\lambda = -1$ and 4.

26. If $\mathbf{A} = \begin{pmatrix} 0 & 1 & 0 \\ 0 & 0 & 1 \\ 1 & 0 & 0 \end{pmatrix}$, show that: (i) $\mathbf{AA}^{\mathrm{T}} = \mathbf{A}^{\mathrm{T}}\mathbf{A} = \mathbf{I}$; (ii) $(\mathbf{A}^{\mathrm{T}})^{-1} = \mathbf{A}$.

APPLICATIONS OF MATRICES

Linear equations

The linear equations

$$a_1x + b_1y = d_1,$$
$$a_2x + b_2y = d_2,$$

can be expressed as

$$\mathbf{AX} = \mathbf{D},$$

where

$$\mathbf{A} = \begin{pmatrix} a_1 & b_1 \\ a_2 & b_2 \end{pmatrix}, \quad \mathbf{X} = \begin{pmatrix} x \\ y \end{pmatrix}, \quad \mathbf{D} = \begin{pmatrix} d_1 \\ d_2 \end{pmatrix}.$$

Similarly the equations

$$a_1x + b_1y + c_1z = d_1,$$
$$a_2x + b_2y + c_2z = d_2,$$
$$a_3x + b_3y + c_3z = d_3,$$

can be expressed as

$$\mathbf{AX} = \mathbf{D},$$

where

$$\mathbf{A} = \begin{pmatrix} a_1 & b_1 & c_1 \\ a_2 & b_2 & c_2 \\ a_3 & b_3 & c_3 \end{pmatrix}, \quad \mathbf{X} = \begin{pmatrix} x \\ y \\ z \end{pmatrix}, \quad \mathbf{D} = \begin{pmatrix} d_1 \\ d_2 \\ d_3 \end{pmatrix}.$$

In both cases, the solution is given by

$$\mathbf{X} = \mathbf{A}^{-1}\mathbf{D}.$$

Geometrical interpretation

In two-dimensional geometry, the linear equations in x, y represent two straight lines and the solution gives the coordinates of their common point. Special cases arise when either the lines are parallel or coincident; in both cases $\det \mathbf{A} = 0$ and as a consequence $\mathbf{A}^{-1}$ does not exist.

In three-dimensional geometry, the linear equations in x, y, z represent three planes and the solution gives the coordinates of their common point. Special cases arise when: (i) at least two of the planes are parallel; (ii) the planes intersect in three parallel lines; (iii) the planes have a common line of intersection; (iv) at least two of the planes are coincident; in all these cases $\det \mathbf{A} = 0$ and $\mathbf{A}^{-1}$ does not exist.

Example 7. Solve the systems of equations: (i) $2x+5y = 6$, $x-2y = -5$; (ii) $2x+2y+z = 1$, $x+2z = -3$, $2x+y+2z = 4$.

(i) The equations are expressed in the form

$$\mathbf{AX} = \mathbf{D},$$

where $\mathbf{A} = \begin{pmatrix} 2 & 5 \\ 1 & -2 \end{pmatrix}$, $\mathbf{X} = \begin{pmatrix} x \\ y \end{pmatrix}$, $\mathbf{D} = \begin{pmatrix} 6 \\ -5 \end{pmatrix}$

$\det \mathbf{A} = -9;$ $\quad \mathbf{A}^{-1} = -\frac{1}{9}\begin{pmatrix} -2 & -5 \\ -1 & 2 \end{pmatrix}.$

$$\therefore \quad \mathbf{X} = -\frac{1}{9}\begin{pmatrix} -2 & -5 \\ -1 & 2 \end{pmatrix}\begin{pmatrix} 6 \\ -5 \end{pmatrix},$$

$$= -\frac{1}{9}\begin{pmatrix} 13 \\ -16 \end{pmatrix};$$

i.e. $\quad x = -\frac{13}{9}, \; y = \frac{16}{9}.$

(ii) In this case,

$$\mathbf{A} = \begin{pmatrix} 2 & 2 & 1 \\ 1 & 0 & 2 \\ 2 & 1 & 2 \end{pmatrix}, \quad \mathbf{X} = \begin{pmatrix} x \\ y \\ z \end{pmatrix}, \quad \mathbf{D} = \begin{pmatrix} 1 \\ -3 \\ 4 \end{pmatrix}.$$

$$\det \mathbf{A} = 1; \quad \mathbf{A}^{-1} = \frac{1}{1}\begin{pmatrix} 2 & -3 & 4 \\ 2 & 2 & -3 \\ 1 & 2 & -2 \end{pmatrix}.$$

$$\therefore \quad \mathbf{X} = \begin{pmatrix} -2 & -3 & 4 \\ 2 & 2 & -3 \\ 1 & 2 & -2 \end{pmatrix}\begin{pmatrix} 1 \\ -3 \\ 4 \end{pmatrix},$$

$$= \begin{pmatrix} 23 \\ -16 \\ -13 \end{pmatrix};$$

i.e. $\quad x = 23, \; y = -16, \; z = -13.$

Transformations

Given a coordinate system in a plane in terms of the coordinates (x, y), or position vector $\begin{pmatrix} x \\ y \end{pmatrix}$, of a point P, a new coordinate system $\begin{pmatrix} x' \\ y' \end{pmatrix}$ can be defined by means of a transformation where $x' = a_1x+b_1y+c_1$, $y' = a_2x+b_2y+c_2$, $a_1b_2-a_2b_1 \neq 0$. The new pairs (x', y') or $\begin{pmatrix} x' \\ y' \end{pmatrix}$ determine the position of a point P′, *the image point* of P under the transformation, relative to a new origin O′ given by the values of x and y which satisfy the equations $a_1x+b_1y+c_1 = 0$, $a_2x+b_2y+c_2 = 0$; the new x-axis is the original line, $a_1x+b_1y+c_1 = 0$ and the new y-axis the original line $a_2x+b_2y+c_2 = 0$. It should be noted that the new axes will be perpendicular if $a_1a_2+b_1b_2 = 0$.

Note

(i) A point P is called a *fixed* or *invariant point* under the transformation if $x' = x$, $y' = y$ at P;

(ii) if every point in the plane is a fixed point, the transformation has the equations $x' = x$, $y' = y$ and is the *identity transformation*;

(iii) if all points on a line are transformed onto points, not necessarily the same points, on the line, then the line is a *fixed or invariant line*; i.e. an invariant line is a line which is mapped onto itself.

Translations

In a translation, axes remain parallel to themselves and the origin is moved. $x' = x+a$, $y' = y+b$, or in matrix notation $\begin{pmatrix} x' \\ y' \end{pmatrix} = \begin{pmatrix} x \\ y \end{pmatrix} + \begin{pmatrix} a \\ b \end{pmatrix}$, represents a translation through distances a, b parallel to the axes; the new origin is the point $(-a, -b)$. The transformation is a translation with vector $\begin{pmatrix} a \\ b \end{pmatrix}$.

Linear transformations

A linear transformation from coordinates (x, y) to coordinates (x', y') is defined by

$$x' = a_1x+b_1y; \quad y' = a_2x+b_2y.$$

Note

(i) All linear transformations in a plane can be represented by the matrix equation

$$\mathbf{x}' = \mathbf{T}\mathbf{x}, \text{ where } \mathbf{T} = \begin{pmatrix} a_1 & b_1 \\ a_2 & b_2 \end{pmatrix};$$

(ii) in these transformations, if A' is the image area of a region of area A, then

$$A':A = |\det \mathbf{T}|:1.$$

Dilations

A dilation is effected by equations of the form $x' = ax$, $y' = by$ or in matrix notation $\begin{pmatrix} x' \\ y' \end{pmatrix} = \begin{pmatrix} a & 0 \\ 0 & b \end{pmatrix}\begin{pmatrix} x \\ y \end{pmatrix}$; the origin and axes are unchanged and areas are magnified by a factor ab.

Reflections

(a) $x' = -x$, $y' = y$, or in matrix notation $\begin{pmatrix} x' \\ y' \end{pmatrix} = \begin{pmatrix} -1 & 0 \\ 0 & 1 \end{pmatrix}\begin{pmatrix} x \\ y \end{pmatrix}$, gives a reflection in the y-axis;

(b) $x' = x$, $y' = -y$, or in matrix notation $\begin{pmatrix} x' \\ y' \end{pmatrix} = \begin{pmatrix} 1 & 0 \\ 0 & -1 \end{pmatrix}\begin{pmatrix} x \\ y \end{pmatrix}$, gives a reflection in the x-axis;

(c) $x' = y$, $y' = x$, or in matrix notation $\begin{pmatrix} x' \\ y' \end{pmatrix} = \begin{pmatrix} 0 & 1 \\ 1 & 0 \end{pmatrix}\begin{pmatrix} x \\ y \end{pmatrix}$, gives a reflection in the line $y = x$;

(d) $x' = -y$, $y' = -x$, or in matrix notation $\begin{pmatrix} x' \\ y' \end{pmatrix} = \begin{pmatrix} 0 & -1 \\ -1 & 0 \end{pmatrix}\begin{pmatrix} x \\ y \end{pmatrix}$, gives a reflection in the line $y = -x$.

Rotations

$x' = ax - by,\ y' = bx + ay,$ where $a^2 + b^2 = 1$, or in matrix notation $\begin{pmatrix} x' \\ y' \end{pmatrix} = \begin{pmatrix} a & -b \\ b & a \end{pmatrix}\begin{pmatrix} x \\ y \end{pmatrix}$, where $\det\begin{pmatrix} a & -b \\ b & a \end{pmatrix} = 1$, gives a rotation about the origin, with axes fixed, through an angle $\tan^{-1} b/a$, measured positive in the counter-clockwise direction, where $\cos\theta = a$, $\sin\theta = b$.

Shears

(a) $x' = x + ky,\ y' = y$, or in matrix notation $\begin{pmatrix} x' \\ y' \end{pmatrix} = \begin{pmatrix} 1 & k \\ 0 & 1 \end{pmatrix}\begin{pmatrix} x \\ y \end{pmatrix}$, gives a shear in which the line $y = 0$ is invariant and all points other than those on this line move parallel to this line; in this as with all shears, area is preserved;

(b) $x' = x,\ y' = kx + y$, or in matrix notation $\begin{pmatrix} x' \\ y' \end{pmatrix} = \begin{pmatrix} 1 & 0 \\ k & 1 \end{pmatrix}\begin{pmatrix} x \\ y \end{pmatrix}$, gives a shear in which the line $x = 0$ is invariant;

(c) $x' = a_1x + b_1y,\quad y' = a_2x + b_2y,\quad b_1 \neq 0$, or in matrix notation $\begin{pmatrix} x' \\ y' \end{pmatrix} = \begin{pmatrix} a_1 & b_1 \\ a_2 & b_2 \end{pmatrix}\begin{pmatrix} x \\ y \end{pmatrix}$, gives a shear with invariant line $y = (b_2 \mp 1)x/b_1$, so long as $a_1 + b_2 = \pm 2$ and $a_1b_2 - a_2b_1 = 1$.

Inverse transformations

If a transformation is defined by the relationship $\mathbf{x}' = \mathbf{T}\mathbf{x}$, then the inverse transformation is defined by the relationship $\mathbf{x}' = \mathbf{T}^{-1}\mathbf{x}$.

Example 8. A linear transformation of a plane has matrix $\mathbf{T}\begin{pmatrix} 4 & 2 \\ 3 & 5 \end{pmatrix}$. *Find: (i) the ratio of the area of the image under* $\mathbf{T}$ *of a region R to the area R; (ii) the equations of the lines through the origin each of which is mapped onto itself by the transformation.*

(i) The transformation is given by $\begin{pmatrix} x' \\ y' \end{pmatrix} = \mathbf{T}\begin{pmatrix} x \\ y \end{pmatrix}$, so the ratio of areas under the transformation is $|\det \mathbf{T}|:1$, i.e. $14:1$.

(ii) We have

$$x' = 4x + 2y,$$
$$y' = 3x + 5y.$$

Let the equation of a line through the origin which maps onto itself be $y = mx$ or $y' = mx'$; substituting for y and y' in the above equations and dividing,

$$m = \frac{3 + 5m}{4 + 2m},$$

$$2m^2 - m - 3 = 0,$$

$$m = -1, \frac{3}{2}.$$

The equations of the required lines are $y + x = 0$, $2y - 3x = 0$.

Multiple transformations

If separate linear transformations in a plane are represented by the matrix equations

$$\mathbf{x}' = \mathbf{T}_1\mathbf{x},\ \ \mathbf{x}'' = \mathbf{T}_2\mathbf{x}',\ \ \mathbf{x}''' = \mathbf{T}_3\mathbf{x}'' \text{ and so on,}$$

then $\quad \mathbf{x}'' = \mathbf{T}_2\mathbf{T}_1\mathbf{x},\ \ \mathbf{x}''' = \mathbf{T}_3\mathbf{T}_2\mathbf{T}_1\mathbf{x}$ and so on.

Example 9. Given $\mathbf{T}_1 = \begin{pmatrix} \cos\theta & -\sin\theta \\ \sin\theta & \cos\theta \end{pmatrix}$, $\mathbf{T}_2 = \begin{pmatrix} 1 & 0 \\ 0 & -1 \end{pmatrix}$, *find* $\mathbf{T}_\theta = \mathbf{T}_1\mathbf{T}_2\mathbf{T}_1^{-1}$.

$$\det \mathbf{T}_1 = 1;\ \ \mathbf{T}^{-1} = \begin{pmatrix} \cos\theta & \sin\theta \\ -\sin\theta & \cos\theta \end{pmatrix}.$$

$$\begin{aligned} \mathbf{T}_\theta &= \begin{pmatrix} \cos\theta & -\sin\theta \\ \sin\theta & \cos\theta \end{pmatrix}\begin{pmatrix} 1 & 0 \\ 0 & -1 \end{pmatrix}\begin{pmatrix} \cos\theta & \sin\theta \\ -\sin\theta & \cos\theta \end{pmatrix}, \\ &= \begin{pmatrix} \cos\theta & -\sin\theta \\ \sin\theta & \cos\theta \end{pmatrix}\begin{pmatrix} \cos\theta & \sin\theta \\ \sin\theta & -\cos\theta \end{pmatrix}, \\ &= \begin{pmatrix} \cos^2\theta - \sin^2\theta & 2\sin\theta\cos\theta \\ 2\sin\theta\cos\theta & \sin^2\theta - \cos^2\theta \end{pmatrix}, \\ &= \begin{pmatrix} \cos 2\theta & \sin 2\theta \\ \sin 2\theta & -\cos 2\theta \end{pmatrix}. \end{aligned}$$

Special linear transformations

(i) A rotation in a plane through an angle α about the origin with axes fixed is represented by the matrix equation $\mathbf{x}' = \mathbf{T}_1\mathbf{x}$, where $\mathbf{T}_1 = \begin{pmatrix} \cos\alpha & -\sin\alpha \\ \sin\alpha & \cos\alpha \end{pmatrix}$;

(ii) a rotation through an angle $-\alpha$ about the origin is represented by the equation $\mathbf{x}' = \mathbf{T}_1^{-1}\mathbf{x}$, where $\mathbf{T}_1^{-1}$ is the inverse of $\mathbf{T}_1$;

(iii) reflection in the line $y = x\tan\alpha$ is given by the repeated transformation represented by $\mathbf{T}_1\mathbf{T}_2\mathbf{T}_1^{-1}$ where $\mathbf{T}_1$ is as defined in (i) and $\mathbf{T}_2 = \begin{pmatrix} 1 & 0 \\ 0 & -1 \end{pmatrix}$, or by the equivalent matrix $\begin{pmatrix} \cos 2\alpha & \sin 2\alpha \\ \sin 2\alpha & -\cos 2\alpha \end{pmatrix}$.

Example 10. Given $\quad \mathbf{T}_1 = \begin{pmatrix} \cos\alpha & -\sin\alpha \\ \sin\alpha & \cos\alpha \end{pmatrix}$,

$\mathbf{T}_2 = \begin{pmatrix} \cos 2\alpha & \sin 2\alpha \\ \sin 2\alpha & -\cos 2\alpha \end{pmatrix}$, *show geometrically that* $\mathbf{T}_2\mathbf{T}_1\mathbf{T}_2 = \mathbf{T}_1^{-1}$.

Geometrically the transformation associated with $\mathbf{T}_1$ gives a rotation about the origin through an angle α and $\mathbf{T}_2$ gives a reflection in the line $y = x\tan\alpha$. In Fig. 37, the successive positions of a point P arising from the transformations $\mathbf{T}_2$, $\mathbf{T}_1$, $\mathbf{T}_2$ are P_1, P_2, P_3. Clearly the final position P_3 is equivalent to a single rotation of $-\alpha$; i.e. the transformation associated with $\mathbf{T}_1^{-1}$.

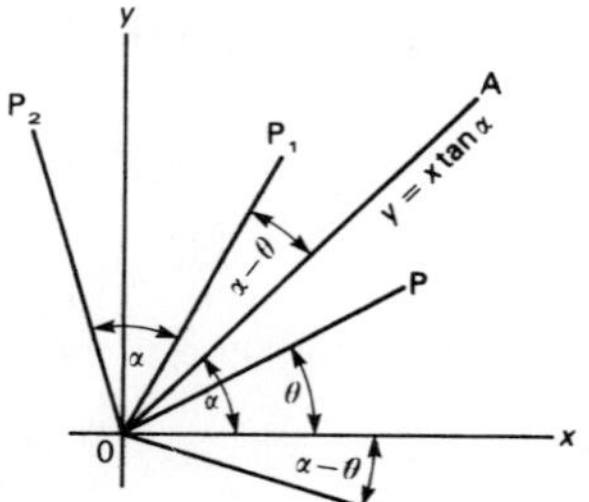

Fig. 37

Transformation produced by a singular matrix

In the transformation $\mathbf{x}' = \mathbf{T}\mathbf{x}$, where $\mathbf{T} = \begin{pmatrix} a_1 & b_1 \\ a_2 & b_2 \end{pmatrix}$, $a_1b_2 - a_2b_1 = 0$, and excluding the case $\mathbf{T} = \mathbf{0}$, all points of the plane are mapped onto a line. In the case where $a_1, a_2 \neq 0$, the line has the equation $a_2x - a_1y = 0$ and when $b_1, b_2 \neq 0$, the line has the equation $b_2x - b_1y = 0$. In other cases the line will be one or other of the coordinate axes.

Example 11. A linear transformation in a plane has matrix $\mathbf{T}\begin{pmatrix} 4 & 2 \\ -2 & -1 \end{pmatrix}$, *state why* $\mathbf{T}$ *has no inverse and find the equation of the line onto which* $\mathbf{T}$ *maps all points of the plane. Also show that* $\mathbf{T}$ *maps all points of a certain line onto the point (2, −1) and give the equation of this line.*

$\mathbf{T}$ has no inverse because $\begin{pmatrix} 4 & 2 \\ -2 & -1 \end{pmatrix}$ is a singular matrix, i.e. $\det \mathbf{T} = 0$.

We have
$$x' = 4x + 2y,$$
$$y' = -2x - y.$$

So for all values of x, y, $x' = -2y'$ and consequently all points of the plane map onto the line $x + 2y = 0$.

When $x' = 2$, $y' = -1$,
$$2 = 4x + 2y,$$
$$-1 = -2x - y,$$

showing that all points of the line $2x + y = 1$ map onto the point $(2, -1)$.

(A) EXAMPLES 37

Solve the following systems of equations:

1. $2x - y = -3$, $x + 3y = 1$.
2. $x + y + 6 = 0$, $2x + 4y + 5 = 0$.
3. $2x + 4y + 3 = 0$, $x - 2y + 7 = 0$.
4. $7x + 3y = 11$, $2x - 5y = 7$.
5. $11x - 15y - 1 = 0$, $7x + 11y + 3 = 0$.
6. $3x - 5y + 10 = 0$, $6x - 9y + 17 = 0$.
7. $2x - y - z = 6$, $x + 3y + 2z = 1$, $3x - y - 5z = 1$.
8. $x + 2y - 3z = 0$, $3x + 3y - z = 5$, $x - 2y + 2z = 1$.
9. $2x + 2y + z - 1 = 0$, $x + 2z + 3 = 0$, $2x + y + 2z - 4 = 0$.
10. $x + 2z + 1 = 0$, $3x - y - 3 = 0$, $-x + 2y + z = -4$.
11. $x + 4y + 11z = 7$, $2x + 8y + 16z = 8$, $x + 6y + 17z = 9$.
12. $3x + 2y - z = 0$, $x + 7y - 5z = 0$, $-x + z = 11$.
13. Find the coordinates of the image point of the point $(2, -3)$ under the transformation $\mathbf{x}' = \begin{pmatrix} 2 & -1 \\ 3 & 4 \end{pmatrix}\mathbf{x}$. Also find the coordinates of the point whose image point is $(0, 11)$.
14. Find the coordinates of the fixed point in the transformation $\begin{pmatrix} x' \\ y' \end{pmatrix} = \begin{pmatrix} 2 & 1 \\ 1 & -1 \end{pmatrix}\begin{pmatrix} x \\ y \end{pmatrix} + \begin{pmatrix} -3 \\ 3 \end{pmatrix}$.
15. Under the transformation $\begin{pmatrix} x' \\ y' \end{pmatrix} = \begin{pmatrix} a_1 & b_1 \\ a_2 & b_2 \end{pmatrix}\begin{pmatrix} x \\ y \end{pmatrix}$ the image points of the points $(2, -3)$, $(0, 1)$ are respectively the points $(3, -5)$, $(1, 1)$. Find the image point of the point $(-1, 2)$.

16. Give the geometrical significance of the transformation associated with each of the following relationships: (i) $\mathbf{x}' = \mathbf{x} + \begin{pmatrix} 3 \\ -2 \end{pmatrix}$; (ii) $\mathbf{x}' = \begin{pmatrix} 5 & 0 \\ 0 & 5 \end{pmatrix}\mathbf{x}$; (iii) $\mathbf{x}' = \begin{pmatrix} -1 & 0 \\ 0 & 1 \end{pmatrix}\mathbf{x}$; (iv) $\mathbf{x}' = \begin{pmatrix} 2 & 0 \\ 0 & -2 \end{pmatrix}\mathbf{x}$; (v) $\mathbf{x}' = \begin{pmatrix} 0 & 1 \\ 1 & 0 \end{pmatrix}\mathbf{x}$; (vi) $\mathbf{x}' = \begin{pmatrix} 3 & -1 \\ 4 & -1 \end{pmatrix}\mathbf{x}$.

17. A triangle ABC is mapped under the transformation $\mathbf{x}' = \begin{pmatrix} 3 & 0 \\ 0 & 3 \end{pmatrix}\mathbf{x}$ onto the triangle A′B′C′. Find the ratio of the area of triangle A′B′C′ to the area of triangle ABC and show that the triangles are similar. If triangle ABC is now mapped under the transformation $\mathbf{x}' = \begin{pmatrix} 0 & 3 \\ 3 & 0 \end{pmatrix}\mathbf{x}$ onto triangle A″B″C″, show that the triangles A′B′C′, A″B″C″ are congruent.

18. Write down the matrix representations of the following transformations: (i) origin moved to the point $(2, -3)$; (ii) a magnification factor of a; (iii) reflection in the x-axis and a magnification factor of 2; (iv) rotation through an angle of $\pi/4$.

19. A linear transformation of a plane has matrix $\mathbf{T}\begin{pmatrix} 3 & 2 \\ 2 & 3 \end{pmatrix}$. Find: (i) the ratio of the area of the image under $\mathbf{T}$ of a region R to the area of R; (ii) the equations of the lines through the origin each of which is mapped onto itself by the transformation.

20. A transformation $\mathbf{T}_1$ is a magnification by a factor 4; a transformation $\mathbf{T}_2$ is a translation with vector $\begin{pmatrix} -1 \\ -2 \end{pmatrix}$; find: (i) the matrix of the transformation $\mathbf{T}_1\mathbf{T}_2$; (ii) the image of the point $(0, 1)$ under this transformation.

21. A linear transformation has matrix $\mathbf{A}\begin{pmatrix} 4 & 2 \\ 1 & 1 \end{pmatrix}$; find the coordinates of the point which is mapped onto the point $(1, 0)$ by the inverse transformation $\mathbf{A}^{-1}$.

22. Under the transformation $\mathbf{x}' = \mathbf{A}\mathbf{x}$, where $\mathbf{A}$ is a 2×2 matrix, $(0, 1)$ is the image point of the point $(2, 3)$ and $(1, 4)$ is the image point of the point $(-1, 2)$. Find $\mathbf{A}$.

23. Under the transformation $\mathbf{x}' = \mathbf{T}\mathbf{x}$, where $\mathbf{T} = \begin{pmatrix} a_1 & b_1 \\ a_2 & b_2 \end{pmatrix}$, the lines $y = x$, $y = 2x$ are mapped onto themselves. Show that: (i) $a_1 = (3a_2 + 2b_2)/2$; (ii) $b_1 = -a_2/2$.

24. A geometrical transformation $\mathbf{T}$ is given by $\begin{pmatrix} x' \\ y' \end{pmatrix} = \begin{pmatrix} 3 & 2 \\ 1 & 2 \end{pmatrix}\begin{pmatrix} x \\ y \end{pmatrix}$. Find the area of the image OA′B′C′ of a rectangle OABC of area $10\,\text{cm}^2$ under this transformation and also find the area of OA″B″C″ the image of OA′B′C′ under the transformation. Also find the matrix of the transformation which maps OABC onto OA″B″C″.

25. A linear transformation of the plane has matrix $\begin{pmatrix} 3 & 4 \\ 1 & 2 \end{pmatrix}$, state the scale factor for the change in area produced by the transformation. Also find: (i) the coordinates of the image point of the point $(-1, 2)$; (ii) the coordinates of the point which is mapped onto the point $(1, 1)$ by the transformation.

26. Identify geometrically, transformations associated with the matrices: (i) $\begin{pmatrix} \cos\pi/5 & -\sin\pi/5 \\ \sin\pi/5 & \cos\pi/5 \end{pmatrix}$; (ii) $\begin{pmatrix} 1/2 & -\sqrt{3}/2 \\ \sqrt{3}/2 & 1/2 \end{pmatrix}$; (iii) $\begin{pmatrix} 1/2 & \sqrt{3}/2 \\ -\sqrt{3}/2 & 1/2 \end{pmatrix}$; (iv) $\begin{pmatrix} \sin\alpha & -\cos\alpha \\ \cos\alpha & \sin\alpha \end{pmatrix}$.

27. A linear transformation $\mathbf{T}$ has matrix $\begin{pmatrix} 6 & 3 \\ -2 & -1 \end{pmatrix}$; state why $\mathbf{T}$ has no inverse transformation. Show: (i) that all points in a certain line, whose equation should be given, are mapped onto the point $(3, -1)$; (ii) that all points of the plane are mapped onto the line $3y + x = 0$.

28. Write down the matrices $\mathbf{T}_\alpha$, $\mathbf{T}_\beta$, $\mathbf{T}_{\alpha+\beta}$ associated with rotations through angles of α, β, $\alpha+\beta$ respectively and verify that $\mathbf{T}_{\alpha+\beta} = \mathbf{T}_\alpha\mathbf{T}_\beta$.

29. If $\mathbf{A} = \begin{pmatrix} \cos\alpha & -\sin\alpha \\ \sin\alpha & \cos\alpha \end{pmatrix}$, show that $\mathbf{A}^{\mathrm{T}} = \mathbf{A}^{-1}$ and hence state the geometrical transformation associated with the matrix $\mathbf{A}^{\mathrm{T}}$.

(B) MISCELLANEOUS EXAMPLES

1. If $\mathbf{A}$ is an orthogonal matrix show that: (i) $\det(\mathbf{A}\mathbf{A}^T) = 1$; (ii) $\det \mathbf{A} = \pm 1$. Verify these results in the case where $\mathbf{A} = \begin{pmatrix} a & -b \\ b & a \end{pmatrix}$, where $a^2+b^2 = 1$.

2. Given $\mathbf{A} = \begin{pmatrix} \cos\alpha & -\sin\alpha \\ \sin\alpha & \cos\alpha \end{pmatrix}$ and $\mathbf{A}^4 = \mathbf{A}$, find α in the range $0 < \alpha < \pi$.

3. For what values of λ have the equations $2x-(\lambda+2)y = 1$, $(4-2\lambda)x-3y = \lambda$ not got a unique solution? State the geometrical significance. Solve the equations in the case where $\lambda = 3$.

4. If $\mathbf{S} = \begin{pmatrix} a_1 & b_1 \\ a_2 & b_2 \end{pmatrix}$, $\mathbf{I} = \begin{pmatrix} 1 & 0 \\ 0 & 1 \end{pmatrix}$, show that the condition for $\mathbf{S}$ to be singular is that at least one root of the equation $\det(\mathbf{S}-\lambda\mathbf{I}) = 0$ in λ is zero.

5. Given that $\mathbf{A} = \begin{pmatrix} \cos\theta & -\sin\theta \\ \sin\theta & \cos\theta \end{pmatrix}$, show geometrically that: (i) $\mathbf{A}^2 = \begin{pmatrix} \cos 2\theta & -\sin 2\theta \\ \sin 2\theta & \cos 2\theta \end{pmatrix}$; (ii) $\mathbf{A}^T = \begin{pmatrix} \cos n\theta & -\sin n\theta \\ \sin n\theta & \cos n\theta \end{pmatrix}$, where n is a positive integer.

6. Show that if $\mathbf{A} = \begin{pmatrix} a_1 & b_1 \\ a_2 & b_2 \end{pmatrix}$, $\mathbf{B} = \begin{pmatrix} p_1 & q_1 \\ p_2 & q_2 \end{pmatrix}$ are non-singular matrices, then $(\mathbf{AB})^{-1} = \mathbf{B}^{-1}\mathbf{A}^{-1}$.

7. Given $\mathbf{B} = \mathbf{P}^T\mathbf{A}\mathbf{P}$ where $\mathbf{P} = \begin{pmatrix} 1 & -1 \\ 0 & 1 \end{pmatrix}$, find: (i) $\mathbf{B}$ when $\mathbf{A} = \begin{pmatrix} 3 & 2 \\ -1 & 1 \end{pmatrix}$; (ii) $\mathbf{A}$ when $\mathbf{B} = \begin{pmatrix} 3 & 2 \\ -1 & 1 \end{pmatrix}$.

8. State the 2×2 matrices which lead to the following transformations in the plane: (i) reflection in the y-axis; (ii) rotation through an angle of $\pi/3$ about the origin; (iii) reflection in the line $y = -x$; (iv) reflection in the line $\sqrt{3}y = x$.

9. Points A, B have coordinates (x_1, y_1), (x_2, y_2) respectively and O is the origin. Show that the area of $\triangle$OAB is the numerical value of $(1/2)\det\begin{pmatrix} x_1 & y_1 \\ x_2 & y_2 \end{pmatrix}$. In a linear transformation of the plane associated with the matrix $\begin{pmatrix} a_1 & b_1 \\ a_2 & b_2 \end{pmatrix}$, the image points of A, B are A′, B′, show that the area of $\triangle$OA′B′ is the numerical value of $(1/2)\det\begin{pmatrix} a_1 & b_1 \\ a_2 & b_2 \end{pmatrix}\det\begin{pmatrix} x_1 & y_1 \\ x_2 & y_2 \end{pmatrix}$.

10. Given $\mathbf{T} = \begin{pmatrix} 1 & 0 \\ 0 & -1 \end{pmatrix}$, $\mathbf{T}_\alpha = \begin{pmatrix} \cos\alpha & -\sin\alpha \\ \sin\alpha & \cos\alpha \end{pmatrix}$, $\mathbf{T}_\beta = \begin{pmatrix} \cos\beta & -\sin\beta \\ \sin\beta & \cos\beta \end{pmatrix}$, state the linear transformations associated with: (i) $\mathbf{T}$; (ii) $\mathbf{T}_\alpha$; (iii) $\mathbf{T}_\alpha^{-1}$; (iv) $\mathbf{T}_\alpha\mathbf{T}_\beta$; (v) $\mathbf{T}_A = \mathbf{T}_\alpha\mathbf{T}\mathbf{T}_\alpha^{-1}$; (vi) $\mathbf{T}_B = \mathbf{T}_\beta\mathbf{T}\mathbf{T}_\beta^{-1}$. Deduce that $\mathbf{T}_B\mathbf{T}_A$ represents a rotation through an angle $2(\beta-\alpha)$.

11. If $\mathbf{A} = \begin{pmatrix} 1 & 1 \\ 1 & 1 \end{pmatrix}$; $\mathbf{B} = \begin{pmatrix} 1 & 1 \\ 1 & 0 \end{pmatrix}$, show that it is not possible to find a nonsingular 2×2 matrix $\mathbf{X}$, such that $\mathbf{A} = \mathbf{X}^{-1}\mathbf{B}\mathbf{X}$.

12. A transformation $\mathbf{T}$ of three-dimensional space is defined by $\mathbf{r}' = \mathbf{A}\mathbf{r}$, where
$$\mathbf{r}' = \begin{pmatrix} x' \\ y' \\ z' \end{pmatrix}, \quad \mathbf{r} = \begin{pmatrix} x \\ y \\ z \end{pmatrix}, \quad \mathbf{A} = \begin{pmatrix} 2 & 0 & 1 \\ 0 & 3 & -1 \\ 1 & 1 & 1 \end{pmatrix}.$$
Find: (i) the image point of the point $(1, 1, 1)$; (ii) the point which has the point $(5, -4, 2)$ as its image point under the transformation.

13. Linear transformations $\mathbf{T}_1$, $\mathbf{T}_2$ of the plane are respectively reflections in the lines $y = x$, $y = x\tan(\pi/3)$. Write down the matrix representations of $\mathbf{T}_1$ and $\mathbf{T}_2$. Find the matrix representation of the transformation $\mathbf{T}_2\mathbf{T}_1$, and interpret the combined transformation geometrically.

14. Find the values of λ for which the equations $\lambda x+y+z = 1$, $x+\lambda y+z = \lambda$, $x+y+\lambda z = \lambda^2$ have not a unique solution and solve the equations in the case where $\lambda = -1$.

15. If $\mathbf{A} = \begin{pmatrix} \cos\alpha & -\sin\alpha \\ \sin\alpha & \cos\alpha \end{pmatrix}$, $\mathbf{I} = \begin{pmatrix} 1 & 0 \\ 0 & 1 \end{pmatrix}$, show that $\mathbf{I}+\mathbf{A} = 2\cos(\alpha/2)\begin{pmatrix} \cos(\alpha/2) & -\sin(\alpha/2) \\ \sin(\alpha/2) & \cos(\alpha/2) \end{pmatrix}$ and obtain a similar expression for $\mathbf{I}-\mathbf{A}$. If α is not an odd multiple of π, deduce that $(\mathbf{I}-\mathbf{A})(\mathbf{I}+\mathbf{A})^{-1} = \tan(\alpha/2)\begin{pmatrix} 0 & 1 \\ -1 & 0 \end{pmatrix}$.

16. If $\mathbf{A} = \begin{pmatrix} \cos\alpha & -\sin\alpha \\ \sin\alpha & \cos\alpha \end{pmatrix}$, $\mathbf{B} = \begin{pmatrix} \cos 2\beta & \sin 2\beta \\ \sin 2\beta & -\cos 2\beta \end{pmatrix}$ where $0 < \beta < \pi/2$, describe the transformations of points in a plane associated with $\mathbf{A}$ and $\mathbf{B}$. Establish that $\mathbf{BAB} = \mathbf{A}^{-1}$ and find the least positive value of α for which $\mathbf{BA}^4\mathbf{B} = \mathbf{A}^{-1}$.

17. The 2×2 matrices $\sigma_1, \sigma_2, \sigma_3, \mathbf{I}$ are defined by $\sigma_1 = \begin{pmatrix} 0 & 1 \\ 1 & 0 \end{pmatrix}$, $\sigma_2 = \begin{pmatrix} 0 & -\mathrm{i} \\ \mathrm{i} & 0 \end{pmatrix}$, $\sigma_3 = \begin{pmatrix} 1 & 0 \\ 0 & -1 \end{pmatrix}$, $\mathbf{I} = \begin{pmatrix} 1 & 0 \\ 0 & 1 \end{pmatrix}$ where $\mathrm{i}^2 = -1$. Prove that: (i) $\sigma_1^2 = \sigma_2^2 = \sigma_3^2 = \mathbf{I}$; (ii) $\sigma_1\sigma_2 = -\sigma_2\sigma_1 = \mathrm{i}\sigma_3$; (iii) $\sigma_2\sigma_3 = -\sigma_3\sigma_2 = \mathrm{i}\sigma_1$; (iv) $\sigma_3\sigma_1 = -\sigma_1\sigma_3 = \mathrm{i}\sigma_2$.

18. If $\mathrm{P}'(x', y')$ is the reflection of $\mathrm{P}(x, y)$ in the line $y = x\tan\alpha$ and $\begin{pmatrix} x' \\ y' \end{pmatrix} = \mathbf{A}\begin{pmatrix} x \\ y \end{pmatrix}$, show that $\mathbf{A} = \begin{pmatrix} \cos 2\alpha & \sin 2\alpha \\ \sin 2\alpha & -\cos 2\alpha \end{pmatrix}$. If $\mathrm{P}''(x, y)$ is the reflection of P in the line $y = x\tan\beta$ and $\mathbf{B}$ is the matrix associated with this transformation, show that the matrix $\mathbf{BA}$ gives a rotation of OP about the origin O and state the angle of rotation.

19. In the case of the matrix $\mathbf{A} = \begin{pmatrix} a & h & g \\ h & b & f \\ g & f & c \end{pmatrix}$, show that: (i) $\mathbf{A}^{\mathrm{T}} = \mathbf{A}$; (ii) $(\operatorname{adj}\mathbf{A})^{\mathrm{T}} = \operatorname{adj}\mathbf{A}$; (iii) $(\mathbf{A}^{\mathrm{T}})^{-1} = \mathbf{A}^{-1}$.

20. In three dimensions, a transformation of space is given by $\mathbf{x}' = \mathbf{R}\mathbf{x}$ where $\mathbf{x}' = \begin{pmatrix} x' \\ y' \\ z' \end{pmatrix}$, $\mathbf{x} = \begin{pmatrix} x \\ y \\ z \end{pmatrix}$. Show that: (i) $\mathbf{R} = \begin{pmatrix} 1 & 0 & 0 \\ 0 & 1 & 0 \\ 0 & 0 & -1 \end{pmatrix}$ gives a reflection in the plane $z = 0$; (ii) $\mathbf{R} = \begin{pmatrix} 1 & 0 & 0 \\ 0 & \cos\alpha & -\sin\alpha \\ 0 & \sin\alpha & \cos\alpha \end{pmatrix}$ gives a rotation through an angle α about the positive x-axis.

Vectors

DEFINITIONS AND FUNDAMENTAL PROCESSES

In print a vector quantity is shown in heavy type, **a**; in written work it is denoted by a letter over a bar, $\underset{\sim}{a}$. Displacement vectors related to points P, Q, say, are shown as $\overline{\mathrm{PQ}}$ or $\overrightarrow{\mathrm{PQ}}$.

The *modulus* or magnitude of a vector **a** is shown as italic a or $|\mathbf{a}|$; the modulus of the vector $\overline{\mathrm{PQ}}$ is PQ or $|\overline{\mathrm{PQ}}|$.

Unit vectors

Unit vectors are vectors of unit magnitude; unit vectors in the directions $\overline{0x}$, $\overline{0y}$, $\overline{0z}$ of a right-handed system of coordinate axes are denoted by **i**, **j**, **k** respectively. Generally, the unit vector in the direction of the vector **a** is written $\hat{\mathbf{a}}$; so $\mathbf{a} = a\hat{\mathbf{a}}$.

Equal vectors

Vectors are equal when they are in the same direction and have equal magnitudes; e.g. if ABCD is a parallelogram, vectors $\overline{\mathrm{AB}}$ and $\overline{\mathrm{DC}}$ are equal as are vectors $\overline{\mathrm{AD}}$ and $\overline{\mathrm{BC}}$.

Negative vectors

The negative of **a** is $-\mathbf{a}$; it is a vector of modulus a and a direction opposite to that of **a**.

Cartesian components of a vector

Two-dimensional vector; if the magnitudes of the components of **a** in the directions $\overline{0x}$, $\overline{0y}$ are a_1, a_2, then $\mathbf{a} = a_1\mathbf{i} + a_2\mathbf{j}$; three-dimensional vector; if the magnitudes of the components of **a** in the directions $\overline{0x}$, $\overline{0y}$, $\overline{0z}$, are a_1, a_2, a_3, then $\mathbf{a} = a_1\mathbf{i} + a_2\mathbf{j} + a_3\mathbf{k}$.

Note As mentioned in the previous section, a *generalised vector* can be defined as a matrix of two or three elements which has only one row or one column. The algebra of matrices is developed in such a way that this type of vector behaves in the same way as a physical vector. Throughout this section the notation of physical vectors will be used, but readers should be familiar with the alternative notations:

(a_1, a_2) a line vector;

$\begin{pmatrix} a_1 \\ a_2 \end{pmatrix}$ a column vector with components a_1, a_2;

(a_1, a_2, a_3) a line vector;

$\begin{pmatrix} a_1 \\ a_2 \\ a_3 \end{pmatrix}$ a column vector with components a_1, a_2, a_3.

Modulus of a vector in terms of its components

If $\mathbf{a} = a_1\mathbf{i}+a_2\mathbf{j}$, $\quad |\mathbf{a}| = \sqrt{(a_1^2+a_2^2)}$;
if $\mathbf{a} = a_1\mathbf{i}+a_2\mathbf{j}+a_3\mathbf{k}$, $\quad |\mathbf{a}| = \sqrt{(a_1^2+a_2^2+a_3^2)}$.

Vector addition and subtraction

If $\qquad \mathbf{a} = a_1\mathbf{i}+a_2\mathbf{j},\ \mathbf{b} = b_1\mathbf{i}+b_2\mathbf{j}$,

then $\qquad \mathbf{a}+\mathbf{b} = (a_1+b_1)\mathbf{i}+(a_2+b_2)\mathbf{j}$;

$$\mathbf{a}-\mathbf{b} = (a_1-b_1)\mathbf{i}+(a_2-b_2)\mathbf{j},$$

with corresponding results for three-dimensional vectors.

Note Geometrically these definitions lead to the well-known parallelogram and triangle laws of vector addition as illustrated in Fig. 38 (i) and (ii).

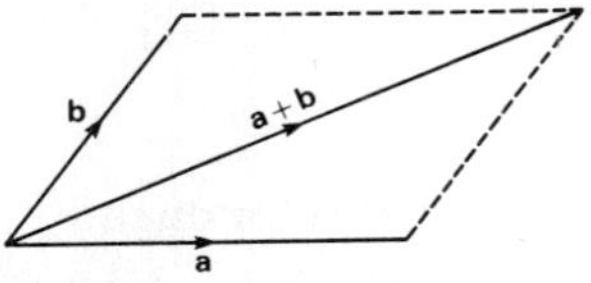

Fig. 38(i)

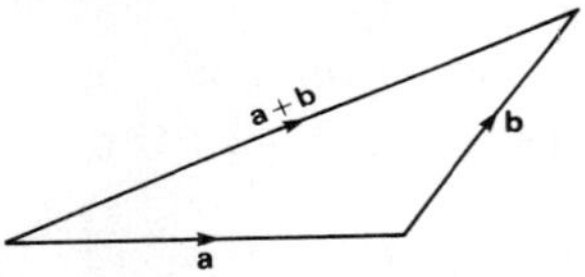

Fig. 38(ii)

Product of a vector and a scalar

If $\mathbf{a} = a_1\mathbf{i}+a_2\mathbf{j}+a_3\mathbf{k}$ and λ is a scalar,

$$\lambda\mathbf{a} = \lambda a_1\mathbf{i}+\lambda a_2\mathbf{j}+\lambda a_3\mathbf{k}.$$

Note The vector $\lambda\mathbf{a}$ is parallel to and in the direction of $\mathbf{a}$ if λ is positive and in the opposite direction if λ is negative.

Example 1. Given $\mathbf{a} = \mathbf{i}+2\mathbf{j}$, $\mathbf{b} = -3\mathbf{i}+5\mathbf{j}$, *find the value of* $|\mathbf{a}-\mathbf{b}|$.

$$\mathbf{a}-\mathbf{b} = 4\mathbf{i}-3\mathbf{j};$$
$$|\mathbf{a}-\mathbf{b}| = \sqrt{(4^2+(-3)^2)} = 5.$$

Example 2. Find the vector $\mathbf{r}$ *which is of magnitude 12 units and in the direction of the vector* $\mathbf{s} = 2\mathbf{i}-\mathbf{j}+2\mathbf{k}$.

Magnitude $\qquad \mathbf{s} = \sqrt{(2^2+(-1)^2+2^2)} = 3$;

So the unit vector in the direction of $\mathbf{s}$,

$$\mathbf{s} = \frac{1}{3}(2\mathbf{i}-\mathbf{j}+2\mathbf{k}).$$

$\therefore \qquad \mathbf{r} = 12 \cdot \frac{1}{3}(2\mathbf{i}-\mathbf{j}+2\mathbf{k}) = 4(2\mathbf{i}-\mathbf{j}+2\mathbf{k}).$

Ratio theorem

If vectors **a**, **b** are represented by the line vectors $\overline{\mathrm{OA}}$, $\overline{\mathrm{OB}}$ respectively and m, n are scalar constants, then

$$m\mathbf{a}+n\mathbf{b} = (m+n)\mathbf{c},$$

where vector **c** is represented by $\overline{\mathrm{OC}}$; C being the point dividing AB in the ratio $n:m$.

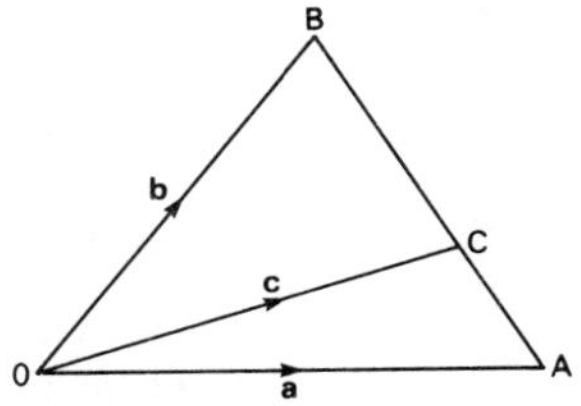

Fig. 39

Note If $m = n$, $\mathbf{a}+\mathbf{b} = 2\mathbf{c}$, where C is the mid-point of AB.

Example 3. A, B are the points with coordinates (3,0), (0,4) respectively. Express the vector $\overline{OC}$ in terms of **i**, **j** *when: (i) C is the mid-point of AB; (ii) C divides AB internally in the ratio 2:3.*

(i)
$$\overline{\mathrm{OA}} = 3\mathbf{i},\ \overline{\mathrm{OB}} = 4\mathbf{j};$$
$$\overline{\mathrm{OC}} = \frac{1}{2}(3\mathbf{i}+4\mathbf{j}).$$

(ii)
$$5\overline{\mathrm{OC}} = 3(3\mathbf{i})+2(4\mathbf{j}),$$
$$\overline{\mathrm{OC}} = \frac{1}{5}(9\mathbf{i}+8\mathbf{j}).$$

Example 4. On a diagram, vectors **a**, **b** *are represented by line vectors $\overline{OA}$, $\overline{OB}$, respectively; show the point C where $\overline{OC}$ represents the vector* $\mathbf{c} = 2\mathbf{a}+\mathbf{b}$. *If $a = 2$, $b = 3$, $\cos \angle AOB = 1/3$, find the modulus of* **c**.

In Fig. 40, $\mathrm{OA'} = 2\mathrm{OA}$ and OA′CB is a parallelogram.

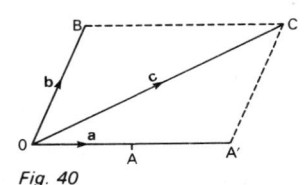

Fig. 40

$$\overline{\mathrm{OC}} = \mathbf{c} = 2\mathbf{a}+\mathbf{b}.$$

In $\triangle$OA′C

$$\mathrm{OC}^2 = \mathrm{OA'}^2+\mathrm{A'C}^2-2\cdot\mathrm{OA'}\cdot\mathrm{A'C}\cos\angle\mathrm{OA'C},$$

where

$$\mathrm{OA'} = 2a = 4,\ \mathrm{A'C} = \mathrm{OB} = b = 3,\ \cos\angle\mathrm{OA'C} = -\frac{1}{3}.$$

$$\therefore \quad \mathrm{OC}^2 = 16+9+8 = 33,$$
$$c = \mathrm{OC} = \sqrt{33}.$$

(A) EXAMPLES 38

1. Given $\mathbf{a} = 3\mathbf{i}-\mathbf{j}$, $\mathbf{b} = \mathbf{i}+2\mathbf{j}$, find the values of: (i) $2\mathbf{a}$; (ii) $-\mathbf{b}$; (iii) $\mathbf{a}+2\mathbf{b}$; (iv) $3\mathbf{a}-2\mathbf{b}$.
2. Find the modulus of each of the following vectors: (i) $3\mathbf{i}+4\mathbf{j}$; (ii) $\mathbf{i}-\mathbf{j}$; (iii) $\sqrt{3}\mathbf{i}+\mathbf{j}$; (iv) $5\mathbf{i}-12\mathbf{j}$.
3. Find the unit vector in the direction of the vector **r** if: (i) $\mathbf{r} = -3\mathbf{i}+4\mathbf{j}$; (ii) $\mathbf{r} = 2\mathbf{i}-\mathbf{j}$; (iii) $\mathbf{r} = 7\mathbf{i}+24\mathbf{j}$.

4. Represent the vectors $\mathbf{a} = \mathbf{i}+2\mathbf{j}$, $\mathbf{b} = -2\mathbf{i}$ on a Cartesian diagram and show on the same diagram the vectors: (i) $\mathbf{a}+\mathbf{b}$; (ii) $\mathbf{a}-2\mathbf{b}$; (iii) $\mathbf{a}+2\mathbf{b}$.
5. Find $|\overline{AB}|$ given that $|\overline{OA}| = 3$, $|\overline{OB}| = 4$ and angle AOB $= 60°$.
6. Show that $\cos\alpha\mathbf{i}+\sin\alpha\mathbf{j}$ is a unit vector included at an angle α to the x-axis.
7. Find the vector of modulus 15 in the direction of the vector $4\mathbf{i}-3\mathbf{j}$.
8. Given $\mathbf{a} = 2\mathbf{i}+2\mathbf{j}$, $\mathbf{b} = 3\mathbf{i}-\mathbf{j}$ and $\mathbf{a}+2\mathbf{b}+\mathbf{c} = 0$, find the value of $|\mathbf{c}|$.
9. In a diagram, vectors $\mathbf{a}$, $\mathbf{b}$ are represented by $\overline{OA}$, $\overline{OB}$ respectively. Illustrate on the diagram the vectors which represent: (i) $2\mathbf{a}$; (ii) $-3\mathbf{b}$; (iii) $2\mathbf{a}+\mathbf{b}$; (iv) $\mathbf{a}-3\mathbf{b}$.
10. Find the modulus of $\mathbf{c}$ where $\mathbf{c} = 2\mathbf{a}-\mathbf{b}$, given that the magnitudes of $\mathbf{a}$, $\mathbf{b}$ are 2, 3 respectively and that the angle of inclination of $\mathbf{a}$ and $\mathbf{b}$ is $\cos^{-1}(1/4)$.
11. Find: (i) the modulus of the vector $\mathbf{r} = 6\mathbf{i}+3\mathbf{j}-2\mathbf{k}$; (ii) the unit vector in the direction of $\mathbf{r}$.
12. Find the vector of magnitude 14 units in the direction of the vector $3\mathbf{i}-2\mathbf{j}+6\mathbf{k}$.
13. Show that the vectors $\mathbf{a} = 4\mathbf{i}-2\mathbf{j}+2\mathbf{k}$, $\mathbf{b} = -6\mathbf{i}+3\mathbf{j}-3\mathbf{k}$ are parallel and in opposite directions. What is the ratio of their magnitudes?
14. Given $\mathbf{r} = \mathbf{a}+\lambda\mathbf{b}$, find $|\mathbf{r}|$ when $\mathbf{a} = 2\mathbf{i}-\mathbf{j}+3\mathbf{k}$, $\mathbf{b} = \mathbf{i}+\mathbf{j}+\mathbf{k}$, $\lambda = 2$.
15. If $\overline{OA} = \mathbf{a}$, $\overline{OB} = \mathbf{b}$, what vectors are represented by $\overline{OC}$, where C is the point dividing AB: (i) internally in the ratio 3:4; (ii) externally in the ratio 3:5?
16. Find the unit vector in the direction of the vector $2\mathbf{a}-\mathbf{b}$ where $\mathbf{a} = 2\mathbf{i}+\mathbf{j}-\mathbf{k}$, $\mathbf{b} = -2\mathbf{i}+\mathbf{k}$.
17. If $\lambda(\mathbf{a}+\mathbf{b}) = \mathbf{a}+\mu\mathbf{b}$, what are the values of the scalars λ, μ?
18. Given $\overline{OA} = 2\mathbf{i}+4\mathbf{j}+\mathbf{k}$, $\overline{OB} = \mathbf{i}-\mathbf{j}-2\mathbf{k}$, find $\overline{OC}$ where: (i) C is the mid-point of AB; (ii) C divides AB internally in the ratio 1:2.
19. The vector $(a-3)\mathbf{i}-b\mathbf{j}$, where a, b are constants, is parallel to the axis $\overline{Oy}$ and the vector $(a+1)\mathbf{i}+2b\mathbf{j}$ is parallel to the vector $\mathbf{i}+\mathbf{j}$. Find the values of a and b.
20. Find the constants λ, μ if $2\mathbf{i}-\mathbf{j}+\mathbf{k}+\lambda(3\mathbf{i}+\mathbf{j}) = -\mathbf{i}+\mathbf{j}+\mathbf{k}+\mu(-3\mathbf{i}+2\mathbf{j})$.
21. Find the unit vector in the direction of the vector $\mathbf{a}+2\mathbf{b}$ where $\mathbf{a} = 3\mathbf{i}-\mathbf{j}+5\mathbf{k}$, $\mathbf{b} = -\mathbf{i}+2\mathbf{j}+\mathbf{k}$.
22. Vectors $\mathbf{a}$, $\mathbf{b}$ are such that their moduli are 2, 3 respectively and the angle between their directions is $\cos^{-1} 1/3$. Find the moduli of the vectors: (i) $2\mathbf{a}-\mathbf{b}$; (ii) $2\mathbf{a}+\mathbf{b}$.
23. If $\overline{OP} = \mathbf{a}+\mathbf{b}$, $\overline{OQ} = 2\mathbf{a}+3\mathbf{b}$, $\overline{OR} = 5\mathbf{a}+9\mathbf{b}$, where $\mathbf{a}$, $\mathbf{b}$ are given vectors, show that the vectors $\overline{PQ}$, $\overline{QR}$ act in the same line and have magnitudes in the ratio 1:3.
24. Given $\mathbf{a}+s\mathbf{b} = \mathbf{c}+t\mathbf{d}$, where s, t are scalar constants, find the values of s and t in each of the cases: (i) $\mathbf{a} = \mathbf{i}+2\mathbf{j}$, $\mathbf{b} = 2\mathbf{i}-\mathbf{j}$, $\mathbf{c} = 4\mathbf{i}-3\mathbf{j}$, $\mathbf{d} = 3\mathbf{i}+2\mathbf{j}$; (ii) $\mathbf{a} = 2\mathbf{i}+\mathbf{j}-\mathbf{k}$, $\mathbf{b} = 3\mathbf{i}-\mathbf{j}-2\mathbf{k}$, $\mathbf{c} = 3\mathbf{i}-2\mathbf{j}+\mathbf{k}$, $\mathbf{d} = \mathbf{i}+\mathbf{j}-2\mathbf{k}$.

Scalar or inner product of two vectors

For two physical vectors $\mathbf{a}$, $\mathbf{b}$ inclined at an angle θ, the scalar product $\mathbf{a}\cdot\mathbf{b}$ is defined by the result $\mathbf{a}\cdot\mathbf{b} = ab\cos\theta$.

Note

(i) Clearly $\mathbf{b}\cdot\mathbf{a} = ba\cos\theta = ab\cos\theta = \mathbf{a}\cdot\mathbf{b}$;

(ii) $\mathbf{a}\cdot\mathbf{b} = 0$ if the vectors $\mathbf{a}$, $\mathbf{b}$ are perpendicular and conversely assuming $\mathbf{a}, \mathbf{b} \neq 0$; in particular $\mathbf{i}\cdot\mathbf{j} = \mathbf{j}\cdot\mathbf{k} = \mathbf{k}\cdot\mathbf{i} = 0$;

(iii) $\mathbf{a}^2 = \mathbf{a}\cdot\mathbf{a} = a^2$; in particular, $\mathbf{i}^2 = \mathbf{j}^2 = \mathbf{k}^2 = 1$;

(iv) the angle θ between two vectors $\mathbf{a}$, $\mathbf{b}$ is given by $\cos\theta = \mathbf{a}\cdot\mathbf{b}/ab$.

Scalar product in terms of components

If $\mathbf{a} = a_1\mathbf{i}+a_2\mathbf{j}$, $\mathbf{b} = b_1\mathbf{i}+b_2\mathbf{j}$, then $\mathbf{a}\cdot\mathbf{b} = a_1b_1+a_2b_2$ with a corresponding result for two three-dimensional vectors.

In the case of generalised vectors, these results are used as the definition of a scalar or inner product.

Example 5. Given that $\mathbf{r}\cdot\mathbf{s} = 25$ *where* $\mathbf{s} = 3\mathbf{i}-4\mathbf{j}+2\mathbf{k}$ *and* $\mathbf{r} = \mathbf{i}+2\mathbf{j}+3\mathbf{k}+\lambda(4\mathbf{i}+\mathbf{j}+2\mathbf{k})$, *find the value of the scalar constant* λ.

$$\mathbf{r}\cdot\mathbf{s} = (\mathbf{i}+2\mathbf{j}+3\mathbf{k})\cdot(3\mathbf{i}-4\mathbf{j}+2\mathbf{k})+\lambda(4\mathbf{i}+\mathbf{j}+2\mathbf{k})\cdot(3\mathbf{i}-4\mathbf{j}+2\mathbf{k}),$$
$$= 3-8+6+\lambda(12-4+4) = 1+12\lambda.$$
$$\therefore \qquad 1+12\lambda = 25,$$
$$\lambda = 2.$$

Example 6. *If a, b are perpendicular vectors, show that* $(\mathbf{a}+\mathbf{b})^2 = (\mathbf{a}-\mathbf{b})^2 = a^2+b^2$.

$$(\mathbf{a}+\mathbf{b})^2 = (\mathbf{a}+\mathbf{b})\cdot(\mathbf{a}+\mathbf{b}) = \mathbf{a}^2+2\mathbf{a}\cdot\mathbf{b}+\mathbf{b}^2,$$
$$= a^2+b^2, \text{ as } \mathbf{a}\cdot\mathbf{b} = 0, \mathbf{a}^2 = a^2, \mathbf{b}^2 = b^2.$$

Similarly $\qquad (\mathbf{a}-\mathbf{b})^2 = a^2+b^2.$

Component of a vector in the direction of another vector

Magnitude of the component of **a** in the direction of **b** equals

$$OC = OA\cos\theta, \quad \text{(Fig. 41)}.$$
$$= \frac{1}{b}\mathbf{a}\cdot\mathbf{b}.$$

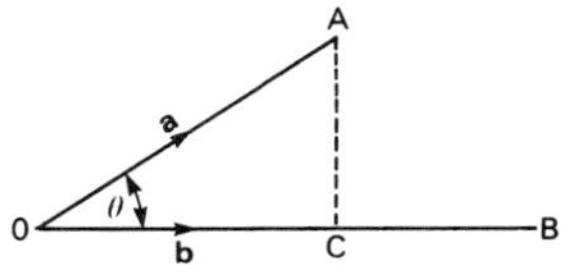

Fig. 41

Component of **a** in the direction of $\mathbf{b} = (\mathbf{a}\cdot\mathbf{b})\mathbf{b}/b^2$.

Example 7. *Find the resolved part of the vector* $\mathbf{r} = 2\mathbf{i}+\mathbf{j}+3\mathbf{k}$ *in the direction of the vector* $\mathbf{s} = 6\mathbf{i}+3\mathbf{j}+2\mathbf{k}$.

$$\text{Resolved part of } \mathbf{r} \text{ in the direction of } \mathbf{s} = \frac{1}{s^2}(\mathbf{r}\cdot\mathbf{s})\mathbf{s},$$
$$= \frac{1}{49}(21)(6\mathbf{i}+3\mathbf{j}+2\mathbf{k}),$$
$$= \frac{3}{7}(6\mathbf{i}+3\mathbf{j}+2\mathbf{k}).$$

(A) EXAMPLES 39

1. Vectors **a**, **b** are inclined at an angle θ, find the value of $\mathbf{a}\cdot\mathbf{b}$ in each of the cases: (i) $a = 3$, $b = 4$, $\theta = 60°$; (ii) $a = 1$, $b = \sqrt{2}$, $\theta = \pi/4$; (iii) $a = \sqrt{3}$, $b = 2$, $\theta = \cos^{-1}(-1/\sqrt{3})$.
2. Find the values of $\mathbf{r}\cdot\mathbf{s}$ when: (i) $\mathbf{r} = \mathbf{i}+\mathbf{j}$, $\mathbf{s} = \mathbf{i}-\mathbf{j}$; (ii) $\mathbf{r} = 3\mathbf{i}-\mathbf{j}$, $\mathbf{s} = 2\mathbf{i}+2\mathbf{j}$; (iii) $\mathbf{r} = 2\mathbf{i}-\mathbf{j}+\mathbf{k}$, $\mathbf{s} = \mathbf{i}+\mathbf{j}+2\mathbf{k}$; (iv) $\mathbf{r} = 2\mathbf{j}+3\mathbf{k}$, $\mathbf{s} = \mathbf{i}-\mathbf{j}$.
3. Verify the result $\mathbf{a}\cdot(\mathbf{b}+\mathbf{c}) = \mathbf{a}\cdot\mathbf{b}+\mathbf{a}\cdot\mathbf{c}$ in each of the cases: (i) $\mathbf{a} = \mathbf{i}+2\mathbf{j}$, $\mathbf{b} = 3\mathbf{i}+4\mathbf{j}$; (ii) $\mathbf{a} = -\mathbf{i}+2\mathbf{j}-\mathbf{k}$, $\mathbf{b} = 3\mathbf{i}+\mathbf{j}+4\mathbf{k}$.
4. Show that the vectors $p\mathbf{i}+q\mathbf{j}$, $-q\mathbf{i}+p\mathbf{j}$ are perpendicular and of equal moduli.
5. If $\overline{OA} = \mathbf{a}$, $\overline{OB} = \mathbf{b}$, find $\cos\angle AOB$ in each of the following cases: (i) $\mathbf{a} = 3\mathbf{i}-\mathbf{j}$, $\mathbf{b} = \mathbf{i}+\mathbf{j}$; (ii) $\mathbf{a} = 2\mathbf{i}-3\mathbf{j}$, $\mathbf{b} = 3\mathbf{i}+4\mathbf{j}$; (iii) $\mathbf{a} = 3\mathbf{i}-\mathbf{j}-\mathbf{k}$, $\mathbf{b} = \mathbf{i}+2\mathbf{j}-\mathbf{k}$; (iv) $\mathbf{a} = 3\mathbf{i}-2\mathbf{j}+2\mathbf{k}$, $\mathbf{b} = \mathbf{i}-\mathbf{j}+\mathbf{k}$.
6. Show that each of the following pairs of vectors are perpendicular: (i) $\mathbf{i}+\mathbf{j}$, $\mathbf{i}-\mathbf{j}$; (ii) $4\mathbf{i}+3\mathbf{j}$, $-3\mathbf{i}+4\mathbf{j}$; (iii) $\mathbf{i}+4\mathbf{j}+3\mathbf{k}$, $4\mathbf{i}+2\mathbf{j}-4\mathbf{k}$; (iv) $a\mathbf{i}$, $b\mathbf{j}+c\mathbf{k}$.
7. Find the magnitude of the resolved part of the vector **r** in the direction of the vector **s** in each of the cases: (i) $\mathbf{r} = \mathbf{i}+2\mathbf{j}$, $\mathbf{s} = 2\mathbf{i}-\mathbf{j}$; (ii) $\mathbf{r} = 3\mathbf{i}-4\mathbf{j}$, $\mathbf{s} = \mathbf{i}+\mathbf{j}$; (iii) $\mathbf{r} = \mathbf{i}+2\mathbf{j}+\mathbf{k}$, $\mathbf{s} = 2\mathbf{i}-\mathbf{j}-2\mathbf{k}$; (iv) $\mathbf{r} = \mathbf{i}-2\mathbf{j}-2\mathbf{k}$, $\mathbf{s} = \mathbf{j}+2\mathbf{k}$.

8. Find the value of the scalar multiple λ if the vectors $2\mathbf{i}+\mathbf{j}+\mathbf{k}$, $\lambda\mathbf{i}+(1-\lambda)\mathbf{j}+(1+\lambda)\mathbf{k}$ are perpendicular.
9. Given $\mathbf{a} = 9\mathbf{i}+6\mathbf{j}+8\mathbf{k}$, $\mathbf{b} = 7\mathbf{i}+4\mathbf{j}+6\mathbf{k}$, $\mathbf{c} = 4\mathbf{i}-5\mathbf{j}+\mathbf{k}$, show that the vectors $(\mathbf{a}-\mathbf{b})$ and $\mathbf{c}$ are perpendicular.
10. Find, in each of the following cases, the resolved component of the vector $\mathbf{r}$ in the direction of the vector $\mathbf{a}$: (i) $\mathbf{r} = 3\mathbf{i}+\mathbf{j}$, $\mathbf{a} = 4\mathbf{i}-3\mathbf{j}$; (ii) $\mathbf{r} = 2\mathbf{i}+\mathbf{j}+5\mathbf{k}$, $\mathbf{a} = 3\mathbf{i}$; (iii) $\mathbf{r} = \mathbf{i}-3\mathbf{j}+2\mathbf{k}$, $\mathbf{a} = 2\mathbf{i}+3\mathbf{j}+\mathbf{k}$.
11. If $\hat{\mathbf{a}}$, $\hat{\mathbf{b}}$ are unit vectors inclined at an angle of $\pi/3$, show that $(\hat{\mathbf{a}}+\hat{\mathbf{b}})^2 = 3$.
12. Find the resolved part of the vector $2\mathbf{i}-3\mathbf{j}+\mathbf{k}$ in the direction of the vector $-\mathbf{i}+2\mathbf{j}+2\mathbf{k}$.
13. Given $\mathbf{r} = -\mathbf{i}+\mathbf{j}+\mathbf{k}+\lambda(2\mathbf{i}-\mathbf{j}+3\mathbf{k})$, $\mathbf{s} = 3\mathbf{i}+2\mathbf{j}+2\mathbf{k}$, find the value of the scalar constant λ for which $\mathbf{r}\cdot\mathbf{s} = 21$.
14. Show that the magnitudes a, b, c of the components of the vector $\mathbf{r} = a\mathbf{i}+b\mathbf{j}+c\mathbf{k}$ are given by $a = \mathbf{r}\cdot\mathbf{i}$, $b = \mathbf{r}\cdot\mathbf{j}$, $c = \mathbf{r}\cdot\mathbf{k}$.
15. If $\mathbf{r} = 2\mathbf{a}+\mathbf{b}$, $\mathbf{s} = \mathbf{a}-2\mathbf{b}$ where $\mathbf{a}$, $\mathbf{b}$ are perpendicular vectors of equal moduli, show that the vectors $\mathbf{r}$, $\mathbf{s}$ are also perpendicular.
16. Find the value of the scalar product $\mathbf{P}\cdot\mathbf{s}$ when $\mathbf{P}$ is a vector of modulus 14 in the direction of the vector $2\mathbf{i}-3\mathbf{j}+6\mathbf{k}$ and $\mathbf{s}$ is a vector of modulus 6 in the direction of the vector $2\mathbf{i}-\mathbf{j}+2\mathbf{k}$.
17. Given $\mathbf{a}\cdot\mathbf{r} = \mathbf{b}\cdot\mathbf{r}$, where $\mathbf{r} \neq 0$ and $\mathbf{a} \neq \mathbf{b}$ prove that the vectors $\mathbf{r}$ and $(\mathbf{a}-\mathbf{b})$ are perpendicular.
18. If $a\mathbf{i}+b\mathbf{j}+\mathbf{k}$ is perpendicular to each of the vectors $2\mathbf{i}+\mathbf{j}-\mathbf{k}$, $-\mathbf{i}+3\mathbf{k}$, find the values of the constants a and b.

POSITION VECTORS

The position vector of a point P relative to an origin O is the vector $\overline{OP}$. *If P has coordinates* (x, y), *then the position vector of P relative to the origin O is* $x\mathbf{i}+y\mathbf{j}$.

In three dimensions when the coordinates of P are (x, y, z), *its position vector relative to the origin is* $x\mathbf{i}+y\mathbf{j}+z\mathbf{k}$.

Basic results

Taking the position vectors of the points A, B, C, D relative to an origin O to be $\mathbf{a}$, $\mathbf{b}$, $\mathbf{c}$, $\mathbf{d}$ respectively:

(i) *vector* $\overline{AB} = \mathbf{b}-\mathbf{a}$, *vector* $\overline{BA} = \mathbf{a}-\mathbf{b}$;

(ii) *the position vector of the mid-point of AB* $= (\mathbf{a}+\mathbf{b})/2$;

(iii) *the position vector of the point dividing AB in the ratio m:n is* $(n\mathbf{a}+m\mathbf{b})/(m+n)$; *(as a special case of this result it follows that the point with position vector* $\lambda\mathbf{a}+(1-\lambda)\mathbf{b}$ *lies on the line AB, dividing it in the ratio* $(1-\lambda):\lambda$);

(iv) *lines AB, CD are perpendicular if* $(\mathbf{b}-\mathbf{a})\cdot(\mathbf{d}-\mathbf{c}) = 0$ *and parallel if* $\mathbf{d}-\mathbf{c} = \lambda(\mathbf{b}-\mathbf{a})$ *where* λ *is a scalar multiple;*

(v) *lines AB, CD are equal in length if* $(\mathbf{b}-\mathbf{a})^2 = (\mathbf{d}-\mathbf{c})^2$.

Example 8. The points A, B, C have coordinates (4, −1, 5), (8, 0, 6), (5, −3, 3) respectively. Write down the position vectors of A, B, C relative to the origin and show that angle BAC = 90°. Also find the cosine of angle ACB.

The position vectors of A, B, C are $4\mathbf{i}-\mathbf{j}+5\mathbf{k}$, $8\mathbf{i}+6\mathbf{k}$, $5\mathbf{i}-3\mathbf{j}+3\mathbf{k}$ respectively.

So $$\overline{AB} = (8\mathbf{i}+6\mathbf{k})-(4\mathbf{i}-\mathbf{j}+5\mathbf{k}) = 4\mathbf{i}+\mathbf{j}+\mathbf{k};$$

$$\overline{AC} = (5\mathbf{i}-3\mathbf{j}+3\mathbf{k})-(4\mathbf{i}-\mathbf{j}+5\mathbf{k}) = \mathbf{i}-2\mathbf{j}-2\mathbf{k}.$$

$\therefore$ $$\overline{AB}\cdot\overline{AC} = 4-2-2 = 0, \text{ consequently angle BAC} = 90°.$$

Also $$\cos ACB = \frac{\overline{CA} \cdot \overline{CB}}{CA \cdot CB}$$

$$< \frac{(>\mathbf{i}+2\mathbf{j}+2\mathbf{k}) \cdot (3\mathbf{i}+3\mathbf{j}+3\mathbf{k})}{\sqrt{((-1)^2+2^2+2^2)}\sqrt{(3^2+3^2+3^2)}},$$

$$= \frac{9}{9\sqrt{3}} = \frac{1}{\sqrt{3}}.$$

Example 9. The position vectors **a**, **b**, **c** *of three points A, B, C are given by* $\mathbf{a} = \mathbf{i}+\mathbf{j}+\mathbf{k}$, $\mathbf{b} = \mathbf{i}+2\mathbf{j}+3\mathbf{k}$, $\mathbf{c} = \mathbf{i}-3\mathbf{j}+2\mathbf{k}$. *Find: (i) the unit vector parallel to* $\mathbf{a}+\mathbf{b}+\mathbf{c}$*; (ii) the position vector of the point P which divides BC in the ratio* $(1-\lambda):\lambda$*; (iii) the value of* λ *for which AP is perpendicular to BC.*

(i) $\mathbf{a}+\mathbf{b}+\mathbf{c} = 3\mathbf{i}+6\mathbf{k}; |\mathbf{a}+\mathbf{b}+\mathbf{c}| = \sqrt{(3^2+6^2)} = 3\sqrt{5};$

$\therefore$ unit vector parallel to $\mathbf{a}+\mathbf{b}+\mathbf{c} = \dfrac{1}{3\sqrt{5}}(3\mathbf{i}+6\mathbf{k}) = \dfrac{1}{\sqrt{5}}(\mathbf{i}+2\mathbf{k}).$

(ii) Position vector of $P = \lambda\mathbf{b}+(1-\lambda)\mathbf{c} = \lambda(\mathbf{i}+2\mathbf{j}+3\mathbf{k})+(1-\lambda)(\mathbf{i}-3\mathbf{j}+2\mathbf{k}),$

$$= \mathbf{i}+\mathbf{j}(5\lambda-3)+\mathbf{k}(\lambda+2);$$

$\therefore$ $$\overline{AP} = \mathbf{j}(5\lambda-4)+\mathbf{k}(\lambda+1),$$

and $$\overline{BC} = -5\mathbf{j}-\mathbf{k}.$$

(iii) As AP is perpendicular to BC, $\overline{AP} \cdot \overline{BC} = 0,$

i.e. $$-5(5\lambda-4)-(\lambda+1) = 0; \quad \lambda = \frac{19}{26}.$$

Example 10. ABCD is a square and E, F are the mid-points of sides AD, DC respectively. Show that lines BE, AF are perpendicular.

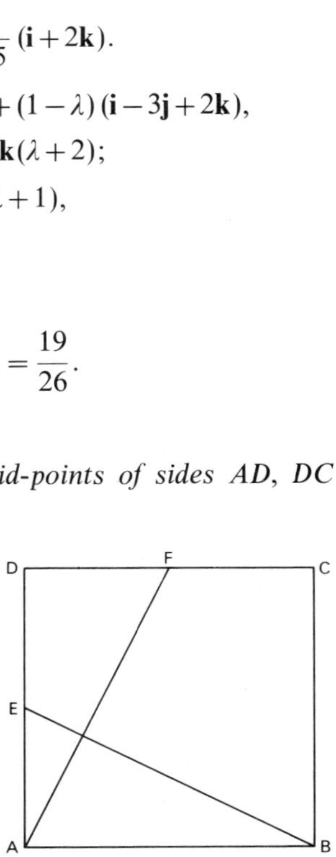

Fig. 42

With A as origin, let the position vectors of B and D be **b**, **d**; i.e. $\overline{AB} = \mathbf{b}$, $\overline{AD} = \mathbf{d}$; so $\overline{AC}$, the position vector of $C = \mathbf{b}+\mathbf{d}$.

Position vector of $E = \mathbf{d}/2$; position vector of $F = (\mathbf{b}+2\mathbf{d})/2$; $\overline{BE} = \mathbf{d}/2-\mathbf{b}$; $\overline{AF} = (\mathbf{b}+2\mathbf{d})/2$,

$$\overline{BE} \cdot \overline{AF} = \left(\frac{\mathbf{d}}{2}-\mathbf{b}\right) \cdot \frac{(\mathbf{b}+2\mathbf{d})}{2},$$

$$= \frac{(\mathbf{d}-2\mathbf{b})}{4} \cdot (\mathbf{b}+2\mathbf{d}),$$

$$= \frac{(2\mathbf{d}^2-3\mathbf{b}\cdot\mathbf{d}-2\mathbf{b}^2)}{4}.$$

But $\mathbf{d}^2 = d^2$ and $\mathbf{b}^2 = b^2$, so as AD = AB, $\mathbf{d}^2 = \mathbf{b}^2$; also $\mathbf{b}\cdot\mathbf{d} = 0$ as BAD = 90°.

$\therefore$ $\overline{BE} \cdot \overline{AF} = 0$ and consequently BE, AF are perpendicular.

Skew lines

In three-dimensional geometry, lines which are not parallel and which do not intersect, i.e. they are not in the same plane, are said to be *skew*.

Common perpendicular

Two skew lines AB, CD have a common perpendicular PQ (Fig. 43); PQ is the shortest distance between the skew lines.

If PR is drawn parallel to CD, angle BPR is an angle between the skew lines.

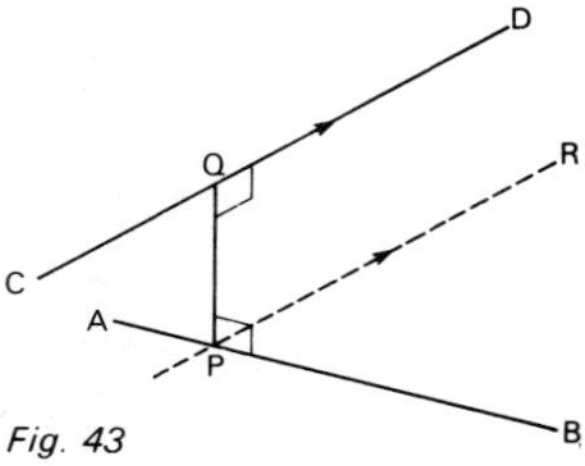

Fig. 43

Example 11. AB is the common perpendicular of two skew lines AP, BQ; the mid-points of AB, PQ are H and M respectively. Prove that HM is perpendicular to AB.

Take A as origin and let the position vectors of B, P, Q be **b**, **p**, **q** respectively.

Then H, M have position vectors $\mathbf{b}/2$ and $(\mathbf{p}+\mathbf{q})/2$,

so $$\overline{HM} = \frac{(\mathbf{p}+\mathbf{q}-\mathbf{b})}{2}.$$

∴ $$\overline{AB}\cdot\overline{HM} = \mathbf{b}\cdot\frac{(\mathbf{p}+\mathbf{q}-\mathbf{b})}{2},$$

$$= \frac{(\mathbf{b}\cdot\mathbf{p}+\mathbf{b}\cdot\mathbf{q}-\mathbf{b}^2)}{2}.$$

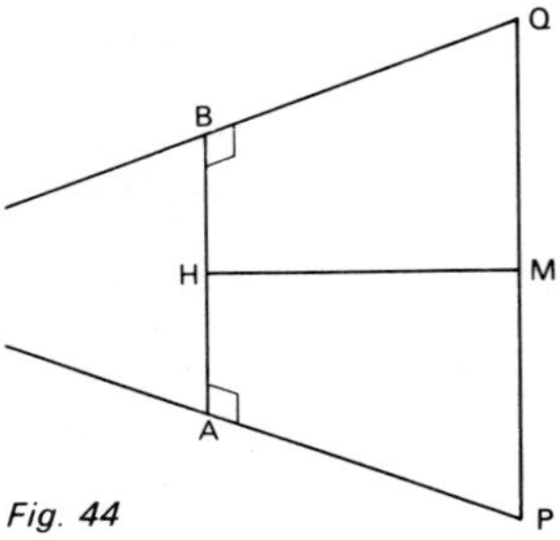

Fig. 44

As AP, AB are perpendicular, $\mathbf{b}\cdot\mathbf{p} = 0$; as BQ, AB are perpendicular $\mathbf{b}\cdot(\mathbf{q}-\mathbf{b}) = 0$, i.e. $\mathbf{b}\cdot\mathbf{q}-\mathbf{b}^2 = 0$.

∴ $\overline{AB}\cdot\overline{HM} = 0$ and consequently AB, HM are perpendicular.

(A) EXAMPLES 40

1. Points P, Q have coordinates (3, 2), (1, −4) respectively. Write down in terms of the unit vectors **i**, **j**, the position vectors relative to the origin O of: (i) P; (ii) Q; (iii) M, the mid-point of PQ; (iv) the point R which divides PQ internally in the ratio 3:2; (v) the point N which divides OM in the ratio $1-\lambda:\lambda$.
2. Points A, B have position vectors $2\mathbf{i}+\mathbf{j}$, $4\mathbf{i}-3\mathbf{j}$ relative to an origin O. By evaluating the product $\overline{OA}\cdot\overline{AB}$, show that OA, AB are perpendicular.
3. Find (a) the modulus, (b) the unit vector in the direction of the vector $\overline{AB}$ in each of the cases where the coordinates of A, B are respectively: (i) (2, −1), (5, 3); (ii) (3, 0, 4), (1, 1, 2); (iii) (−4, 2, 1), (2, −1, 3).
4. Points A, B have position vectors **a**, **b** relative to an origin O; find the position vectors of: (i) the point C, where OACB is a parallelogram; (ii) the mid-point M of BC; (iii) the point dividing OC internally in the ratio 2:1; (iv) the point dividing AM internally in the ratio 2:1. Deduce that OC, AM trisect each other.
5. The coordinates of the points A, B are (2, 0, 3), (−3, 5, 2) respectively. Use the scalar product $\overline{OA}\cdot\overline{OB}$, where O is the origin, to show that OA, OB are perpendicular. Also find the area of triangle AOB.
6. The position vectors of the points A, B, C, D are **a**, **b**, $3\mathbf{a}-\mathbf{b}$, $\mathbf{a}+\mathbf{b}$ respectively. Show that $\overline{CD}$ is parallel to $\overline{AB}$ and find the ratio AB:CD.
7. In each of the following cases where the coordinates of points A, B, C are given, show that the points

are collinear by establishing that the vectors $\overline{AB}$, $\overline{BC}$ are parallel: (i) A(2, 1), B(3, 4), C(0, −5); (ii) A(1, 2, 1), B(2, 0, 3), C(0, 4, −1); (iii) A(0, 3, −1), B(2, 1, 1), C(−2, 5, −3).

8. Show that the vector $4\mathbf{i}-5\mathbf{j}+\mathbf{k}$ is perpendicular to the line joining the points with coordinates (7, 4, 6), (9, 6, 8).
9. Find the cosine of the angle of inclination of the vectors $\overline{AB}$, $\overline{CD}$ where A, B, C, D have coordinates (1, −1, 1), (0, 1, 2), (3, 1, 0), (1, 4, −1) respectively.
10. The vertices of a triangle have coordinates A(0, 1, 1), B(2, −1, 2), C(1, 3, 3). Show that the angle BAC = 90° and find the angle ABC.
11. Triangle ABC is right-angled at A and the position vectors of B, C relative to A are **b**, **c** respectively. By expressing $\overline{BC}^2$ in terms of **b** and **c**, deduce that $BC^2 = AB^2 + AC^2$.
12. Prove that the points with position vectors $\mathbf{a}+2\mathbf{b}$, $2\mathbf{a}-\mathbf{b}$, $3\mathbf{a}-4\mathbf{b}$ are collinear.
13. The position vectors of A, B, C, D are $\mathbf{a} = \mathbf{i}+\mathbf{j}+\mathbf{k}$, $\mathbf{b} = 2\mathbf{i}+3\mathbf{j}$, $\mathbf{c} = 3\mathbf{i}+5\mathbf{j}-2\mathbf{k}$, $\mathbf{d} = -\mathbf{j}+\mathbf{k}$. Show that: (i) $\overline{AB}$, $\overline{CD}$ are parallel and determine the ratio AB:CD; (ii) find the cosine of the angle of inclination of the vectors $\overline{AC}$, $\overline{BD}$.
14. Find the value of λ for which the line joining the origin to the point with coordinates $(1+2\lambda, 1+2\lambda, 1-\lambda)$ is perpendicular to the vector $2\mathbf{i}+2\mathbf{j}-\mathbf{k}$.
15. The position vectors **a**, **b**, **c** of the points A, B, C are given by $\mathbf{a} = \mathbf{i}+\mathbf{j}+\mathbf{k}$, $\mathbf{b} = \mathbf{i}-\mathbf{j}+3\mathbf{k}$, $\mathbf{c} = \mathbf{i}-2\mathbf{j}+2\mathbf{k}$. Find: (i) the cosine of the angle between the vectors **a** and $\mathbf{a}+\mathbf{b}+\mathbf{c}$; (ii) the position vector of D where ABCD is a parallelogram having AC as one diagonal.
16. Points P, Q have position vectors **p**, **q** with respect to an origin O. If the angle POQ = θ, show that $p^2q^2\sin^2\theta = p^2q^2-(\mathbf{p}\cdot\mathbf{q})^2$.
17. In triangle ABC, the position vectors of B, C relative to A are **b**, **c** respectively. By expressing $\overline{BC}^2$ in terms of **b** and **c**, deduce the Cosine Rule for BC^2.
18. The vertices A, B, C of a triangle have position vectors **a**, **b**, **c** respectively and the point H has position vector **h**. Express in terms of these position vectors the condition that: (i) AH is perpendicular to BC; (ii) BH is perpendicular to AC. Deduce that CH is perpendicular to AB.
19. The position vector **r** of a variable point P relative to the origin is given by $\mathbf{r} = 6\mathbf{i}+8\mathbf{j}+6(\mathbf{i}\cos\theta+\mathbf{j}\sin\theta)$. Show that the locus of P is a circle and state the centre and the radius.
20. In the rectangle ABCD, AB = 2AD and P is the point on DC such that DP = 3PC. Taking $\overline{AB} = \mathbf{b}$, $\overline{AD} = \mathbf{d}$, express $\overline{AC}$, $\overline{BP}$ in terms of **b** and **d** and hence show that the lines AC, BP are perpendicular.
21. In the tetrahedron OABC, edges OA, OB are perpendicular respectively to edges BC, CA. Taking the position vectors of A, B, C, relative to O as **a**, **b**, **c** establish the results: (i) OC is perpendicular to AB; (ii) $OA^2+BC^2 = OB^2+CA^2 = OC^2+AB^2$.
22. A cube, edge $2a$, has opposite faces ABCD, PQRS joined by edges AP, BQ, CR, DS; the mid-points of BC, RS are M, L respectively. Taking A as origin and letting unit vectors in the directions of axes $\overline{AB}$, $\overline{AD}$, $\overline{AP}$ be **i**, **j**, **k** respectively, show that: (i) $\overline{ML} = -a\mathbf{i}+a\mathbf{j}+2a\mathbf{k}$; (ii) the cosine of the angle between $\overline{AP}$ and $\overline{ML}$ is $2/\sqrt{6}$.

VECTOR EQUATION OF A LINE

The equation of the line passing through the point, position vector **a**, *and parallel to the vector* **b** *is* $\mathbf{r} = \mathbf{a}+\lambda\mathbf{b}$, *where* λ *is a scalar parameter. The equation of the line passing through two points, position vectors* **a** *and* **b** *is* $\mathbf{r} = \mathbf{a}+\lambda(\mathbf{b}-\mathbf{a})$, *where* λ *is a scalar parameter, or* $\mathbf{r} = \mathbf{b}+\mu(\mathbf{b}-\mathbf{a})$, *where* μ *is a scalar parameter.*

Intersecting or non-intersecting lines

Let the equations of two lines be $\mathbf{r} = \mathbf{a}_1+\lambda\mathbf{b}_1$, $\mathbf{r} = \mathbf{a}_2+\mu\mathbf{b}_2$; then the lines intersect if values of the scalar parameters λ, μ can be found such that $\mathbf{a}_1+\lambda\mathbf{b}_1 = \mathbf{a}_2+\mu\mathbf{b}_2$.

If this is not possible the lines are non-intersecting, i.e. skew.

The angle θ between the two lines is determined by noting that it is also the angle between the directions of the vectors $\mathbf{b}_1$ and $\mathbf{b}_2$.

Example 12. Find the coordinates of the common point of the lines with equations $\mathbf{r} = 5\mathbf{i}+7\mathbf{j}-3\mathbf{k}+\lambda(4\mathbf{i}+4\mathbf{j}-5\mathbf{k})$, $\mathbf{r} = 8\mathbf{i}+4\mathbf{j}+5\mathbf{k}+\mu(7\mathbf{i}+\mathbf{j}+3\mathbf{k})$, *where* λ, μ *are scalar parameters.*

Collecting the terms in **i**, **j**, **k**, the equations of the two lines are

$$\mathbf{r} = \mathbf{i}(5+4\lambda)+\mathbf{j}(7+4\lambda)+\mathbf{k}(-3-5\lambda);$$

and $$\mathbf{r} = \mathbf{i}(8+7\mu)+\mathbf{j}(4+\mu)+\mathbf{k}(5+3\mu).$$

For the lines to have a common point the three equations

$$5+4\lambda = 8+7\mu,\ 7+4\lambda = 4+\mu,\ -3-5\lambda = 5+3\mu,$$

must be simultaneously satisfied.

Solving the first two equations gives $\lambda = \mu = -1$ and on substitution these values satisfy the third equation.

So the lines have a common point, position vector $\mathbf{i}+3\mathbf{j}+2\mathbf{k}$, coordinates (1, 3, 2).

Example 13. M, N are the mid-points of the sides AB, AD respectively of a parallelogram ABCD. Relative to A as origin, the position vectors of B, D are **b**, **d**. *Write down the equations of the lines NC, MD and find the position vector of P their point of intersection. Verify that P divides NC in the ratio 1:4.*

The position vectors of the points C, M, N are $\mathbf{b}+\mathbf{d}$, $\mathbf{b}/2$, $\mathbf{d}/2$ respectively (Fig. 45).

Equation of NC $$\mathbf{r} = \frac{\mathbf{d}}{2}+\lambda\left(\mathbf{b}+\mathbf{d}-\frac{\mathbf{d}}{2}\right),$$

$$= \mathbf{b}\lambda+\mathbf{d}\left(\frac{1}{2}+\frac{\lambda}{2}\right);$$

equation of MD $$\mathbf{r} = \frac{\mathbf{b}}{2}+\mu\left(\mathbf{d}-\frac{\mathbf{b}}{2}\right),$$

$$= \mathbf{b}\left(\frac{1}{2}-\frac{\mu}{2}\right)+\mathbf{d}\mu.$$

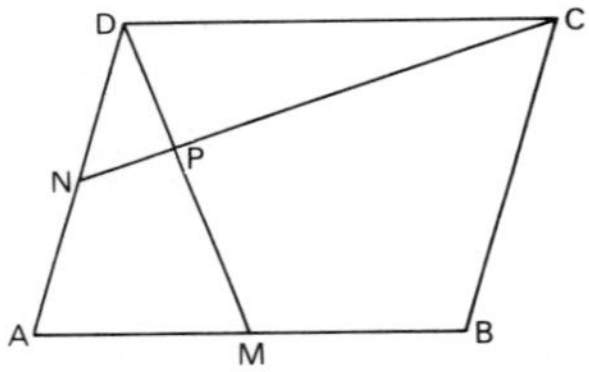

Fig. 45

For P, the values of **r** in the two equations are equal and consequently

$$\lambda = \frac{1}{2}-\frac{\mu}{2} \text{ and } \mu = \frac{1}{2}+\frac{\lambda}{2};$$

solving these equations, $\lambda = 1/5$, $\mu = 3/5$.

$\therefore$ The position vector of P is $\mathbf{b}/5+3\mathbf{d}/5$.

The position vector of the point dividing NC in the ratio 1:4 is $[4(\mathbf{d}/2)+(\mathbf{b}+\mathbf{d})]/(1+4)$, i.e. $\mathbf{b}/5+3\mathbf{d}/5$, the position vector of P.

(A) EXAMPLES 41

1. In each of the following cases write down the equation of the line passing through the point A and in the direction of the vector **p** where: (i) A is the point (2, 3), $\mathbf{p} = 4\mathbf{i}-\mathbf{j}$; (ii) A is the point (1, 2), $\mathbf{p} = -3\mathbf{i}$; (iii) A is the point (1, 0, 3), $\mathbf{p} = \mathbf{i}-2\mathbf{j}+\mathbf{k}$; (iv) A is the origin, $\mathbf{p} = 4\mathbf{i}-3\mathbf{j}-\mathbf{k}$; (v) A has the position vector $\mathbf{a}+2\mathbf{b}$, $\mathbf{p} = \mathbf{a}-\mathbf{b}$.

2. Find the equations of the lines joining the points A, B where: (i) A, B have coordinates (0, 2), (3, 4); (ii) A, B have coordinates (1, 1, 1), (3, −1, 2); (iii) A, B have position vectors $2\mathbf{i}-\mathbf{j}$, $3\mathbf{i}+\mathbf{j}$; (iv) A, B have position vectors $\mathbf{a}-\mathbf{b}/2$, $\mathbf{a}/2+\mathbf{b}$.
3. Find the position vector of the common point of the lines $\mathbf{r} = 2\mathbf{i}+\mathbf{j}+\lambda(\mathbf{i}+\mathbf{j})$, $\mathbf{r} = -\mathbf{i}+4\mathbf{j}+\mu(2\mathbf{i}-\mathbf{j})$, where λ, μ are scalar parameters.
4. Find the vector equation of the line which passes through the point A and is parallel to the line BC in each of the cases where the coordinates are: (i) A(1, 4), B(2, 0), C(4, 1); (ii) A(0, 1, 2), B(−1, 3, 1), C(2, 0, 4); (iii) A(a, 0, 0), B(a, 0, a), C(0, a, a).
5. Show that the equations of the coordinate axes can be taken as $\mathbf{r} = x\mathbf{i}$, $\mathbf{r} = y\mathbf{j}$ and $\mathbf{r} = z\mathbf{k}$, where x, y, z are scalar parameters.
6. Find the equations of the lines parallel to the line $\mathbf{r} = \mathbf{i}+\mathbf{j}+s(2\mathbf{i}-\mathbf{j})$, where s is a scalar, which pass through: (i) the origin; (ii) the point (3, −1).
7. Show that the line with equation $\mathbf{r} = 2\mathbf{i}+\mathbf{j}-\mathbf{k}+\lambda(\mathbf{i}-\mathbf{j}+\mathbf{k})$, where λ is a scalar, cuts the x-axis and find the coordinates of the point of intersection.
8. Find (a) the unit vector in the direction of each of the following lines and (b) the cosine of the angle between the line and the axis of x: (i) $\mathbf{r} = \mathbf{i}+\mathbf{j}+\lambda(3\mathbf{i}-4\mathbf{j})$; (ii) $\mathbf{r} = 2\mathbf{i}+\mathbf{k}+\lambda(2\mathbf{i}-\mathbf{j}+2\mathbf{k})$; (iii) $\mathbf{r} = \lambda(\mathbf{i}+\mathbf{j}+\mathbf{k})$, λ being a scalar parameter.
9. Write down the vector equations of the lines joining: (i) the origin to the point with position vector $3\mathbf{a}+5\mathbf{b}$; (ii) the points with position vectors $\mathbf{a}$ and $3\mathbf{a}-2\mathbf{b}$. Find the position vector of the common point of these two lines.
10. Show that the points A, B, C with position vectors $-2\mathbf{a}+3\mathbf{b}$, $3\mathbf{a}-2\mathbf{b}$, $4\mathbf{a}-3\mathbf{b}$ respectively are collinear and find the ratio AB : BC.
11. Find the cosine of the acute angle between each of the following pairs of lines: (i) $\mathbf{r} = \mathbf{i}-\mathbf{j}+\lambda(\mathbf{i}+\mathbf{j})$, $\mathbf{r} = \mu(\mathbf{i}-\mathbf{j})$; (ii) $\mathbf{r} = 2\mathbf{i}+\mathbf{j}+\mathbf{k}+\lambda(2\mathbf{i}-\mathbf{j}+2\mathbf{k})$, $\mathbf{r} = \mathbf{i}+\mathbf{j}+\mu(\mathbf{i}-2\mathbf{j}+2\mathbf{k})$; (iii) $\mathbf{r} = \lambda(\mathbf{i}-\mathbf{j}+\mathbf{k})$, $\mathbf{r} = \mu(\mathbf{i}+\mathbf{j}-\mathbf{k})$, where λ, μ are scalar parameters.
12. Find the coordinates of the common point of the lines with equations $\mathbf{r} = \mathbf{i}(1+\lambda)+\mathbf{j}(2-\lambda)$, $\mathbf{r} = 2\mu\mathbf{i}+\mathbf{j}(1-\mu)$, where λ, μ are scalars. Also find the cosine of the acute angle between the lines.
13. The position vectors of the coplanar points, P, Q, R, S are $2\mathbf{i}+3\mathbf{j}$, $3\mathbf{i}+2\mathbf{j}$, $4\mathbf{i}-\mathbf{j}$, $\mathbf{i}+5\mathbf{j}$ respectively. Find: (i) the vector equations of the lines PR, QS; (ii) the position vector of their point of intersection.
14. Prove that the points with position vectors $3\mathbf{i}-\mathbf{j}+2\mathbf{k}$, $-\mathbf{i}+\mathbf{j}-2\mathbf{k}$, $5\mathbf{i}-2\mathbf{j}+4\mathbf{k}$ are collinear.
15. Relative to A, the position vectors of the vertices B, C of a triangle ABC are $\mathbf{b}$, $\mathbf{c}$; the mid-points of BC, CA respectively are M and N. Find the position vector relative to A of the common point of BN and the line through C parallel to MA.
16. M, N are the mid-points of the sides AB, CD of a parallelogram ABCD and the position vectors of B, D relative to A are $\mathbf{b}$, $\mathbf{d}$. Write down the equations of DM, BN and the diagonal AC and show that DM and BN trisect this diagonal.
17. Points A, P have position vectors $4\mathbf{i}+6\mathbf{j}$, $2\mathbf{i}\cos\theta+2\mathbf{j}\sin\theta$ respectively. If $\overline{OA}+\overline{OP} = 2\overline{OQ}$, where O is the origin, find the position vector of Q and show that the locus of Q, as θ varies, is a circle.
18. Show that the lines $\mathbf{r} = \mathbf{i}+\mathbf{j}+2\mathbf{k}+s(\mathbf{i}+\mathbf{j}-3\mathbf{k})$, $\mathbf{r} = -2\mathbf{i}-2\mathbf{j}+t(\mathbf{i}+\mathbf{j}+\mathbf{k})$, where s, t are scalar parameters, intersect and find the position vector of the common point.
19. Two lines have equations $\mathbf{r} = \mathbf{i}+2\mathbf{j}-3\mathbf{k}+\lambda(2\mathbf{i}-\mathbf{j}+\mathbf{k})$, $\mathbf{r} = 2\mathbf{i}-3\mathbf{j}-2\mathbf{k}+\mu(-\mathbf{i}-2\mathbf{j})$. Show that the lines are: (i) skew; (ii) perpendicular.
20. In each of the following cases determine whether the lines are coplanar or skew and find the cosine of the acute angle between them: (i) $\mathbf{r} = \mathbf{i}-3\mathbf{k}+\lambda(2\mathbf{i}+\mathbf{j}-\mathbf{k})$, $\mathbf{r} = -2\mathbf{i}+2\mathbf{j}+\mu(3\mathbf{i}-2\mathbf{j}+\mathbf{k})$; (ii) $\mathbf{r} = 2\mathbf{i}+3\mathbf{j}-\mathbf{k}+\lambda(2\mathbf{i}-\mathbf{j}+3\mathbf{k})$, $\mathbf{r} = -2\mathbf{i}+2\mathbf{j}+2\mathbf{k}+\mu(\mathbf{i}+\mathbf{j}-3\mathbf{k})$; (iii) $\mathbf{r} = \mathbf{i}(3+2\lambda)+\mathbf{j}(-1-3\lambda)+\mathbf{k}(4+6\lambda)$, $\mathbf{r} = \mathbf{i}(1+\mu)+\mathbf{j}4\mu+\mathbf{k}(-2+3\mu)$, where λ, μ are scalar parameters.

VECTOR EQUATION OF A PLANE

Perpendicular form of the vector equation of a plane

If $\mathbf{n}$ is a vector normal to a plane, the equation of the plane can be expressed in the form

$$\mathbf{r}\cdot\mathbf{n} = a, \quad \textit{where } a \textit{ is a scalar constant.}$$

More specifically, if $\hat{\mathbf{n}}$ is the unit vector in the direction of the normal to the plane from the origin, the equation of the plane can be taken as

$$\mathbf{r} \cdot \hat{\mathbf{n}} = p, \text{ where } p, \text{ a positive constant,}$$

is the length of the perpendicular from the origin to the plane.

Note

(i) A plane parallel to the plane $\mathbf{r} \cdot \mathbf{n} = a$ has an equation of the form $\mathbf{r} \cdot \mathbf{n} = b$; if a and b are of the same sign, the two planes lie on the same side of the origin, if of opposite signs, the two planes lie on opposite sides of the origin;

(ii) in finding angles of inclination of two planes, find the angles between the normals to the planes; similarly in finding angles of inclination of lines and planes, first find the angles between the lines and the normals to the planes.

Example 14. The equation of a plane is $\mathbf{r} \cdot (\mathbf{i}-2\mathbf{j}+2\mathbf{k})+6 = 0$. *Find: (i) the unit vector in the direction of the normal from the origin to the plane; (ii) the length of the perpendicular from the origin to the plane.*

Write the equation in the form $\mathbf{r} \cdot (-\mathbf{i}+2\mathbf{j}-2\mathbf{k}) = 6$, a positive constant, so the unit vector

$$\hat{\mathbf{n}} = (-\mathbf{i}+2\mathbf{j}-2\mathbf{k})/3,$$

and the equation of the plane is

$$\mathbf{r} \cdot \hat{\mathbf{n}} = \frac{1}{3} \cdot 6 = 2;$$

$\therefore$ the length of the perpendicular from the origin is 2.

Example 15. Find: (i) the equation of the plane parallel to the plane $\mathbf{r} \cdot (\mathbf{i}-\mathbf{j}-\mathbf{k}) = \sqrt{3}$ *and passing through the point* $P(1, 1, 1)$; *(ii) the distance between the two planes.*

The required plane has an equation of the form

$$\mathbf{r} \cdot (\mathbf{i}-\mathbf{j}-\mathbf{k}) = b, \text{ where } b \text{ is a constant.}$$

As it passes through P, the value $\mathbf{r} = \mathbf{i}+\mathbf{j}+\mathbf{k}$ must satisfy the equation, so

$$(\mathbf{i}+\mathbf{j}+\mathbf{k}) \cdot (\mathbf{i}-\mathbf{j}-\mathbf{k}) = b, \text{ i.e. } b = -1.$$

Equation of the parallel plane is $\mathbf{r} \cdot (\mathbf{i}-\mathbf{j}-\mathbf{k})+1 = 0$.

The distance between the parallel planes is determined by finding the lengths of the perpendiculars from the origin to the planes.

The equation of the given plane can be expressed as

$$\mathbf{r} \cdot \frac{1}{\sqrt{3}}(\mathbf{i}-\mathbf{j}-\mathbf{k}) = 1,$$

and that of the parallel plane as

$$\mathbf{r} \cdot \frac{1}{\sqrt{3}}(-\mathbf{i}+\mathbf{j}+\mathbf{k}) = \frac{1}{\sqrt{3}}.$$

The perpendiculars from the origin to the planes are in opposite directions and consequently the distance between the planes is $1+1/\sqrt{3}$.

Example 16. Find the cosine of the acute angle between the planes $\mathbf{r} \cdot (\mathbf{i}+\mathbf{j}+\mathbf{k}) = 3$, $\mathbf{r} \cdot (2\mathbf{i}+2\mathbf{j}-\mathbf{k})+1 = 0$.

If θ is an angle between normals to the planes

$$\cos\theta = \frac{(\mathbf{i}+\mathbf{j}+\mathbf{k})\cdot(2\mathbf{i}+2\mathbf{j}-\mathbf{k})}{\sqrt{(1^2+1^2+1^2)}\sqrt{(2^2+2^2+(-1)^2)}},$$

$$= \frac{3}{\sqrt{3}\cdot 3} = \frac{1}{\sqrt{3}}.$$

So the cosine of the acute angle between the planes is $1/\sqrt{3}$.

Example 17. Find: (i) the position vector of the point of intersection of the line $\mathbf{r} = \mathbf{i}+\mathbf{j}+\mathbf{k}+\lambda(2\mathbf{i}-\mathbf{j})$ *and the plane* $\mathbf{r}\cdot(\mathbf{i}+\mathbf{j}+\mathbf{k}) = 5$*; (ii) the acute angle between the line and the plane.*

Substituting for $\mathbf{r}$ in the equation of the plane,

$$(\mathbf{i}+\mathbf{j}+\mathbf{k}+\lambda(2\mathbf{i}-\mathbf{j})\cdot(\mathbf{i}+\mathbf{j}+\mathbf{k}) = 5,$$

$$1+1+1+\lambda(2-1) = 5,$$

$$\lambda = 2.$$

So the position vector of the common point is $5\mathbf{i}-\mathbf{j}+\mathbf{k}$.

If θ is an angle between the line and a normal to the plane

$$\cos\theta = \frac{(2\mathbf{i}-\mathbf{j})\cdot(\mathbf{i}+\mathbf{j}+\mathbf{k})}{\sqrt{5}\cdot\sqrt{3}},$$

$$= \frac{1}{\sqrt{15}};$$

so the acute angle, $90°-\theta$, between the line and the plane is $\sin^{-1} 1/\sqrt{15}$.

(A) EXAMPLES 42

1. Find for each of the following planes (a) the unit vector in the direction of the perpendicular from the origin to the plane, (b) the length of this perpendicular: (i) $\mathbf{r}\cdot(2\mathbf{i}+\mathbf{j}-2\mathbf{k}) = 6$; (ii) $\mathbf{r}\cdot(3\mathbf{i}-2\mathbf{j}+6\mathbf{k}) = 21$; (iii) $\mathbf{r}\cdot(\mathbf{i}-\mathbf{j}-\mathbf{k})+1 = 0$; (iv) $\mathbf{r}\cdot(\sqrt{2}\mathbf{i}-\mathbf{j}-\mathbf{k})+8 = 0$.
2. Show that the point with coordinates (2, 1, 3) lies on the plane $\mathbf{r}\cdot(\mathbf{i}-2\mathbf{j}-\mathbf{k})+3 = 0$.
3. Find the equation of the plane parallel to the plane $\mathbf{r}\cdot(-\mathbf{i}+3\mathbf{j}+\mathbf{k}) = 1$ which passes through the point with position vector $\mathbf{i}+2\mathbf{j}-\mathbf{k}$.
4. Show that the planes $\mathbf{r}\cdot(2\mathbf{i}+3\mathbf{j}-2\mathbf{k}) = 1$, $\mathbf{r}\cdot(4\mathbf{i}-2\mathbf{j}+\mathbf{k})+2 = 0$ are perpendicular.
5. Find the cosine of the acute angle between the planes $\mathbf{r}\cdot(\mathbf{i}+\mathbf{j}+\mathbf{k}) = 3$, $\mathbf{r}\cdot(-2\mathbf{i}-2\mathbf{j}+\mathbf{k})+1 = 0$.
6. What is the vector equation of the plane passing through the origin and perpendicular to the line with equation $\mathbf{r} = \lambda(-\mathbf{i}+2\mathbf{j}+2\mathbf{k})$?
7. Show that the vector equation of the coordinate plane xOy to $\mathbf{r}\cdot\mathbf{k} = 0$ and find the position vector of the point of intersection of the line $\mathbf{r} = 2\mathbf{i}+3\mathbf{j}+4\mathbf{k}+\lambda(3\mathbf{i}-2\mathbf{j}+2\mathbf{k})$ and this plane.
8. Find the position vector of the common point of the line $\mathbf{r} = \mathbf{i}+\mathbf{j}+\mathbf{k}+\lambda(2\mathbf{i}-\mathbf{j})$ and the plane $\mathbf{r}\cdot(\mathbf{i}+\mathbf{k}) = 4$.
9. Show that the planes $\mathbf{r}\cdot(2\mathbf{i}-\mathbf{j}+2\mathbf{k}) = 6$, $\mathbf{r}\cdot(4\mathbf{i}-2\mathbf{j}+4\mathbf{k})+1 = 0$ are parallel and on opposite sides of the origin. Also find the distance between the planes.
10. Show that the line $\mathbf{r} = (2+\lambda)\mathbf{i}+(1-\lambda)\mathbf{j}+(3-2\lambda)\mathbf{k}$, where λ is a scalar parameter, is parallel to the plane $\mathbf{r}\cdot(2\mathbf{i}+4\mathbf{j}-\mathbf{k}) = 5$.
11. Find the position vectors of the points of intersection of the line $\mathbf{r} = 2\mathbf{i}+\mathbf{j}-\mathbf{k}+\lambda(3\mathbf{i}-2\mathbf{j}-\mathbf{k})$ with the coordinate planes.
12. Find the position vector of the point of intersection of the line $\mathbf{r} = (2+2\lambda)\mathbf{i}+(1-2\lambda)\mathbf{j}+\mathbf{k}$ and the plane $\mathbf{r}\cdot(6\mathbf{i}-2\mathbf{j}-3\mathbf{k}) = 2$. Also find the acute angle between the line and the plane.

13. Show that the plane $\mathbf{r} \cdot (2\mathbf{i}+\mathbf{j}-\mathbf{k})+1 = 0$ is parallel to the line joining the points with coordinates $(3, -1, 0)$, $(4, 2, 5)$.
14. Find the vector equation of the plane which passes through the point $(3, 1, 2)$ and is perpendicular to the line joining the points with coordinates $(2, 0, -1)$, $(1, -1, 0)$.
15. Find the vector equation of the plane which bisects the line joining the origin to the point $(6, -2, 4)$ at right angles.
16. Prove that the equation of the plane perpendicular to the vector $\mathbf{b}$ and passing through the point with position vector $\mathbf{a}$ is $\mathbf{r} \cdot \mathbf{b} = \mathbf{a} \cdot \mathbf{b}$.
17. Determine whether the points with coordinates $(1, -2, 1)$, $(-2, 1, 3)$ are on the same or opposite sides of the plane $\mathbf{r} \cdot (\mathbf{i}+2\mathbf{j}-\mathbf{k}) = 1$, by first finding the equations of the planes through each of these points which are parallel to the given plane.

(B) MISCELLANEOUS EXAMPLES

1. D, E, F are the mid-points of the sides BC, CA, AB respectively of a triangle ABC. Prove that $\overline{AD}+\overline{BE}+\overline{CF} = 0$.
2. Vectors $\mathbf{a}, \mathbf{b}, \mathbf{c}, \mathbf{d}$ are given by $\mathbf{a} = 3\mathbf{i}+4\mathbf{j}+\mathbf{k}$, $\mathbf{b} = -\mathbf{i}+\mathbf{j}+2\mathbf{k}$, $\mathbf{c} = \mathbf{i}+5\mathbf{j}+7\mathbf{k}$, $\mathbf{d} = \mathbf{j}+\mathbf{k}$. Show that it is not possible to find values of scalars s and t for which $\mathbf{a}+s\mathbf{b} = \mathbf{c}+t\mathbf{d}$.
3. Find the possible values of x, y, z if $x\mathbf{i}+y\mathbf{j}+z\mathbf{k}$ is a unit vector perpendicular to each of the vectors $\mathbf{j}+4\mathbf{k}$, $3\mathbf{i}+2\mathbf{j}+4\mathbf{k}$.
4. Given that the vector $\mathbf{x}$ satisfies the equation $\mathbf{x}+[(\mathbf{a} \cdot \mathbf{x})/a^2]\mathbf{a} = \mathbf{b}$, where $\mathbf{a}, \mathbf{b}$ are given vectors, show that $\mathbf{a} \cdot \mathbf{x} = \mathbf{a}/2 \cdot \mathbf{b}$.
5. In a triangle ABC, the mid-point of BC is M. By expressing the vectors $\overline{AM}$ and $\overline{BM}$ in terms of $\mathbf{b}, \mathbf{c}$, the position vectors of B, C relative to A, show that $2AM^2+2BM^2 = AB^2+AC^2$.
6. Show that the component of the two-dimensional vector $\mathbf{r}$ in a direction normal to the two-dimensional vector $\mathbf{a}$ is $\mathbf{r}-(\mathbf{r} \cdot \mathbf{a})\mathbf{a}/a^2$.
7. The point B is the reflection of A in the line OU. If $\hat{\mathbf{u}}$ is the unit vector in the direction $\overline{OU}$ and $\mathbf{a}$ is the position vector of A relative to O, show that the position vector of B is $2(\mathbf{a} \cdot \hat{\mathbf{u}})\hat{\mathbf{u}}-\mathbf{a}$.
8. Find the cosine of the acute angle between the lines $\mathbf{r} = \lambda(2\mathbf{i}+\mathbf{j}-2\mathbf{k})$, $\mathbf{r} = (1-\mu)\mathbf{i}+(1+2\mu)\mathbf{j}+(2\mu-1)\mathbf{k}$, where λ, μ are scalar constants.
9. Three points P, Q, R have non-zero position vectors $\mathbf{p}, \mathbf{q}, \mathbf{r}$ respectively. Show that P, Q, R are collinear if and only if there exist scalars λ, μ, σ, such that $\lambda\mathbf{p}+\mu\mathbf{q}+\sigma\mathbf{r} = 0$ where $\lambda+\mu+\sigma = 0$ and not more than one of λ, μ, σ vanishes.
10. Show that the lines with equations $\mathbf{r} = 3\mathbf{i}+4\mathbf{j}+\mathbf{k}+s(-\mathbf{i}+\mathbf{j}+2\mathbf{k})$, $\mathbf{r} = \mathbf{i}+5\mathbf{j}+7\mathbf{k}+t(\mathbf{j}+\mathbf{k})$ where s and t are scalar constants, are skew and find the acute angle between them.
11. A cube OPQRABCD has edges OA, PB, QC, RD perpendicular to the base OPQR; M is the centre of the face ABCD. Find the vectors $\overline{AB}, \overline{OM}, \overline{OD}$, in terms of $\mathbf{a}, \mathbf{b}, \mathbf{c}$, the position vectors of A, B, C relative to O. If the edge of the cube is 2, express $\overline{OM}$ and $\overline{OD}$ in terms of unit vectors $\mathbf{i}, \mathbf{j}, \mathbf{k}$ along $\overline{OP}, \overline{OR}, \overline{OA}$ respectively and find the cosine of angle MOD.
12. In a diagram, vectors $\mathbf{b}, \mathbf{c}$ are represented by line vectors $\overline{OB}, \overline{OC}$, respectively, show on the diagram the point A where $\overline{OA} = \mathbf{b}-2\mathbf{c}$. If $\mathbf{b}-2\mathbf{c} = 3\mathbf{a}$, where $a = c = 1$, $b = 3$, show that the angle of inclination of $\mathbf{b}$ and $\mathbf{c}$ is $\cos^{-1} 1/3$ and find the cosine of the angle between $\mathbf{a}$ and $\mathbf{c}$.
13. Vectors $\mathbf{a}, \mathbf{b}$ have equal magnitudes and are equally inclined to the unit vector $\hat{\mathbf{n}}$. Show that $\mathbf{a}+\mathbf{b} = 2(\hat{\mathbf{n}} \cdot \mathbf{a})\hat{\mathbf{n}} = 2(\hat{\mathbf{n}} \cdot \mathbf{b})\hat{\mathbf{n}}$.
14. The vertices of a triangle have coordinates A(1, 1), B(5, 5), C(3, 4) and H is the point (x, y). Write down the position vectors relative to the origin of these points in terms of unit vectors along the axes. Given AH is perpendicular to BC and BH is perpendicular to AC, find the values of x and y.
15. The position vectors relative to O of two points A, B are $\mathbf{a}, \mathbf{b}$ respectively. If $\triangle$ is the area of triangle AOB, show that $4\triangle^2 = |\mathbf{a}|^2|\mathbf{b}|^2-(\mathbf{a} \cdot \mathbf{b})^2$ and find the area and angles of triangle AOB in the case where $\mathbf{a} = \mathbf{i}+2\mathbf{j}+2\mathbf{k}$, $\mathbf{b} = 4\mathbf{i}-4\mathbf{j}+2\mathbf{k}$.
16. Find the equation of the plane passing through the point P(1, 1, 1) and parallel to the plane with equation $\mathbf{r} \cdot (\mathbf{i}-\mathbf{j}-\mathbf{k}) = \sqrt{3}$. Also find the lengths of the perpendiculars from the origin to the two planes and deduce the perpendicular distance of P from the given plane.
17. Prove that the lines with equations $\mathbf{r} = (2\lambda+1)\mathbf{i}+(1-\lambda)\mathbf{j}+(1-\lambda)\mathbf{k}$, $\mathbf{r} = (3+\mu)\mathbf{i}-(2\mu+1)\mathbf{j}+(4\mu+2)\mathbf{k}$, where λ, μ are scalar parameters, are both perpendicular and skew.

18. The point O is equidistant from the vertices of a triangle ABC; D, E, F are the mid-points of the sides BC, CA, AB, respectively. If the position vectors of A, B, C relative to O are **a**, **b**, **c** show that: (i) $\mathbf{b}^2 - \mathbf{c}^2 = \mathbf{c}^2 - \mathbf{a}^2 = \mathbf{a}^2 - \mathbf{b}^2 = 0$; (ii) OD, OE, OF are perpendicular to BC, CA, AB respectively.
19. Show that the equation of the plane passing through the point $N(a, b, c)$ and normal to the join of the origin to N is $\mathbf{r} \cdot (a\mathbf{i} + b\mathbf{j} + c\mathbf{k}) = a^2 + b^2 + c^2$.
20. A cube ABCDPQRS with base ABCD has vertical edges AP, BQ, CR, DS; L, M, N are the mid-points of AB, AD, RS respectively. Taking the edge of the cube as $2a$, express the position vectors of L, M, N in terms of unit vectors **i**, **j**, **k** in the directions $\overline{AB}$, $\overline{AD}$, $\overline{AP}$ respectively and hence find the cosine of angle LNM.
21. The position vectors of the vertices A, B, C of a triangle are **a**, **b**, **c**. If **r** is the position vector of a point on the altitude AD, show that $\mathbf{r} \cdot (\mathbf{b} - \mathbf{c}) = \mathbf{a} \cdot (\mathbf{b} - \mathbf{c})$ and write down the corresponding result for a point on the altitude BE. Deduce the result $\mathbf{r} \cdot (\mathbf{a} - \mathbf{b}) = \mathbf{c} \cdot (\mathbf{a} - \mathbf{b})$ and hence that the point of intersection of AD and BE lies on the altitude CF.
22. Given $\mathbf{a} - 2\mathbf{b} = \lambda\hat{\mathbf{n}}$, where λ is a positive scalar, $\hat{\mathbf{n}}$ a unit vector and **a**, **b** are perpendicular vectors, by representing the vectors **a**, **b**, $\mathbf{a} - 2\mathbf{b}$ on a diagram, show that $\lambda = \sqrt{(a^2 + 4b^2)}$. If θ is the angle of inclination of **a** and $\hat{\mathbf{n}}$, by using the product $\mathbf{a} \cdot \hat{\mathbf{n}}$ or otherwise show that $\cos\theta = a/\sqrt{(a^2 + 4b^2)}$.
23. In a tetrahedron OABC, the edges OA, OB are perpendicular respectively to the edges BC, CA. By taking the position vectors of A, B, C relative to O as **a**, **b**, **c** respectively show that: (i) OC is perpendicular to AB; (ii) $OA^2 + BC^2 = OB^2 + CA^2 = OC^2 + AB^2$.
24. Find the equation of the plane passing through point $P(1, 1, 2)$ and parallel to the plane with equation $\mathbf{r} \cdot (2\mathbf{i} - \mathbf{j} - 2\mathbf{k}) = 3$. Show that the origin is equidistant from the two planes and find the perpendicular distance of P from the given plane.
25. A rectangular parallelepiped has opposite rectangular faces ABCD, PQRS joined by edges AP, BQ, CR, DS; $AB = 2a$, $AD = 3a$, $AP = a$. With A as origin and **i**, **j**, **k** as unit vectors in the directions $\overline{AB}$, $\overline{AD}$, $\overline{AP}$ respectively, show that $\overline{BS} = -2a\mathbf{i} + 3a\mathbf{j} + a\mathbf{k}$. Find the position vector of the point L which divides QR internally in the ratio 1:2 and show that AL, BS are perpendicular.
26. The plane with equation $\mathbf{r} \cdot \mathbf{n} = \mathbf{p}$, where $\mathbf{n} = l\mathbf{i} + m\mathbf{j} + n\mathbf{k}$, meets the coordinate axes at the points A, B, C. Find the position vectors of A, B, C.
27. Points A, B have coordinates $(3, 1, 3)$, $(-1, -1, -3)$ respectively; write down in terms of the unit vectors **i**, **j**, **k**, the position vector relative to the origin of the point P which divides AB in the ratio $1:\lambda$. Determine the value of λ for which the line joining P to the point $C(5, 2, -1)$ is perpendicular to AB and hence find the coordinates of the foot of the perpendicular from C to the line AB.
28. Write down the equation of the line passing through the point A, position vector **a**, and in the direction of the vector **b**. If P is the point, position vector **p**, and N is the foot of the perpendicular from P to the line show that: (i) $AN = [(\mathbf{p} - \mathbf{a}) \cdot \mathbf{b}]/b$; (ii) $PN^2 = (\mathbf{p} - \mathbf{a})^2 - [(\mathbf{p} - \mathbf{a}) \cdot \mathbf{b}]^2/b^2$.
29. A rectangular box has opposite rectangular faces ABCD, PQRS joined by edges AP, BQ, CR, DS; $AB = 3$, $AD = 2$, $AP = 1$ units. Taking A as origin and **i**, **j**, **k** as unit vectors in the directions $\overline{AB}$, $\overline{AD}$, $\overline{AP}$ respectively show that $\overline{QS} = -3\mathbf{i} + 2\mathbf{j}$, $\overline{QC} = 2\mathbf{j} - \mathbf{k}$. Find a unit vector $\hat{\mathbf{n}}$ normal to QS and QC and so normal to the plane QSC. Deduce that the equation of the plane QSC is $\mathbf{r} \cdot (2\mathbf{i} + 3\mathbf{j} + 6\mathbf{k}) = 12$ and find the length of the perpendicular from A to this plane.
30. Two skew lines AP, BQ inclined at 60° are intersected by their common perpendicular at A, B. Given that AQ is perpendicular to BP and the position vectors of B, P, Q relative to A are **b**, **p**, **q** respectively, show that $\mathbf{p} \cdot \mathbf{q} = \mathbf{b} \cdot \mathbf{q}$ and $AP \cdot BQ = 2\mathbf{p} \cdot (\mathbf{q} - \mathbf{b})$. Deduce the result $AP \cdot BQ = 2AB^2$.

Answers

(A) EXAMPLES 1

1. (i) $(x-2y)(x+2y)$ (ii) $(x-2y)(x^2+2xy+4y^2)$ (iii) $(x+2y)(x^2-2xy+4y^2)$ (iv) $(x-y)(x+y)(x^2+y^2)$
2. (i) p^2-pq+q^2 (ii) $(p+q)/2$ (iii) $(p^2+pq+q^2)/(p+q)$
3. (i) $1-1/(x+1)$ (ii) $3+3/(x-1)$ (iii) $x-1+1/(x+1)$ (iv) $1-1/(x^2+1)$ (v) $1-5/(x^2+4)$ (vi) $x-x/(x^2+1)$ (vii) $2+[3(2-x)]/[(x-1)(x+2)]$
4. (i) $2\sqrt{5}$ (ii) $7+\sqrt{5}$ 5. (i) 15 (ii) 2 (iii) -3
6. (i) $2\sqrt{3}/3$ (ii) $\sqrt{2}/4$ (iii) $(\sqrt{3}+1)/2$ (iv) $(4-\sqrt{2})/7$ (v) $\sqrt{3}-\sqrt{2}$ (vi) $3-2\sqrt{2}$ (vii) $(2-\sqrt{3})/2$
7. $y = a(p+q)$ 8. $a = 3$ 9. (i) $(x-4)^2-16$ (ii) $(y+5)^2-25$ (iii) $(y+5/2)^2-25/4$ (iv) $2(x+3/2)^2-9/2$ (v) $4-(y-2)^2$ (vi) $2(x-5/4)^2-25/8$ (vii) $a(x+g/a)^2-g^2/a$
11. $c = -1032$ 12. (i) $(x+1)^2+(y-3)^2-7$ (ii) $2(x-1)^2+2(y+3/2)^2-11/2$
13. (i) $(x-1)(x^2+1)$ (ii) $(x+1)(x^2+1)$ (iii) $(x-1)^2(x+2)$ (iv) $(x+2)(x^2-x+1)$
14. 8. 16. $a = 1, b = 2, c = -4$ 17. $7-4\sqrt{3}$
18. $a = 3, b = -25; (x+2)(x-3)(x^2+4x+1)$ 19. $p(p^2-3)$.

(A) EXAMPLES 2

1. (i) (ii) (iii) real, different and of opposite signs (iv) complex (v) real and equal
2. (i) $x > 4/5$ (ii) $x \geqslant 3/2$ (iii) $x \leqslant -2$ (iv) $x < 4/3$
3. (i) 21 (ii) 95 (iii) 433 (iv) $47\frac{1}{2}$ 5. positive
6. $m < 0, m > 2$ (ii) $m \leqslant 0, m \geqslant 2$ (iii) $-1 \leqslant m \leqslant 2$ (iv) $m < -1, m > 3$
7. $x = 1, y = -1, z = 2$ 8. $4x^2-29x+1 = 0$ 9. $m = -2, 14/9$
10. (i) $x < -3, x > 2$ (ii) $-1 < x < 2$ 11. $2a^2 = 9b$
12. (i) $x = 84/25, y = -25$ (ii) $x = -3/2, y = -5/2, x = 2, y = 1$
14. $49x^2-1150x+2500 = 0$ 15. (i) $-2 < x < 1$ (ii) $2 < x < 3$
16. $[(a+kb)^2-2(1-k)(b-ka)]/(1-k)(b-ka)$ 17. (i) $x < 1, x > 2$ (ii) $1 < x < 2, x > 3$
19. $x = -2, y = -1, z = 5$ 20. (i) $-2 < x < 0$ (ii) $0 < x < 4$
21. $p = 2$ 23. (i) p^2-2q (ii) $(p^2-2q)/q$ 24. $1 \leqslant x \leqslant 3$
25. $x < -1, 1 < x < 2$ 26. $x = 2, y = 4/3, z = -1; x = -4/3, y = -8/9, z = 2/3$
28. (i) $3 < x < 3\frac{1}{3}$ (ii) $0 < x < 2, x > 3$
29. $x^2-(q^2-2r+2q+2)x+(r+q)^2+2(r+q)+1 = 0$
30. (i) $k > 2$ (ii) $-3 < k < 3$ (iii) $2 < k < 3$
31. (i) $x < 1, x > 2$ (ii) $-5 < x < 1/2$ (iii) $0 < x < 1$

(A) EXAMPLES 3

1. (i) y, x^2 (ii) y^2, x (iii) $y, 1/x$ (iv) $1/y, 1/x^2$ (v) $\lg y, \lg x$ (vi) $\ln y, x$ (vii) $\lg y, x$ (viii) $y, 1/x^2$ (ix) $y/x, x$ (x) xy, x^2
2. $a \approx 105, b \approx 0.38$ 3. $a \approx 0.73, n \approx 0.29$ 4. $k = 3, n = 2$
5. $a = 1, b = 1.5$ 6. $x = 0.4y + 0.2y^2$

(A) EXAMPLES 4

2. (i) $(x+1)^2+1$, positive (ii) $(x-3)^2+1$, positive (iii) $-(x-1)^2-2$, negative (iv) $2(x+2)^2+1$, positive (v) $4(x-1/2)^2+2$, positive (vi) $-2(x-1/2)^2-5/2$, negative
4. $x = 4, 1$ 5. (i) $(x+2y)^2+y^2$ (ii) $2(x+y/2)^2+y^2/2$ (iii) $-(x-3y/2)^2+5y^2/4$
6. $(x-3)^2-4;\ -4$ 7. (i) $a = 3$ (ii) $a > 3$
8. (i) $x = 1, y = 2$ (ii) $x = 0, y = 3$ (iii) $x = 2, y = 0$ (iv) $x = 1, y = -3$ (v) $x = -2, y = 1$
9. $k = 1/2, 9/2$ 10. $-(x-2)^2+3$; maximum $(2, 3)$
11. (i) $-4 \leqslant x \leqslant 6$ (ii) $-1 \leqslant x \leqslant 3$ 12. $y > 0$
14. $k = 0; a = 9, b = -2/3; k = 16; a = 25, b = -6/5$ 16. $\lambda < -1, \lambda > 1/2$

(A) EXAMPLES 5

1. (i) 2^{x+3y} (ii) -1 (iii) $1/2$ (iv) x (v) $[\ln(1+x)-\ln(1-x)]/2$ (vi) $\sqrt{2}$ (vii) $\sqrt{x}$ (viii) 3
2. (i) 4 (ii) 256 3. $x = 2.105$ 4. $\log_2 x + 3\log_2 y/2$ 5. $2, y = x^2$ 6. $4, 1/4$
7. (i) $1/2+n$ (ii) $2n$ (iii) $2/n$ 8. $x = 3, y = 1$ 9. $125, 1/125$
10. $m-1, mn, m(1+n)$ 11. 2.535 13. (i) $-1/2$ (ii) x^2 (iii) $\sqrt{(1+x)}$
14. $(m+2n)/10$ 15. 2.423 16. $x = 2, 16$ 17. $a = 3; n = 5$
18. $x = 0, 1.893.$ 20. $n = 18^3$ 21. $x = 2^{-1/8}$

(A) EXAMPLES 6

1. $x \in \mathbb{R}; f(x) \geqslant -1$ 2. $x \in \mathbb{R}; f(x) > 0$ 3. $x \geqslant 0; f(x) \geqslant 0$
4. $x \in \mathbb{R}; f(x) \geqslant 1$ 5. $-3 \leqslant x \leqslant 3; 0 \leqslant f(x) \leqslant 3$ 6. $x > 0; f(x) > 0$
7. $x \in R \neq 0; f(x) > 0$ 8. $x \in \mathbb{R} \neq -1; f(x) \in \mathbb{R} \neq 0$ 9. $x \in \mathbb{R}; f(x) \geqslant 0$
10. $x > -1; f(x) \in \mathbb{R}$ 11. $x \in \mathbb{R}; f(x) \geqslant 0$ 12. $x > 0; f(x) \geqslant 0$
13. (i) yes for $x \in \mathbb{R}$ (ii) no 14. $-2\sqrt{2} \leqslant x \leqslant 2\sqrt{2}$
15. (i) $y \geqslant -1/4$ (ii) $y \leqslant 4$ (iii) $y \geqslant 1/2$
16. (i) odd (ii) even (iii) even (iv) odd (v) neither (vi) neither (vii) neither (viii) odd
18. (i) $0 \leqslant x \leqslant 1, 0 \leqslant y \leqslant 1/2$ (ii) $0 \leqslant x \leqslant 1, -1/2 \leqslant y \leqslant 0$
21. (i) $x \in \mathbb{R} \neq 2, y \in \mathbb{R} \neq 0$ (ii) $x \in \mathbb{R} \neq -1, y \in \mathbb{R} \neq 1$ (iii) $x \in \mathbb{R} \neq 1, y \geqslant 0, \neq 2$
24. (i) $(x+1)^2$ (ii) $(x+1)^2+2$ (iii) $2(x+1)^2+1$
25. (i) $f^{-1}(x) = (x-1)/3, x \in \mathbb{R}, f^{-1}(x) \in \mathbb{R}$ (ii) $f^{-1}(x) = \ln x, x > 0, f^{-1}(x) \in \mathbb{R}$ (iii) $f^{-1}(x) = (x+1)/x, x \in \mathbb{R} \neq 0, f^{-1}(x) \in \mathbb{R} \neq 1$ (iv) $f^{-1}(x) = e^x - 1, x \in \mathbb{R}, f^{-1}(x) > -1$
26. $x \geqslant 0$, inverse $y = \sqrt{x}$; $x \leqslant 0$, inverse $y = -\sqrt{x}$ 27. $f^{-1}(x) = x/(1-x), x \in \mathbb{R} \neq 1$
28. (ii) $x \geqslant 2, f^{-1}(x) = 2+\sqrt{(4+x)}, x \geqslant -4; x \leqslant 2; f^{-1}(x) = 2-\sqrt{(4+x)}, x \geqslant -4$
29. (i) $(g_0 f)(x) = 2x^2+3, x \in \mathbb{R}, y \geqslant 3; (f_0 g)(x) = 4x^2-4x+3, x \in \mathbb{R}, y \geqslant 2$ (ii) $(g_0 f)(x) = e^x - 2, x \in \mathbb{R}, y > -2; (f_0 g)(x) = e^{x-2}, x \in \mathbb{R}, y > 0$ (iii) $(g_0 f)(x) = 1/(1-x)^2, x \in \mathbb{R} \neq 1, y > 0; (f_0 g)(x) = 1/(1-x^2), x \in \mathbb{R}, x^2 \neq 1, y < 0, y \geqslant 1$

(iv) $(g_0 f)(x) = |\ln x|, x > 0, y \geqslant 0$; $(f_0 g)(x) = \ln|x|, x \in \mathbb{R} \neq 0, y \in \mathbb{R}$
(v) $(g_0 f)(x) = e^{-x/(1+x)}, x \in \mathbb{R} \neq -1, y > 0 \neq e^{-1}$; $(f_0 g)(x) = 1/(e^x + 1), x \in \mathbb{R}, y < 1$
(vi) $(g_0 f)(x) = |\sqrt{x} - 1|, x \geqslant 0, y \geqslant 0$; $(f_0 g)(x) = \sqrt{|x-1|}, x \in \mathbb{R}, y \geqslant 0$

30. $(g_0 f)(x) = -\ln(x+1), x > -1, y \in \mathbb{R}$; $(f_0 g)(x) = 1/(\ln x + 1), x > 0 \neq e^{-1}, y \in \mathbb{R} \neq 0$; $f^{-1}(x) = (1-x)/x, x \neq 0$; $g^{-1}(x) = e^x$; $(g_0 f)^{-1}(x) = e^{-x} - 1$; $(f_0 g)^{-1}(x) = e^{(1-x)/x}, x \neq 0$

(B) MISCELLANEOUS EXAMPLES

1. $a = -1, b = -3$; $f(x) = (x-2)(x+1)(2x^2+x+1)$ 5. $\lambda = -4, 1/8$
6. $f^{-1}(x) = (2x+1)/(x-1), x \neq 1$ 7. (i) $x < -1, x > 1$ (ii) $-1 < x < 1, x > 2$ (iii) $3 < x < 3\frac{1}{3}$ 8. $a \approx 1.98, b \approx 0.72$ 9. $2 < k < 3$; positive
11. 216 14. $-(x-2)^2+3$ (i) (2, 3) (ii) (2, 1/3) 15. (i) $-5 < x < 1/2$ (ii) $-3 < x < 0, x > 1$ 16. $2(x+1)^2+3$ 17. $a = 16, b = 1/8$; $a = 1/64, b = 4$
18. $(x-a)(x-2a)(x+2a)$; $-2a < x < a, x > 2a$
20. $k = 0, 3, 8$ 21. $a = -9, b = 12, c = -5$
22. $g_0 f: y \rightarrow e^{2x} - 1, x \in \mathbb{R}, y > -1$; $(g_0 f)^{-1}: y \rightarrow \ln(x+1)/2, x > -1, y \in \mathbb{R}$
23. $x = y = 2$; $x = \sqrt{2}, y = 2\sqrt{2}$ 24. $(-b, c)$ (i) $c = 0$ (ii) $ac > 0$
25. $9/5 < x < 2$ 26. $x = \pm 4a, y = \pm a$; $x = \pm 8a/3, y = \pm a/3$
27. $0 < f(x) < 1, g(x) > 0, 1/2 < (g_0 f)(x) < 1$; $y = f^{-1}(x) = -\ln x/2, 0 < x < 1, y > 0$; $y = g^{-1}(x) = (2x-1)/x, x > 0, y < 2$; $y = (g_0 f)^{-1}(x) = \ln[x/(2x-1)]/2, 1/2 < x < 1, y > 0$
28. $a = 4, b = 1, c = -6$; $x = -3, -2, 1$
29. $k = 3, a = b = -2$; $k = -7, a = 8, b = 1/2$
30. f neither, g odd; g is not one-one; $f^{-1}(x) = (2x+1)/x$
32. 3, 6; $a = -1, b = 5$

(A) EXAMPLES 7

1. (i) $x^5 + 10x^4y + 40x^3y^2 + 80x^2y^3 + 80xy^4 + 32y^5$ (ii) $81a^4 + 108a^3b + 54a^2b^2 + 12ab^3 + b^4$ (iii) $64r^6 - 192r^5s + 240r^4s^2 - 160r^3s^3 + 60r^2s^4 - 12rs^5 + s^6$ (iv) $x^3 + 3x + 3x^{-1} + x^{-3}$
2. (i) 715 (ii) $126.2^4.3^5$ (iii) 10
3. $x^3 + y^3 - z^3 + 3x^2y - 3x^2z + 3xy^2 - 3zy^2 + 3xz^2 + 3yz^2 - 6xyz$
4. 1792 5. $41 + 29\sqrt{2}$ 6. $x^6 - 6x^5y + 15x^4y^2 - 20x^3y^3 + 15x^2y^4 - 6xy^5 + y^6$; 59348.10^3
7. -12 8. 1260 9. $n = 6$
10. $1 + nx + n(n+1)x^2/2 + n(n-1)(n+4)x^3/6$ 11. 10084
12. 7560 13. -3 15. $a = -3, b = 1/2$ 16. $n = 6$

(A) EXAMPLES 8

1. $u_1 = 1/3, u_2 = 5/6, u_3 = 4/3$
2. $u_1 = 3/2, u_2 = 2/3, u_3 = 5/12$; $u_{r+1} = (r+3)/[(r+1)(r+2)]$; $u_{2n} = (n+1)/[n(2n+1)]$
3. $u_1 = 4, u_2 = 6, u_3 = 8, u_r = 2(r+1)$; arithmetic
4. $d = -1$; $S_n = n(5-n)/2$ 5. $r = 1/3$ (i) 18 (ii) $27(1-(1/3)^n)$; 27
6. (i) 120 (ii) $2^n - 1$ (iii) 1 8. $u_1 = 6, u_2 = 2, u_3 = 2/3$; $u_n = 6(1/3)^{n-1}$; $r = 1/3, S = 9$
9. (i) $(4m+1)/2$ (ii) $(4m+1)(6m+1)/4$ 10. 13
11. $d = 3\frac{1}{3}$; $3733\frac{1}{3}$ 15. $d = 1/3, r = 3$ 16. $2a^2/b$
17. 23/99 19. $n(4n^2-1)/3$ 21. 24 000 22. $0 < x < 1$; 3/4

(A) EXAMPLES 9

1. $\dfrac{4}{7(2x+1)}+\dfrac{5}{7(x-3)}$ 2. $1+\dfrac{10}{3(x-2)}+\dfrac{2}{3(x+1)}$ 3. $\dfrac{3}{4x}-\dfrac{3}{4(x-2)}+\dfrac{3}{2(x-2)^2}$

4. $-\dfrac{1}{2x}+\dfrac{3}{2(x-1)}+\dfrac{5}{6(x+2)}$ 5. $-\dfrac{4}{x}+\dfrac{7x}{1+x^2}$ 6. $1+\dfrac{2}{x-1}+\dfrac{1}{(x-1)^2}$

7. $1-\dfrac{12}{5(x+4)}+\dfrac{2}{5(x-1)}$ 8. $\dfrac{7}{9(x-1)}-\dfrac{7}{9(x+2)}+\dfrac{2}{3(x+2)^2}$

9. $\dfrac{1}{4x}-\dfrac{x}{4(x^2+4)}$ 10. $-\dfrac{1}{x}+\dfrac{1}{x+1}+\dfrac{1}{x-1}$ 11. $\dfrac{1}{4x^2}+\dfrac{4x-1}{4(x^2+4)}$

12. $1-\dfrac{1}{3(x+1)}+\dfrac{x-2}{3(x^2-x+1)}$ 13. $\dfrac{1}{x-a}-\dfrac{1}{x+a}$ 14. $\dfrac{2}{x}-\dfrac{2x}{x^2+a^2}$

15. $\dfrac{a-b}{(a+b)(x+a)}-\dfrac{a-b}{(a+b)(x-b)}+\dfrac{a-b}{(x-b)^2}$

(A) EXAMPLES 10

1. (i) $1+x-x^2/2;\ |x|<1/2$ (ii) $1+2x+4x^2;\ |x|<1/2$ (iii) $1-2x+3x^2;\ |x|<1$
(iv) $(1+x/2+x^2/4)/2;\ |x|<2$ (v) $-(1+x/2+x^2/4)/2;\ |x|<2$
(vi) $(1-x/8+3x^2/128)/2;\ |x|<4$
2. (i) $1+x/2-5x^2/8-3x^3/16$ (ii) $1-2x+2x^2-2x^3$ (iii) $1-x-x^2-x^3$
(iv) $1+3x+5x^2+7x^3$ (v) $1+x^2-x^3$ (vi) $1+2x^2$ (vii) $x/2-x^3/16$
(viii) $1+3x+5x^2/2+x^3/2$ (ix) $1+5x/2+23x^2/8+45x^3/16$
3. 1.41421
4. $1, (-1)^r, (r+1), (-1)^r(r+1)$ (i) 2^r (ii) $(-3)^r$ (iii) $(r+1)2^r$ (iv) $(-1)^r(r+1)(1/2)^{r+2}$
5. 3.332222 6. (i) $1+3x+7x^2;\ |x|<1/2$ (ii) $x+x^2+2x^3;\ |x|<1$
(iii) $1-3x/2+13x^2/4;\ |x|<1/2$ (iv) $-4x+4x^2-8x^3;\ |x|<1$
7. $1-x/2-3x^2/8+3x^3/16$
9. (i) $x+1/2x-1/8x^3$; (ii) $1/x-2/x^2+4/x^3$; (iii) $1/x-2/x^3$
10. (i) $1-x-x^2+3x^3$ (ii) $1-x^2+x^3$ (iii) $1-x/2-x^2/8+7x^3/16$
(iv) $1/\sqrt{2}(1-x/2+x^2/8+x^3/16)$ 12. $a=-1/2, b=-9/8$ 13. $[1+(6n+7)(-1)^n]/4$
14. $1+x/5-2x^2/25;\ 1+x(a-b)+x^2(b^2-ab)$

(B) MISCELLANEOUS EXAMPLES

1. (i) 2/3 (ii) 6 2. $n=2,3$
3. $1/(x-2)-(x+2)/(x^2+1);\ -5/2-5x/4+15x^2/8+15x^3/16-65x^4/32$
5. $[n(n+1)/2]/\log_3 x$ 6. $1-2x+2x^2-2x^4$ 7. $r=3/4$
8. $21/[16(3x-1)]-7/[16(x+1)]+7/[4(x+1)^2];\ (-1)^n7(4n+3)/16-21/16\cdot 3^n;\ |x|<1/3$
10. $a=11/20, b=-1/10$ 11. $1/(x-2)+(1-x)/(x^2+1);\ -(1+(1/2)^7)$
13. $n(2n-1)b^2+$ higher powers of b 14. $[p\pm\sqrt{(p^2+4)}]/2$
17. $x>-1/2$ (i) 3/2 (ii) $x=2$ 18. $1+2x-6x^2+28x^3;\ 55/53$
19. (i) $|x|<1/2, 1/(1-2x)$ (ii) $x<0, 1/(1+e^x)$ (iii) $1/2<x<1, 1/(4x-2)$
20. 1/8 21. $(1-3x+27x^2/4-14x^3)/4;\ (-1)^n[2^{n+4}-2^{-n}(3n+7)]/36$
22. $[a^2(c-b)]/(1-ax)+[b^2(a-c)]/(1-bx)+[c^2(b-a)]/(1-cx)$
24. $u_1=a/2, u_2=a/2+d/6, u_3=a/2+d/3, u_4=a/2+d/2$
25. $2^{n+1}-2-n$ 26. $-1/3<x<1;\ x=1/2$

27. $[r(r+1)]/2$; $[(r+1)(r+2)]/2$ 28. $1+2x+3x^2+4x^3+5x^4$; $(1-x)^{-2}+2(1-x)^{-1}$
29. $n+(n-1)(2^n-1)$ 30. $(3^{r+1}-1)/2$

(A) EXAMPLES 11

1. (i) 0 (ii) -1 (iii) $-1/2$ (iv) 1 (v) $-1/2$ (vi) -1 (vii) 0 (viii) $\sqrt{2}/2$ (ix) 0
2. (i) 1 (ii) $1+\cos^2\theta$ (iii) $2\sec^2\theta$ (iv) $2+2\sin\theta$ (v) 1
3. (i) $2\sin\theta/2\cos\theta/2$ (ii) $2\cos^2\theta/2$ (iii) $2\sin^2\theta/2$
   (iv) $(2\tan\theta/2)/(1-\tan^2\theta/2)$ (v) $\cot^2\theta/2$ (vi) $\tan\theta/2$
4. $-\sin\theta, \cos\theta, -\tan\theta$ 5. (i) $3, -3$ (ii) $\sqrt{5}, -\sqrt{5}$ (iii) $3, -1$ (iv) $2+\sqrt{3}, 2-\sqrt{3}$
6. (i) $(\sqrt{6}+\sqrt{2})/4$ (ii) $(\sqrt{6}+\sqrt{2})/4$ (iii) $2+\sqrt{3}$ (iv) $(\sqrt{6}+\sqrt{2})/4$
7. (i) $(1-\cos 2x)/2$ (ii) $(3-4\cos 2x+\cos 4x)/8$
8. (i) $(\cos 2x-\cos 4x)/2$ (ii) $(\cos 7x+\cos 3x)/2$ (iii) $(\sin 7x+\sin x)/2$
   (iv) $(\sin 6x-\sin 4x)/2$ (v) $[\sin(\pi+2x)+\sin\pi]/2 = \sin(\pi+2x)/2$
9. (i) $5\sin(x+\alpha)$, $\tan\alpha = 3/4$ (ii) $2\sin(2\theta-\alpha)$, $\alpha = \pi/6$ (iii) $3\cos(x/2-\alpha)$, $\tan\alpha = \sqrt{5}/2$
10. $2+\sqrt{3}$ 11. (i) 1 (ii) 1/2 13. $[\sqrt{2}(1-\sqrt{3})]/4$
14. (i) $[\sin(2\theta+\pi/6)+\sin\pi/6]/2$, 3/4 (ii) $[\cos(2\theta+\pi/4)+\cos\pi/4]/2$, $(2+\sqrt{2})/4$
   (iii) $(\cos\pi/2-\cos(2\theta+\pi/2))/2$, 1/2
19. 0 20. (i) $\sqrt{2}, -\sqrt{2}$ (ii) $5, -5$ (iii) $2, -2$

(A) EXAMPLES 12

1. (i) $x = 180n+35°$ (ii) $360n\pm 60°$ (iii) $90n+(-1)^n 135°$ (iv) $120n+30°$
2. (i) 153°26′, 333°26′ (ii) 53°8′, 233°8′ (iii) 66°12′, 246°12′
3. (i) $\pi/6, 5\pi/6, 7\pi/6, 11\pi/6$ (ii) $0, \pi/6, 5\pi/6, \pi, 2\pi$ (iii) $\pi/6, \pi/2, 5\pi/6, 3\pi/2$
   (iv) $0, 0.7226, \pi, 2\pi-0.7226, 2\pi$
4. (i) $n\pi+(-1)^n(\pi/2-0.2)$ (ii) $n\pi\pm(\pi/4-0.1)$ 5. $7\pi/8, 15\pi/8$
6. (i) 0, 120°, 240°, 360° (ii) 120°, 240° (iii) 0°, 30°, 150°, 180°, 210°, 330°, 360°
7. $x+y = \pi/2$; $\pi/12$ 8. 60°, 300° 9. 16°10′, 145°24′
10. −8°8′, 142°54′ 11. 40°, 180° 12. 0°, 90° 13. 30°
14. $n\pi/3, n\pi/2\pm\pi/12$ 15. $-3 \leqslant k \leqslant 3$; 9°6′, 129°6′, 189°6′, 309°6′

(A) EXAMPLES 13

1. (i) $1-2\theta^2$ (ii) $1+4\theta+4\theta^2$ (iii) $1-3\theta$ (iv) $-1-\theta^2$ (v) $1+4\theta+4\theta^2$ (vi) $2+2\theta-\theta^2/2$
   (vii) $1-3\theta^2/2$
4. 120°; 6 cm 5. 72/97 8. (i) 0.99875 (ii) 0.7415 (iii) 1.1053
10. $x = 8k/3$ 12. 1.15 cm 19. $r^2(\sqrt{3}-\pi/3)$

(A) EXAMPLES 14

1. (i) odd (ii) even (iii) odd (iv) neither (v) odd (vi) even (vii) even (viii) odd
   (ix) neither (x) odd (xi) even (xii) even (xiii) odd (xiv) odd (xv) even (xvi) even
2. (i) yes, $4\pi/3$ (ii) yes, 2π (iii) yes, 2π (iv) no (v) yes, 2π (vi) yes, π (vii) yes, 3π
   (viii) no (ix) yes, 2π (x) yes, 2π (xi) yes, $\pi/3$
3. (i) $\pi/4$ (ii) $\pi/3$ (iii) $\pi/4$ (iv) $-\pi/6$ (v) $5\pi/6$ (vi) $-\pi/6$ (vii) 1 (viii) 3/5

5. (i) $7\sqrt{2}/10$ (ii) $3/5$ 6. $1/2$
7. (i) $f, 2\pi$; $g, 4\pi$ (ii) f, even; g, neither; 4π
9. (i) 2π (ii) π (ii) $4\pi/3$ (iv) π (v) π (vi) $\pi/2$
13. (i) 4π (ii) $\pi/2$ (iii) 2π (iv) 2π (v) 2π (vi) 12π (vii) 4π (viii) π (ix) π (x) π
(xi) 2π (xii) π (xiii) π (xiv) π (xv) $\pi/2$ (xvi) π
14. (i) $\sin^{-1} x/2, \pi/4$ (ii) $\cos^{-1}(x/2), \pi/3$ (iii) $2\tan^{-1}\pi x, 2\tan^{-1}\pi$ (iv) $\sin^{-1}(x/2)-\pi/4$; $-\pi/12$
15. $\sin^{-1}(x/\sqrt{2})-\pi/4$

(B) MISCELLANEOUS EXAMPLES

1. $x = \sqrt{3}\sin(\theta+45°)/2$, $y = \cos(\theta+45°)/2$; $4x^2+12y^2 = 3$
3. $\sqrt{5}\sin(x+\alpha)$, $\alpha = \tan^{-1} 1/2$ (i) 140°31′, 346°21′ (iii) 0, 63°26′, 180°, 243°26′
4. 0, 0.848, 2.294, $3\pi/2$, 2π
7. (i) max $(11\pi/6, 2)$, min $(5\pi/6, -2)$ (ii) max $(5\pi/6, 3)$, min $(11\pi/6, -1)$ (iii) min $(11\pi/6, 1/4)$
8. $2n\pi/5 \pm \pi/10$, $n\pi \pm \pi/2$ 9. 22°30′, 60°, 67°30′, 112°30′, 120°, 157°30′
10. $2-\sqrt{3}$ 12. (i) $f, 2\pi$; $g, 3\pi$ (ii) f, even; g, neither; yes, 6π
14. (i) 78°28′, 106°36′ (ii) 0°, 75°31′, 180°
16. $-\sqrt{3} \leqslant c \leqslant \sqrt{3}$; 24°44′, 275°16′ 17. 18° 18. $(\pi-1):1$
19. f, odd; g, even; h, odd; $F(x) = 4\cos x$, even, 2π
21. $2\cos 3\theta - 1$; 2.879, 0.6528, -0.5320 23. 2/11
24. $x = 0.1197$ 26. (i) 63°26′, 116°34′ (ii) 18°26′, 123°41′
27. $-\pi/4 \leqslant x \leqslant \pi/4$, $f^{-1}(x) = \sin^{-1}(x/2)$; $\pi/4 < x < 3\pi/4$, $f^{-1}(x) = \pi(2-x)/4$

(A) EXAMPLES 15

1. (i) $3+i$ (ii) $3+4i$ (iii) $(1+i)/2$ (iv) $(1-5i)/13$
(v) $-(3+4i)/25$ (vi) $-2(1+i)$ (vii) $-7-24i$
2. $(-78+96i)/25$ 3. 0 4. $x = 1, y = -1$ 5. $(68+24i)/13$
6. (i) $(1-3i)/5$ (ii) $3(1-2i)/5$ 7. $x = 2, y = -4$
8. (i) $1 \pm i\sqrt{3}$ (ii) $(1 \pm i\sqrt{3})/2$ (iii) $(1 \pm i\sqrt{31})/4$
10. $p = 10/17, q = 19/17$ 11. $1-10a^2+5a^4+i(5a-10a^3+a^5)$; $a = 0, \pm\sqrt{(5 \pm \sqrt{20})}$
12. (i) $(7-i)/50$ (ii) $c^4-6c^2+1+i(4c^3-4c)$ 13. $a = \pm 2, b = \pm 1$
14. $x^2+y^2+10x+16 = 0$ 18. $z = \pm 2+i$ 19. $(1 \pm i\sqrt{3})/2$
20. $p = \pm\sqrt{2}, q = -2 \mp 2\sqrt{2}$ 21. $a = 2/3, b = -5/3$ 22. $z = 1+2i, t = 2-3i$

(A) EXAMPLES 16

2. (i) $1+i$ (ii) $-1+i$ 5. (i) $5+4i$; $(7+7i)/2$
6. (i) $3-2i$ (ii) $-1+2i$ (iii) $2+3i$ 7. $6-2i$
8. $1-2i$; $3\sqrt{2}$ 9. $x = 3\lambda$, $y = 2\lambda$; $3y = 2x$ 10. $a = 4, b = -5$; 5
11. $z_1 = 2(2+i\sqrt{2})/3$; $z_2 = 2(1+i2\sqrt{2})/3$ 12. $x^2+y^2+7x+6 = 0$

(A) EXAMPLES 17

1. (i) $\sqrt{2}(\cos\pi/4+i\sin\pi/4)$ (ii) $\sqrt{2}(\cos 3\pi/4+i\sin 3\pi/4)$ (iii) $2(\cos\pi/2+i\sin\pi/2)$
(iv) $\cos 0+i\sin 0$ (v) $\cos\pi+i\sin\pi$ (vi) $\cos(-\pi/2)+i\sin(-\pi/2)$

(vii) $5[\cos(-\theta)+i\sin(-\theta)]$ where $\theta = \tan^{-1} 3/4$ (viii) $2[\cos(-5\pi/6)+i\sin(-5\pi/6)]$

2. (i) $2\sqrt{5}, \tan^{-1} 1/2$ (ii) $5, -\tan^{-1} 4/3$ (iii) $\sqrt{2}/2, \pi/4$
(iv) $\sqrt{10}/2, \tan^{-1} 1/3$ (v) $2\sqrt{5}/5, -\tan^{-1} 1/2$
3. (i) $-\pi/3$ (ii) 0 (iii) $-\pi/3$ (iv) $3\pi/14$ (v) $-\pi/10$
4. (i) $\cos 3\theta + i\sin 3\theta$ (ii) $\cos 5\theta + i\sin 5\theta$
(iii) $\cos(-\theta)+i\sin(-\theta)$ (iv) $\cos(-2\theta)+i\sin(-2\theta)$
5. (i) $9, 2\pi/5$ (ii) $27, 3\pi/5$ (iii) $1/3, -\pi/5$
6. (i) $16(\cos 2\pi/3 + i\sin 2\pi/3)$ (ii) $[\cos(-\pi/6)+i\sin(-\pi/6)]/2$
(iii) $8(\cos \pi/2 + i\sin \pi/2)$ (iv) $8(\cos \pi/2 + i\sin \pi/2)$
8. $-8i$ 9. (i) $2^5[\cos(-5\pi/6)+i\sin(-5\pi/6)]$ (ii) $-16(\sqrt{3}+i)$
10. (i) 16 (ii) 64 (iii) $-(1+i\sqrt{3})/32$
13. (i) $2^{10}[\cos(-2\pi/3)+i\sin(-2\pi/3)]$ (ii) $-2^9(1+i\sqrt{3})$ 14. $2\cos\theta/2, \theta/2$
15. $2\sin\theta/2, \pi/2-\theta/2$; $8\sin^3\theta/2[\cos(3\pi/2-3\theta/2)+i\sin(3\pi/2-3\theta/2)]$
16. (i) $2\cos\theta$ (ii) $2\cos n\theta$

(A) EXAMPLES 18

1. (i) $\cos 5\theta + i\sin 5\theta$ (ii) 1 (iii) $\cos 5\theta + i\sin 5\theta$ 2. $\cos 4\theta + i\sin 4\theta$
3. (i) $\cos\theta - i\sin\theta$ (ii) $2\cos\theta$ (iii) $2\cos 3\theta$ (iv) $2i\sin 3\theta$ (v) $2\cos 3\theta + 2\cos 2\theta + 2\cos\theta$
5. (i) $4\cos^3\theta - 3\cos\theta$ (ii) $8\cos^4\theta - 8\cos^2\theta + 1$
(iii) $16\cos^5\theta - 20\cos^3\theta + 5\cos\theta$ (iv) $32\cos^5\theta - 32\cos^3\theta + 6\cos\theta$
6. (i) $3\sin\theta - 4\sin^3\theta$ (ii) $8\sin^4\theta - 8\sin^2\theta + 1$
(iii) $16\sin^5\theta - 20\sin^3\theta + 5\sin\theta$ (iv) $16\sin^4\theta - 12\sin^2\theta + 1$
7. (i) $(\cos 3\theta + 3\cos\theta)/4$ (ii) $(\cos 4\theta - 4\cos 2\theta + 3)/8$
(iii) $(\cos 5\theta + 5\cos 3\theta + 10\cos\theta)/16$ (iv) $-(\sin 4\theta - 2\sin 2\theta)/8$
(v) $-(\sin 7\theta + \sin 5\theta - 3\sin 3\theta - 3\sin\theta)/64$
8. (i) $\pm 1, \pm i$ (ii) $-3/2, 3(1\pm i\sqrt{3})/4$ (iii) $-1, \cos\pi/5 \pm i\sin\pi/5, \cos 3\pi/5 \pm i\sin 3\pi/5$
9. $z = \cos r\pi/4 + i\sin r\pi/4, r = 0, 1, \ldots, 7$ 11. $z = \pm 2, 1\pm i\sqrt{3}, -1\pm i\sqrt{3}$
12. -2^8

(A) EXAMPLES 19

3. $2, \pi/2$; $2, \pi/3$ 9. $(2, 0), (-1, 0)$; $x = 1/2$

(B) MISCELLANEOUS EXAMPLES

1. $5(1+i)/2$; $5\sqrt{2}/2, \pi/4$ 2. $4, 2+4i$
3. (i) $(i-1)/2i = (1+i)/2$ (ii) $1/2i = -i/2$; $-6i$ 4. $1+2i$; $5\sqrt{2}$; $a = -2, b = -1$
5. $z = 1, (-1\pm i\sqrt{3})/2$; $z = 3, \pm i\sqrt{3}$ 7. -2^8
8. $p = \pm 3, q = \pm 1$ 9. $x = \lambda + 1/5\lambda$, $y = (-\lambda + 1/5\lambda)/2$
10. (i) $x = -1$ (ii) $3x^2 + 3y^2 + 10x + 3 = 0$. 12. $4\cos\theta/2, \theta/2$
13. $2\cos(\pi/4 - \phi/2)$ 14. $\sqrt{2}(\cos\theta + i\sin\theta), \theta = \pi/12, 3\pi/4, -7\pi/12$ 15. $-3/2+2i$
16. (i) $(x-3)^2 + y^2 = 16$ (ii) portion of line $y = x - 1$ in + quadrant
(iii) $3x^2 + 3y^2 - 16x + 16 = 0$
19. $2^{1/4}(\cos\theta + i\sin\theta), \theta = -\pi/24, 11\pi/24, 23\pi/24$ 20. $(3\cos\theta - 3\cos 3\theta - \cos 5\theta + \cos 7\theta)/8$
21. $5\pi/12, 11\pi/12$ 23. $(\sqrt{3}-i)/2$ 24. $(13+13i)/3$ 26. $1+2i, 2\sqrt{5}$

(A) EXAMPLES 20

1. $4x-2x^{-3}$ 2. $6(2x-1)^2$ 3. $-1/(x+1)^2$ 4. $x/[\sqrt{(x^2+1)}]$
5. $3\cos 3x$ 6. $3\sin^2 x\cos x$ 7. $-1/(x-1)^2$ 8. $-4e^{-4x}$
9. $(\sec^2 x/2)/2$ 10. $(1-x)^3(1-5x)$ 11. $\cos x - x\sin x$
12. $xe^x(2+x)$ 13. $2/(2x+1)$ 14. $2/[\sqrt{(1-4x^2)}]$ 15. $-3/[\sqrt{(1-9x^2)}]$
16. $2x/(1+x^4)$ 17. $2x/(x^2+1)$ 18. $e^{-2x}(1-2x)$ 19. $\ln x$ 20. $x(1-x^2)^{-3/2}$
21. $(x\cos x-\sin x)/x^2$ 22. $1/[2\sqrt{x}(1+x)]$ 23. $x/(x^2+1)$ 24. $e^{2x}(2\sin 3x+3\cos 3x)$
25. $2\sec 2x\tan 2x$ 26. $-(\operatorname{cosec}^2 x/2)/2$ 27. $\tan^{-1}x+x/(1+x^2)$
28. $-6\cos 3x\sin 3x$ 29. $e^{-x^2}(2x-2x^3)$ 30. $-1/\cos x\sin x$
31. $-1/(1-\cos x)$ 32. $\sin x\cos^2 x(2\cos^2 x-3\sin^2 x)$ 33. $\cos^{-1}x-x/[\sqrt{(1-x^2)}]$
34. $\cos x/(1+\sin x)$ 35. $e^{\sin x}\cos x$ 36. $1/[(1+x)^{1/2}(1-x)^{3/2}]$ 37. $1/x\ln 10$
38. $\cos x/(1+\sin^2 x)$ 39. $1/[2\sqrt{x}\sqrt{(1-x)}]$ 40. $2x^3/(1+x^4)$
41. (i) $-x/y$ (ii) $(4-3x^2)/3y^2$ (iii) $-y/x$ (iv) $-y/[2(x+1)]$
(v) $[y(2x-\ln y)]/x$ (vi) $(6-2xy-y^2)/(2xy+x^2)$ (vii) $(e^y-ye^x)/(e^x-xe^y)$
(viii) $-(\sin 2y+y\cos x)/(2x\cos 2y+\sin x)$ (ix) $-(2e^x+ye^{xy})/(xe^{xy}-e^y)$
42. (i) $dy/dx=1/t$, $d^2y/dx^2=-1/2t^3$ (ii) $dy/dx=t$, $d^2y/dx^2=1/6t$
(iii) $dy/dx=-3\cot t/4$, $d^2y/dx^2=-3\operatorname{cosec}^3 t/16$
(iv) $dy/dx=(t^2+1)/[2(t^2-1)]$, $d^2y/dx^2=-t^3/[(t^2-1)^3]$ 43. $2^x\ln 2$
44. (i) $dy/dx(xe^y+e^x)+e^y+ye^x$ (ii) $-\sin(xy)(y+x\,dy/dx)$ (iii) $e^{x^2y}(2xy+x^2\,dy/dx)$
(iv) $(y+x\,dy/dx)/\sqrt{(1-x^2y^2)}$ 45. $2e^{\sqrt{3}x}\sin(x+\pi/6)$
46. $x/[(1+2x^2)(1+x^2)]$; $[x(1+2x^2)^{1/2}(1+x^2)^{-1/2}]/[(1+2x^2)(1+x^2)]=x/[(1+2x^2)^{1/2}(1+x^2)^{3/2}]$
48. $-\operatorname{cosec} x$ 49. $x=-1, y=3$; $x=17^{-1/3}$, $y=3.17^{-1/3}$
50. (i) $2\,dx/dt+dy/dt$ (ii) $y\,dx/dt+x\,dy/dt$ (iii) $(y\,dx/dt-x\,dy/dt)/y^2$
(iv) $2x\,dx/dt+2y\,dy/dt$ (v) $(x\,dy/dt-y\,dx/dt)/(x^2+y^2)$
52. (i) $2xy+x^2\,dy/dx$ (ii) $dy/dx+x\,d^2y/dx^2$ (iii) $2\,dy/dx\,d^2y/dx^2$

(A) EXAMPLES 21

1. (i) 5 ml/s (ii) 7 ml/s 2. $y-33x+96=0$ 3. 0.08
5. max $(-1, 15)$, min $(2, -12)$ 6. $(1, 1)$ 7. 1; $y-x=4$ 8. $-x$
9. $\alpha\cos\theta$ (i) 0.8665 (ii) 0.500 25 10. max $(-1/\sqrt{2}, 1/4)$, min $(0, 0)$, max $(1/\sqrt{2}, 1/4)$
11. $a=1/2, b=-1$ 12. $x=20$ 13. $x\cos\phi/a+y\sin\phi/b=1$
15. (i) $\delta y\approx 2e^{2x}\delta x$ (ii) $\delta y\approx(\sin x+x\cos)\delta x$ (iii) $\delta y\approx[(\cos x+x\sin x)/\cos^2 x]\,\delta x$
(iv) $\delta y\approx[6(x+2)^2/(y+1)]\,\delta x$ (v) $\delta y\approx 2xy\,\delta x$
16. $(2, 2e^{-2})$; $-e^{-2}$ 17. tangent $y\sin\theta-x+a\cos\theta=0$; normal $y+x\sin\theta=2a\tan\theta$
18. $(\pi/3, 4)$ 19. $32\pi/81$ 20. $x<3/2$
21. $2(1+y)^3$ 22. 1/3 unit/s 23. $-e^{-1}/2$
24. (i) 2/3 unit/s (ii) 1 unit/s (iii) $19/\sqrt{73}$ unit/s (iv) 32/73 rad/s
25. $2\pi l^3/9\sqrt{3}$ 26. $(0, 0), (\pi, \pi), (2\pi, 2\pi), (3\pi, 3\pi), (4\pi, 4\pi)$
27. max $(1, e^{-1/2})$, min $(-1, -e^{-1/2})$ 28. 0.09 %
29. (i) 10π cm²/s (ii) 3:2 (iii) $t=3$ s

(A) EXAMPLES 22

1. (i) $1+3x+9x^2/2$, all values (ii) $1+x^2+x^4/2$, all values (iii) $1-2x+2x^2$, all values
(iv) $2x-2x^2+8x^3/3$, $-1/2<x\leqslant 1/2$ (v) $-(x/2+x^2/8+x^3/24)$, $-2\leqslant x<2$
(vi) $x^2-x^4/2+x^6/3$, $-1\leqslant x\leqslant 1$ (vii) $2x-4x^3/3+4x^5/15$, all values
(viii) $2x^2-2x^4/3+4x^6/45$, all values (ix) $1-x^2+x^4/3$, all values
2. (i) $1+1+1/2!+1/3!$ (ii) $1-1+1/2!-1/3!$ (iii) $1+1/2+(1/2)^2/2!+(1/2)^3/3!$
(iv) $2(1+2^2/2!+2^4/4!+2^6/6!)$ (v) $2(2^2/2!+2^4/4!+2^6/6!+2^8/8!)$
3. $\sqrt{2}(1-x-x^2/2+x^3/6)/2$

4. (i) $-2-x+x^3/6$ (ii) $2x+2x^3/3$ (iii) $x+5x^3/6$ (iv) $3-2x+x^2/2$
6. (i) $\ln 2+x/2-x^2/8,\ -2<x\leqslant 2$ (ii) $\ln 3-x/3-x^2/18,\ -3\leqslant x<3$
(iii) $-x^2-x^4/2-x^6/3;\ -1<x<1$ (iv) $\ln 2+x/2-5x^2/8;\ -1<x\leqslant 1$
(v) $-2x-5x^2-26x^3/3,\ -1/3\leqslant x<1/3$ (vi) $x+x^3/3+x^5/5,\ -1<x<1$
7. (i) 4/3 (ii) 1/48 (iii) $e/6$ 8. $1-3x^2/2+7x^4/8$
10. (i) $4x^2+4x^3$ (ii) $4x^3$ 11. (i) $x+x^2+x^3/3$ (ii) $1-x+x^3/3$
12. (i) $2^r/r!$ (ii) $[(-1)^r]/r!$ (iii) $(-1)^{r+1}2^r/r$ (iv) $-3^r/r$
(v) $(r+1)/r!$ (vi) $1/[r(r-1)]$ (vii) $[(-1)^r]/r!+[2(-1)^{r-1}]/[(r-1)!]$
13. $\sqrt{2}(1+x-x^2-2x^3/3+x^4/3+2x^5/15-2x^6/45)/2$
15. $2x-2x^2+2x^3/3;\ x^{2r}[(-1)^{2r+1}-(-1)^{r+1}]/r$
16. (i) $x+x^2/2-2x^3/3$ (ii) $x/2+x^2/4-x^3/3$
17. (i) $(1-x/2+x^3/24)/2,\ x<0$ (ii) $\ln 2+x/2+x^2/8,\ x\leqslant 0$ (iii) $x-x^2/2+x^3/6,\ \sin x\neq -1$
(iv) $e(1-x^2/2+x^4/6)$, all values of x

(A) EXAMPLES 23

2. $-2, -1; 0, 1; 1, 2$ 3. (i) 1 (ii) 1 (iii) 1 (iv) 3 4. 2.77
6. (i) (a) 2, (b) 1.15 (ii) (a) 1, (b) 0.45 (iii) (a) 1, (b) 0.30
10. 1.2 11. 0.79 12. $-2, -1; -1, 0; 2, 3$ 14. 1.9 15. 0.79
16. 2.07 18. 1.11 19. 1.516 20. 1.370 21. $x_9\approx 1.45$

(B) MISCELLANEOUS EXAMPLES

1. $3y-5x+8a=0$ 3. (i) $\ln 2+x^2/2-x^4/12$ (ii) $x+x^2+x^3/3$ (iii) $1-x^2-5x^4/6$
(iv) $1+x^2/2+5x^4/24$ 5. (i) 0.79 (ii) 0.792
6. $a=-3, b=-9, c=9$; max $(-1, 14)$, min $(3, -18)$; $(1, -2)$
7. $3y-4x+2a=0$ 9. min $(1, 1)$
10. $y=3x-3x^2/2+3x^3-15x^4/4$ (i) $-1/2<x\leqslant 1/2$ (ii) $[1+(-1)^{r+1}2^r]/r$
11. $x_4=0.750$
12. (i) $[2(\cos x+\sin x)]/(\sin x-\cos x)$ (ii) $-x(1-x^2)^{-1/2}\arcsin x+1$ (iii) $(2x^3-6x)/[(1+x^2)^3]$
13. $y\sin\theta-x+a\cos\theta=0;\ y+x\sin\theta=2a\tan\theta$ 14. $x^2-x^4/3;\ 1+x^2+x^4/6$
16. $(a, 1+\ln a);\ a>e^{-1}$ 17. 2.071 18. $-2/3, -10/27$
19. (i) $(-1)^r(1+r)/r!$ (ii) $e^2/r!$ (iii) $(r+1)(1/2)^r/4$ (iv) $-2^r/r-2^{r-1}/(r-1)$
20. -8 21. min $(1, 0)$, max $(1/5, 4^4/5^5)$ 22. $(xy-y^2)/(x+xy\ln x);\ e+\varepsilon(e-e^2)$
23. $3x/2+x^2/4+x^3/2;\ a=-1/6, k=1/2$ 25. $x_{n+1}=\sqrt[3]{(5-x_n)}$; 1.52
26. min $x=0$; max $x=\pm\pi/2$ 27. $(1+x)^{-2};\ 11y+7x-18=0$
28. (i) $3\sqrt{3}a/\sqrt{7}$ (ii) 15/7 rad/s 30. 2.49; not convergent

(A) EXAMPLES 24

1. $\sqrt{(2x+3)}+c$ 2. $\ln(2x+1)/2+c$ 3. $-(1-x)^7/7+c$
4. $-\cos 5x/5+c$ 5. $1/[2(1-2x)]+c$ 6. $2\tan x/2-x+c$
7. $(e^{2x}+e^{-2x})/4+c$ 8. $\sin^{-1}x/2+c$ 9. $(\tan^{-1}x/3)/3+c$
10. $-\cos^4 x/4+c$ 11. $2(\tan x)^{3/2}/3+c$ 12. $\ln(1+x^2)/2+c$
13. $\ln\sin x+c$ 14. $(1+x^2)^5/10+c$ 15. $-e^{-x^2}/2+c$
16. $\ln(1-\cos x)+c$ 17. $\tan^{-1}x+\ln(1+x^2)/2+c$ 18. $\sin^{-1}(2x/3)/2$
19. $\tan^{-1}(2x/3)/6+c$ 20. $-\ln(9-x^2)/2+c$ 21. $110\frac{5}{6}$ 22. 1/6
23. $\ln 2/4$ 24 $\pi/4\sqrt{2}$ 25. $\sqrt{5}-1$ 26. $5\frac{5}{6}$ 27. 1 28. $\ln[(1+e)/2]$

29. (i) $-\sqrt{(1-x^2)}-2\sin^{-1}x+c$ (ii) $2\tan^{-1}x/2-\ln(1+x^2)/2+c$
(iii) $3\sin^{-1}x/3+2\sqrt{(9-x^2)}+c$
30. (i) $x+\ln(x-1)+c$ (ii) $x^2/2+x+\ln(x-1)+c$ (iii) $x+2\ln(x-1)+c$
(iv) $x-\sqrt{2}\tan^{-1}(x/\sqrt{2})+c$

(A) EXAMPLES 25

1. $\sin^2(x/2)+c$ 2. $-\cos 4x/8-\cos 2x/4+c$ 3. $\sin 3x/6+\sin(x/2)+c$
4. $-\cos 7x/14+\cos 3x/6+c$ 5. $-\sin 5x/10+\sin(x/2)+c$ 6. $-\cos x+\cos^3(x/3)+c$
7. $\sin x-2\sin^3(x/3)+\sin^5(x/5)+c$ 8. $\tan^2(x/2)+\ln\cos x+c$
9. $-\cos^3 x/3+\cos^5 x/5+c$ 10. $x/2+\sin 4x/8+c$ 11. $2\ln\sin(x/2)+c$
12. $x/8-\sin 4x/32+c$ 13. $\tan 2x/2-x+c$ 14. $\sin^4(x/4)-\sin^6(x/6)+c$
15. $-\cos 4x/8+c$ 16. $-2\cos(x/2)+2\cos^3(x/2)/3$ 17. $\pi/8$ 18. $-1/2$ 19. $4/3$
20. $1-\pi/4$ 21. $\sqrt{3}/4$ 22. $1/8$ 23. $\pi/4-2/3$ 24. $1/3$
25. (i) $\tan(x/2)+c$ (ii) $-\cot(x/2)+c$ (iii) $2\tan(x/2)-x+c$

(A) EXAMPLES 26

1. $\ln[(x+1)/(x+2)]+c$ 2. $x\sin x+\cos x+c$ 3. $\ln[(x-1)/x]+1/x+c$
4. $(e^x+1)^3/3+(e^x+1)^2/2+e^x+1+x+c$ 5. xe^x-e^x+c
6. $x\ln x-x+c$ 7. $\ln(x-1)+\ln(1+x^2)/2+\tan^{-1}x+c$
8. $x^4\ln x/4-x^4/16+c$ 9. $(1-x)^6/6-(1-x)^5/5+c$
10. $-x\cos 2x/2+\sin 2x/4+c$ 11. $x+\ln[(x-1)/(x+1)]/2+c$ 12. $x\tan x+\ln\cos x+c$
13. $2(x+1)^{3/2}+2(x+1)^{1/2}+c$ 14. $e^{2x}(2x^2-2x+1)/4+c$
15. $\ln[(1+x)(1-x)^2]+2(1-x)^{-1}+c$ 16. $-\sqrt{(1-x^2)}+c$ 17. $4\ln 4-3\ln 3$
18. $\pi\sqrt{2}/2+2\sqrt{2}-4$ 19. $3/2-2\ln 2$ 20. $\ln 9/8$ 21. π
22. $\pi/4-\ln 2/2$ 23. $\pi/4-1/2$ 24. $\pi/8$ 25. $5/3-4\ln 3/2$
26. $3\ln 3-2$ 27. $\sqrt{3}$ 28. $2(\tan^{-1}2-\pi/4)$ 29. $\ln(32/17)/4$
30. (i) $x\sin^{-1}2x+(1-4x^2)^{1/2}/2+c$ (ii) $x\ln(1+x^2)-2x+2\tan^{-1}x+c$
31. $\sqrt{2}/2$ 32. $I=e^x(\sin x-\cos x)/2$, $I'=e^x(\sin x+\cos x)/2$
33. $-1/(2-x)-(x-1)/(1+x^2)$; $\pi/4-3\ln 2/2$ 34. $\ln(1+e)/2+1/(1+e)-1/2$ 35. $\pi/2$

(A) EXAMPLES 27

1. $e-2$ (i) $\pi(e^2-4e+5)/2$ (ii) $1/[2(e-2)]$ 2. $4\sqrt{2}/\pi$
3. (i) $5/3$ (ii) $20\pi/7$ 4. $\pi p^8/4$ 5. $3/2+4/\pi$ 6. $6\frac{3}{4}$
8. $-4\sqrt{2}/3$ 9. $1-2/\pi$ 10. $4-2\sqrt{e}$ 11. $\pi(e^{2a}+4a-e^{-2a})/8$
12. $3^5/10$; $6/7$ 13. $2\pi/3$ 14. π; $(\pi^2-4)/\pi$ 15. $2\pi/3$
17. $\pi(2\pi-3\sqrt{3})$ 18. $2e^{-1}$ 19. $(0,0)$, (m^2,m^3) 20. $20\ln 2/3$; 4
21. $4/5$; $(0,2/7)$ 23. (i) $1/2$ (ii) $2/3$

(A) EXAMPLES 28

1. 2.961 2. 0.881 3. 4.344 4. 3.417 5. 3.091
6. 3.407 7. 5.653 8. 1.434 9. 8.655 10. 2.285

11. 0.785; 3.14 12. $-16/15; -1.083$ 13. 0.810
14. (i) 0.5241 (ii) $\pi/6$; 3.145 15. 0.6946

(A) EXAMPLES 29

1. $y = 2x^2+c$ 2. $y = 1/x+c$ 3. $y = ce^x$ 4. $y^2 = x^2+c$
5. $3y^2 = 2x^3+c$ 6. $y^3 = 3x^2+3x+c$ 7. $-1/y = \ln x+c$
8. $y^2 = 2\ln x+c$ 9. $y = c(x+1)$ 10. $\ln(y+1) = x+2\ln(x-2)+c$
11. $\ln(y^2-1)/2+1/x = c$ 12. $\tan^{-1} y = \ln(1+x^2)/2+c$ 13. $x\ln(y-1) = 1$
14. $V = (g/k)(1-e^{-kt})$ 15. $y = ce^{-x^2/2}/x$ 16. $y = e^x/(1+e^x)$
17. $p = 2/(2-t)$ 18. $q+1 = 3e^{-kt}$ 20. $y = (2\sqrt{C}-kt)^2/4$ 21. $p = 1/(1-t)$

(B) MISCELLANEOUS EXAMPLES

1. (i) $\ln 4/3$ (ii) $5/24$ (iii) $\pi/6\sqrt{2}$ 2. 1
3. (i) $\tan^{-1} y = \tan^{-1} x+\tan^{-1} 1/3$ (ii) $y-\ln y = 2\ln x+c$
4. (i) $2+\ln 4/3$ (ii) $\ln 3/4$ 5. $1/\sqrt{3a^2}$ 7. $\pi^2(\pi^2+6)/48$
8. (i) $1/495$ (ii) $e^4/4+4e^3/3+3e^2+4e-7\frac{7}{12}$ (iii) $8\ln 2-3/4$
9. (i) $3(\ln 2)^2/2 \approx 0.721$ (ii) 0.719 11. (i) 1.72 (ii) $\ln 3/4$
12. $y-x+4 = 0$; 8.1 13. $2\ln x/x$; $(e^2-1)/4$ 15. $1/7\ln 9/2$
16. $A = n_0, k = \ln 5/2$ 17. (i) $2(\ln 3-1)$ (ii) $\ln 2/2+1/4$ (iii) $\pi/3-\sqrt{3}/2$
18. (i) $(e^2+4-e^{-2})/2$ (ii) $2(1-e^{-1})$ 19. (i) $\pi ab/4$ (ii) $2\pi ab^2/3$ (iii) $4a/3\pi$
20. 0.488; $2(\ln 5/3-4/15) \approx 0.4886$ 21. $4/3\ln 8/7$ 23. (i) $2-\ln 2$ (ii) $7\pi/4$
24. (i) 1.944 (ii) 1.948114 25. $A = 2, B = 1, C = a$
26. (i) $2/35$ (ii) $\pi/4-1/2$ (iii) $e-1-\ln[(1+e)/2]$ 28. (i) $a = 1/3$

(A) EXAMPLES 30

1. $3\sqrt{2}$ 2. 3 3. (i) $2/(p+q)$ (ii) $(p+q)y-2x = 2apq$
4. $4y-5x = 0$ 5. (i) $(2cp/3, 2c/3p)$ (ii) $(2cp, 2c/p)$ 6. $(0, a/m)$
7. (i) $2ax-2by = a^2-b^2$ (ii) $[(a^2-b^2)/2a, 0]$ 8. $(-21/4, -11/16)$
9. (i) 2 (ii) 1; 3 10. (1, 3) 11 $\tan^{-1} 15/8$
12. $16x-7y = 0$ 13. $[(5+3\lambda)/\lambda, (2+2\lambda)/\lambda]$ 14. $m = 0, 4/3$
15. $(d \sim c)/[\sqrt{(1+m^2)}]$ 16. $11x+33y = 43$ 17. (6, 1)
18. $[3(2m-3)/5m, 2(3-2m)/5]$ 19. (i) $2y-5x+10 = 0$; (ii) $\tan^{-1} 3/7, \tan^{-1} 19/4$
20. $x-3y+2 = 0, 5x+2y-3 = 0$ 21. $5y-x = 10$ 22. 7
23. (i) (6, 7) (ii) 16/15 (iii) $8\sqrt{2}$ (iv) 80.
24. $(-1/2, 11/2), (11/2, 5/2)$ 25. (i) (7, 7); $\tan^{-1} 3$

(A) EXAMPLES 31

1. $(1, -3/2)$; $\sqrt{19}/2$ 2. $y = 3x-1$ 4. $(-1, 0), (0, 2/3)$ 5. $3x+4y+17 = 0$
6. $x^2+y^2+2x-4y = 0$ 7. $2y+x = 1, y-2x = 8$ 10. (1, 0), (5, 4)
11. $x^2+y^2-5x-4y+4 = 0$ 12. $3x^2+3y^2-13x-11y+10 = 0$

13. $(14, 5)$ 14. $2x^2+2y^2-17x-21y+34 = 0$
15. $x^2+y^2-6x-6y+9 = 0$, $x^2+y^2-30x-30y+225 = 0$; (i) $x = 6$, $3x+4y-30 = 0$ (ii) $\tan^{-1} 4/3$
16. $(x-2)^2+(y+4)^2 = 9$ 17. $X+Y+2 = 0$
18. $25(x^2+y^2)-50y+9 = 0$, $25(x^2+y^2)-150x-100y+244 = 0$
19. $m = 0, 24/7$ 20. $(2/5, 11/5), 1; (2, 1)$

(A) EXAMPLES 32

1. $x^2+y^2+8x+12 = 0$ 2. $x^2+10y+5 = 0$ 3. $5(x^2+y^2)+52x-18y+29 = 0$
4. $y^2 = 4ax$ 5. $5x^2+9y^2 = 45$ 6. $x^2+y^2 = k^2-a^2$
7. (i) $xy = 16$ (ii) $4y = (1+x)^2$ (iii) $x = 3y-1$ (iv) $x^3 = y^2$ (v) $x^2-y^2 = 4$
(vi) $x^2+y^2 = 9$ (vii) $x^2+16y^2 = 16$ (viii) $2y = x^2-2$ (ix) $9(x-1)^2+16(y-2)^2 = 144$
(x) $x+y = 1$ (xi) $y(1-x^2) = 2x$ (xii) $x^3+y^3 = xy$
8 $x+2y = 2xy$ 9. $x-2y = 1$ 10. $x^2-2xy+y^2+4ax+4ay-4a^2 = 0$
11. $xy = 2x-y$ 12. $x = y^2+1$ 13. $[(2x-a)/a]^2+(2y/b)^2 = 1$
14. $y^2 = 4a(x+a)$ 15. $x = 2y+6$; $t = 5$ 16. $y = -x(2x-3)$

(A) EXAMPLES 33

3. $yp-x = 2p^2$; $yp-xp^2 = 2$ 4. $1/t$; $(1/m^2, 2/m)$
5. tangent $xy-y = t^2$; normal $x+ty = 2t+t^3$
6. $y+px = 2ap+ap^3$ 7. (i) $(p+q)y-2x = 2apq$ (ii) $pq = -1$
8. $yt-x = t^2$; $t = 1, 2$; $y-x = 1$, $2y-x = 4$ 10. $(2/m^2, 4/m)$
11. $(pq, p+q)$ 16. $yt-x = t^2$; $2y+x+4 = 0$ 17. $x = 2a$
18. $y+px = 4p+2p^3$ (i) $(6+2p^2, -2p)$ (ii) $y^2 = 2x-12$ 19. $(2ap^2, 3ap)$; $2y^2 = 9ax$

(A) EXAMPLES 34

4. $t^2y+x = 2t$; $(2, 1/2), (-2, -1/2)$ 5. $(10, 2/5), (-2, -2)$ 6. $[(2m-3)/m, 3-2m]$
10. $t^2y+x = 4t$ (i) $(8t/5, 12t^{-1}/5)$ (ii) $25xy = 96$
13. $t = -4$; $4y+x+16 = 0$ 15. $ypq+x = c(p+q)$ 16. $(cp/2, 2cp^{-1})$

(A) EXAMPLES 35

2. (i) $x^2+4y^2 = 4$ (ii) $2x^2+y^2 = 4$ (iii) $(x-1)^2+3y^2 = 3$ 3. $2x+3y = 5$; $25/12$
4. $6y-8x+7 = 0$ (ii) $(7/8, 0), (0, -7/6)$ 5. $\phi = \pi+\theta$
6. $2x\cos\phi+3y\sin\phi = 6$; $\theta = \pi/2-\phi$, $2x\sin\phi+3y\cos\phi = 6$
8. $(3\cos\theta, 4\sin\theta)$; $16x^2+9y^2 = 144$
9. $\pi/3, 4\pi/3$ 11. $\sqrt{3}x\sin\theta-y\cos\theta = 2a\sin\theta\cos\theta$; $\theta = \pi/6$
13. $\theta = \pi/12, 5\pi/12, 13\pi/12, 17\pi/12$; $(a\cos\pi/12, b\sin\pi/12)$, $(a\cos 5\pi/12, b\sin 5\pi/12)$,
$(-a\cos\pi/12, -b\sin\pi/12)$, $(-a\cos 5\pi/12. -b\sin 5\pi/12)$
15. $x\cos\theta+\sqrt{2}y\sin\theta = \sqrt{2}$; $(\pm 2\sqrt{3}/3, \sqrt{3}/3)$
17. $(a\cos\phi/2\sqrt{2}, -a\sin\phi/2)$; $8x^2+4y^2 = a^2$ 19. a, $3a/5$

(B) MISCELLANEOUS EXAMPLES

2. $(5/3, 4/3)$ 3. (i) $x(x-1)+y(y-1) = 3(x+y-1)$ (ii) $c = 1$ 5. $x^2+y^2 = 2x+3y$
6. (ii) $2y^2 = x-1$ 8. rectangular hyperbola; centre $(2/3, 1/3)$
9. AB, $y-2x+1=0$; AD, $2y+x-3=0$; CD, $y-2x-9=0$; BC, $2y+x-18=0$
10. $(2p\cos\alpha, 2p\sin\alpha)$ 11. circles through the common points of S and L
12. $2y^2 = 9ax$ 13. $(cp, c/q), (cq, c/p)$ 14. $25x^3 = 27y^2$ 15. $yt-x = at^2$
16. $[(3k+9)/(1+k), (4k+1)/(1+k)]$; $k = 2$; $(5, 3)$ 17. $x^2+y^2-4y-33 = 0$
18. $2x^2+y^2 = (x^2+y^2)^2$ 19. $y+x = 3a$ 21. -2; $2y+x+4 = 0$
22. (i) $(x-3)^2+(y-4)^2 = 25$ (ii) $16x^2+9y^2 = 144$ (iii) $x\sqrt{3}-y = 3\sqrt{3}-4$
23. $5/2, 10$ 25. $p+q = 2/m$, $pq = 2$; $h = 4a/m^2$, $k = -4a/m$
26. $(p^2+pq+q^2, pq(p+q))$; $pq = 1$; $x = y^2-1$
27. $x^2+y^2-6x-10y+9 = 0$, $x^2+y^2-22x-26y+121 = 0$
29. $q = -(2+p^2)/p$; $y^2(x+2a)+4a^3 = 0$ 32. $y\cos\phi+x\sin\phi\cos\phi = 2a\sin\phi$
33. $p+q = Y/a$, $pq = Y^2/2a^2-X/a$

(A) EXAMPLES 36

1. (i) $\begin{pmatrix} -1 & 6 \\ 2 & 3 \end{pmatrix}$ (ii) $\begin{pmatrix} -2 & 0 \\ 7 & 0 \end{pmatrix}$ (iii) $\begin{pmatrix} -2 & 0 \\ -1 & 14 \end{pmatrix}$ (iv) $\begin{pmatrix} 12 & 4 \\ 7 & 0 \end{pmatrix}$

2. (i) (5) (ii) $\begin{pmatrix} 4 \\ 13 \end{pmatrix}$ (iii) $\begin{pmatrix} 11 & -14 \\ 11 & 26 \end{pmatrix}$

(iv) $\begin{pmatrix} 3 \\ -54 \\ 6 \end{pmatrix}$ (v) $\begin{pmatrix} 24 & -14 \\ 29 & 6 \end{pmatrix}$ (vi) $\begin{pmatrix} 1 & 0 & 0 \\ 0 & 1 & 0 \\ 0 & 0 & 1 \end{pmatrix}$

3. (i) $\begin{pmatrix} 0 & 0 \\ 0 & 0 \end{pmatrix}$ (ii) $\begin{pmatrix} 0 & 0 \\ 0 & 0 \end{pmatrix}$ (iii) $\begin{pmatrix} 0 & 0 \\ 0 & 0 \end{pmatrix}$

7. $\begin{pmatrix} 0 & -1 \\ 1 & 0 \end{pmatrix}, \begin{pmatrix} -\sqrt{2}/2 & -\sqrt{2}/2 \\ \sqrt{2}/2 & -\sqrt{2}/2 \end{pmatrix}, \begin{pmatrix} -1 & 0 \\ 0 & -1 \end{pmatrix}$

8. $\begin{pmatrix} 1 & 2a \\ 0 & 1 \end{pmatrix}, \begin{pmatrix} 1 & 3a \\ 0 & 1 \end{pmatrix}, \begin{pmatrix} 1 & na \\ 0 & 1 \end{pmatrix}$ 9. (i) $\begin{pmatrix} 1 & 0 & 0 \\ 0 & 1 & 0 \\ 0 & 0 & 0 \end{pmatrix}$; $\begin{pmatrix} 0 & 0 & 0 \\ 0 & 1 & 0 \\ 0 & 0 & 1 \end{pmatrix}$

10. (i) 5 (ii) 8 (iii) 1 (iv) 0 (v) -2 (vi) 0 (vii) 1
11. (i) -2 (ii) 0 (iii) 705 (iv) 66 (v) 1710 (vi) 0 (vii) 871 (viii) 0

13. (i) $\frac{1}{11}\begin{pmatrix} 4 & -3 \\ 1 & 2 \end{pmatrix}$ (ii) $\begin{pmatrix} 1/2 & \sqrt{3}/2 \\ -\sqrt{3}/2 & 1/2 \end{pmatrix}$ (iii) $\begin{pmatrix} \cos\alpha & -\sin\alpha \\ \sin\alpha & \cos\alpha \end{pmatrix}$

(iv) $-\frac{1}{18}\begin{pmatrix} -1 & -7 & 5 \\ -7 & 5 & -1 \\ 5 & -1 & -7 \end{pmatrix}$ (v) $\begin{pmatrix} 1 & 0 & 0 \\ 0 & \cos\alpha & \sin\alpha \\ 0 & -\sin\alpha & \cos\alpha \end{pmatrix}$

(vi) $-\begin{pmatrix} 0 & -\cos 2\alpha & -\sin 2\alpha \\ 0 & -\sin 2\alpha & \cos 2\alpha \\ -1 & 0 & 0 \end{pmatrix}$ 17. $ab = -1$

18. $\begin{pmatrix} -11 & -15 \\ 9 & -14 \end{pmatrix}$; $\alpha = -\frac{3}{17}$, $\beta = \frac{1}{17}$ 19. $\begin{pmatrix} 1 & 1/2 \\ 3 & 0 \end{pmatrix}$ 20. $b = \frac{a}{2}$

(A) EXAMPLES 37

1. $x = -8/7, y = 5/7$ 2. $x = -19/2, y = 7/2$ 3. $x = -17/4, y = 11/8$
4. $x = 76/41, y = -27/41$ 5. $x = -17/113, y = -20/113$ 6. $x = 5/3, y = 3$
7. $x = 3, y = -2, z = 2$ 8. $x = y = z = 1$ 9. $x = 23, y = -16, z = -13$
10. $x = 5/9, y = -4/3, z = -7/9$ 11. $x = 4, y = -2, z = 1$
12. $x = -3/2, y = 7, z = 19/2$ 13. $(7, -6), (1, 2)$ 14. $(1, 2)$ 15. $(-1, 3)$
16. (i) translation, new origin $(-3, 2)$ (ii) dilation, lengths magnified by a factor of 5
(iii) reflection in the y-axis (iv) reflection in the x-axis and magnification by factor of 2
(v) reflection in the line $y = x$ (vi) shear with invariant line $y = 2x$

17. 9:1 18. (i) $\mathbf{x}' = \mathbf{x} + \begin{pmatrix} -2 \\ 3 \end{pmatrix}$ (ii) $\mathbf{x}' = \begin{pmatrix} a & 0 \\ 0 & a \end{pmatrix}\mathbf{x}$ (iii) $\mathbf{x}' = \begin{pmatrix} 2 & 0 \\ 0 & -2 \end{pmatrix}\mathbf{x}$

(iv) $\mathbf{x}' = \begin{pmatrix} \cos \pi/4 & -\sin \pi/4 \\ \sin \pi/4 & \cos \pi/4 \end{pmatrix}\mathbf{x}$ 19. (i) $5:1$; $y = \pm x$

20. (i) $\begin{pmatrix} 4 & 0 \\ 0 & 4 \end{pmatrix}\left[\mathbf{x} + \begin{pmatrix} -1 \\ -2 \end{pmatrix}\right]$ (ii) $(-4, -4)$ 21. $(4, 1)$ 22. $\frac{1}{7}\begin{pmatrix} -3 & 2 \\ -10 & 9 \end{pmatrix}$

24. $40\,\text{cm}^2$; $160\,\text{cm}^2$; $\begin{pmatrix} 11 & 10 \\ 5 & 6 \end{pmatrix}$ 25. 2 (i) $(5, 3)$ (ii) $(-1, 1)$

26. (i) rotation through $\pi/5$ (ii) rotation through $\pi/3$
(iii) rotation through $-\pi/3$ (iv) rotation through $\pi/2 - \alpha$

27. $\det\begin{pmatrix} 6 & 3 \\ -2 & -1 \end{pmatrix} = 0$ (ii) $2x + y = 1$

28. $\begin{pmatrix} \cos\alpha & -\sin\alpha \\ \sin\alpha & \cos\alpha \end{pmatrix}, \begin{pmatrix} \cos\beta & -\sin\beta \\ \sin\beta & \cos\beta \end{pmatrix}, \begin{pmatrix} \cos\overline{\alpha+\beta} & -\sin\overline{\alpha+\beta} \\ \sin\overline{\alpha+\beta} & \cos\overline{\alpha+\beta} \end{pmatrix}$

29. rotation through $-\alpha$

(B) MISCELLANEOUS EXAMPLES

2. $2\pi/3$ 3. $\lambda = \pm 1$; the lines are parallel; $x = -3/4, y = -1/2$

7. (i) $\begin{pmatrix} 3 & -1 \\ -4 & 3 \end{pmatrix}$ (ii) $\begin{pmatrix} 3 & 5 \\ 2 & 5 \end{pmatrix}$

8. (i) $\begin{pmatrix} -1 & 0 \\ 0 & 1 \end{pmatrix}$ (ii) $\begin{pmatrix} \cos \pi/3 & -\sin \pi/3 \\ \sin \pi/3 & \cos \pi/3 \end{pmatrix}$ (iii) $\begin{pmatrix} 0 & -1 \\ -1 & 0 \end{pmatrix}$ (iv) $\begin{pmatrix} \cos \pi/3 & \sin \pi/3 \\ \sin \pi/3 & -\cos \pi/3 \end{pmatrix}$

10. (i) reflection in the x-axis (ii) rotation through α (iii) rotation through $-\alpha$
(iv) rotation through $\alpha + \beta$ (v) reflection in the line $y = x \tan\alpha$
(vi) reflection in the line $y = x \tan\beta$

12. (i) $(3, 2, 3)$ (ii) $(2, -1, 1)$

13. $T_1 = \begin{pmatrix} 0 & 1 \\ 1 & 0 \end{pmatrix}$; $T_2 = \begin{pmatrix} \cos 2\pi/3 & \sin 2\pi/3 \\ \sin 2\pi/3 & -\cos 2\pi/3 \end{pmatrix}$;

$T_2 T_1 = \begin{pmatrix} \sin 2\pi/3 & \cos 2\pi/3 \\ -\cos 2\pi/3 & \sin 2\pi/3 \end{pmatrix}$, rotation through $\pi/6$

14. $\lambda = 1, -2$; $x = 0, y = 1, z = 0$ 15. $2 \sin\alpha/2 \begin{pmatrix} \sin\alpha/2 & \cos\alpha/2 \\ -\cos\alpha/2 & \sin\alpha/2 \end{pmatrix}$

16. $\alpha = 2\pi/3$ 18. $2\beta - 2\alpha$

(A) EXAMPLES 38

1. (i) $6\mathbf{i}-2\mathbf{j}$ (ii) $-\mathbf{i}-2\mathbf{j}$ (iii) $5\mathbf{i}+3\mathbf{j}$ (iv) $7\mathbf{i}-7\mathbf{j}$
2. (i) 5 (ii) $\sqrt{2}$ (iii) 2 (iv) 13
3. (i) $(-3\mathbf{i}+4\mathbf{j})/5$ (ii) $(2\mathbf{i}-\mathbf{j})/\sqrt{5}$ (iii) $(7\mathbf{i}+24\mathbf{j})/25$ 5. $\sqrt{13}$
7. $3(4\mathbf{i}-3\mathbf{j})$ 8. 8 10. $\sqrt{19}$ 11. (i) 7 (ii) $(6\mathbf{i}+3\mathbf{j}-2\mathbf{k})/7$
12. $2(3\mathbf{i}-2\mathbf{j}+6\mathbf{k})$ 13. 2:3 14. $\sqrt{42}$ 15. (i) $(4\mathbf{a}+3\mathbf{b})/7$ (ii) $(5\mathbf{a}-3\mathbf{b})/2$
16. $(6\mathbf{i}+2\mathbf{j}-3\mathbf{k})/7$ 17. $\lambda=\mu=1$ 18. (i) $(3\mathbf{i}+3\mathbf{j}-\mathbf{k})/2$ (ii) $(5\mathbf{i}+7\mathbf{j})/3$
19. $a=3, b=2$ 20. $\lambda=0, \mu=-1$ 21. $(\mathbf{i}+3\mathbf{j}+7\mathbf{k})/\sqrt{59}$
22. (i) $\sqrt{17}$ (ii) $\sqrt{33}$ 24. (i) $s=3; t=1$ (ii) $s=1, t=2$

(A) EXAMPLES 39

1. (i) 6 (ii) 1 (iii) -2 2. (i) 0 (ii) 4 (iii) 3 (iv) -2
5. (i) $1/\sqrt{5}$ (ii) $-6/5\sqrt{13}$ (iii) $2/\sqrt{66}$ (iv) $7/\sqrt{51}$
7. (i) 0 (ii) $-1/\sqrt{2}$ (iii) $-2/3$ (iv) $-6/\sqrt{5}$ 8. $\lambda=-1$
10. (i) $9(4\mathbf{i}-3\mathbf{j})/25$ (ii) $2\mathbf{i}$ (iii) $-5(2\mathbf{i}+3\mathbf{j}+\mathbf{k})/14$ 12. $-2(-\mathbf{i}+2\mathbf{j}+2\mathbf{k})/3$
13. $\lambda=2$ 16. 76 18. $a=3, b=-5$

(A) EXAMPLES 40

1. (i) $3\mathbf{i}+2\mathbf{j}$ (ii) $\mathbf{i}-4\mathbf{j}$ (iii) $2\mathbf{i}-\mathbf{j}$ (iv) $(9\mathbf{i}-8\mathbf{j})/5$ (v) $(1-\lambda)(2\mathbf{i}-\mathbf{j})$
3. (i) (a) 5, (b) $(3\mathbf{i}+4\mathbf{j})/5$ (ii) (a) 3, (b) $(-2\mathbf{i}+\mathbf{j}-2\mathbf{k})/3$
(iii) (a) 7, (b) $(6\mathbf{i}-3\mathbf{j}+2\mathbf{k})/7$
4. (i) $\mathbf{a}+\mathbf{b}$ (ii) $(\mathbf{a}+2\mathbf{b})/2$ (iii) $2(\mathbf{a}+\mathbf{b})/3$ (iv) $2(\mathbf{a}+\mathbf{b})/3$ 5. $\sqrt{494}/2$
6. 1:2 9. $7/2\sqrt{21}$ 10. 45° 13. (i) 1:3 (ii) $-23/\sqrt{609}$ 14. $\lambda=-1/3$
15. (i) $1/\sqrt{3}$ (ii) $\mathbf{i}$ 18. (i) $(\mathbf{h}-\mathbf{a})\cdot(\mathbf{c}-\mathbf{b})=0$ (ii) $(\mathbf{h}-\mathbf{b})\cdot(\mathbf{c}-\mathbf{a})=0$
19. (6, 8), 6. 20. $\overline{AC}=\mathbf{b}+\mathbf{d}$; $\overline{BP}=(-\mathbf{b}+4\mathbf{d})/4$

(A) EXAMPLES 41

1. (i) $\mathbf{r}=2\mathbf{i}+3\mathbf{j}+\lambda(4\mathbf{i}-\mathbf{j})$ (ii) $\mathbf{r}=\mathbf{i}+2\mathbf{j}+\lambda(-3\mathbf{i})$ (iii) $\mathbf{r}=\mathbf{i}+3\mathbf{k}+\lambda(\mathbf{i}-2\mathbf{j}+\mathbf{k})$
(iv) $\mathbf{r}=\lambda(4\mathbf{i}-3\mathbf{j}-\mathbf{k})$ (v) $\mathbf{r}=\mathbf{a}+2\mathbf{b}+\lambda(\mathbf{a}-\mathbf{b})$
2. (i) $\mathbf{r}=2\mathbf{j}+\lambda(3\mathbf{i}+2\mathbf{j})$ (ii) $\mathbf{r}=\mathbf{i}+\mathbf{j}+\mathbf{k}+\lambda(2\mathbf{i}-2\mathbf{j}+\mathbf{k})$
(iii) $r=2\mathbf{i}-\mathbf{j}+\lambda(\mathbf{i}+2\mathbf{j})$ (iv) $\mathbf{r}=\mathbf{a}-\mathbf{b}/2+\lambda(-\mathbf{a}/2+3\mathbf{b}/2)$
3. $3\mathbf{i}+2\mathbf{j}$ 4. (i) $\mathbf{r}=\mathbf{i}+4\mathbf{j}+\lambda(2\mathbf{i}+\mathbf{j})$ (ii) $\mathbf{r}=\mathbf{j}+2\mathbf{k}+\lambda(3\mathbf{i}-3\mathbf{j}+3\mathbf{k})$ (iii) $\mathbf{r}=a\mathbf{i}+\lambda(-a\mathbf{i}+a\mathbf{j})$
6. (i) $\mathbf{r}=\lambda(2\mathbf{i}-\mathbf{j})$ (ii) $\mathbf{r}=3\mathbf{i}-\mathbf{j}+\lambda(2\mathbf{i}-\mathbf{j})$ 7. (3, 0, 0)
8. (i) (a) $(3\mathbf{i}-4\mathbf{j})/5$; (b) 3/5 (ii) (a) $(2\mathbf{i}-\mathbf{j}+2\mathbf{k})/3$; (b) 2/3
(iii) (a) $(\mathbf{i}+\mathbf{j}+\mathbf{k})/\sqrt{3}$; (b) $1/\sqrt{3}$
9. (i) $\mathbf{r}=\lambda(3\mathbf{a}+5\mathbf{b})$ (ii) $\mathbf{r}=\mathbf{a}+\mu(2\mathbf{a}-2\mathbf{b})$; $(3\mathbf{a}+5\mathbf{b})/8$ 10. 5:1
11. (i) 0 (ii) 8/9 (iii) 1/3 12. (4, -1); $3/\sqrt{10}$
13. PR, $\mathbf{r}=2\mathbf{i}+3\mathbf{j}+\lambda(2\mathbf{i}-4\mathbf{j})$; QS, $\mathbf{r}=3\mathbf{i}+2\mathbf{j}+\mu(-2\mathbf{i}+3\mathbf{j})$; $\mathbf{i}+5\mathbf{j}$
15. $(-\mathbf{b}+2\mathbf{c})/3$ 16. DM, $\mathbf{r}=\mathbf{b}/2+\lambda(\mathbf{d}-\mathbf{b}/2)$; BN, $\mathbf{r}=\mathbf{b}+\mu(-\mathbf{b}/2+\mathbf{d})$; AC, $\mathbf{r}=\gamma(\mathbf{b}+\mathbf{d})$
17. $\mathbf{i}(2+\cos\theta)+\mathbf{j}(3+\sin\theta)$ 18. $(3\mathbf{i}+3\mathbf{j}+11\mathbf{k})/4$
20. (i) skew, $3/2\sqrt{21}$ (ii) coplanar, $8/\sqrt{154}$ (iii) coplanar, $8/7\sqrt{26}$

(A) EXAMPLES 42

1. (i) (a) $(2\mathbf{i}+\mathbf{j}-2\mathbf{k})/3$, (b) 2 (ii) (a) $(3\mathbf{i}-2\mathbf{j}+6\mathbf{k})/7$, (b) 3
   (iii) (a) $(-\mathbf{i}+\mathbf{j}+\mathbf{k})/\sqrt{3}$, (b) $1/\sqrt{3}$ (iv) (a) $(-\sqrt{2}\mathbf{i}+\mathbf{j}+\mathbf{k})/2$, (b) 4
3. $\mathbf{r}\cdot(-\mathbf{i}+3\mathbf{j}+\mathbf{k}) = 4$ 5. $1/\sqrt{3}$ 6. $\mathbf{r}\cdot(-\mathbf{i}+2\mathbf{j}+2\mathbf{k}) = 0$
7. $-4\mathbf{i}+7\mathbf{j}$ 8. $3\mathbf{i}+\mathbf{k}$ 9. 13/6
11. $-\mathbf{i}+3\mathbf{j}$, $7\mathbf{i}/2-3\mathbf{k}/2$, $7\mathbf{j}/3-\mathbf{k}/3$ 12. $(11\mathbf{i}+13\mathbf{j}+8\mathbf{k})/8$; $\sin^{-1} 4\sqrt{2}/7$
14. $\mathbf{r}\cdot(\mathbf{i}+\mathbf{j}-\mathbf{k}) = 2$ 15. $\mathbf{r}\cdot(3\mathbf{i}-\mathbf{j}+2\mathbf{k}) = 14$ 17. same side

(B) MISCELLANEOUS EXAMPLES

3. $x = \pm 4/13$, $y = \mp 12/13$, $z = \pm 3/13$ 8. 4/9 10. 30°
11. $\overline{AB} = \mathbf{b}-\mathbf{a}$; $\overline{OM} = (\mathbf{a}+\mathbf{c})/2$; $\overline{OD} = \mathbf{a}+\mathbf{c}-\mathbf{b}$; $\overline{OM} = \mathbf{i}+\mathbf{j}+2\mathbf{k}$, $\overline{OD} = 2\mathbf{j}+2\mathbf{k}$; $\sqrt{3}/2$
12. $\cos^{-1}(-1/3)$ 14. A, $\mathbf{i}+\mathbf{j}$; B, $5\mathbf{i}+5\mathbf{j}$; C, $3\mathbf{i}+4\mathbf{j}$; H, $x\mathbf{i}+y\mathbf{j}$; $x = -4$, $y = 11$
15. area = 9; 90°, $\cos^{-1} 1/\sqrt{5}$, $\cos^{-1} 2/\sqrt{5}$ 16. $\mathbf{r}\cdot(\mathbf{i}-\mathbf{j}-\mathbf{k})+1 = 0$; $1+1/\sqrt{3}$
20. $a\mathbf{i}$, $a\mathbf{j}$, $a\mathbf{i}+2a\mathbf{j}+2a\mathbf{k}$; $\sqrt{3}/2$ 24. $\mathbf{r}\cdot(2\mathbf{i}-\mathbf{j}-2\mathbf{k})+3 = 0$; 2 25. $2a\mathbf{i}+a\mathbf{j}+a\mathbf{k}$
26. $p\mathbf{i}/l$, $p\mathbf{j}/m$, $p\mathbf{k}/n$ 27. $(3\lambda-1)/(\lambda+1)\mathbf{i}+(\lambda-1)/(\lambda+1)\mathbf{j}+(3\lambda-3)/(\lambda+1)\mathbf{k}$; $\lambda = 3$; (2, 1/2, 3/2)
28. $\mathbf{r} = \mathbf{a}+\lambda\mathbf{b}$ 29. $\pm(2\mathbf{i}+3\mathbf{j}+6\mathbf{k})/7$; 12/7

Index